Miriam Peretz

Miriam's Song

The Story of Miriam Peretz

SMADAR SHIR

Translated by Jessica Setbon

gefen
publishing house בית הוצאה לאור גפן
JERUSALEM • NEW YORK   Est. 1981

Scripture quotations are modified from The Holy Scriptures According to
the Masoretic Text, published by the Jewish Publication Society in 1917.

COVER DESIGN: Dragan Bilic - Pixel Droid Design Studio
TYPESETTING: Benjie Herskowitz, Etc. Studios

Paperback ISBN: 978-965-229-835-5
Hardcover ISBN: 978-965-229-875-1

3 5 7 9 8 6 4 2

Gefen Publishing House Ltd.   Gefen Books
6 Hatzvi Street   11 Edison Place
Jerusalem 94386, Israel   Springfield, NJ 07081
972-2-538-0247   516-593-1234
orders@gefenpublishing.com   orders@gefenpublishing.com

www.gefenpublishing.com

Printed in Israel   *Send for our free catalogue*

This book is dedicated with love to my dear family:

*To the souls of my sons Uriel and Eliraz –
may they always live with me and within me.*

*To my sons and daughters –
Hadas, Avichai, Elyasaf, and Bat-El – who bear
the pain and the longing with me, and continue the
Peretz family's song of life.*

*To my sons-in-law and daughters-in-law –
Avichai, Matan, Noa, and Chani – who bound their
fate to ours, and who breathe new life into our
home and lives.*

*To my grandsons and granddaughters, who light a
thousand suns of comfort and hope within me.*

*To my daughter-in-law Shlomit, whose soul is
interwoven with my own.*

And last but most importantly,

*To my beloved husband Eliezer, of blessed
memory, who built a home and family with me,
and implanted in me an everlasting love that
renews my spirit each and every day.*

Contents

Preface vii

Acknowledgments... xv

Part One: How It All Began

Chapter 1: Morocco Isn't Ours – My Childhood in Casablanca 1

Chapter 2: Dialna! Hatzerim Immigrant Camp................................ 15

Chapter 3: Shikun Dalet – The Move to Be'er Sheva 29

Chapter 4: Will You Marry Me? Meeting Eliezer............................. 40

Chapter 5: Uriel Is Born 60

Chapter 6: My Romance with Sharm el-Sheikh – Life in Sinai 69

Chapter 7: A New Beginning – The Move to Givat Ze'ev 82

Part Two: Uriel

Chapter 8: The Magician – Uriel Is Drafted..................................... 99

Chapter 9: For Every Descent There's an Ascent – Uriel's Last
Summer 116

Chapter 10: I Knew Uriel Would Die.. 123

Chapter 11: Uriel's Lookout – Life in One Sentence 136

Part Three: Eliezer

Chapter 12: Covenant of Disaster – A Marriage in Grief............. 143

Chapter 13: "Hang On" – Parting from Eliezer............................... 152

Chapter 14: Mama Diali – My Younger Brother Charly 164

Part Four: Eliraz

Chapter 15: "Mother, What Are You Worried About?" Eliraz
Enters the Army 179

Chapter 16: "Israel, My Land" – Eliraz Is Wounded 204

Chapter 17: At First Sight – Eliraz and Shlomit...........................213

Chapter 18: I Knew Eliraz Would Live...223

Chapter 19: Forgive Me, My Sons 236

Part Five: My Family Tells Their Story

Chapter 20: Hadas Peretz Eitam 241

Chapter 21: Avichai Peretz...247

Chapter 22: Elyasaf Peretz 274

Chapter 23: Bat-El Peretz Issachar 288

Chapter 24: Shlomit Gilboa Peretz – Parting from Eliraz...........309

Chapter 25: Where's Dad? Or-Chadash Begins First Grade.......311

Part Six: And Now

Chapter 26: Dancing with God – Faith in the Shadow
of Death...319

Chapter 27: A Living Tombstone – My Mission...........................324

Chapter 28: A New Path – A Principal No Longer 336

Chapter 29: There Is an Eden 341

Five Years Later..349

Preface

On Shabbat eve, hours before the sky becomes painted in orange, Miriam Peretz sets the candles in the candlesticks.

Eight candlesticks. Just like before. "Six children, a husband, and a wife."

Eight candles. Even though three members of the family are no longer with her.

"Then I reach toward the printed blessings that stand on the shelf, but I can't find any blessing that fits," she says, tugging the tablecloth straight. "One says, 'May it be Your will that You act compassionately and have mercy on my husband.' How can I say that? Because He didn't have mercy, nor did He act compassionately. Eliezer, my husband, couldn't cope with the death of Uriel, our oldest son, and his heart failed. On the other hand, perhaps God did in fact have mercy and compassion? Because Eliezer didn't witness the death of Eliraz. Sometimes I change it to, 'Act compassionately and have mercy on me,' but that doesn't fit either. I've never prayed for anything for myself. I don't even know what that means. In another prayer book, I find the prayer 'May God grant me the privilege of raising children and grandchildren, wise and God-fearing scholars of Torah' – and I feel resentful. After all, I had raised them to be Torah scholars, and fear of God was part and parcel of their everyday lives. So why didn't I merit raising all of the sons I'd brought into this world?"

As Miriam Peretz has learned from personal experience, each Shabbat eve is different from the one before. So when none of the written blessings seem to fit, she sometimes makes one up. "I say, 'Protect them all for me,' and I recite the names of my children and grandchildren. Sometimes I get mixed up and make mistakes – I repeat the name of a certain grandson or skip a granddaughter, and then I get scared and start over again. Later as well, when I sit down at the table, I'm spooked by a breeze that blows out one of the flames. I'm filled with a sense of foreboding. Whose candle was extinguished? Why? What can I do in order to rekindle the flame? The candle represents a person's soul. So every Shabbat is different. Like every visit to Mount Herzl. Sometimes I get there and see both of them, Uriel and Eliraz, standing before me and walking toward me, and I catch my breath. Sometimes the stillness is so profound that I hear the fluttering of a bird's wings and the rustling of a branch, and I feel that I've joined them in Eden. Sometimes I stand in front of the stone, and it's just a stone. Cold and silent. Sometimes I spend time doing things that might bring them closer – I light a candle, clean and touch the stone, water the plants. Sometimes I take out the little book of Psalms that I placed under the head of each tombstone, and each page I open to speaks to me as if it were written especially for me, Miriam Peretz. I read the verse 'Even when I walk in the valley of darkness' (Psalms 23:4), and I glance up at the heavens. What does 'even' mean? I'm already walking in the valley of darkness. 'I will fear no evil,' I read. I live the verses of Psalms and take comfort. Maybe it wasn't just coincidental? Maybe it was no accident that God's computer got stuck specifically on the Peretz family?"

First Lieutenant Uriel Peretz (1976–1998) dreamed of becoming the first Moroccan chief of staff, but his mother is sure he knew he would never realize this dream. She also knew that Uriel, a combat soldier in the Golani Brigade, would not leave Lebanon unharmed. At two thirty a.m., when she heard footsteps outside her house, she opened the second-floor window and saw the "three angels," bringing to her mind the angels who visited Abraham. She called out to them, "I know!" Minutes later, she opened the door and begged, "Please tell me he was injured."

Some twelve years later, the three angels returned to Miriam to inform her of the death of her second son, Eliraz (1978–2010).

"They visited our forefather Abraham to inform him that his wife would bear a son, but they came to me to announce that my son was no longer alive," she said in a choked voice. "Even before I saw them, I knew it. I closed the door and pulled the latch, closed all the blinds, shut the back door, and declared, 'No one's coming into this house!' Then I stood before the photo of Eliezer in the entrance hall. 'What did you do to Eliraz?!' I shouted at him. 'You went there to keep watch over him, but I'm down here watching over all the rest of them!' When they came in, they found the house clean and ready for Passover, the table set for Shabbat. One of them tried to talk to me, but I wouldn't let him. 'Wait a minute,' I begged, 'just a second, give me a moment.' He fidgeted, embarrassed. 'Miriam,' he said, 'I have to do this.' I pleaded with him: 'Another minute. As long as you haven't finished your sentence, my son is still alive.' Finally he overcame my resistance and said his piece."

Eight candles. Eight candlesticks. Each morning, after washing her hands and reciting the blessing, she spends a few moments standing close to the mezuzah, following the custom of her departed mother. Death was the landscape of her mother's childhood; she had grown up in a shack inside the Jewish cemetery of Sus in the Atlas Mountains.

"This is the image that informs my life, from Casablanca and from the *ma'abarah* [immigrant camp] in Be'er Sheva," she says, and her expression clouds over. "Mother cups the mezuzah in both her hands, bows her head, and spends ten minutes in silent prayer. As a child, I watched in awe as she united with the sacred. When Mother prayed, we children didn't dare open our mouths. We didn't even dare come close. Later, we could hear a single sentence that Mother said: 'Don't let me witness the deaths of my children and grandchildren.' Mother knew in her soul that as soon as Uriel became a commander, he would go out to lead his soldiers and would not come back alive. She couldn't stand the thought, and a few months before he was killed, she passed away. I also grasp the mezuzah each morning, but usually I remain silent. I pray for my loved ones who are still alive, and for the souls of those no longer with us."

My first visit to Miriam's house in Givat Ze'ev, where an Israeli flag waves out front, was in April 2009, ten years after her eldest son was killed in an ambush. I heard that during the Second Lebanon War, Miriam hung up a sign: "Here we give only good news," to keep the Angel of Death away from her doorstep. I heard how in 2008–2009, during Operation Cast Lead, she almost went out of her mind because three of her sons were on the front lines.

"There's no way to speak of the pain of losing a child. All the words of the best writers don't even come close to expressing the power of grief," she said to me then. "I don't picture Uriel at the door, because he's in the house. He's here. I live him every single moment and die with him every single second. I breathe him, smell him, speak to him and with him. With every bite I take, I think how sad that he isn't tasting this new dish. I can't touch him or kiss him, but every morning I ask God to give me the strength to continue living him."

A spark of joy danced in her eyes when she told me how happy Uriel had been, when after two months of service in the army kitchens, he was asked to join the selection process for an elite reconnaissance unit of the Golani infantry brigade. "Out of hundreds of soldiers, only twenty were chosen, the crème de la crème, and he was overjoyed. Uriel didn't say much about the program. He came home exhausted, and I sat beside his bed and pulled the thorns out of his hands, one by one. When I hung up his socks to dry, I prayed, 'Please, God, give me socks with thorns,' because each thorn represents a step Uriel takes on this land." As proof, she shows me a framed piece of paper. "Here," she says, beaming at me, "this is Uriel's handwriting. He wrote this himself: 'With all the thorns and barbs that have scratched my body, you could put together a three-foot hedge. But these aren't just ordinary thorns – they're thorns from the Land of Israel, and whoever lives in this country must know how to accept these thorns with love.'"

Something inside me rebelled. Even recoiled. After all, I'm also a mother of six.

Is that how you raised your children? I wondered. On heroic stories?

"Not at all," she protested. "We raised them on patriotism, faith, and love. We taught them that to be a fighter is a privilege, an honor, and a mitzvah. I didn't know anything about the army; I came from Morocco to the *maʾabarah* in Hatzerim. The rabbi in the camp decided that according to Jewish law, young women should not serve. For many years I chastised myself for not doing enough for my country. When we lived in Sharm el-Sheikh, I met a woman of the Palmach generation who told me tales of heroism, and I felt a twinge of conscience. Each time I sang the patriotic song [written by Natan Alterman] with the words 'We'll dress you in a robe of concrete and cement,' I felt like I was faking it, because I hadn't given anything. I didn't pave any roads or dry up any swamps. After Uriel fell in combat, a woman sent me a letter. 'Nu Miriam,' she wrote, 'now do you understand what you've given?'

"But I still didn't understand. Or else I understood but I wasn't able to internalize it.

"It wasn't just a meaningless death," she said, raising her head high. "My children endanger their lives on behalf of the land that my great-great-grandparents dreamed about in the Atlas Mountains, but never reached. Our country was earned through struggle, and my sons fight so that we can realize our dreams and aspirations, those of the previous generations, and those of generations to come."

"Her Golani" – this was the title of the article about Miriam Peretz published in the special section of *Yediot Aharonot* newspaper for Yom Hazikaron, Israel's Memorial Day, in April 2009.

In the photo, her children stand beside her. Eliraz, her second son – with dark skin and piercing eyes – rests one arm on her shoulder, while his other arm hugs a framed photo of Uriel, his older brother. Eliraz followed Uriel into the Golani reconnaissance unit, one of the IDF's special combat forces. When Uriel was killed, Eliraz was sixth months into the training program. Who would ever have imagined that this photo of Eliraz holding a picture of his brother Uriel would be his last?

Major Eliraz Peretz (1978–2010), married and the father of four, including a two-month-old baby, was killed on March 26, 2010, just before the start of Passover, in an exchange of fire in the Gaza Strip. He died almost twelve years after he eulogized his older brother Uriel with these words: "Sometimes we pay a price for doing the right thing. The price of life."

I returned to Miriam, to her outstretched arms, to the warm embrace.

"Is this normal?" Again she took me in her arms. "I already gave Uriel, and my husband Eliezer followed him. Is it logical to give two sons?"

Eventually I discovered that I wasn't the only one who needed that embrace. The sharp contrast between the sequence of tragedies and Miriam's resilience transformed her into a kind of national heroine. A one-woman pilgrimage site. In December 2010, she was awarded the Menachem Begin Prize, along with the navy special forces unit, Shayetet 13, "In recognition of a special contribution to the Jewish people and its homeland." Chief of Staff Gabi Ashkenazi said that "Miriam's ability to continue to express her deep pain and channel it into a contribution to the education and development of future generations serves as an example and model of inspiration for us all."

Almost every day, Miriam visits IDF bases throughout Israel. On her own initiative, she visits the homes of those who have joined the community of grieving families. But she finds it hard to adjust to this role, which was not one she sought out. She protests, "People ask me to come to strengthen them, and I just want to ask, 'What does that mean, to strengthen?' Why am I, who experienced so many tragedies, considered a person who strengthens others? Touch me – I'm a flesh and blood human being. I just say what I think, feel, and believe. How can you tell I'm a strong person? By the fact that I continue living? We live whether we want to or not. Every day you wake up, and the question is what you do with your life, what meaning you put into it."

During one of our meetings, she had the idea that this strength that she is known for might derive from her name – Miriam. "It contains an element of bitterness – *mar*. It also has *meri*, which means rebellion. It has a bit of the calm sea, *yam*, as well as something that lifts upward – *merim*, and perhaps this expresses hope. It also recalls the biblical Miriam, with whom I strongly identify myself. She was the sister of the great leader Moses, and the one who protected him. She was also the one who led the Israelites in song: 'Miriam the prophetess, Aaron's sister, took a timbrel in her hand' (Exodus 15:20). Not that I'm comparing myself to the biblical Miriam," she is quick to demur, "but I've always felt a special connection to her character, and in the past few years that connection has grown stronger.

"What do I have in my life? I sat shivah three times – for my two sons and for my husband Eliezer. Then I sat shivah three more times – for my brother Charly, and again for my father and for my mother. What does the Torah say about King David when he found out that all his sons had been killed? 'The king rose up' (II Samuel 13:31). According to Jewish law, the first thing you have to do after the end of the shivah is to get up. In order to get up from shivah, someone has to lift you up. You don't get up on your own. But as for me, Miriam, every day I pick myself up, by myself, to a new battle for existence."

Miriam and Eliezer gave their first two sons the names of angels. "But did it help?" she asks. "I think that heaven does exist. I believe in it. In my imagination I picture them beside their father, beside their grandmothers and grandfathers, and I feel that they are being carefully guarded and that somebody is watching over them. But the first rain brings a river of tears, as well as the hot wind of the *hamsin*. Are they cold? Or hot? I talk to them and cry out to them. Not to Eliraz yet, but to Uriel and Eliezer.

"Sometimes I hear Eliraz saying to me, 'Keep going, Mom, it's okay.' Sometimes I hear his voice in my ears, apologizing: 'I had to go, I was asked to go.' I hope so much that they are in a place that is wholly good, better than the place where I am. Because I'm the one who's walking in the valley of death, in the place of soul-searching and inner torment."

Are you sorry you were named Miriam? I ask.

"God forbid. It's a meaningful name, and I can't blame my fate on it. But in my childhood in Casablanca, as well as in school in Be'er Sheva, everyone called me Yamna-Mari. Yamna after my maternal grandmother, and Mari with a melodic French sound. When I turned sixteen, my teacher announced, 'Yamna-Mari is too complicated and tedious. It sounds foreign. From now on, we'll call you Miriam.' Then my parents, who never managed to learn Hebrew, told me in Moroccan Arabic, 'Actually, Miriam is your name, from back there…'"

– **Smadar Shir**, *August 2015*

Acknowledgments

The decision to publish an English edition was not an easy one as my English is far from fluent. Every word in my book is of great significance to me; it was critical that the English edition faithfully transmit the core messages of carrying on with life and strengthening others. The fact that the book you see before you conveys those values accurately and eloquently is a reflection on all those who assisted with this book.

First and foremost I would like to thank my family, for supporting me throughout the process.

So many dedicated individuals contributed to the creation of this book. Since I do not want to mistakenly leave out anyone who helped make this book a reality, I will take this opportunity to thank all of you who have invested much time, effort, and thought into producing a book that I am very proud of. Thank you.

I would like to give a special thank-you to Howard Jonas. Though I only met him once, he immediately offered to generously contribute to make the publishing of the English edition possible.

And last but not least – I would like to thank God for giving me the strength to continue.

PART ONE

How It All Began

CHAPTER 1

Morocco Isn't Ours –
My Childhood in Casablanca

Casablanca. A narrow alley in the heart of the *mellah*, the Jewish ghetto, leads to a courtyard. Our last name, Ohayon, does not appear on the door, because my parents, Ito and Ya'akov, were illiterate, but a mezuzah is affixed to the doorpost. This is where I, the eldest of five children, was born, and where I spent the first ten beautiful years of my life.

My mother, Ito (short for *étoile*, "star" in French), was born in the village of Sus in the Atlas Mountains. Her mother died when she was three. Her father, Machluf, made a living by sewing mattresses, until the straw and dust damaged his eyes and his sight failed. As a widower bringing up three young daughters, he was given a hut in the Jewish cemetery, as well as the job of cemetery custodian. "Every day I saw dead people," my mother told me as a child. "As long as I can remember, I've lived in the shadow of death."

I didn't enjoy hearing these stories. I was a lively, vivacious child – I wanted to swallow the entire world. But Mother kept drifting off into bitter memories. "Yamna-Mari, *ya binti*, listen to me," she insisted, telling me how at a young age, she had to step into her father's shoes and take care of him as well as her sisters. I didn't know that along with her mother's milk, her strength had seeped into me as well.

As I learned from another story she told me, Mother's strength was revealed in full force when she was fourteen. A match was arranged for her. She was taken to the man's home, and preparations were made for the wedding. But on the wedding day, while she was wearing her white dress, she heard the groom's sisters gossiping about the modest dowry she had brought with her. She decided she would not join this family that was humiliating her father, who had provided her with a sack filled with *fakya* – precious almonds, peanuts, raisins, and dates. She fled from their house without a backward glance. This was a daring, dangerous act. At that time in Morocco, who would have heard of a young bride crossing wadis and hills in the middle of the night to flee from the man she was supposed to marry? But Mother was not afraid. She walked off in the night, alone, while everyone, including her father, searched for her. The rumor circulated that Ito had disappeared – perhaps she had been kidnapped. For many days she wandered the villages on the back of a donkey, until she reached Agadir and sent word to her father that she was still alive.

"How did you do it? How did you dare?" I asked her. Mother had continued to Casablanca, where she met my father, Ya'akov Ohayon, who was born in Marrakesh. To a girl's ears, this story sounded like the stuff of legend. "There are many things that a woman must accept," she replied, "but no man will ever insult me. That I refuse to take." I never dreamed that these mythical stories, which resonated in my ears from my childhood, were fortifying me in preparation for the future.

On the right side of our courtyard lived two childless sisters in their fifties, whom we nicknamed "the seamstresses." A few steps from their apartment, in the center of the courtyard, stood a well that served as a bountiful source for my fears. It was open, with no barrier around it, and from the day I learned to walk I clung to the wall, frightened of falling in. The end of the courtyard opened onto a rectangular corridor. We lived on one side, and on the other was a Muslim family with whom we maintained a good neighborly relationship. The father had been in prison, and on the day of his release there was a celebration. The women made couscous, and when he reached the top of the alley, they placed the giant sifter on his head, where it eventually tore. When his eyes appeared from inside the sifter, everyone broke into applause and shouted with joy, "Hey, he's been reborn!"

Next to this family lived a young couple without children, whom Father called "the magicians." Strange and mysterious scents wafted from their apartment, and we were forbidden to go near it. Even without Father's prohibition, I wouldn't have tried to get close. I was afraid of them, especially the man. I was also afraid of the rain. Each winter, the entire alley flooded, and I was afraid the water would flood our small apartment.

The home in which I grew up was one small room of twenty-one square feet (two square meters), with another narrow rectangular room attached to it that served as a kitchen. Father stood there with the *raboz*, a bellows that opened and closed accordion-style, to kindle the coal fire. The bathroom was outside, and shared by all the residents. At one end of the room stood a large bed, and beside it a wooden cradle with two bow-shaped handles, in which we rocked the babies, mainly my brother, Charly. The main room also had a clothes closet, while the kitchen had a dish cupboard and a small table, although we usually sat on the floor and ate what Father cooked: a piece of vegetable wrapped in a hunk of bread, which on a good day had a little butter on it.

When the peddler passed through the alley and shouted, "*Il gerba delma lehlo*" (A skin of sweet water), Father would go out to him and buy some cold water. He heated it on the fire and filled the big iron tub, and that's how we bathed, one after the other. Grandfather, Mother's father, also bathed in the tub. He was blind and lived with us. Every morning, Father would take his hand and lead him to the synagogue for prayers, and blind Grandfather was also the one who took care of us when Father went out.

Where was Mother? We almost never saw her. She worked as a servant in the home of Baba La'aziz, great-grandson of Rabbi David Ben Baruch, one of the great rabbis of Morocco. She came home very late at night.

Another girl might have complained that her mother was gone most of the time, or about her inferior status as the daughter of a servant, but I remember the excitement of our visits to the rabbi's home. It was in a wealthy neighborhood near the main road. Palm trees and green grass adorned the entrance, and when I climbed the stairs to the door, my eyes widened taking in every detail: the room on the right served as a library, while on the left the rabbi received visitors. The kitchen was enormous, with a gas range, oven, and refrigerator – I had never seen such appliances. Two servants worked in the rabbi's home: the Arab woman cooked, while the Jewish woman – that was my mother – cleaned. The stairs leading to the second floor wound up toward the attic, where there was a small room allotted to my mother. This was where she received me, surprising me with a slice of cake she had set aside for me.

But before I reached her room, an entire world revealed itself to me: this house was very different from those of the *mellah*. I peeked into the rooms, astounded by the shelves full of books – hundreds, even thousands of them. When the rabbi's wife gave my mother clothes that were too small for her daughters, I tried them on and felt like a princess. I felt honored to wear the pink dress that the rabbi's daughter had worn.

Sometimes, when I missed her terribly, I slept over in the attic with Mother. In the morning, I would find a black car, shiny and elegant, standing in front of the house, with a chauffeur. He drove the rabbi's daughters to the Alliance School, and the rabbi instructed him to take me as well. Why should I complain about status and discrimination? Here I was, little Miriam from the *mellah* of Casablanca, sitting in a fancy car, crossing the city avenues on wheels.

I always believed that everything was a matter of perspective, of point of view. You are the one who decides whether to focus on the cup that is half-empty or half-full. My mother worked as a servant, but she was a servant in the rabbi's house, and that was a big honor. Thanks to her job, we became like family to the rabbi, and he hugged us as if we were his own children.

One day, the rabbi invited me and my sister Zehava to go with his children to the movie theater. The chauffeur drove us. I enjoyed seeing the film and basked in the rabbi's liberal attitude. In his library, sacred books stood alongside secular ones, and he read *Snow White and the Seven Dwarfs* in French to his children. This openness seeped into my blood, and this is what eventually pushed me to teach in the secular school system in Israel instead of the national religious schools. In the rabbi's house, I learned that you could be a Jew but still be educated and modern, and open to the outside world.

"Why doesn't Mother tuck me in at night?" I asked Father in a moment of longing. In my friends' homes, I saw how their mothers took care of them and sang to them before bedtime.

Father was silent. When I directed the question to Mother, she explained: "Father hasn't found work, and someone has to make a living. You should be grateful that I have work. I bring more than just a salary from the rabbi's house. I bring food and clothing, and more importantly, blessings."

Every morning Father accompanied me to school. It was a forty-minute walk, perhaps more. Father wore a black *jalabiya* (he wore the white one only on Shabbat) and pointy shoes, and early in the morning we were on our way. I held Father's hand, while my sister Zehava sat on his shoulders. Grandfather took care of our younger brothers, Charly and Machluf, who stayed home.

We walked through the market as it awoke. Sometimes we came across an acquaintance driving a car, and he would give us a ride, but I enjoyed walking. It was a healthy morning jaunt, and I was particularly happy on the days when I reached the classroom before the Jewish teacher, who stood on a platform in a white robe. School was a place of discipline and aloofness, and I was not an outstanding student. I had trouble with the Hebrew lessons, yet the teachers wrote that I was "above average," praising my serious attitude and diligence. I didn't dare show up in class without having done my homework.

We had a break between two and four p.m., and my teacher would take me in her car to her apartment. It had a living room with a small balcony, a spacious kitchen, and a bathroom – not outside, but right inside the apartment, and with a bathtub to boot! She asked me to clean while she cooked in the kitchen with her sister. As I dusted, I took in the furnishings: two armchairs, a piano, a radio, a large gramophone with a loudspeaker, a carpet, vases, and bric-a-brac.

I wasn't afraid of breaking things, as I was very careful. By the time I got married, I had cleaned countless houses and become an expert at corners. Each ornament called out to me and fueled my imagination. I wiped the dust from a horse figurine and imagined myself galloping away on it. To where? My thoughts churned. As I washed the floor, I glanced out into the street. I saw people and cars, and they also called to me, as the curtain flapped in the wind. What was it saying to me? Was it asking me to come closer and kick it with all my might to get a view of the world outside, or was it suggesting that I brush it gently as I held it and the world at a distance?

Today people would criticize such an arrangement and accuse the teacher of exploiting her position. But I didn't have any problem with it; on the contrary, I was proud of the fact that the teacher had chosen me to clean her apartment. It was a sign that she liked me, trusted and valued me. I gave the money I earned to my parents and was quite pleased. For me, these were not just two hours of cleaning work, but two hours of seeing the world, discovering the street, living life.

After I finished working, the teacher served me a meal. I didn't like what she made, but I ate it anyway because I was hungry. There was only one dish that I refused to put in my mouth: potato salad with mayonnaise. So as not to offend her, I put the plate aside and hid the offending chunks in a secret place in the bathroom. The next day I cleaned it up, and no one ever knew. The teacher also never knew how thrilling it was for me to touch the drawers in her bedroom, and she never suspected that once I gave in to temptation and used her lipstick on my lips.

At four o'clock, the teacher drove me back to school, where she treated me like a regular student, as if I had never visited her apartment. At six o'clock, Father came to take me home. For a while, Father worked as the school janitor, and Zehava and I helped him clean the empty classrooms. I liked wiping the blackboard with a cloth, and when we found an abandoned pencil, it was cause for celebration.

One day, when I went home by myself, I walked through the market and bought an ear of corn for my brothers, as well as a cup of deliciously sweet yogurt poured from the barrel. My brothers were pleased to have the corn, and I enjoyed every sip of the yogurt, and mainly the knowledge that I had purchased this surprise with my own money. I felt grown-up and independent.

But not always. Sometimes at the end of the school day, I would stand in line at the corner store and the Arab vendor would ignore me. I was pushed aside, and I looked back and waited until all the Arab children passed in front of me. I realized that the vendor was treating me like air because I was second-class, a Jew. I felt insulted, and bit my lips impatiently to contain my fury. At the time, I was already certain that one day I would go to a place where I could live as an equal among equals, the place where no one would dare treat me poorly because of my religion and beliefs.

At another stand, outside the store, they sold grasshoppers fried over coals, considered a delicacy fit for kings. Once the children swarming around the stand pushed me, and I was badly burned. Mother rushed me to the hospital and I stayed there overnight. It hurt and stung, but I was ecstatic because Mother remained beside my bed. The bed was raised, and she cared for me gently, making sure not to move my left arm. Although I was young and afraid, I marveled at the doctors, admiring them. In my imagination, I frequently changed professions. I pictured myself as a doctor, then as a lawyer, then a teacher, professions that share a common denominator: they're all based on caring and giving to others.

Shabbat was Mother's day off, and on that day she compensated us for her absence during the rest of the week. We got up early and went out for a walk in the park. We packed picnic baskets and blankets, and wandered around until evening, enjoying the scenery and eating on a bench.

Baba La'aziz had a summer home on the seashore, and every year during summer vacation we went there for two or three weeks: Mother, my siblings and I, and the rabbi and his children. Although we didn't ride in the esteemed rabbi's car, he provided another one for us, and the trip was an exhilarating experience. I swallowed the beautiful landscapes of Morocco, burning them into my memory one by one until we arrived at the house, which stood right on the oceanfront. All around us stretched sand and more sand. A shower stood at the entrance to the house, and every morning we woke up and ran down to the beach, to gather shells and swim.

As always, every outing was accompanied by work. I helped Mother cook and clean, and when the vacation was over, the rabbi gave me a double gift – one of his daughter's dresses, and money.

One summer, though, left a bitter taste in my mouth. Mother didn't go back home with us; she remained in the summer home for a few more days, while an unfamiliar driver took us home. When I got back, I discovered that I had forgotten my money in the car. And where was the driver? He disappeared as if he had never existed.

The disappointment stung. To this day, I can't forget the image of the back seat where I had forgotten the envelope full of money. I had planned to use it to buy fancy notebooks and writing implements. I wanted to be able to choose them for myself, according to my taste, and not have to use the ones Mother would bring me from the rabbi's house. But I consoled myself by dreaming of the next summer, when we would again visit the house by the sea.

When we returned, I again helped Mother cook, used kerosene to remove the tar from my feet and those of the rabbi's daughters, and polished the silver using a mixture of sand and lemon. After each of these vacations, I returned home tanned and full of memories. I never dreamed of thinking about or asking why the rabbi's daughters had more than I did. Such thoughts, although natural and understandable, show that a person is not happy with what he has. But we, despite our poverty and separation from Mother, felt perfectly happy, and didn't lack anything.

Today, when I sift through these sweet memories, I ask myself what I enjoyed so much, since our life was so simple. But it was the very simplicity that charmed me. I learned to enjoy the little things in life. Just as I was proud of the fact that the teacher had chosen me to clean her apartment, I was proud of the fact that we were the ones who stayed in the homes of the honored rabbi.

Then came the news that we were going to Jerusalem – to the Holy Land.

A representative of the Jewish Agency announced it in a whisper, and the news was spread quietly, so that it wouldn't reach the neighbors' ears. I didn't know what the Land of Israel was. People only said that it was our land, and that things would be good for us there, fun and pleasant, but that we mustn't tell anyone. Again and again they warned us that it was a secret, and if we revealed it – God forbid – the plan would be cancelled. I asked when it would happen, as I wanted to say goodbye to my friends at school, but the edict was clear: keep your mouth shut.

Mother told the rabbi that she was planning to leave. She wouldn't dream of making such an important move without obtaining the permission and blessing of the great *tzaddik*. At first he made a face, because he valued her and her work, and he regretted having to part with her. But in the end Baba La'aziz ruled that going to live in the Land of Israel was a great mitzvah, and he gave her the wayfarer's blessing and a gift – a Kiddush cup. But this cup was not for making Kiddush. Rather, Mother filled it with oil and added a wick, which turned into a steady flame after she lit it. Every single day, until the last day of her life, Mother would put that cup on the windowsill, light the wick, and say a blessing and pray. Everyone who came to our home, from near and far, was invited to "light the rabbi's cup."

Eventually, I also adopted the custom of lighting a wick inside the cup and praying for the safety of Uriel and Eliraz. When one was sick, or the other had a test, I knew that the light would protect them from harm.

On Shabbat eve, before they left for synagogue, they would pause by the door and bend their heads. I would take another precious item, the tobacco box that had belonged to the Baba Sali and been given to my husband Eliezer's father, and pass it over my sons' heads. The Baba Sali used to breathe its aroma and say that it could raise the dead. When a woman was about to give birth, he would pass the box over her head and bless her. So I would pass the box over my sons' *kippot* and recite a silent prayer.

That prayer still burns in my mind. It's a prayer of faith, but today it's combined with searing questions that won't leave me until the day I die: since I prayed and recited blessings, how can it be that I wasn't able to protect Uriel and Eliraz? Perhaps I didn't pray enough?

Uriel and Eliraz followed my mother's path, as I had done. At eleven p.m. on that last Passover eve, a Thursday night, Eliraz came to Netivot, to the home of my sister Elisheva, to wish her a happy holiday. He lit a wick in the Kiddush cup, which she had inherited after my mother's death (and still uses to this day), and prayed along with her. She prayed for his safe return, but we will never know what Eliraz prayed for.

Did he know that he would be killed the next day?

In Casablanca we waited a long time for the journey to Israel. Inside, I felt that I was vacillating between sadness and joy. The Holy Land was like a hazy dream in my mind, while the separation from home, from the land of my birth, was real. If we had suffered from expressions of anti-Semitism, I think it might have been easier for us to leave Casablanca. But such incidents were rare, and our daily routine was simple and pleasant. Grandfather was the only one who spoke of Jerusalem. Morocco, Grandfather said, is not ours. Jerusalem is *dialna* (ours) – but he always said *dialna* in Arabic.

One day in late 1963 when I came home from school, I saw a giant crate that filled the entire room. I needed no explanations; I understood that the day of our departure was approaching. Mother filled the crate with blankets and clothes. I wanted to take one item that would remind me of the childhood I was about to leave behind, and I stuffed my schoolbag and notebooks into the crate. When we finally reached Israel and received the crate, I pulled out my schoolbag and flipped through the notebooks, but

I didn't feel disconnected or uprooted anymore. The notebooks were solid proof of the life that we had left behind, which would never return.

The evening after we packed the crate, after dark, Father announced, "We'll leave tonight." We waited until the neighbors went to bed, and then we went out to the courtyard in front of the house, walking on tiptoes. Mother spread a blanket over us, but we couldn't sleep. "Soon they'll come get us," Father whispered, "soon." I just stared at the silent alley with eyes wide open. My ears were cocked, waiting to hear steps.

We waited tensely in the thick darkness. I felt prickling all over my body, like knives, and then two men came into the alley. They held out their hands to us and silently led us to the entranceway, and from there to a bend in the road, where finally we saw a truck waiting for us, packed with people. Suddenly I heard someone calling my mother's name. It was her sister, Alya. She kissed and hugged us all goodbye, and promised to join us soon. Two months later she indeed fulfilled her promise, but at that very moment, the separation from her felt like a wound in our flesh.

In the middle of the night, we boarded a boat that took us to a transit camp in Gibraltar. It looked like a military base, with dozens of bunks that housed our group of four hundred Jews. The Jewish Agency cared for us with devotion. I had my own bed, and we were given as much as we wanted to eat. I don't recall how long we were there. The days turned into weeks, and I lost track of time. The second boat took us on a longer voyage than the first, and brought us to Naples. Many years later, I went to a medical clinic in the Ramat Eshkol neighborhood of Jerusalem for an X-ray. The Romanian X-ray technician looked at my identity card and said, "According to the number, I got off the same boat just before you." But he couldn't recall any other details.

In Naples, they took us to a hotel. My brother Machluf had rubella, so he was sent to quarantine. My mother stayed with him far away from us in a room in the basement, and we weren't allowed to go there. Every morning I stood in line for breakfast, and brought them a plate of food, which I set outside their room. They gave us butter, a taste I will never forget – what a treat! To this day I have a weakness for butter.

During the third voyage, with Israel as our final destination, I wore a red dress. All the travelers wore red. The sea was stormy, and we believed that the bold red color would calm the waves. We gathered on deck. I saw people crying and praying, and I was afraid. Why had we left Casablanca? Only to be swallowed up by the sea? "Pray," Father told me, and so I did, until the sea's anger abated, and on the distant horizon we caught a glimpse of land – Haifa.

The boat shook with cries of joy. Endless ululations. Mother covered her hair with a colorful embroidered Moroccan scarf, and Father disembarked in his elegant *jalabiya*. He was standing straight, his head held high as he descended from the boat. Then suddenly I saw him fall. *Father, what's wrong?* Then I saw that my father wasn't the only one lying down. All the men were bowing, bending, lying flat on the ground. And kissing. *Father, what are you kissing?*

"I'm kissing the earth of the Holy Land!" Father exclaimed. "*Dialna…*" he said, his voice choked.

Some of the women imitated what the men were doing, and even some of the children followed their parents' lead. I didn't lie down or kiss the ground. I stood aside, frozen, wondering: *Where am I? Is this my new home?*

We were led into an enormous hangar – men, women, and children – and someone gave me a piece of candy. *What's this? Do I chew it, bite it, or suck it? Can I have another one? I want to taste the red one.* Father was given a loaf of dark bread, and he recoiled.

Why is the bread dark? Since when does a Jew eat black bread? Is it permitted? There was no time for questions. We were loaded onto a truck, perhaps a minibus. We sat in three rows. *Mother, where are you? Mother, where am I?* Then someone said in Moroccan Arabic, "We're taking you to your home." It sounded encouraging. If he spoke Arabic, was it a sign that in my new home – my new country – everyone spoke Arabic? Was it a sign that someone here would understand me?

CHAPTER 2

Dialna!
Hatzerim Immigrant Camp

We left Morocco in the middle of the night, and we arrived at Hatzerim immigrant camp in Be'er Sheva in the middle of the night, too. We entered a hut. Wow! To me it looked like an entire kingdom. There was a sink in the kitchen with running water. The bathroom was outside, but inside there was a small square table with four legs, and iron beds with mattresses and blankets. It wasn't just one room; there was a bedroom and a living room. Above all, it was ours. *Dialna!*

But it was so hot. We arrived in the Holy Land in summer, in the middle of an intense *hamsin*, a heat wave, in the Negev Desert. Hoping to catch a breeze, Father and Grandfather Machluf sat on the three steps in front of the hut, which became their regular spot. Meanwhile, Mother and we kids began to get organized. We were still exhausted from the journey, and we weren't sure how to begin. We collected some wood nearby, and I suggested that Father build a fence to mark off our area. He liked the idea, and when the fence was finished, he proposed turning the plot into a garden. He took a tomato, threw it on the ground, and just like that, tomatoes began to grow. Someone brought him some mint and he threw it down, watered it, and just like that, we began to see green. If we already had a vegetable garden, he suggested, expanding on his dream, why not a chicken coop as well? He went to the market, bought a chick, and when the chicken laid eggs, everyone came to see.

I followed my father's lead and looked for new ideas. If he was growing things in the ground, then I could build a play area for my little brothers. I saw abandoned houses in the camp, and I went inside, collected broken tiles and brought them to our hut. All summer I sat on my knees and used the simple tiles to pave a small patio. I didn't have any cement, just broken tiles and mud. After paving a path to the doorway, I took a flat tire I found in a pile of junk and placed it in the middle of the patio. The children sat on it, rocking and playing. We got so much joy out of that tire! We learned how to say the word *keff* in Hebrew – "fun."

The camp housewives baked bread in a clay and mud oven called *frena* in Moroccan Arabic. My mother built the biggest *frena* in the camp, and anyone who wanted fresh challah for Shabbat came to our yard. Each woman brought a wooden tray covered with a white cloth. On it rested balls of dough covered with another white cloth. The house was filled with the scent of baking bread. I was nervous: What if Mother made a mistake and one of the women didn't get her tray? What would she put on her table on Shabbat eve?

My righteous mother never charged money for the use of the *frena*. She could neither read nor write, and she never marked the loaves with secret signs. With her natural resourcefulness, she knew which challah belonged to which woman. When they started to bring her their pots of *chamin* (Shabbat stew), because there weren't any electric hot plates in the huts yet, she knew how to tell them apart as well: one woman spread glue on the edge of the pot lid so that the steam wouldn't escape, another tied a wire to the handle. Mother also knew what each woman cooked and how much wood we should place under the coals. Quickly, the name Ito, owner of the big *frena*, spread beyond the camp perimeter, and even people who lived in the southern neighborhood of Be'er

Sheva would come to her with their trays. Slowly, our small hut became a neighborhood meeting place.

We children collected wood for the *frena*, helped place and remove the loaves and pots, and so we felt that we were taking part in the mitzvah of giving. But one role was reserved for Mother alone: she was the one who took a round piece of metal and placed it over the door of the *frena* so it would be completely sealed.

One Shabbat, disaster struck. We woke up in the morning and discovered that the *frena* had been broken into, and all the pots had been stolen. What could we do? The Shabbat prayer service was about to end and the men would be coming to take the pots of *chamin*. What would they eat for the Shabbat meal? Efficient housewives were already sending their kids over to us, equipped with towels with which to hold the burning pot handles.

Mother wrung her hands. Tears of distress streamed from her eyes. That Shabbat, every resident of the camp went hungry, and Mother took full responsibility on herself. How could she not have guarded her *frena*? Every time another man or child showed up, armed with a towel, the stream of tears began to flow again. Eventually, the pots were found in the cemetery near the camp, empty. The thieves had abandoned them among the graves, but only after filling their bellies with *chamin*.

As the days went by, we became accustomed to the simple daily routine. We didn't dream of a better life, because we didn't know what to dream about. Every little thing made us happy. I improvised toys for my little brothers from boards and wheels. I built them a makeshift cart and pushed them down to the wadi behind the house, which to me was magical and haunted. We played hide-and-seek, the seeker leaning his forehead on an electrical pole. "We're so lucky to have electricity," I thought, thrilled.

But there were times of sadness as well, for example, when Israeli spy Eli Cohen was caught in Syria and hung. The neighbor's phonograph played a beautiful Moroccan song: *"Lah ya'atik ya Nadia sber"* (May God give you strength, Nadia). Over and over again, I heard how the Syrians had tortured him mercilessly, and my thoughts wandered to his wife Nadia, who was widowed. I felt that I was a partner in her mourning, and this tragedy taught me that there is a price to pay for love of the Land of Israel.

When summer was over, some people came to our hut and took us to the school that had been set up in the camp. I don't recall its name, as we attended for only two days. At the end of the second day, someone came and told Mother that it wasn't proper for us to attend a secular school, and that she should transfer us to Ohel Sarah. At first, I regretted the move. The camp school was just a few minutes' walk from our hut, while the Ohel Sarah school was far away in the southern neighborhood of Be'er Sheva. I cringed at the thought that every day I would have to go down into the wadi and climb back up. But on the first day when I climbed up the hill, I saw a synagogue in front of me, and behind it, the school. I saw a large courtyard and my teacher, Mazal Seroussi, welcoming me with a broad smile.

Mazal, who came to comfort me after the deaths of Uriel and Eliraz, was an influential person in my life. At the time, she herself was also a new immigrant, and she spoke Tunisian and Moroccan with the parents. She was an example to us all of successful integration. I entered the sixth grade and began to learn Hebrew using the classic Dvora Levanon workbooks for new immigrants. Every day, Mazal would take me out of the classroom for a private lesson, where I tried to prove that I remembered every word.

In history and geography classes, I sat hypnotized thanks to the teacher, Carmela, whose family name was never revealed to us. The moment she entered the classroom, silence reigned. In every class, she took us on an amazing voyage to countries around the world. Eventually, when I decided to study history for my undergraduate degree, I knew it was because of her.

We ate lunch in the school cafeteria: meatballs and *ptitim*, Israeli toasted pasta. I always volunteered for cleaning duty, because after I finished they gave me a giant pot of red *ptitim* or a pot of the drink that was new to us – *petel*, sweet raspberry-flavored juice. I proudly carried these treats up and down the wadi, and my little brothers would stand in the door of the hut, waiting. I would put the juice into the refrigerator with ice, and in the evening we all enjoyed the cold raspberry drink.

I was afraid of Shoshanna, the school nurse. She was the first to discover that my hair was full of nits. Once a week she entered the classroom and stood in the center, holding two knitting needles. She called out the names of the students in order, and using the needles she examined their heads and declared who had lice, who had nits, and who had both. I was paralyzed by the fear that she would announce my name, as it was very shameful.

Luckily for me, my mother's cousin Phoebe Weizmann lived in the camp. On Shabbat, we would visit her and she would pick the nits from our heads. She taught my mother how to prepare the "holy trinity": one tablespoon of oil, one tablespoon of vinegar, and one tablespoon of kerosene. Every evening, Mother rubbed this magic formula into our hair and wrapped our heads in scarves, and then we went to sleep that way. In the morning before we went to school, she washed our hair so that we wouldn't stink, and on Shabbat Aunt Phoebe checked my head. When she announced that it was clean, I was on cloud nine.

We were a welfare family, so my parents didn't pay rent or tuition. Sometimes I went with Mother to the welfare office and translated for the social worker.

"We have no blankets," Mother said, and I permitted myself to add, "We have no table, either."

"We have no schoolbags," Mother said, and I added, "We have no pencils or pens, either."

I wasn't embarrassed about padding the picture a bit, but considered my cup half-full. I was proud of the state and the people in the welfare office, as both took care of us. How wonderful it is to be here, I thought, how lucky that we don't live in a country that abandons its poor.

We never went hungry. We ate the simple bread that came from the *frena* and the vegetables from our garden. Sometimes Father slaughtered a chick or a rooster, and Mother cooked it with vegetables. Sometimes we got semolina for couscous. But our home was poor in furniture, clothing, and books. For homework, Carmela, the geography teacher, asked us to place transparent paper over the atlas and trace the Mediterranean countries. I had no such special paper, so I took regular paper and wet it with kerosene so that when it dried, it became transparent.

Before Passover we received food coupons. Mother woke me up early in the morning so I could run to school to be first in line for the distribution of *matzot*, oil, and sugar. Today, many immigrants who came to Israel when we did say that they suffered from prejudicial attitudes during their aliyah and integration. I feel amazed that I underwent exactly the same experiences they describe, but instead of feeling offended, I internalized them as positive ones. I wanted to be first in line! Once, when someone threw down his chit and left, I got a double portion. From then on, every time I stood in line, I searched the floor for lost chits. I was so pleased to return home with the food, as I made my siblings happy and helped support the family.

When Father came to school, I did feel a little embarrassed, a tiny bit. My classmates' fathers all wore pants, but he was faithful to the *jalabiya* to his dying day. Underneath he wore wide Turkish pants and Moroccan shoes. When I asked him to dress like the other fathers, he objected strenuously. "I'm comfortable like this," he said. Mother also continued to wear the few dresses she had brought from Morocco or received second-hand from other people, and she never dreamed of buying a new one. "What for?" she remonstrated.

"In Israel we need to dress like Israelis," I answered her in Arabic.

"Really?" she protested. "So why don't they bring an Ashkenazi to our camp so that we can learn from him how to dress and behave?"

On the day we arrived in Israel, Mother and Father exchanged roles. In Casablanca, she had worked outside the home, but now she almost never left the door of the hut. While in Morocco, Father had been responsible for raising the children, but in Israel he found a job with the Hameshakem organization. Sometimes they sent him to sweep the streets; at other times he would clean buildings in neighborhoods built for new immigrants from the United States, South America, England, or France, but not Morocco. They were wealthy, or at least well-off, and he would bring their castoffs to the camp.

That's how we got bedspreads in our hut, and the biggest treasure of all, a small transistor radio. Every time we changed the station, we would get an electric shock. The radio quickly became the most important and valuable item in our home. Every week I waited with anticipation for Effi Netzer's program, in which he taught the listeners an Israeli song. I sat on the steps in front of the hut and sang, "These are birds that fly over the sea." Everyone knew this was my special private time, and my little brothers knew that they couldn't bother me or ask me any questions. They said, "Now it's Miriam's time. Miriam's program is on." That's how I learned to sing "We'll build our country, our homeland," and "Royal Hermon." I didn't know what the Hermon was, but I felt like a bird that had flown to Israel from a foreign land.

Everyone knew we were poor. Even in the camp, there were people whose financial situation was better than ours, and good people from the southern neighborhood of Be'er Sheva gave us clothes. When friends from class invited me to their homes, I felt as if I had entered a new world, just as I had on my first visits to the rabbi's house back in Morocco. In their homes I saw real refrigerators and washing machines, and private bathrooms inside the house, not behind it like in our hut. But I didn't feel even the slightest speck of jealousy. I was happy that I had the luck to see both worlds and to move between the simple life of the camp and visits to "dream houses."

In the home of my good friend Dalia Cohen, I saw a salad bowl and cutting board for the first time. Until then I had eaten cucumbers and tomatoes that Mother cut while holding them in her hands. Before I went back to the hut, my friends' parents would stuff a sweater or coat into my schoolbag. Since I was happy with what I had, I didn't feel humiliated at all. On the contrary, I knew that although now they were giving to me, one day, when I was able, I would give to others. I grew up in second-hand clothing. Twice a year, before Rosh Hashanah and Passover, Father would take us to the old market in Be'er Sheva and buy us festive cloth- ing: a blue pleated skirt, a white shirt, and black patent-leather shoes, which I cared for as my most precious possessions. I never felt underprivileged, because here, as opposed to Morocco, I was an excellent student, and the achievements I attained by putting my brains to use empowered me and gave me a feeling of strength.

At school I acted in plays. I also loved to dance and was accepted into the Israeli dancing troupe. For Chanukah, Carmela taught us a dance set to a Russian tune, and I – born and bred Moroccan – hummed it cheerfully. On the eve of Independence Day, Mother took us all to the main outdoor show in Be'er Sheva. As for any outing, she packed delicacies in plastic baskets, this time in double quantities, since after the first show, we went on to another one. The next day we packed the baskets again for a picnic in the park. Father stayed home with Grandfather Machluf, who died after the Six-Day War.

I was in eighth grade when the war broke out. Someone in uniform came to the camp and ordered us to dig a trench in the shape of the Hebrew letter *lamed*, and to cover the windows with black cloth. "Blackout" was a new term for us, as well as for my sabra (native Israeli) classmates. We helped Father dig a trench, filled it with sandbags, and at the first wail of the siren we had to run from the hut. A Piper airplane flew right over our heads, but Father sat on a chair in the kitchen and announced that he wasn't about to move an inch.

"They may want to bury us, but I'm not going anywhere," he insisted.

Mother grabbed his hand and shouted, "There's a war going on!" She dragged us by force to the bomb shelter in the Ohel Sarah School, but Father stayed home.

We had no newspapers, and television was only a dream. But the rumor spread like wildfire that our air force had bombed all the Egyptian planes. In the crowded shelter, everyone celebrated: "Victory!" they cheered. Ululations echoed throughout the camp. My cousin Phoebe, the delousing champion, took us on a victory trip to Rachel's Tomb, and for the first time in my life, I kissed the stones of the Western Wall. When the victory festivities died down, the grief over the fallen soldiers began to reach us. Each time Mother heard of a soldier who had been killed, she lit candles and mourned, and not just for soldiers from Be'er Sheva or those she had known personally. Each soldier who was martyred for protecting the homeland opened a new wound in her soul.

Later, when tens of thousands of people shared my pain over the loss of my sons, I realized that death had always been a regular visitor in our home. My mother, Ito, was born in a hut in the cemetery of Susa, and lost her mother when she was only three. Funerals were the landscape of her childhood. In Be'er Sheva, the cemetery was next to our camp. Although Mother was unlettered, she would lead us among the tombstones and say, "This is

Rabbi Massoud. Poor soul, he passed on before his time. And this is Sulika, may the Lord have mercy on her. She suffered greatly before she passed." She didn't speak of death as something frightening, but as part of life, and she wept for each soldier as if he were her own son.

We first experienced death in uniform when Yona Seroussi, of blessed memory, brother of my beloved teacher Mazal, was killed during an IDF attack on PLO headquarters in the Jordan Valley. This was the first time I had ever seen a military funeral. Mother wailed and cried. To this day, every time I visit the cemetery in Be'er Sheva to pray at the graves of my parents and my brother Charly, I go to the military cemetery and visit his grave, too. He was the first to show me what it means to fight for Israel and to pay the price of life.

In seventh grade, I started to work during vacations. Mother's sister, Aunt Alya, lived in Ofakim, and she told us that in the nearby *moshavim* (cooperative settlements) of Bitcha, Mabu'im, and Tidhar, one could earn good money doing summer work. That's how I got to work in potato and tomato fields. When I worked as a contract laborer, and not for hourly wages, I picked quickly in order to fill as many crates as possible.

The relentless July-August sun beat down on my head, turning my hair auburn. When more freckles appeared on my cheeks, I felt like saying: "Look at these, I earned them with sweat. These freckles didn't just pop out of nowhere." I enjoyed the physical labor, the feeling that I, the new immigrant, was connecting to the land. My employers were kind people. During the break they brought me food, a cup of yogurt and green onions, which was strange to me at first. My mother had only regular onions in her kitchen, the white ones.

One day I was picking green peppers on one of the *moshavim*, and the owner pressed us to hurry, as an intense *hamsin* wind was blowing. He watched us as we bent and picked the peppers, but he was not satisfied.

"Who are you?" he asked me. "What's your name?"

I straightened my back, frightened, and answered, "Miriam Ohayon."

"Whose daughter are you?" he asked in Moroccan Arabic.

"I'm the daughter of Ya'akov Ohayon," I answered.

"Who is your mother?"

"Ito."

"What is her *waldiha*, her parents' name?" he continued.

"Vaknin."

"You're Ito Vaknin's daughter?" he exclaimed. "She ran away from my uncle on their wedding day! And to this day he's never been married!"

A vague memory echoed somewhere inside my head, something I had once heard in passing. Mother had recounted that on her wedding night, wearing her white dress, she had fled from the man who was about to become her husband.

"Your mother was supposed to marry him, and at the last minute, she ran off," the owner of the field told me. "I promised that if I ever met her one day, I would choke her. She shamed our whole family." He looked me over from head to toe, and said, "Your mother had grit, and her daughter has grit, too."

"I have grit?" I questioned, hesitant.

"You sure do," he answered. "A girl without grit wouldn't come to work in the fields."

That day, when I went home, I told Mother about the encounter.

She was silent.

"Why did you run away from him?" I asked.

"A good thing I got away," she muttered. "He hurt me."

"How did he hurt you?" I insisted. "Was it something he said? Or did?"

"Forget about it, *ya binti*," she pronounced, and that was the end of it.

At the end of that summer, I used the money I had earned with my own hands to buy myself a wristwatch. This was the first wristwatch in our family. Until then, we had relied on the radio to tell us the time. With my remaining money, I bought a table and chairs for the house. I went to Be'er Sheva with Father, and we came home together with the furniture. From the money I saved in subsequent summers, I organized a bar mitzvah celebration for my brothers Machluf and Charly, and in honor of the occasion I had a dress sewn for myself by a seamstress, Mazal Dahan. Slowly, I became the breadwinner in the home, and my siblings would say, "Miriam's here, everything's okay."

But as I advanced to the upper grades of elementary school, the teachers' demands grew, and I didn't know what to do. I didn't have any textbooks, and in our hut there was no corner where I could sit and do homework. Fortunately, one of my friends took me to the Beit Yatziv municipal library in Be'er Sheva, and it became my second home. At the end of each school day, I would go home, organize my things, and go to the library, where I enjoyed the company of the books until seven in the evening. On rainy days, I carried my schoolbag on my head when I crossed the wadi, and asked myself, "What are a few raindrops compared to an education?"

But at the end of eighth grade, we had to take an evaluation exam, which was challenging even for the sabra students. I was scared. How could I manage so many questions in Hebrew? I was a new immigrant; I had only been in Israel for two years. I was sure that I would fail, not because I didn't know how to solve the math problems, but because I didn't know what they were about. There was a question about a swimming pool that was filled with water. I stared at the page. What was a swimming pool? Another question asked about the speed of a train. What was a train? I barely knew what a car was. All my life I'd been a pedestrian, and the only trip I had taken in Israel was the yearly pilgrimage to Mount Meron by bus. I didn't know how to approach the questions. They were like riddles to me.

The results of the evaluation exam indicated that I was not suitable for the academic stream, so I was accepted to the vocational class of Comprehensive High School "B" in Be'er Sheva. The teacher told Father, who showed up in his *jalabiya* and pointed shoes, "She can be a secretary or a nurse."

I translated his words into Moroccan Arabic, and Father was pleased. "Great! So you'll work, you'll have a profession. Good for you," he answered, and kissed the teacher, on both cheeks, in the Moroccan expression of esteem.

I stared at both of them in surprise. I had thought that Father knew what was good for me, and Father thought that the teacher knew what was good for me. So how could it be that they were both wrong? I already felt the inner drive to help others, but why should I aspire to be only a nurse? To this day, whenever I go into a hospital, the thought crosses my mind that I could have been a good doctor.

They both decided for me, and I accepted their decision. I was accepted into a technical drawing class, and bought a long drawing ruler. Every day I boarded the bus with the ruler, which was taller than me and symbolized my entrance into the professional world. As I stood among the passengers flourishing the ruler, I felt like shouting with joy, "Look at me, I'm going to study!"

The vocational class teacher was Mr. Benson, who eventually became principal of the high school. After the first semester of ninth grade, he recognized my potential. He saw that I was a diligent student, that I prepared my homework and participated in class, and he called Father in for a talk. When he said, "I want your daughter to transfer into the academic class," my mouth felt dry. How could I translate the Hebrew word for "academic," *iyuni*, into

Arabic? The same word in Arabic means "my eyes," and there is no word for "academic." I told the teacher that Father agreed, and that's how I transferred into the academic class.

Mr. Benson was the teacher who decided my fate. Had he not moved me to the academic class, I would never have passed the matriculation exams or attended university, and who knows where life would have taken me. Today when people describe me as a strong woman, I recoil. In my opinion, a strong woman is someone who recognizes her own strengths and pushes herself forward. But as a child, I wasn't like that at all. Other people pushed me, and I merely followed their lead. Eventually, when I became a homeroom teacher, I recalled Mr. Benson as an example of a teacher who made a change and saved a world.

I began my first day in the academic class with mixed feelings. I was very happy, but also very scared. Even before the class began, I knew it would be difficult. I, a student from the vocational class, was thrown into the deep water, and had to swim with the achievers. But something inside me burned, urging me on, "You can do it!"

CHAPTER 3

Shikun Dalet – The Move to Be'er Sheva

The students were already sitting in their seats when I walked in. I found an empty seat at the last desk. I was pleased. If I sat in the back row, maybe no one would notice that my legs were shaking with fear. If no one noticed me, maybe I could observe from the side, quietly, until I became part of the class.

The first class was chemistry, and the teacher wrote "H_2O" on the board. I looked at the letters in confusion. We hadn't studied chemistry in the vocational class. I knew what "2" was, but what were those Latin letters? What were they doing in this classroom, and what was I supposed to do with them? Maybe Mr. Benson was wrong, and I didn't really belong here?

But luckily for me, the second class was Tanach. We studied the book of Isaiah, and slowly my self-confidence returned. I gathered my courage and raised my hand, and even gave the right answer. Then came literature class. We studied the poem "Tehillah" (Praise) by Shai Agnon, and I felt that I was in my element. Then we had history, at which I excelled, and I also raised my hand in geography class. Day by day, my fears subsided and I began to feel that if I really worked and tried hard, I might actually be able to fit in.

I also began to get to know the other students. In the humanities subjects I was considered a strong student, but science and math were difficult for me, so I had to find private tutors from among the students. I got to know Yitzchak, who became my first boyfriend. He helped me with math, and I helped him with literature and history. My parents couldn't help me at all with my studies. They barely understood what was going on in my class. When I came home they would ask, "What did you learn today?"

Once I replied, "Today we learned about Chaim Nachman Bialik and his poem 'If You Would Like to Know.'" When we read the poem in class, I had felt as if I were flying off to the ancient *beit midrash* (study hall). But Mother and Father exchanged astonished glances and asked, "Who's Bialik? We never heard of him in Morocco. What else did you learn?"

Another day, I told them that we had studied a poem by Saul Tchernichovsky, which struck the deepest chords within me: "You see, O earth / We were very wasteful… For you, the best of our sons."

Father was furious: "What are they teaching you in that school?! Why don't they teach you about Rabbi Chaim Pinto or Rabbi David Ben Baruch? Now *those* are wise men." I was ashamed. Was it my fault that the wise men of Morocco weren't part of the curriculum? Father became angry, and I felt as if I had been reprimanded.

Every evening before bedtime, Father used to tell us stories from memory. Each tale began with "Once upon a time," and contained a moral lesson and principles of faith. Even when he told us fables about a king's daughter who went on a journey to search for her happiness, I knew that the happy ending would be found along the paths of the Talmud and religious faith. Suddenly I realized that the two worlds in which I was growing up didn't always fit together, and sometimes even clashed.

In order to minimize the growing gap between my parents and myself, I decided to tell them about the new literature I was studying in class. I tried to translate Agnon and Antigone into Arabic, retelling the stories for them using Moroccan names that would sound familiar to their ears. But they preferred short stories.

One story – after I translated it and added my own embellishments – captured Mother's heart, and she waited all week to hear the next installment; it was "Three Gifts" by Y. L. Peretz. I recounted the story by heart, sometimes changing the details, although I kept the book in my lap so as not to lose the thread. The first time that I told it to my children was only after Eliraz was killed, and then Elyasaf asked me, "Mother, why did you keep this to yourself? Why didn't you ever tell it to us before?"

This is how I told the story to my mother, on consecutive Shabbatot:

> *Once a soul went up to heaven, but it wasn't accepted into the Garden of Eden. The angels asked it to go back down to earth and bring up three gifts, which would allow it to open up the longed-for gates of Eden. The soul went back down to earth and took a simple pin. A young Jewish girl had used it to pin her skirt, when she was tied to the tail of a horse that galloped through the city streets. The girl was so modest that she didn't want anyone to see any part of her flesh, and though the pin had pricked her and caused her to bleed, she continued to wear it to protect her modesty. The soul took that pin, which was soaked with her blood. It went up to heaven, and the gift was accepted.*

> *On its second journey, the soul brought a single thread from the kippah of a Jew who stood between two rows of men who whipped him. They flogged him mercilessly, and when they had had their fill, he lifted his hand up to his head, felt that his kippah had fallen off, and bent down to pick it up. The round of beatings began again, until he gave up his soul to his Creator. The soul*

took a single thread from the kippah up to heaven, and this gift was also accepted.

On its third journey, the soul reached the wastelands of Siberia, coming to the home of a Jew just as a gang of robbers was breaking into his home. The Jew stood beside a small chest, and as he watched the robbers burst in, he protected the chest with his body. The robbers pushed him, as they thought a treasure must be hidden inside the chest. He fought them until he collapsed, because inside the chest was a box, and inside the box was dust from the ground of the Land of Israel. The soul flew with this dust up to heaven, and the gates of Eden opened. Through the dust of the Land of Israel, the soul entered the World to Come.

This is the story I used to tell Mother in Moroccan Arabic on Shabbat, and we would both cry, but only after Eliraz was killed did I feel that it was really my own. When Uriel, my eldest son, fell in battle, I wanted to bring the Master of the Universe just one of the many thorns that had pierced his hands and feet as he walked the land, and say, "Please accept my small offering, a thorn from the Land of Israel, from the body of my son Uriel." When my husband Eliezer died because his heart could not withstand the grief, I wanted to bring a single thread from his *tallit* and say, "Please accept my humble offering. You know how much he prayed for the safety of this boy, and how his *tallit* was soaked with tears." After Eliraz fell in battle, I wanted to bring some dust from Mount Herzl – dust from the graves of Uriel and Eliraz – and say to the Creator, "Don't force any other mothers to make this choice when they come to kneel at the graves of their sons. Don't make them choose which stone will be the first they kiss. I have already given you three gifts – what more do You want?"

* * *

During summer vacation after ninth grade, my cousin Chavah asked me to come to Zefat to babysit her son Ashi, then four years old. I traveled to Zefat by bus, and Chavah picked me up at the central bus station and took me to her apartment. Here again another new world unfolded before my eyes: there was a television, bookcase, oven, gas range, and refrigerator. Order and cleanliness reigned. In the morning, while my cousin went to work in a hotel, I played with Ashi, and when she came home I stood beside her in the kitchen and watched her cook and bake. Previously, I had known only Mother's *frena* and the lone pot she placed on the gas burner. I was enchanted by more surprises: trays of cakes peeked from inside the oven! Ever the diligent student, I sat with my notebook and recorded each recipe: ingredients, quantities, temperature, cooking and baking times.

When summer vacation ended, I received my salary. Chavah paid me generously, and because I spent not one penny while in her home, I hoped it would be enough to buy a refrigerator. Happy and full of pride, I made the journey home. But when I got off the bus at the camp and stood at the entrance to our hut, my legs froze: it was empty.

"Where are Father and Mother?" I asked the neighbors. "Where is everyone?"

"What, don't you know?" they laughed expansively. "Your family got a key to an apartment in Shikun Dalet in Be'er Sheva. They've moved to a new home!"

Today, psychologists would no doubt have a field day with this and diagnose me with abandonment trauma, but on the contrary, I felt drunk with joy. A key! An apartment! I understood that my parents had not been able to share this news with me because they had no telephone. So I ran to the bus and rode to Shikun Dalet.

When I got off at the bus stop, I realized I didn't know their address. I walked down Sanhedrin Street and asked random passersby, "Do you perhaps know where Ya'akov Ohayon lives?" Finally someone directed me to apartment building number 150. I climbed the stairs to the second floor, and my sister Elisheva (whom we called Batsheva) ran toward me and led me into our new palace: living room, kitchen outfitted with cabinets, toilet and shower, and even a balcony with laundry cords already strung. Father hugged me and announced that the Amidar public housing company had begun to move everyone out of the camp. Mother's eyes shone with tears, and we both stood on the balcony and looked down at the street.

I stood there for the first few minutes, delighted and enchanted, then quickly went to work. I chose my own room, as I was the oldest, and began by making my brothers' and sisters' beds. I promised myself that I would invest every *lira* I earned in the new apartment. I bought a shower curtain and hung up a mirror, and with the money I had earned from the job in Zefat, I bought a refrigerator – Amcor 16 – as well as an oven and gas range.

In the new neighborhood, I discovered a new job opportunity: every day after school, I began to clean stairwells of the apartment buildings. Soon I recruited Mother for the job as well. Some homes were already known as "Miriam's homes," and other cleaners didn't dare enter them. But Mother didn't know how to clean Israeli-style – that was my specialty. I earned my doctorate in cleaning supplies. In our home we had only bleach and soap, but the apartment owners taught me which products were for windows and which for doors, and what to scrub with what.

I proved myself to be a thorough, energetic cleaner, and I did it with love, all the while discovering new worlds. When I scrubbed a refrigerator, I took a peek inside and discovered new foods. When I dusted a bookcase, I leafed through the books. With the money I earned, I bought my parents a washing machine.

Mother was intimidated by the fancy machines I brought home. "Why do we need an oven? What do I do with it?" She missed the *frena* in the camp. She looked all over Be'er Sheva for a *frena* in which to bake her bread, but didn't find one. This made her very unhappy. In her worldview, food was a demonstration of love. Every day she cooked a simple, hearty meal, and to this day I can't replicate the flavor – the taste of Mother.

My parents were not excited by the fact that I had transferred to the academic class, and so I had to continue to push myself on my own. I picked out a few students who excelled at science and math, and made a deal with them: "You teach me everything you know, and I'll help you in the humanities."

The most dedicated of these "teachers" was Yitzchak, my boyfriend during high school. I don't remember if he asked me to be his girlfriend or if I ever said yes – that wasn't done in our crowd. We began to meet in the afternoons, and gradually we neglected our homework. Yitzchak was a sabra, but I didn't sense that his family was condescending toward me. On the contrary, his parents considered me a serious, friendly student. He used to call me "carrot-top." I was a bit offended by this label and told him that I had earned all the freckles with sweat.

Before each test, I would tell my parents: "Tomorrow I have to do well!" and they would spring into action. Mother would light candles, Father would go to synagogue. He prayed before the Torah scroll and put money for charity in the *tzedakah* box. I knew he was praying "for Miriam to succeed on her test," and I also knew I couldn't disappoint – not God, but Father. What sort of face would he make at home if he couldn't boast that his prayer had been accepted?

When the *bagrut* (matriculation) exams began, Mother realized that she had to double her efforts, so she went to the Be'er Sheva cemetery to pray for me. When my group of friends came to study on the floor in my room, she made sure that my siblings were quiet, and brought us food and drinks. To this day, when my own children have to take a test, I light a candle for their success.

I take the amulet that Eliezer got from the Baba Sali and pass it over their heads, and pray that with God's help, they will achieve success in any undertaking.

While continuing my studies and daily cleaning jobs, I also helped furnish my parents' new apartment. I bought curtains, ordered kitchen cabinets, and on Passover Eve, I painted the doors and door frames white. Father left his job as a cleaner and went to work in the Be'er Sheva branch of Tnuva, a major Israeli food manufacturer. He would bring home chickens and fruit, and our small apartment was filled with plenty, even though the crate he brought home had a strong smell of kerosene, a sign that the food might have been designated unfit for consumption. When I came home, he would greet me by saying, "Go to your room, there's a surprise for you." I would find an orange or other juicy piece of fruit waiting for me in the closet. Sometimes my brothers and sisters felt jealous and said that Father loved me best, but I hope they understood that this was his way of thanking me for my hard work and devotion.

"Mother has holes in her hands," Father would say when he brought home his wages in an envelope. "We're lucky that the four table legs are stuck to the tabletop. Otherwise your mother would cut off one of the legs and give that away, too." A well-known rabbi from Morocco came to Israel, and Mother went downstairs to meet him bearing two kilos of flour, two liters of oil, and a picture she took off the wall, a straw image of a boat, like the one in which he had come to Israel. "Take the oil and the flour, but leave the picture at home!" I said. "It's the only one we have in the house, and you're not taking it, not even to the rabbi."

I noticed that Mother was hurt, but I also realized the extent of her generosity.

In eleventh grade, thanks to my good grades in history and literature, I was chosen outstanding student. The school organized a ceremony and invited the parents. I went to Father to tell him the news, but in the middle, I stopped. There was no word for "outstanding" in Moroccan. "*Anna m'zhiana*," I said to Father. "I'm doing fine."

"Okay," he retorted.

"What do you mean, 'okay'? They want you to come to the school."

"What happened?" he asked, worried. "What did you do wrong?"

Father arrived in his *jalabiya* and pointed shoes, while Mother stayed home, as usual. She never went out to events. Father sat in the front row, right in the center. The auditorium filled with people. When the principal called "Miriam Ohayon," I went up onstage. Shalom Sharabi, my teacher, presented me with the prize: a Hebrew-English dictionary. I was so proud, but Father lowered his eyes in disappointment as if to ask, "That's the prize? A book? Why didn't they give you money?"

On the eve of elections for the Knesset, I got off the bus at the Egged station in Be'er Sheva, and who did I see right in front of me? My father, who was still working at Tnuva at the time. He was sitting behind a table, handing out leaflets for Rafi – Reshimat Poalei Yisrael, David Ben-Gurion's center-left party. "Father, what are you doing here?" I asked him in Arabic.

"The boss told me to sit here and hand these out," he answered. For him, the boss was on the same level as God.

"Father," I pressed, "do you know what you're handing out?"

"This is what the boss gave me," he shrugged. "The boss told me to do it," he repeated. For him, what the boss said was holy.

"But those are Rafi leaflets," I insisted. Father didn't get it. He was unlettered.

He stuffed the remaining slips of paper into his pocket and the next day, handed them out at morning services in the synagogue. The congregants shouted at him. "Rabi Ya'akov," they said, using the honorary appellation, "what's wrong with you? Those fliers aren't for us religious people!" Father was completely confused. Why was everyone attacking him about these slips of paper? Why were they trying to keep him from carrying out the boss's orders? He couldn't imagine that the boss might have deceived him.

That year, I began to be active in the neighborhood committee, although this was not universally approved of. The adults thought I was too young to join them, while the young people were jealous. Because I didn't like conflicts, I forced myself to focus on the job at hand. I gathered all the children who were wandering aimlessly around the streets in the afternoons and took them to after-school programs where they would do their homework. Eventually, the municipality appointed me as the social worker of north Shikun Dalet in Be'er Sheva.

That was gratifying, and also an honor. Our neighborhood had poor people who were kind and charitable, but disreputable people also lived there. Father worried about me when I worked until late at night. He would stand on the narrow balcony and wait. But I felt safe. I got off the bus, knowing I had quite a ways to walk, but I knew that the drunks sitting on the bench under our apartment building would do me no harm. When they saw me approaching, they would toss their bottles on the ground and say, "Here's our school gal, our smart one."

At the end of twelfth grade, I began to manage the Beit Hatalmid after-school program at Degania School, and it was then that I began to feel that my mission in life was education. In high school I thought I would choose either medicine or law, but when I stood in front of these students and felt how much I loved them, I said to myself, I'll be a good teacher, like the good teachers I had – Carmela, Mazal, and Mr. Benson. I was aware of the powerful impact of a good teacher who becomes an educator for life.

Enlisting into the army was not an option, because the rabbi in our synagogue warned the congregants that girls should not go into the army. I accepted his decision, but every time I passed a woman soldier in the street, I was filled with envy. On the bus, when I sat next to a female officer, I saluted her.

I registered to study Jewish history and literature at Ben-Gurion University, and the flexible schedule permitted me to combine my studies with after-school activities and cleaning work. I did my homework in the library, where I also met new friends.

Father didn't understand what university was or what I was studying. When the neighbors asked him what I was up to, he replied that every morning I went to the big building next to the hospital. Everyone thought I was going to nursing school. "Father," I tried to explain in Arabic, "It's a university, not a nursing school" – but to no avail.

I didn't tell my parents that as part of the course on the Second Temple period, I was studying Christianity. I got a 100 in Christianity. I became an expert on Jesus, and I hid my copy of the New Testament in a drawer in my room. These studies actually strengthened my Judaism, as I became aware that the source of Christianity was Judaism. But I knew that Mother and Father wouldn't approve of me wandering in foreign fields.

My status rose in my father's eyes and in the neighborhood when Rabbi Shlomo Alkabetz visited our home. I told him that I was studying the Second Temple period. We discussed minutiae of Talmudic passages and studied tractate *Baba Metzia* together, and he told my father, "Rabi Ya'akov, your daughter is a *rabbanit*, a smart girl." Such a compliment, when given by the honored rabbi, was a reason to be proud.

CHAPTER 4

Will You Marry Me?
Meeting Eliezer

During my third year at the university, I was on a bus in Be'er Sheva, when a young man wearing a knitted *kippah* sat down beside me. He had long sideburns in the style of the Israeli pop singer Mike Brant, as all young men did in those days. He tried to begin a conversation with me and asked my name, but I conveyed disinterest. He looked too old and serious for me – his hair was already gray. He got off the bus a few stops before mine, and I didn't give him more than a moment's thought. But I hadn't noticed that a notebook with a sticker saying "Miriam Ohayon, Degania School" – where I was working as a substitute teacher – was peeking out of the knapsack perched on my knees.

If he told me his name during the ride, I forgot it immediately. But it turned out that this was Eliezer.

The next day, a young man called Degania School and asked to speak to Miriam. The secretary went to look for Miriam the first-grade teacher, who was sixty years old. She brought her to the telephone. Eliezer said, "Hello, Miriam. We met yesterday on the bus, and I'd like to talk to you." She attacked him with a cry of indignation: "You've got cheek!"

Eliezer replied, "Excuse me, I didn't mean to offend you. It's just that I'm looking for a young lady." I didn't yet know how polite and friendly he was. The other teacher replied, "Ah, you probably mean Miriam the redhead, who works here as a substitute." When they called me to the phone, he said, "I'm Eliezer, from yesterday on the bus."

I didn't want to talk to him. What did we have in common? But he asked me to give him a chance. "Let's meet, just once."

I was embarrassed. Why didn't he understand that "no" meant "no"? Did I have to express my refusal in a more assertive manner, so that he would understand that I wasn't interested and that he couldn't force me to meet him? True, I was already twenty-one, and the norm then was to marry young. But I was in no rush, and even after my younger sister Zehava got married, my parents didn't pester me with questions about when was I getting married. On the other hand, I knew that there was no way I would go out with boys just for fun, and that the first one I went out with would be the one I was supposed to bring home to ask Father for my hand.

On the other end of the line, Eliezer repeated, "Just once." I asked where. He suggested, "The Egged station in Be'er Sheva." My embarrassment growing, I mumbled, "How will I recognize you? I don't remember what you look like. What will you wear?" He replied, "I'll wear a beige shirt and brown pants."

Oh dear, I shuddered, what unattractive colors. Eliezer added that he would have no problem recognizing me by my red hair. We arranged to meet the next day, and I went to a store and bought a blue embroidered corduroy dress with a micro mini-skirt, as was the fashion then. I harbored no expectations for the date, but I was always careful about my appearance.

At four p.m. I arrived at the Egged station, and from afar I recognized the youth in the beige shirt, wide, brown bell-bottomed pants, and Mike Brant sideburns. I told myself, "He's not for you – run away," but Eliezer had already noticed me and approached. "*Shalom*, Miriam," he said, while I muttered a limp "*Shalom*." We were strangers.

I looked around and felt as if my dreams were shattering, one by one. I was a bookworm of unusual tastes: on the one hand, I was addicted to books about the Holocaust, particularly *Sunrise over Hell* by Ka-Zetnik (the pseudonym of Yehiel Dinur). I liked to pretend that I had experienced the suffering of Jews who crawled through sewage pipes to escape the Germans. On the other hand, I also read many history books, and in between I gobbled romantic fiction, which carried me off into a world of illusion. Swayed by these stories, I had anticipated that my first date would take place in a romantic setting – in a picturesque café surrounded by nature, with the trickling of a stream and birds chirping in the background. But here we were, standing in the burning desert sun, in the midst of the uproar, soot, and smoke of the Be'er Sheva central bus station.

We stood there opposite each other, silent, and then Eliezer shifted his gaze toward the square, where something greenish-yellow was growing, and asked me, "Do you know the difference between grass and weeds?"

At that moment, my heart sank. No romantic novel I had ever read contained such a question. Who would think of such a strange question? That's what you ask a girl on your first date? I was shocked. "No," I said, "I don't know the difference between grass and weeds." Again we fell silent.

Later, after we were engaged, I asked Eliezer to explain why he had asked this question. He said, "I'm a man of the land. I wanted to know if you understood the land, if you knew how to plant your feet on the ground." Suddenly that strange question from our first date took on a powerful meaning. He hadn't asked me about the weather, or complained, "It's so hot." His first question harbored an entire world. Especially after Uriel and Eliraz were drafted, I began to sense the difference between a thistle and a thorn.

I looked for a place to sit down, as I felt uncomfortable standing. "I'm sorry, I don't know Be'er Sheva," Eliezer apologized. He explained that he was from Moshav Gadish in the Ta'anach region near Afula. He was working in Sharm el-Sheikh, in Sinai, which Israelis affectionately called "Sharm." Once a month he flew to Sde Dov and took a bus to Be'er Sheva to visit his grandmother. "Is there a café near here?" he asked. "No," I answered, "but there's a public park nearby."

We sat on a bench in that very unenchanted and unromantic park. Eliezer told me about himself, and I told him about myself and my studies. The date ended an hour and a half later. He had to catch his flight back to Sharm, and I went home feeling that this was not it. I told no one about our meeting. What was there to tell? There would be no continuation.

But the next day, Eliezer called the school again to arrange our second date, four weeks from then, when he would again be coming for his monthly visit to his grandmother. I said "Okay," completely uninterested, and again I had the feeling that I was being led around by the nose. I was hardly floating on the clouds of an exciting romance.

A month later we met in the same park next to the Be'er Sheva central bus station. This time, he made more of an effort with his clothes, and his external appearance was much improved. I also took pains with my looks: I put white nail polish on my fingernails – never in my life would I wear red – and sat on the bench with my hands under my knees. At one point during our conversation, I lifted my hands and he looked at them and said, "What beautiful, delicate fingers."

I smiled, contented. During our first meeting, he had complimented me on the fact that I was a teacher and a university student, but this was the first time he had complimented me on how I looked. Then he added quietly, "I'd like to place a ring on those fingers."

I froze. I didn't think he was joking – he looked too serious. But who had ever heard of a marriage proposal on the second date? Without a second thought, I replied right away: "Yes." Why? Because I was already twenty-one, and my younger sister Zehava had bypassed me and gotten married, and I was afraid I wouldn't find any other man who would propose. Deep inside, I knew I had a strong desire to build my own home and family. I also knew that my parents were praying for me. So when Eliezer made his offer, I said yes by default. But still I was shocked – a marriage proposal on the second date?

"Yes," Eliezer said, "I've found what I've been looking for. A teacher from a good home."

I straightened my back. That's what was important to him, the teaching profession and a girl from a good home.

"I've already chosen a date," he said, continuing to amaze me. "October 13." Apparently he had come to our second meeting prepared, after checking the calendar and finding an appropriate date, just after the Jewish holiday season. He had even bought an engagement ring. When I said yes again, because I liked the ring, he put it back in his pocket.

This date also lasted for about an hour and a half, and after it was over I went home and informed my parents: I've met a young man. Father gave me a look, and said in Arabic, "You have to bring him home." I knew that's what he would say, since for a Moroccan father, it was shameful to have your daughter walk in the streets with a boy, where everyone could see and hear. People would talk about you! If he was serious, he should come to my parents and ask for my hand. But how could I tell Eliezer that? He had already gone back to Sharm.

Every neighborhood had one public payphone, and I went down to it every evening with a handful of phone tokens, and called him. Sometimes I called the office he had been given when he was appointed Health Ministry supervisor of the Shlomo district, which extended from Sharm el-Sheikh to Santa Katerina and Abu Rudeis. Sometimes I dialed the number of his rented apartment.

Each conversation was as difficult as the parting of the Red Sea. People crowded around the payphone, which was in the neighborhood shopping area. On one side were the local drunks with their wine bottles, on the other shouting children. A beauty salon to the right, merchants to the left. I stood in the midst of it all, holding the receiver, for everyone to see and hear. What kind of intimate conversation could I have with the man who was going to be my husband?

Since there was no other choice, we began to write letters. I still have the bundle of letters, his to me, and mine to him. I worked hard on the visual aspect of my missives. I bought blue stationery and carefully traced each letter of each word. When I looked at them again years later, I realized that these were letters from a young woman in love. My rational side still opposed it, but my heart, from letter to letter, was warming up.

Eliezer's letters, by contrast, revealed terribly messy handwriting. The first time I opened an envelope and stared at a letter from him, I thought this was a good reason to call off the wedding. But when I managed to decipher it, word by word and fragments of sentences at a time, I sensed that those words had come from the heart of a man in love to the very depths of his soul.

To the day he died, Eliezer's love for me was all-encompassing, bordering on idolization. In those letters he described how he imagined our home and the children we would bring into the world. He wanted twelve children, just as Eliraz said to Shlomit years later. I still hadn't digested the fact that we were getting married, and that the date was approaching. But, like Herzl who envisioned the Jewish state, Eliezer envisaged the idyllic atmosphere that would reign over our nascent family.

I informed Eliezer that Father had invited him to our home, and he was pleased. I had three weeks until his return from Sharm, and the entire family began to get organized for his visit. It was like preparing for a military operation. The first mission was to teach Father to eat with a knife and fork. Until then, he had always eaten with his hands, ripping off a piece of bread and dipping it into the spicy sauce of the fish. With my groom finally visiting our home, this was unacceptable.

Mother devoted herself to cleaning the apartment. While she scoured and scrubbed, I demonstrated to Father how to hold the knife in the left hand and the fork in the right. Poor Father, he practiced and suffered. What wouldn't he do in honor of his oldest daughter's fiancé? My sister Zehava prepared delicacies, decorating them with garnishes I could only begin to imagine, such as cucumber circles with olives speared on toothpicks. All my siblings joined in the preparations, hanging curtains and spreading a white tablecloth on the table. Then, the groom arrived!

Eliezer walked in, and their excitement was boundless. Mother welcomed him with a shy expression, then slipped away into the kitchen, as usual. Father shook his hand, said "*Shalom,*" and fell silent. That was the only Hebrew word he knew. Then I elbowed Father's side and whispered to him, "You can speak to him in Arabic. He's a Moroccan." The ice was broken.

Mother came out of the kitchen when she heard the familiar, welcome sounds. My parents asked Eliezer, "Who are your parents? Where are they from?" He related that his parents came from the city, as opposed to a village, and that his father Eliyahu was a Torah scholar and his mother Rivka a God-fearing woman. They lived on a *moshav,* and he had come to Israel when he was six years old.

But Moroccans have no time for idle talk; when conversation begins to flow, the plates come out of the kitchen and everyone sits down at the table. I saw my father, sitting across from me, pick up the knife and fork and begin to squirm. He tried to hold the utensils one way, then another, but to no avail. He was hungry and

Father, Ya'akov Ohayon, in Casablanca

Mother, Ito Ohayon, in Casablanca

In Hatzerim immigrant camp in Be'er Sheva. From left:
Miriam (rear), *Charly* (front), *Zehava, Machluf Ohayon.*

*Shikun Dalet in Be'er Sheva. Bar mitzvah of Machluf and
Charly. Miriam* (sitting) *with her mother Ito, and sister Zehava*
(standing).

Miriam and Eliezer at their wedding

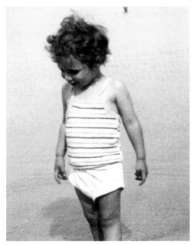

Uriel in Sharm-el-Sheikh

Two fish in Sharm: Eliraz (left) *and Uriel*

Eliraz and Uriel (with mask and snorkel) *at Na'ama Beach*

Uriel and Eliraz wearing T-shirts from Gan Ofira, at a gathering in Eilat after the evacuation of Sharm. In the rear: *Eliezer.*

Miriam (front row, center) *as a homeroom teacher in Sharm. The sign reads: "Ofira School."*

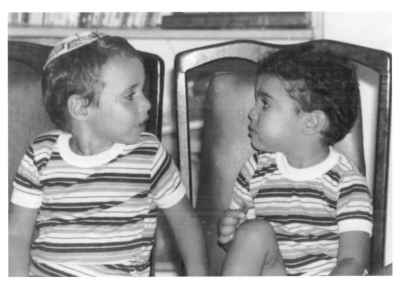

Uriel and Eliraz, at home in Sharm

Family outing. Uriel, Eliezer, Eliraz.

*Uriel on a family outing in northern
Israel*

*With Grandfather Ya'akov Ohayon in Shikun Dalet,
Be'er Sheva*

Eliraz and Uriel at the Western Wall

Uriel (left) *on his fifth birthday, with Eliraz, in Givon*

Uriel and Eliraz

First day of school. Uriel entering second grade, Eliraz entering first.

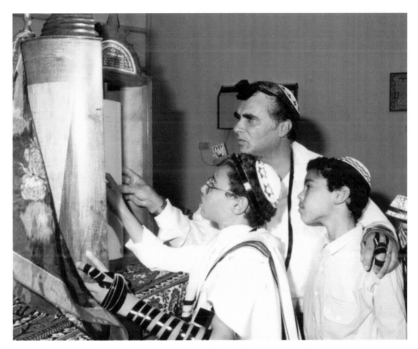

Uriel has an aliya to the Torah. Behind him: *Eliezer and Eliraz.*

Joint bar mitzvah party. Eliraz, Uriel, Avichai.

Eliraz on 12th grade trip to Poland

Eliraz in Poland with teacher Jeremy Stavitzky

*Inauguration of Darchei Noam synagogue, later named after Uriel. Eliraz,
Miriam, Uriel, Hadas.*

Uriel with Eliezer in front of the wadi behind our home in Givat Ze'ev

In our yard in Givat Ze'ev. Elyasaf, Uriel, Eliezer, Eliraz.

Uriel as commander of Golani backup company

Uriel in Golani reconnaissance unit

*Uriel on training course with his
backup company*

*Uriel at concluding ceremony of
officer training course*

*Concluding ceremony of Uriel's officer training course at Bahad 1. From left,
front row: Bat-El, Elyasaf. Back row: Eliezer, Avichai, Uriel, Eliraz, Hadas.*

Sukkot 1998. Eliraz, Eliezer, Uriel. All three are gone.

Last summer with Uriel, at Yehudiya
waterfall. Hadas, Batel, Uriel (rear), *Elyasaf.*

Uriel's funeral. Elyasaf and Eliezer.

Uriel's funeral. City military officer, Miriam, Eliraz.

Mourners pay their respects during shiva for Uriel. From left: Eliezer; IDF Chief of Staff Shaul Mofaz; Eliraz; Commander of the Northern Command Gabi Ashkenazi.

Miriam and Eliezer at a gathering for bereaved families at Givat Olga with Commander of the Northern Command Gabi Ashkenazi, and Golani battalion commander Shmuel Zakkai.

Eliezer and Miriam at surprise party for their twentieth wedding anniversary

Miriam and Eliezer on the "Lebanon Lookout Walk" in memory of Uriel. Between them: *Oded Bashan.*

frustrated. My heart went out to him, and I said, "Father, what are you doing? Eliezer is also a *shluchi* [a Berber Moroccan, from the desert]. Eat like you usually do." Father raised his eyes from his plate and looked at Eliezer, who was sitting beside him. He abandoned his knife and fork, tore out the *ftata*, the soft inside of the bread, dipped it into the fish sauce and ate with gusto.

But the meal wasn't the only reason for our gathering. Father said to Eliezer, "You have to ask for Miriam's hand." Eliezer pulled out the ring, placed it on my finger in front of my parents, and gave them the date. Mother and Father were teary-eyed. "*Mazal tov, mazal tov*! May you enjoy blessings and happiness."

That night Eliezer slept in our apartment. It was late, and we made his bed in the most important room of our home, the living room, as we only had two bedrooms. In his honor, we made up the bed with our best sheets. My mother slept with me, and my brothers, who usually slept in the living room, went to sleep with my father in the double bed. Later, each time we visited my parents and found the apartment in a state of disorder, Eliezer would tease me: "You really tricked me that night of our engagement, when you took me to a pleasant, neat home with tasty food."

The next morning we said goodbye, and he went on his way. The neighbor women came to see Mother immediately. "Ito," they asked, "who was that?"

"That's *la'arus*," she replied – the groom.

Then they said, "He's *shibani* [old]," because Eliezer, who was ten years older than me, already had some white hair. Miriam needs someone younger, they told her, offending her gravely.

April, May, June, July, August, September: we had six more dates during the period leading up to the wedding. On our fourth date, I took Eliezer to see Ben-Gurion University. He had a practical engineering degree, and he was proud of his university student fiancée. It was important for me to show him that I wouldn't be just a housewife, but that I was at home in the university as well.

That week our exam grades were posted. I went with Eliezer from one bulletin board to another, and gave him the task of looking for my grades, listed according to my identity number, which he had memorized. My scores were all over ninety, and Eliezer beamed. "Of course, you couldn't get less than that." At the end of the day he announced that we would be married in the Neptune Hall in Bat Yam, a location in the middle of the country, between our two homes, Be'er Sheva and Afula. He invited me to spend Shabbat with his parents.

A month later, I put on a fancy pair of slacks – he had seen me in pants when we first met, and he had no problem with the way I dressed – and we took the bus from Be'er Sheva to Afula. He told me that his mother liked drinking glasses, so I bought her a nice set. The journey was long and took almost an entire day. During the trip, my fiancé told me about the hills and the plants, *kibbutzim* and villages, and slowly I discovered his knowledgeable side.

In Afula, we boarded a bus to Moshav Gadish. To my disappointment, it was a *moshav* that looked old and neglected, as if it had not advanced since its founding in 1956. But I didn't allow disappointment to ruin my mood. I was still floating on the cloud of romantic fiction. I dreamed of a knight who would lead me to a house that was the height of perfection – a palace!

My knight led me to a simple, modest home. Eliezer's ten brothers and sisters were lining the path outside the house, waiting for his bride. In contrast to my mother, who had hidden in the kitchen, his mother, Rivka, stood outside with the others, wearing traditional Moroccan dress with an embroidered kerchief. A *balabusta* (housewife) in an apron, hands calloused from working the land, she had taken a break from her Shabbat cooking to welcome her son's bride. Eliezer's sisters couldn't believe that I was Moroccan. When they saw that I was a redhead, they thought I must be Ashkenazi. One of them murmured, "*Mzhyana!*" (Nice) while another quickly shushed her with *"Dialna"* – She's one of ours. I listened to their whispers and laughed to myself. Ashkenazi? Me?

Mother Rivka led me into the house, showed me the room where I was to sleep – the pillow and blanket already waiting for me on the bed – and invited me to sit at the table. Eliezer's father, Rabi Eliyahu, stood up and shook my hand. "Welcome," he said simply. I sat down, and in keeping with our rules of politeness, said I wasn't hungry. But his mother, just like my mother and all good Moroccans, wouldn't take no for an answer when it came to food. She served me meat dishes the likes of which I couldn't remember ever tasting: organ meats of lamb and beef that had just been slaughtered, and the big *frena* bread that reminded me of the immigrant camp. Then she returned to the kitchen to finish the Shabbat preparations.

The family members all went out of their way to spoil me and make me feel like a princess. When they asked me what I did and I told them I was a teacher and university student, his sisters swallowed me up with their looks of admiration.

For the Shabbat meal, I wore the flower-print dress I had bought for the occasion. I glanced at the table out of the corner of my eye. It wasn't yet set for dinner, and I wondered how it would hold all the brothers and sisters, including the married ones who had come to meet me and a brother who arrived with a new girlfriend. But when we sat down, wonder of wonders, there was room for everyone, and the sounds of singing rose up to the ceiling – the traditional Shabbat melodies of "Lecha Dodi" and "Eshet Hayil." Instead of two *challot* that came out of the *frena*, twelve loaves were spread out on the tablecloth, representing the Twelve Tribes of Israel. Mother Rivka didn't rush around carrying plates, like my mother. She sat at the table beside her husband while her daughters served the meal, and she supervised and whispered, "Bring this to her, give that to her," meaning me. Eliezer sat beside me, happy and proud as a peacock.

After the meal, he said, "Come, Miriam, I'll show you the *moshav*," and we went out for an evening stroll. He pointed out the sites and explained, "Here's the store. Here's where my older brother Moshe lives. Those are homes of *moshav* members." He showed me the onion fields and told me about the challenges of establishing the *moshav*. He also spoke about the skirmishes with the *fedayeen*, the Arab peasants, as the *moshav* was near the borders of the Arab towns of Shechem and Jenin.

We walked together along the paths that he had walked as a child, and slowly we dared to hold hands. I began to get used to the subtle scent of Brut, the aftershave that he always wore.

On Shabbat morning, Eliezer woke up before me, and when I walked into the living room, he was already scrubbed and polished, ready to go off to synagogue. After services, he took me to the stable behind the house and showed me the cows and sheep. "This is my dream," he said. "When I get old, I hope to have my own herd. Every day I'll take the animals out to pasture, sit on the banks of a stream or in some quiet place, and you'll come sit beside me." I admit I was surprised. We hadn't yet stood under the *chuppah* and he already knew what he would be doing in his old age?

Eliezer also described how he enjoyed helping the ewes give birth, and the wonderful feeling he had during the process. The young version of me mumbled, "Wow, I'm so afraid of giving birth! It must be so painful," but he put his hand on my shoulder and said, "Don't worry, I'll be there if you need help. I'm an expert." As he spoke these calming words, the lambs came up to us, licking his hands and making loving sounds.

We had some fascinating conversations that Shabbat. I learned that Eliezer had begun working when he was only seven years old. Each morning he would rise at five a.m. and take the livestock out to pasture. At six thirty, he would go home, shower, and get ready for school. He was the third child, but his family treated him as the oldest. They did nothing without consulting him first. He was the one who called the shots in his family, just as I was the one who wore the trousers in my family.

He described the back-breaking work in the fields that his parents awoke to each morning, even then when they were getting old. He described them as satisfied tillers of the soil. When I expressed my doubts, he took me behind the house to see "Mother Rivka's garden," which contained the best the land had to offer: tomatoes, coriander, celery, parsley, and pumpkin. Not just any old pumpkins, but enormous ones that she used to make the soup served with couscous, and it was even tastier than my mother's. Everything on the *moshav* was fresh. By noon, the chicken that had stood on the doorstep just that morning was slaughtered and served at the table, after Mother Rivka had plucked its feathers one by one and passed it through a flame to singe off the rest.

During Shabbat, I also learned that Eliezer had gone to high school at the Amit Youth Village in Petach Tikva. In the army, he served in a battalion later known as the 12th "Barak" Battalion, the same unit in which Eliraz was, years later, deputy battalion commander. I had no clue about the army, so I didn't know that Barak was a Golani unit. Once, a long time after our marriage, when I was invited to give a lecture at an army base near Kiryat Shemona, Eliezer went with me and saw a photo of his army buddies on the wall. Who could imagine that Barak would be the battalion in which Eliraz would go to his death?

After the army, with a practical environmental engineering certificate in hand, Eliezer began to work in the *kibbutzim* of the Jezreel Valley, near his *moshav*. On our trips to the *moshav*, he would point and say, "Here's where we fenced in the pond, and here we sprayed for mosquitoes when they dried up the swamp."

Later, he won a tender for managing the sewage department in Kiryat Malachi, and went to live there. He rented an apartment and led the life of a young, independent bachelor. I found this quite charming; he knew how to cook and clean, do the laundry and iron. Suddenly I realized why my romantic dreams had been of a man older than me. I don't think I would have managed with someone as young and inexperienced as myself.

As part of his work, he met managers and supervisors of hospitals and other institutions. He had a rare ability to develop relationships and maintain them over time. Up until he died, he kept up with a wide-ranging, colorful circle of friends.

A few years after obtaining the position in Kiryat Malachi, he was appointed Health Ministry supervisor for the Shlomo district, and rented a room in a bachelors' apartment in Sharm el-Sheikh. This was a new challenge, as he was the only religiously observant man in all of Sharm. On Shabbat and holidays, he told me, he went to the nearby army base in order to pray in a minyan. "What about love?" I asked him. The open conversation helped us feel more at ease with each other. Eliezer related that he had been searching for "someone special," but hadn't found her there. When I raised an eyebrow, he asked, "Where could I have found my one and only? On the nude beach at Sharm? On my monthly visits to the *moshav* for a long weekend?"

On Saturday night, *motzaei Shabbat* after the Havdalah ceremony, we began to discuss the wedding in concrete terms. Eliezer told his parents the date, and said to me, "Don't worry about a thing. Whatever you want, it's yours." He knew that I had not one *agora* to my name. With a casual gesture, he handed me some cash and instructed, "Go look for the prettiest dress. Buy nightgowns, and blankets and housewares for the apartment."

It was the beginning of the academic year, my fourth and last before earning my teaching certificate, and Eliezer said, somewhat regretfully, that he was willing to leave Sharm for my sake. He began to look for work in the center of the country, and rented a furnished apartment in Rehovot. He gave me the key so that I could start moving our things. Mother went to the Bedouin market, and with the money she earned cleaning stairwells she bought plates and pots. I traveled by bus to Rehovot with the heavy baskets. Mother had begun to act like Father, who always saved the juiciest apple in the crate for me. Every time she saw an attractive item, she would say, "That's for Miriam – that's for the bride."

The day of the wedding drew closer, but it was not until we went to choose the invitations that the penny dropped, and suddenly I realized that I was going to marry this man. What if he wasn't right for me? Maybe it wasn't so good that he was ten years older than me? On the way to the print shop, I found a host of reasons to humiliate him.

"I don't want to marry you," I said.

"Okay," he quipped, and continued walking.

"What do you mean, 'okay'? Didn't you hear me? I don't want to marry you!" I whined and complained like a baby, while he nodded. "Yes, I heard, it's all right," and he grasped my arm and continued walking.

I still don't understand how he had the resilience and patience to put up with my nonsense. Not that I object to differences of opinion between spouses – that's natural. But when one makes a statement and the other throws out an answer, they begin to argue. When conflict rages, it's so easy to break the rules of the game. Perhaps Eliezer, with his quiet wisdom, realized that my behavior came from fear. Perhaps he understood that I still hadn't decided what I wanted from life and the world. Either way, he held his tongue and neither argued nor protested.

At the print shop, he gave me free reign, and I designed a silly invitation with four hearts, the height of kitsch. Later, my children turned white when they saw it, but that was the fashion at the time, shiny hearts. We invited some three hundred people, and Eliezer organized two buses, one to bring my guests from Be'er

Sheva and the other for his from the *moshav*. Then he accompanied me to a bridal shop in Rehovot to choose a dress.

We bought the wedding rings in Be'er Sheva, simple gold bands. His uncle recommended a disco band. I invited all my friends from university, and the neighbors exclaimed, "Miriam's getting married at the Neptune Hall in Bat Yam! Not just any hall – a hall that advertises on the radio!"

Then came the hardest part of the wedding preparations: buying clothes for Father. He had never worn pants or a shirt. He had spent his whole life wearing a *sharwal* (loose-fitting pants), *jalabiya*, a black *tarboosh* instead of a *kippah*, and pointed roach-killer shoes. At the store, he was lost. He didn't even know how to push his arm through a shirt sleeve. I didn't ask him to wear a tie, just pants and a shirt. But Father complained. "What do I need this for?" he pointed to the zipper. "I need ventilation." He was so skinny that when he went into the dressing room, the pants slipped off. When I threaded a belt in the belt loops, he pulled it up to his neck and almost choked. "What do you want from me?" he whined in Arabic, when the tailor came to mark the hems. "What does the length matter? Who will notice? I'll sit down, I promise I won't get up from the chair, I promise."

After the clothes, it was time for the shoes. No shoe was as comfortable to him as the pointy ones. One was too closed, one was too tight, another was too heavy. "What's wrong with my shoes? The pants will cover them up anyway."

I didn't buy any clothes for Mother, because I knew she wouldn't come to the wedding. I begged and cried, but she said, "It wouldn't be fair, as I didn't go to your sister Zehava's wedding, either." This pierced my heart. How could I walk down the aisle to the *chuppah* without my mother beside me? But I sensed that she was praying for me, with all the blessings in the world.

I arranged for the henna celebration to be held in the WIZO hall on Sanhedrin Street, near my home, the night before the wedding. I was very excited, because this was the first time my parents would meet Eliezer's father and mother. Mazal Dahan – our intellectual neighbor, a Moroccan influenced by French culture, who knew how to bake as well as cook – promised to prepare delicacies as if it were her own daughter's wedding. The cooking party lasted for an entire week, to the sounds of the phonograph playing Moroccan songs, and the apartment door remained open so that the sounds of celebration would spill out into the street. The neighborhood women came and went with pots and trays. One peeled the red peppers to fry, another peeled the carrots, and they all sang, "Miriam's getting married." Each woman who came in with a cake also contributed a song in honor of the *arusa*, the bride. There are some beautiful wedding songs in Moroccan: before the bride puts on her white dress, she is told through song that love also means separation, and that joy can be mixed with sadness.

And the giant pots! At one point, a pot was placed on the stovetop, but the gas had been used up. So people began to bring individual Primus stoves, lots of them. One was put in the living room, another in the dining area, with a different pot on each stove – chicken in one, the roast waiting to be sliced in another; this one with mushroom and onion gravy, that one with tomato sauce. And the salads! Dozens of salads in small serving dishes. Spicy roasted peppers, *matbucha* (sweet roasted peppers and tomatoes), Moroccan carrots, eggplant – fried and in mayonnaise – as well as new delicacies I had never tasted before. It was now time to open the jar of pickles that had been bought a month ago and placed on the balcony, waiting for the big day.

Zehava helped with the cooking, and Machluf, Charly, and Batsheva helped me set the table. Disposable dishes? Not in our house, that was considered disgraceful. For the first time in my life, I rented plates and silverware. Dripping with sweat, I carried the pots to the hall. Then I ran home to greet the members of my future husband's family, who had come from the *moshav* to attend the henna and *mikveh* party. "Miriam," Eliezer had advised me the day before, "Put some boxes in your room, on top of the closet." What kind of boxes? I asked. "It doesn't matter, whatever you find. Empty boxes. If someone from my family asks you what the boxes are for, tell them that is where your dowry is being kept."

The Peretz family arrived. My parents and his exchanged kisses and embraces as if they had known each other for a hundred years. Their Moroccan mentality connected them without words. First things first – my parents took out the *br'rad*, the Moroccan teapot. They poured tea into glasses and served nuts and dried fruit – pistachios, raisins, and almonds. That was just the introduction.

Mother urged them to sit down to eat before we went out to the *mikveh*. They avoided her entreaties, saying "Soon," but she didn't give up. As she served, she said, "In the name of Rabbi Shimon bar Yochai, eat just this piece of fish." Then it was, "In the name of Rabbi Meir Ba'al Haness, eat just this little piece of chicken," and she served it. She trotted out all the rabbis over the food, with her "Just taste this" and "Just sample that." The Peretz family sat and ate, and the atmosphere was cheerful and friendly. But I was a bit worried. Would they really go into my room?

Of course they did. "What's this?" they asked, pointing to the crates, and I replied, enjoying the moment, "My dowry! Blankets, pillows, and sheets!"

Eliezer smiled at me, and I at him.

Dusk fell, it was getting dark, and I prepared to go to the *mikveh*. I put on a blouse and skirt, and packed my new carryall with the necessary supplies – soap, shampoo, sponge, a towel, all new. When I opened our door on the second floor, I saw that all the women in our building were waiting for me, one with a tambourine, another with a drum. Each one waved a bag with cookies or candies, and each one also had a tote bag on her shoulder. So what if I was the only one who had paid the entrance fee for the *mikveh*? All the neighborhood women wanted to take showers, and they did so thanks to me, because in our neighborhood, money for the *mikveh* didn't grow on trees.

As I made my way down the stairs, they broke out in song. *Kulululu* echoed from wall to wall, as if we had been thrown into the family of Sallah Shabati, the Mizrachi immigrant in the iconic Israeli film. I marched to the bus stop followed by thirty singing women. We paraded to the bus stop, because how else would I get to the *mikveh*? No one had a car, or even a driver's license. We boarded the bus with our cookies and our drums, and the driver and the other passengers joined in the singing. Strangers hugged me and said, "*Ya binti*, may God bless you and your husband." I was kissed, almost crushed. What joy, what love on that crowded, stuffy bus!

I wanted Mother to come with me to the *mikveh*. I didn't realize that the neighbors and elderly women would immerse themselves along with me. The custom was to immerse oneself seven times, with each dip accompanied by singing and dancing. After the seventh dip, they pelted me with candies, and the unmarried girls were instructed to fish them out of the water, an auspicious sign for finding a groom in the near future.

I left the *mikveh* wearing a different outfit – a traditional Moroccan caftan, black with lots of gold embroidery – and went straight to the WIZO hall, where we had a party with singing and dancing, and a feast fit for a king. After the last guest left, we stayed to clean up until three a.m. The next day would be my wedding, and I was exhausted.

I got dressed for the wedding in the Sarit bridal salon in Rehovot. My sister Zehava took care of dressing my brothers, and Father, who still didn't understand why he was being punished by having to wear pants. We met at the hall in Bat Yam.

Father stood beside me as if waiting for instructions. He honestly didn't know what he was supposed to do. I said, "You have to stand in the entrance and say *shalom* to everyone who comes in." So he stood there and said *shalom*, the only word he knew in Hebrew. When the guests attempted to draw him into conversation, he shrugged his shoulders in helplessness, because he couldn't understand a word. I told him, "When people give you envelopes, keep them safe, as they have money inside," and he folded all of them into his shirt pocket. My brother Charly sat next to Father at the family table of honor, and when the band began to play ballroom tunes, they blushed in embarrassment.

On our wedding night, we stayed at the Hof Hotel in Netanya, the city where Eliezer had studied Arabic. My mother, who hadn't escorted me to the *chuppah*, met us at Eliezer's parents' home along with the rest of the family for the Shabbat following the wedding. I told her that his mother liked drinking glasses, and she lugged a basket with fifty glasses on the bus, all the way from Be'er Sheva to Moshav Gadish.

When we finally went to our nest, the rented apartment in Rehovot, I dreamed of living a quiet life. But again I was forced to travel. I continued taking the bus to university in Be'er Sheva, while working as a substitute teacher at Katzir High School. Eliezer did not acclimate to his job in the center of the country. He missed the sea and the desert landscape. He went back to Sharm, and I returned to my parents' home. Once again we maintained our relationship through the public phone in the neighborhood shopping area. Toward the end of the academic year, I began to hear hints that as his wife, I should follow him. I was overcome with fear. To Sharm? But I was pregnant. How could I leave my parents?

When Uriel, our oldest, was five months old, Eliezer went to my father and said, "Rabi Ya'akov, I want Miriam to come with me."

My dear father didn't hesitate. "Of course, she's your wife," he replied, as tears burst from his eyes and poured down to his chin. I will never forget the day I left my parents' home. It was terrifying.

Both of them, Mother and Father, wept for a whole week. They knew that the break would be harsh, because there was no way they could travel to far-off Sharm. But through the pain, they felt no resentment toward Eliezer, who was effectively cutting me off from them, whereas all my friends were getting married and settling down in Be'er Sheva near their parents.

We packed Uriel into a simple infant carrier, and when I took him out into the hallway toward the stairs, Mother splashed water at me to ensure a safe journey. With each tap of my shoes on the steps, I bid another farewell to the world in which I had grown up.

Sharm brought me closer to my love, but took me far from those who loved me. The day I left my parents' home, their health and financial situation began to deteriorate.

CHAPTER 5

Uriel Is Born

My first pregnancy was shared in letters. Eliezer had returned to Sharm, and I was at my parents' home in Be'er Sheva. I was happy to sit with my growing stomach on the benches at university. I felt that the unborn child inside me was listening to the classes and learning along with me. But how could I tell my husband about my doubts and fears? On the payphone in the neighborhood shopping center? The letters that Eliezer sent me during those months were clear as water. He reassured me, promised that he would help take care of the baby, swore that the only loves in his life were his wife Miriam and the twelve children we would have together.

Twelve?

When Eliezer had mentioned that number before our wedding, it sounded romantic. But in reality, as I carried my first pregnancy, I was lonely and distraught. Mother did everything she could to ease my burden. Although Zehava had already made her a grandmother, she was very excited about her oldest daughter's first pregnancy. She filled me with all sorts of delicacies so that I would be strong and healthy. I had only to mention the scent of the dish that emanated from a neighbor's apartment, and without hesitation, she would knock on their door and demand, "Give some to my girl." Mother also warned me, "If you have a craving for something, don't touch any part of your body, or else the baby will be born with a birthmark in the shape of the food you're thinking about."

I had a craving for cherries. I had only heard about this fruit, but never tasted it. I wrote to Eliezer about this, and he, in Sharm, was stumped. Cherries? In Be'er Sheva? How would he find them? In those days, cherries were a luxury only the wealthy could afford. On one of his monthly visits to the city, we went for a walk. We walked by all the stores and restaurants and peeked into all the display windows, searching desperately for a hint of a cherry.

Finally we passed a small restaurant in the old city, and I saw a jar of preserved cherries in the window. Eliezer didn't bother to ask the price. He pulled out a pile of *lirot* from his pockets, paid, and asked the merchant to permit me to sit down and eat them right there in the store, because I couldn't restrain myself any longer. I can still feel the taste of those cherries on my lips.

In the sixth month of my pregnancy, Eliezer came down with hepatitis, and he was admitted to Soroka Hospital. When I arrived, the doctors wouldn't allow me to get close to him, fearing I might catch the disease. I stood outside the room, crestfallen. The man lying there in the bed was my husband, but he wasn't allowed to hug me! A doctor suggested I have a blood test, and ten days later we received the results. They showed that I was a carrier of the hepatitis gene. That meant that Eliezer and I were permitted to have physical contact, but it also meant potential harm to the fetus. They said clearly, "You must decide what to do with the pregnancy. It would be better to abort, because the fetus has undoubtedly been damaged."

With that sentence, my entire world fell apart. The joy of my first pregnancy soured into fear. In those days ultrasound was not yet available, and Eliezer's hepatitis was serious. What should we do? The doctors surely knew what they were talking about.

"Wait," Eliezer advised. Once every two weeks, I went to the hospital for a blood test, and the doctor passed the stethoscope over my stomach. Those were the tests we had then, very primitive compared to today's. The pessimistic doctors continued to recommend abortion. When Eliezer recovered and was released from the hospital, he told me that we would travel to Netivot to consult with the Baba Sali. I asked how, as I knew it wasn't easy to arrange an audience with the revered rabbi and kabbalist. For one thing, he didn't meet with women. But my father-in-law Eliyahu Peretz pulled some strings. The three of us entered the Baba Sali's room, which was simple and modest. An atmosphere of sanctity prevailed. The Baba Sali, his head wrapped in a white *tallit*, spoke in Moroccan Arabic to my father-in-law. Then I gathered the courage to open my mouth. I told him what they had said to me in the hospital.

"How do those doctors know what will happen to the boy?" the Baba Sali demanded. He answered without looking at me, instead directing his gaze at Eliezer and his father.

Hope flickered in me for a moment. A boy? Was he hinting that there was a male baby in my womb?

"The doctors aren't Elijah the Prophet," the Baba Sali declared, then added, "*K'lshi m'zhian*" (everything's fine). He gave me a bottle of holy water, instructed me to spread it on my stomach and also drink some of it, and concluded by wishing my father-in-law "*mazal tov, mazal tov.*"

I left his room happy and full of faith, hoping with all my heart that the doctors were indeed mistaken, and that soon we would discover that the venerated rabbi was right.

On November 23, 1976, a blustery winter night, the contractions began. I told Mother that I felt an unfamiliar pain, and she advised, "Wait. Don't rush to the hospital. They just stick their hands in and annoy you." She called our upstairs neighbor, Ruby Vaknin – a young, modern woman with whom we often consulted – and she instructed me to watch the clock: "When the contractions come every five minutes, call a taxi." So that's what I did.

When Mother and I got into the taxi, I asked the driver to stop at the shopping center. I called Eliezer from the payphone and told him the baby was on the way. What did he say? "Great."

I boiled with fury. I was still stuck in the romance novel. I was awaiting words of love that would help me overcome the pain, but my far-off husband just said, "Great, good luck."

The birth went on and on – from one a.m. to four p.m. the next day. My firstborn was a son, as the Baba Sali had prophesied, but he sure took his time coming out into the world. I suffered and screamed, while Mother stood behind the door, praying. In the afternoon, Eliezer arrived by plane. He heard from Mother about the difficulty I was in, and joined her in prayer. To either side of me I heard *mazal tov, mazal tov,* as one woman gave birth, and then another, until it seemed I was the only one left who was still in labor.

"Help me!" I begged the doctors, and finally they decided to use vacuum extraction. Amidst the cries coming from my own throat I heard, "*Mazal tov*, Miriam. *Ben zachar* – it's a boy! Three kilos and 250 grams (7.2 pounds)." They whisked him away immediately so I wouldn't infect him with hepatitis. I was exhausted, and my joy was diluted with distress. The nurse whispered in my ears that he was blonde and beautiful, but God in heaven, show me my son! For two days they wouldn't let me touch him. My womb was contracting, each stitch burned, but they wouldn't let me see my baby.

Eliezer came to visit me and related that during the long hours when he had sat in the corridor with my mother, he had read the *siddur*, and had come across the verse that mentions four angels: "Michael on my right, Gabriel on my left, Uriel before me, Raphael behind me, and the Divine Presence upon my head." When he heard my cries of pain, he prayed, "Please God, help her, be like the angel Uriel for her, and we will call our son Uriel." I heard the name Uriel, and tears of exhaustion and joy ran down my cheeks. In those days Uriel was not a common name. I had only heard of Uriel Ofek, an author of children's literature, whose books I loved, and Eliezer's explanation touched me deeply.

After two days of tests, we found out that not only had my firstborn son avoided hepatitis, but he was also free of jaundice. Finally they placed him in my arms, and I couldn't believe that this small, live thing – so beautiful, with chiseled features – was mine. I was afraid I would drop him, and each time I held him, I prayed to God to keep him safe: "Please, please, just as he has no jaundice and was not infected with disease, please let no harm come to him."

Uriel, my firstborn son, came to my parents' home on Sanhedrin Street, into my childhood bedroom, which Mother cleaned and polished, removing every speck of dust. We hadn't prepared anything before the birth because we didn't know the sex of the baby, but mainly because Mother feared the evil eye. Eliezer went out to purchase a bed, cloth diapers, and various types of bottles. I was not allowed to nurse, because the doctors still feared infection. As I was in such pain, I didn't think of nursing as an experience of which I had been deprived. Only after a few weeks had passed, when I got my strength back and saw other women nursing, did I regret that I could not nourish my son from my own body.

As we had no washing machine, Mother boiled the cotton diapers in a giant iron pot she placed on a kerosene burner. She still did not believe in the power of gas, neither for cooking nor for laundry. Early each morning, she filled the pot with water and dropped a stocking filled with soap flakes into it, filling the apartment with a wonderful scent. She rushed to hang the diapers in the sun so that they would dry by sunset. One couldn't leave them on the line during the night, she asserted, because they would attract evil spirits and demons. This custom had to be observed for forty days.

In those days, 1976, it wasn't typical to hold a big party for the *brit milah*. No one had money for such things. But Eliezer, whose joy was unbounded, booked the Argaman Hall in Be'er Sheva for the occasion. Unlike him, I was filled with trepidation. The birth had ended happily, but who could guarantee that the *brit* would be successful as well? Why should I let them hurt my baby son?

Wise, kind Eliezer was able to comfort me this time as well. He spoke inspiringly about the privilege of our son entering the covenant of our forefather Abraham, and promised that my dear father would sit on Elijah's chair and hold his grandson by his firstborn daughter.

On the day of the *brit*, we washed our son in the new plastic tub. Grandmother Rivka, my mother-in-law, and Grandmother Ito, my mother, competed for the honor of being the first to touch him, and with each drop of water they splashed on his back and arms, they blessed him. Then they had the unmarried neighbor girls splash water on him, to bring good luck, but warned them, "Not on the navel!"

Wrapped in a new towel and wearing a lace dress that could be rolled up, my son looked like an angel. It was no coincidence, I felt, that soon they would announce his name – the angel Uriel.

Of course my father had to wear pants when he sat in the seat of honor. My mother, who hadn't attended my wedding, came to the *brit*, and a thread of joy connected us all. From the moment I entered the hall, we were showered with blessings and prayers. God willing, may we be privileged to lead him to the *chuppah*. May this child bring happiness to his parents. Who could imagine that even the best of prayers had a time limit?

During the ceremony, I closed my ears so as to shut out little Uriel's wailing. All of Be'er Sheva celebrated with us. They returned three weeks later to celebrate the *pidyon haben*, the ceremony of the symbolic redemption of the firstborn son, which was held in my parents' home, and was an even bigger celebration than the *brit*. We bought him a new outfit and arranged all the gold jewelry I had received for the wedding – a watch, gold chain, and rings – on a decorative platter. Following the custom, the rabbi asked me if this was my son, and if I was willing to exchange him for property. "Yes," I answered, wearing a broad smile.

In those days, powdered milk was not yet sold in our neighborhood store, and our neighbor Ruby recommended giving Uriel ordinary cow's milk boiled with water. Although we were careful to keep everything very sterile, he vomited and had constant diarrhea. I remember standing in the kitchen, filling up the bottle exactly to the sixty cc line, and hoping that he would keep it down. But he would expel it from both ends.

As if that wasn't enough, he gradually developed a new, worrisome behavior. He cried incessantly, and when he exhausted himself, he lolled his head backwards, rolled his eyes, and stopped breathing.

My husband had gone back to Sharm. New mother that I was, I screamed, "He's dead! He's dead!" All the neighborhood women came running. One said to turn him upside down, another recommended shaking him, while my mother pressed on his bottom. Each woman had her own method. The minutes passed like an eternity until finally he regained consciousness, smiling and acting as if nothing had happened.

At first this happened twice a week, then every day, and sometimes even twice a day. At one point, I broke down on Ruby's shoulder: "I want to die! I'm young, I'm only twenty-one!" I couldn't stand the thought that this child would die in my arms.

The family physician was also at a loss. He advised me to make an appointment at Kupat Holim Gimel, a specialist's clinic. I dressed him in his best clothes. Eliezer came especially from Sharm and we took our five-month-old for an examination. While we were waiting, we went outside, spread a blanket on the lawn, and saw that he was full of life, his eyes dancing curiously from side to side, as if to swallow the whole world. We went in to see the doctor, and I told him that the baby had frequent fainting spells.

"Lady," the specialist reassured me, "It's nothing."

"What do you mean, nothing?" I demanded, incredulous.

"The kid just wants some attention," the doctor explained. "That's his way of getting it. The next time he cries, pay no attention. Just let him cry."

We returned to my parents' home – Eliezer, Uriel, and myself – where Mother was on tenterhooks, waiting to hear what the specialist had said. We were embarrassed. What could we say? That we, out of overwhelming love and dedication to our tiny son, were causing him to faint? That from now on she mustn't rush to him the second he makes a sound?

In the end we had no choice but to tell her. Mother protested, "What kind of doctor would let my grandson cry? Is his heart made of stone? Or iron?" She refused to take the doctor's advice, and continued attending to Uriel when he cried. But deep inside, I felt calmer. My baby was healthy, he was developing properly, and there was no reason to worry.

Then it was time to leave. I went off to be with my husband, and Uriel to be with his father. It was the first time in my life I had ever boarded an airplane. But I wasn't alone – in my arms I held a baby not yet six months old. Once inside the plane, I glanced around me and saw that all the passengers were calm. I was the only one who was paralyzed with fear. Then the plane landed, and who stood on the ground beside it? Eliezer. Sharm was a small place, and thanks to people he knew, he was allowed to meet us on the tarmac at the foot of the stairs. He grabbed the blue infant carrier from my arms, plucked little Uriel from it and boasted to everyone in the airport, "This is my son! This is my Uriel."

When we reached his apartment, I opened up the playpen in the living room and placed Uriel inside. Then I went into the kitchen, and I had not yet managed to put the teapot on the gas burner when I heard him crying. "You're not moving," Eliezer declared. I heard Uriel lose his breath, but Eliezer blocked me. "You're not going, not yet. Wait a minute." I pushed him with all my strength. I had to run to my son. But he was stronger than me, and he didn't give in. A minute passed, then two, and I heard his crying slowly lose momentum.

"Everything's fine," whispered Eliezer. "He's our son; he has to be fine."

That was the last time Uriel lost consciousness after a crying jag.

CHAPTER 6

My Romance with Sharm el-Sheikh – Life in Sinai

My romance with Sharm, which the Israelis also called by its biblical name of Ofira, began just after our wedding. Eliezer encouraged me to come for a visit, and arranged a ride for me with a doctor from Ashkelon. During the trip we had long conversations on topics I was studying, from the destruction of the Second Temple to the history of anti-Semitism. The road refused to end. "When will we get there?" I asked once an hour, and each time he answered, "Soon." The sun was beginning to set, when out of the dry desert landscape I glimpsed a slice of ocean. The ocean! I was thrilled. How I loved that deep blue. But the doctor tempered my excitement. "We've reached Eilat, not Sharm." We had been driving for an entire day.

Eliezer had told me that when I reached Sharm, he would be in Ras Nasrani. He promised to return quickly. In the meantime, he said, I should go to the apartment he was renting with his friends. It was 45°C (113°F) outside, and I was dripping and exhausted. The doctor let me off at the entrance to the building, and I climbed to the third floor and knocked. A young man opened the door, blonde hair cascading down to his shoulders, like an actor out of a film.

"*Shalom*," I said, "I'm Eliezer's wife."

"There's no Eliezer here," he grumbled, and slammed the door shut.

I went down the stairs to the sidewalk and sat in the entrance, in the suffocating heat, after an endless car trip, and thought: my dear husband has tricked me. He said he had an apartment. How can he have an apartment if no one knows him? The redhead in me came out. Just wait, I thought, fuming. I waited for no more than half an hour, but it seemed like an eternity to me. I've come all this way only to have my husband abandon me in the street! I waited impatiently for him to arrive so that I could give him a piece of my mind.

Finally, there he was, walking toward me, all smiles. Instead of hugs and kisses, our reunion began with shouts and accusations: "What's the matter with you! Why did you lie to me? You said you had an apartment!"

Eliezer laughed, "Of course I do." He grabbed my arm and led me up to the third floor. He knocked on the door, and who opened it? The blonde male model again, but this time he slapped Eliezer's shoulders in affection.

"But you told me there wasn't any Eliezer here!" I protested. That was when I found out that all of Sharm el-Sheikh knew my husband by his last name, Peretz, instead of his first. From that day on, until he died, I also called him Peretz, my Peretz.

The Sharm apartment had private rooms and a shared kitchen, and an atmosphere I had never before encountered, a collection of unusual characters, including a young unmarried couple who were living together. Eliezer entered the kitchen, which was equipped with attractive cupboards, and served me a meal fit for a queen. I wandered through the apartment as if in a dream. It had a bathtub – not just a shower, but a real bathtub! The windows were long and narrow, to filter out the powerful sunlight. Each window offered a beautiful view; you could see the ocean from one, the desert from another. A third window looked out onto a rock carved by the wind and rain, which people called the "Kennedy head" due to its resemblance to the famous president. There was a balcony as well, but the cityscape I saw from it was very different from the one in Be'er Sheva, from my parents' balcony. There I sat and watched cars and people go by. Here the streets were empty, as everyone fled the heat and took shelter inside in the air conditioning.

When I returned from that visit, I informed my parents that Eliezer was preparing a lovely third-floor apartment for me in Sharm. They were shocked at the thought of me moving. But, I thought, so what if it was only a rental? So what if it was far away? So what if my husband and I were the only religious couple? Uriel was five months old, and they felt strongly bonded to him. But they bit their lips and helped me pack so that we would be united, far to the south.

At that time, the civil authority of Sharm was headed by Reuven Aloni, of blessed memory, Shulamit Aloni's husband. He sent word that he would send a truck to my parents' home to move my possessions. I laughed – what possessions did I have? I informed the authority that this was an unnecessary waste of money. We agreed that my meager possessions would be loaded onto a truck transporting sewage pipes to Sharm. We loaded the truck with Uriel's baby bed, crates of books, and some clothes. Mother bought some pieces of cloth at the Bedouin souk, and rolled potatoes and onions inside them, until I would have time to sew elastic into the edges and convert them into fitted sheets.

Meanwhile, Eliezer was hard at work trying to furnish our new apartment. There were no double beds to be found in Sharm, so he took two Jewish Agency iron bedsteads, the kind allotted to new immigrants, and fastened them together with wire. He found a sofa and table that someone had discarded and set them up in the living room. He also sent for the electrical appliances we had purchased with the money from the wedding and stored at his parents' home on the *moshav*: a gas range, an oven, a washing machine, and an Amcor 16 refrigerator, which is still in my home to this day. Even if it sputters sometimes, I like the fact that it reminds me of my younger days. It knows it was purchased with love.

One hour after Uriel and I landed in Sharm, I went to a job interview with Nirit Reichel, principal of the local school. She invited me to her home, yet another new world to me. She had sofas and an organ in the living room, and she stood in the kitchen and prepared salad from a can. Who had ever heard of a tin can of carrots and peas? In my parents' home, the food was always fresh. Mayonnaise was never used.

"Right now I don't have a job for you. I don't have hours or a position," Nirit explained after hearing what I had studied. "But I would be happy if you would work in our primary school." I was not put off by the fact that this was a secular school. Degania School in Be'er Sheva, where I had taught, was also secular. I had never worked in a religious school, by my own choice.

The entire school numbered less than one hundred students, who changed each year because their parents were military personnel. In my first year I had to deal with a challenging culture shock: the residents of Sharm shared a language, a military jargon of which I understood not a word. At first I found myself cut off from social life, even lonely, but slowly our home became a community focal point. Students and their parents came to us for Kabbalat Shabbat. Eliezer organized a synagogue in a bomb shelter, where we began to hold bar mitzvah ceremonies. Thanks to our religious uniqueness, we both felt in some ways like pioneers.

The most difficult obstacle we faced in religious life was the *mikveh*. We asked a rabbi, and he said I could immerse in the ocean. Once a month, when darkness fell, Eliezer would drive me over in the jeep. He would park opposite the water so that the headlights would light my way, and I would enter the water wearing a bathing suit and carrying a stick. Why a stick? I would search for a spot on the ocean floor into which I could drive the stick, and then use it to hang up my bathing suit. Each month I dreaded this nighttime dip. Sometimes I shuddered after stepping on a spiny sea creature. I was afraid of what might happen when the water covered my head, as required by halachah.

Four months after I arrived in Sharm, I became pregnant with Eliraz. Perhaps it happened due to my fear of these immersions – a pregnant woman doesn't have to use the *mikveh*. As opposed to the first pregnancy, this one was easy, but I missed Mother's attentions. On the eve of Tisha b'Av, I arrived in Be'er Sheva with Uriel, then eighteen months old, and contractions began. This time I had no need to call our neighbor, Ruby; I knew I had to watch the clock and wait until the contractions came every five minutes. Where was Eliezer when I needed him? In Sharm. When we called him, he behaved exactly as he had during the first delivery. "Good luck," he said, and went back to sleep. This time I wasn't angry. What could he have done to help? There was no need for him to be there, either, as the birth was short and easy. In just three hours it was over. At four a.m. on Friday, 8 Av (August 11, 1978), our second son was born. He was dark and hairy, and cried loudly right away.

He also died on a Friday, the same day of the week on which he was born.

Eliezer arrived from Sharm on Friday afternoon. My family greeted him with "*Mazal tov!* Another son!" Radiant, he rushed to the pay phone to announce the news to the entire world. Sitting beside my bed, my husband said that he would like to name the baby Eliyahu, after his father, as this was an auspicious sign for a long life. "What about Eliya?" I suggested, and he agreed. But I wasn't sure about this choice. I told him that when the contractions started, I had tried to take a nap, and I daydreamed that someone was talking to me, saying I had a secret. I thought this secret should be expressed in the baby's name.

Eliezer gave his interpretation: "Miriam, the secret is Elijah the Prophet; they say he is 'the hidden one.'"

I pulled the blanket toward me, and I said that *raz* was a synonym for "secret." Combining Eliyahu and *raz* produced Eliraz. Eliezer was satisfied, and again booked the Argaman Hall for a lavish *brit milah* celebration. My father wrinkled his nose. "What's this strange name all about?" he asked. "We're all familiar with names like Ya'akov, Yitzchak, Shimon, and Mordecai, but Uriel and Eliraz?" But Eliezer and I revealed the origin of the unusual name to no one.

After the *brit*, I brought Eliraz to Sharm, and he grew sturdy and robust. I nursed him, and when my milk was no longer sufficient, he began to guzzle down bottles, with no vomiting or diarrhea. As opposed to blond, calm Uriel, dark Eliraz was mischievous and full of life, sometimes even wild. One day, they were both playing with Lego bricks in the living room, when Uriel grabbed his younger brother's bag of Bamba, the popular Israeli peanut-butter snack. Eliraz didn't think twice – he took a bite out of his brother.

In my second year in Sharm, I became a homeroom teacher, and Principal Nirit allowed me to implement new ideas and initiatives. With her support and encouragement, I began to organize the school ceremonies. I felt that the town offered me room for personal growth, in addition to the breathtaking scenery and vibrant social life. Almost every day, I took the children to the library, which reminded me of Beit Yatziv from my childhood. Shosh Chen-Tov, the librarian, told me about days past, and I said, "Wow, I'm so jealous of you for taking part in building the state! I've done nothing." She exposed me to books about the years that led to Israel's founding. Only one thing bothered me: the distance from my family. When Mother's longing grew too intense to bear, she went up to our neighbor Ruby, who had a phone in her apartment, and called us. At the sound of her voice, I missed her even more.

Before the major Jewish holidays in the months of Tishrei and Nissan, we left Sharm and alternated visits to my parents and my in-laws. I was used to being in my parents' home, and I missed them terribly. I invited them to visit us. On Shabbat in Be'er Sheva, when my father went to synagogue, people would ask, "Where does your eldest daughter live?" But he didn't even know how to reply. The fathers would brag – my daughter lives in Ofakim, mine lives in Netivot – even though these were small towns. My father would boast, "My daughter lives in a place you can only get to *par avion*, by airplane."

As expected, Mother refused to fly down to visit us. But Father came. My sister Zehava made sure he wore pants, and he boarded the plane like a bridegroom. We had come to the Holy Land by boat, and now, for the first time in his life, he was flying! I was so excited to see him. But when he got off the plane he looked around and asked, "Where am I? Where are the houses? There's nothing here."

I held his arm and said, "Just a minute, Baba, *shwaye-shwaye* (slowly, slowly)." He complained, "*Ya binti, l'chla*" (This is a back-water, my daughter). Disappointment and concern were written all over his face. He couldn't understand why I was living there.

Then we drove to the residential area, and slowly the light returned to his eyes. When he walked into our apartment, he was more positive. "How lovely! What fresh air." He didn't realize that the fresh air was coming from the air conditioner. He called the bathtub a *hammam*, and refused to believe that it could be used on an ordinary weekday, not just in preparation for Shabbat or a holiday. Moroccan songs were playing on our record player, and I served the giant locus fish that Eliezer had bought directly from the fishermen. Father was used to carp. "Where did you get this enormous fish?" he marveled.

"It's from here, Father," I answered. "Everything's from here."

He returned to Be'er Sheva after a week, and told Mother and our neighbor Ruby that "Miriam lives in a palace." Of course this was an exaggeration, as we lived in an 80 square meter (860 square foot) apartment with tattered furniture. In synagogue on Shabbat, he told Rabbi Shlomo Alkabetz, "My daughter lives in a place fit for kings," and all the congregants congratulated him for the royal honor he had enjoyed.

In Sharm, Uriel and Eliraz had a magical childhood. They were children of freedom, of the sea, sand, and waves. I bought them a washtub and took it to a glazier who made a glass bottom for it. They sat in the water and watched the fish on Na'ama Beach or the IDF navy beach. They collected shells and stones on the coral reefs. The ocean remained in their bones from their days in Sharm. Later, long after we had moved on from there, they both learned to dive, and Eliraz bought himself a surfboard. While in Sharm, they also experienced military life, observing planes, tanks, and boats all around. On Yom Ha'atzmaut, Israel Independence Day, we rode out to Ras Mohammad on a Dabur boat, a pod of dolphins trailing behind. We visited the air force, armored corps, and navy bases many times.

Their favorite song was "*Bo'j, Ima*" (Come, Mother), and true to the song's lyrics, they wanted me beside them constantly. Above each bed we hung a sign with the verse *Hamalach hago'el oti* – "May the angel who has redeemed me from all harm bless these children" (Genesis 48:16). At Mother's advice, I stuffed *chamsa* charms against the evil eye under their mattresses and pillows. She told me to put *rota* leaves there as well, as this plant was effective in warding off evil. Every Passover she prepared a bag with salt and a piece of matzah, to be kept under the bed until the following Passover – another good luck charm.

Teaching in school and working in summer camp helped me develop warm relations with the students and their parents, and to integrate into the military community. My social circle was also broadened thanks to the connections my sons made in preschool. Uriel liked visiting Shelly Ben-Zvi, his friend from kindergarten, and when I saw her room, which was fully equipped with crayons and educational toys, I bought him the exact same things at a toy factory in Sharm. Eliezer nailed a large board with hooks onto the wall in their room. On each hook I hung a blue bucket, the kind that Ama dishwashing detergent comes in, and filled these containers with toys. Raising our two sons kept me busy round the clock.

Calm Uriel would enter the preschool room quietly and sit down to play, humming the popular children's song "Perach natati l'Nurit" (I gave Nurit a flower) to himself. Eliraz the mischief maker would burst in like the wind, pushing and making a racket. But when Dvora Elazari, the legendary nurse of Sharm, gave him a vaccination, he fainted, and she called a doctor. I was in shock. How could this be? Eliraz was so strong! We discovered that he was sensitive to one of the vaccination components, and that was the last vaccination he ever received. One day he disappeared from my sight while playing with David, the son of our neighbor Daniela Shopan. Daniela and I searched for the boys with growing alarm until we came to the area near the library, where we found the two of them sitting on a cliff, dangling their legs. I approached them on tiptoe, worried that if they heard me, they might be startled and fall off the cliff. I reached out and grabbed them both at the same time.

During my seven years in Sharm, 1975–1982, several military personnel who were also religious came to live there, including the Eliya and Giladi families, who are my neighbors in Givat Ze'ev today. We formed a group of observant people that met on Shabbat. I felt comfortable there; it had become my home. I never considered the possibility that the settlement might be evacuated. There was no television in Sharm, and radio reception was poor, so we were quite cut off and had no way of following the news on a daily basis. When we heard of Anwar Sadat's upcoming visit to Israel, we were very excited. Peace was coming!

But soon there was talk of evacuation, and the word "farewell" was blowing in the wind amid the golden sands. As the questions multiplied, our gloom intensified. We were young parents with two children. Where would we live? How would we make a living? Our reaction to Menachem Begin's momentous speech was mixed. On the one hand, we were happy about the upcoming visit of the Egyptian president. On the other hand, we had our suspicions. The day before the historic visit, when we heard that the residents of Yamit were demonstrating, we collected the children and held a quiet, polite demonstration. We didn't dare raise our voices, perhaps because we didn't quite believe the worst would happen.

By then Uriel was almost six years old, and he asked, "Why must we leave our home?" Eliraz protested as well, "This is our home. Where will we go?" Eliezer and I, like all the other inhabitants who were beginning to pack, explained to our children that we didn't want it, but that this was the price we had to pay for peace. "No!" they objected, stamping their feet. "We don't want to leave!"

"It's not in our hands," I replied tenderly, looking at my two flowers, imagining a pink cloud of hope and optimism floating above their heads. I promised, "If we have peace, you won't have to go to the army. There won't be any wars."

Holding on to that belief, I sat down to prepare the leave-taking ceremony and the last yearbook for the Ofira School. I didn't have to spend much time packing, because we didn't have many belongings. Most of the residents left before Passover 1982. We were among the few who decided to celebrate our last Seder night in Sharm. Ten families participated in the Seder, which we held in the portable prefab home of preschool teacher Edna Kedem, which was already empty. As I was the only one who had kosher-for-Passover pots, I cooked for everyone. We sat at a large table set with disposable plates and read the Haggadah with tears in our eyes, feeling as if we were literally leaving Egypt. After we finishing singing "*V'hi she'amdah*" (This is the promise that sustained our forefathers and us) and "*be'chol dor va'dor omdim aleinu la'chaloteinu*" (in every generation our enemies rise up against us to destroy us), we collected our children and walked down the long path between the abandoned prefab houses.

Ten families walked with their children, singing and crying.

For several weeks after the Seder, our hearts broke as the Israeli army began to blow up the military installations. We were ordered to go to Na'ama Beach, and while we sat there with Uriel and Eliraz, they shivered and asked, "Mom, why are they blowing up the ocean?"

Our farewell ceremony to Sharm was very difficult for the children. I framed their certificates from preschool, and they both star in the film that was made about Ofira. They were so proud to go to preschool in the T-shirts bearing the slogan "Gan Snapir, Ofira." Even after we left, Uriel wouldn't let me throw away those shirts. I kept them in my home in Givat Ze'ev, where many photos of Sharm hang on the walls. I gave the shirts to Eliraz's children. I had hoped he would be the one to pull them over their heads when they grew up and asked to hear about his memories of the landscape of his early childhood.

Our last day in Sharm was drowned in tears. Uriel and Eliraz could not stop crying. We got into the car and looked back at the view. No one knew if we would ever see it again. I said, trying to sound optimistic, "Children, look in front of you! We're going on a new journey. We'll build a new home."

About six months before the evacuation, Eliezer began to look for a new job. He heard that there was a good chance of finding one in Jerusalem. Then we saw a notice in a newspaper about a new communal settlement, and I tried to be enthusiastic. It was clear to me that after the endless open spaces of Sharm el-Sheikh, I could not live in a city. Our acclimation would be easier in a small, new place. That's how we got to Givat Ze'ev. Eliezer went to Jerusalem for the housing lottery that determined which plot we would receive – the plot where my family still lives today. Until the land was prepared and the house was built, we were allotted a prefab caravan home in the nearby settlement of Givon.

The trip up from Sharm was long and exhausting. We traveled from Dahab Beach to the crossing at Eilat, and from there turned north, while the kids fell asleep in the back seat of the car. We reached Givon at midnight. I opened the car door, and a cold wind slapped me in the face. What was this? It was March already, and we had left Sharm in short-sleeved T-shirts and sandals, while in Givon it was still freezing cold. I opened the door of our caravan home for the very first time and I wanted to run away: one bedroom, a small living room, a tiny kitchen, and a shower. Where was the bathtub? There was none. We put the children to bed in the bedroom, opened the living-room couch, which converted into a double bed, and I began a new tradition: every morning at dawn, I took a chair out to the yard and tried to catch the rays of sun.

We felt the change in ways far more significant than the climatic conditions, but we didn't complain. We felt like pioneers once more. I went to the elementary school in Givon and began to work as a substitute teacher on a voluntary basis, since the government was still paying my salary until the end of the school year. On Shabbat we took Uriel and Eliraz to see something new to them, the ancient tomb of the prophet Samuel at nearby Nabi Samuel. Eliezer took them to tennis and swimming lessons in Jerusalem. At Givon I gave birth to a baby girl, Hadas, and a year later we moved to the house in Givat Ze'ev, where Avichai, Elyasaf, and Bat-El were born.

The names we chose for our children have symbolic significance. Hadas was born at Purim time, so we named her after Hadassah, another name for Queen Esther. Avichai was born in 1984, the year my father Ya'akov died. On the Shabbat after his birth, we read the Torah portion *Miketz*, where Joseph meets his brothers in Egypt, and asks, *"ha'od avi chai?"* (is my father still alive?). Elyasaf was born in late 1987, when I thought I was probably no longer able to bear children. We felt that God had added to our family; *El yasaf* means "God adds." Because we thought he would be the last child, we chose Binyamin, the biblical Jacob's last child, as his second name. Three years later I held another new baby in my arms. We considered her a gift from God, and Eliezer suggested the name Bat-El, daughter of God.

My husband had dreamed of twelve children, and if I could have, I would have continued. Raising them was easy, and Eliezer truly served as my right hand in every way. But God gave us no more. The year Bat-El was born, Eliezer fell ill with cancer. I prayed that he would recover, win the battle against the illness, and walk her down the aisle to the *chuppah*.

CHAPTER 7

A New Beginning –
The Move to Givat Ze'ev

In 1983, a secular elementary school was founded in Givat Ze'ev. It took in students from Givon, and I was homeroom teacher for the first class. This was the fourth school I had worked in, after Degania in Be'er Sheva and the schools in Ofira and Givon. The choice to work in the secular school was no coincidence. I felt that teaching in a religious school was like preaching to the converted, while I preferred to acquaint secular students with the Jewish sources.

I felt their thirst to learn about our religious heritage, and my own desire equaled theirs. I wanted to open a window for them onto the world of faith, while at the same time, giving them the opportunity to choose, develop an inquisitive mind, and forge a new path out of knowledge.

The principal of the school, Avi Harari, became a significant person in my life. He appointed me as his vice principal, and I was pleased to take on all the duties he assigned me: social activities coordinator, Jewish studies coordinator, literacy coordinator, and the list went on. When the principal recommended that I register for a principal's course, I reacted as my father had when given an assignment by his manager at Tnuva – as if hearing the word of God. I said, "If the principal says so, then I should follow his decision." I had five children when I began to study for my master's degree.

When Harari left the school, Idit Tabak, his first vice principal, was appointed to take his place, and I continued as her vice principal. I felt that I was still at the beginning of my career. I derived great satisfaction from my job as a homeroom teacher and community coordinator for the school, as this offered me contact with the new residents who were coming to live in Givat Ze'ev. I was involved in naming the streets and the first planting ceremonies, and this made me feel that I was taking part in establishing the settlement and creating its history.

But for many years, the highpoint of my involvement in the Givat Ze'ev community, as in Ofira, was the memorial ceremony for fallen IDF soldiers held on Yom Hazikaron. Preparations would begin before school let out for Passover vacation. Each year, I searched for meaningful passages that would express the deep pain of losing the sons of our nation. No two ceremonies were ever alike. At home I have a thick file labeled "Yom Hazikaron," in which I keep all the materials I've collected over the years. I can still recite entire passages by heart. Over the intermediate days of Passover, the melodies of classic Israeli songs sung on Memorial Day, such as *"Ahi hatza'ir Yehuda"* (My younger brother Yehuda), *"Hare'ut"* (Friendship), and *"Anachnu shneinu me'oto hakfar"* (We're both from the same village) issued from our house, as I prepared for the ceremony with Hannah Aharoni, the music teacher. She loved Uriel so much that she gave his name to her son as well.

Everyone knew that the Yom Hazikaron ceremony belonged to Miriam Peretz. Why did I feel so connected to this sacred, dreadful day? I can't be sure, but perhaps I inherited it from my mother, who mourned every soldier who fell in the line of duty.

At school, I initiated projects that were considered innovative. When we planned the annual school field trip, I never collected money from the parents, but instead organized a student car wash to raise funds. We printed flyers and distributed them to the local homes. On a Friday afternoon, the students went around with buckets and rags. Even those who laughed at "the teacher from Sharm" were impressed by the results. As in Ofira, I pursued an open-door policy, welcoming the children in my home. I encouraged them to participate in the Givat Ze'ev Bible quiz and taught them in my living room. My children Hadas and Avichai played their opponents, as they were representing the religious school in the quiz. Hadas won the first Bible quiz held in Givat Ze'ev, and Avichai came in second.

In the mid-1980s, when the tension between religious and secular Jews in Israel became razor-sharp, I decided to teach the *siddur*, the prayer book, in the secular school. As expected, the parents were alarmed. "Religious coercion! It's scandalous!" they protested.

I took a deep breath and asked the children to bring prayer books to class. Some came to school and said they had no such thing in their homes. But some parents dug into old crates and found *siddurim* they had received upon becoming bar mitzvah, bearing the once-familiar scents of the old family home and the study hall. The older the *siddur*, the more I felt like it was crying out to be opened. The students placed the books on their desks. I had also invited the parents to attend the event. They arrived with mixed feelings, fearing an attempt to convince them to become more observant. But I began with a popular song that is also a prayer, Hannah Senesh's "*Eli, Eli, she'lo yigamer l'olam*" (My God, my God, may it never end). I taught them the song in historical context, as well as from the perspective of prayer.

Prayer, I explained to the parents, is a conversation between the individual and something that one person may call God, while another may think of it as a higher power. It is speech that flows from a place of pain or joy, speech that can be expressed in a whisper or a shout.

I continued by slipping from this song to another type of prayer from the prayer book. I remarked that Jews begin the day by giving thanks, with the prayer Modeh Ani: "I thank You, living and enduring King, for You have graciously returned my soul within me." For me, appreciation is a central value in the education of my children and my students. Even today, when I visit the graves of my two sons and my husband, it is only after I have begun my day with Modeh Ani. I thank God for being able to wake up, stand up, and keep on going, and for the fact that I can see the world, hear the sounds, and walk to the graves on my own two feet.

There is another aspect to my understanding of prayer. Communication with God teaches us about communication with other human beings. You don't just go up and ask someone for something; you have to begin with words of praise. Before we can shout, "Heal us!" we must first declare, "You are powerful." Similarly, between individuals, a positive word will smooth the way.

In the first few moments of the school prayer event, I felt as if I had been thrown into a cold bath, but as the minutes passed, I was enveloped with waves of warmth. I gave everyone time to write a personal prayer, and asked them to give a thought to "the other" as well. Through prayer, I opened a door for my students to a world of ethical behavior, of values and culture. For example, what do you wear when you visit the synagogue? How does one comfort a person in mourning? How does concern for others create mutual respect? Slowly, the students fell in love with the siddur as a way of life, as a tool that enabled them to become better human beings.

I waited for the day when I could reinforce Judaic studies within the framework of the school system. But I could not be the one to initiate this step, because in Givat Ze'ev, I was considered a representative of the religious crowd.

During Idit's second year as principal, we scheduled a meeting with the parents before the beginning of the school year. At seven thirty p.m., just before I had to leave for the meeting, Eliezer came in and reported that at that very moment, Rabbi Yosef Toledano was being interviewed for the position of rabbi of Givat Ze'ev, and that his wife was waiting for him in the park.

I got the hint. Rebbetzin Margalit Toledano was a member of the Abuhatzeira family, which is highly esteemed among Moroccan Jews. She was the sister of Rabbi David Abuhatzeira of Nahariya and Rabbi Eleazar Abuhatzeira of Be'er Sheva, and of Rabbi Yekutiel Abuhatzeira of Ashdod. It wasn't proper for such a well-respected woman to sit alone in a park.

"I'm bringing her here," Eliezer said.

"How?" I protested. "I have to go out to a parents' meeting." I was already dressed in pants, purse in hand. But Eliezer left to get her, and without being asked, I went up to the second floor and changed into a skirt, the usual garb of observant women in Israel. I sat with her for a few minutes, served her something to drink, and from that day on, I never wore pants again.

In 1990, the school superintendent called me and informed me that the principal was leaving, and that he considered me as her natural replacement. I was shocked. By that time, the school numbered twelve hundred students, and I had six children of my own. Bat-El was only two months old, and Eliezer was undergoing chemotherapy. This was hardly ideal timing, but when I went home and told Eliezer about the offer, he said, "Yes, fine."

My astonishment grew. "What do you mean, fine? How can I manage such a big school when I have a baby, and you are ill at home, and..."

"You'll manage," Eliezer interrupted. "You can do it."

The superintendent gave me a week to think about it. I barely slept a wink during those seven days. I turned the whole thing over in my mind, wavering and doubting. On the day I was supposed to give him my answer, I woke up confused. I didn't know what to say. But at seven thirty a.m., when he called, the doubts disappeared in a flash. I said yes without hesitation, just like when Eliezer had proposed to me. From the moment I said yes, I began to feel the weight of the responsibility I had been given.

During summer vacation I was busy with frantic preparations, with Eliezer's help. He didn't stand behind me, he stood beside me, acting like a third hand. One week before the beginning of the 1989 school year, he said, "Miriam, I'm taking the kids to a hotel in Tiberias – little Bat-El, too – so that you can have some time to yourself." On the first night in the hotel, Avichai and Elyasaf became ill. But Eliezer said on the phone, "Yeah, they're not feeling well, but everything's fine. How about you, are you making progress? Don't forget to eat. Eat something!"

I wrote my first speech to the school teachers at the table in the dining area. I began with a sentence from Pirkei Avot (Ethics of the Fathers): "Know from where you have come, and where you are going," a favorite maxim of mine. I wrote that I knew from where I came – from among them, the staff. Now that I was principal, I knew what I was aiming for, and how much I valued their cooperation in working toward our shared goal. I wrote that I had the students' interests in mind, and that I wanted them to come to school happy. I prayed that I would be able to return this deposit back to their parents healthy and whole in body and in spirit. I presented my personal educational credo, with faith in God as my foundation. I wrote to the teachers: "We have been given a great privilege, the privilege of shaping a generation. Let us consider our everyday labor, even in the most difficult and demanding moments, as a privilege, the privilege of influencing the future citizens of our country." I practiced reading my speech dozens of times, and each time, I could feel the butterflies in my stomach.

The day before the first day of school, I came home and found a package on the table. Inside were a skirt and blouse. Eliezer had gone through my closet and looked for the tag of the clothing chain where I usually shopped. He took a blouse and skirt from home to show the saleswoman my size, and said, "Find me a suit for my wife. Tomorrow she's starting a new position as school principal, and she's got to look her best."

The next day, he attended the opening ceremony. He continued to act as the wind beneath my wings. When I worked long days and nights, as all principals do, he would calm me down: "Miriam, put it into perspective." Every morning he would prepare my special sandwich. He knew exactly what I liked – an omelet made without oil, lettuce and two peeled olives, inside a roll that he wrapped with love.

Every day he would call my secretary, Sima, of blessed memory, and ask, "How's my redhead?" When he noticed that I was annoyed or stressed, he would go to the corner store and buy some cheese pastries. Then he would stop by the guard at the school entrance and say, "Give these to the redhead." Sometimes he would deliver them via the kids who came late to class, and a few hours later he would call and ask, "How were the cheese pastries?"

On the day I accepted the position of principal, I stopped sleeping soundly at night. Every morning before I left home, I prayed to God to help me watch over my twelve hundred children. I was petrified that one of them would get hurt – physically in a fight, or emotionally by a critical comment from one of the teachers or myself. This fear accompanied me throughout my twenty-two years as principal. When the children went on a field trip, I couldn't fall asleep until I received a phone call from the teacher reporting that all the students had returned home safely.

Throughout my years as a teacher and principal, I knew that Eliezer was standing at my side, supporting me, offering encouragement and praise. He attended all the school events and ceremonies. He always sat in the back of the hall and applauded, waiting until the parents had finished talking to me before he would approach, proud as a peacock. He developed ties with the teachers and Ministry of Education staff. Eliezer died on 4 Elul 5765 (September 8, 2005), the year that hot lunches began to be served in schools. As a Ministry of Health employee, he wanted to make sure that my children received a nourishing lunch. On the day before he died, he came to the school, checked the catering delivery, and wished the teachers and students success.

I was lucky that in my second year as principal, a proposal was made to add a supplemental Jewish studies program in our school. The initiative came from the parents' association, and I was very pleased.

As principal, I continued to teach the *siddur* and Mishnah. When the parents' initiative failed due to "suspicions of religious coercion," I realized that conditions were not yet ripe. I was satisfied with the knowledge that at least Pirkei Avot had become an integral part of the curriculum. Still, I couldn't help but see the symbolism in the fact that in 1998 – the very year Uriel was killed – my secular school joined the TALI network of schools offering augmented Jewish studies. Uriel was dead, but something new was born. Uriel's death sapped all my strength, but TALI forced me to gather new strength to begin this new path.

Uriel was very proud of his mother the school principal. When our school won a national prize for road safety education, he encouraged me to continue on for my doctorate. "Your talent is being wasted," he told me, echoing his father. "You should go study." I just smiled. Why were they encouraging me to get a PhD? I had not qualified for my MA, because I hadn't managed to turn in one final assignment. In the evenings I had my six children to take care of, and during the school year I volunteered to help other students write papers. "So turn in that missing paper," Eliezer urged, but again I grinned, arguing that it was impossible. Two years had passed since I had completed the courses for an

MA in educational administration, and there was no chance that the university would accept the credits I had earned. "They are no longer valid," I told my husband, "and my mind is no longer there."

Then Eliezer decided to take action, in secret, behind my back. He had never earned a college degree himself, but he went to the Hebrew University, asked for the chairman of the department, knocked on his door, and went inside. He related that his wife had studied there for two years, but had not yet received her MA because of one missing paper. Returning home, he said, "Miriam, I spoke to someone high up, and they've called you in for a meeting on Tuesday."

I was astonished. What was he up to? Who had he spoken to? I argued that I couldn't possibly go to the meeting. But Eliezer didn't even let me finish my sentence. "There's no such thing as 'I can't,'" he asserted. Remarkably, at the meeting they agreed to a compromise: if I turned in the last paper within one month, they would give me credit for my course work and I could sit for the final exam. I reported this offer to Eliezer by phone, and added, "It's impossible. It's May, we're getting ready for the end of the school year."

In the evening he came home, gathered all the kids together, and announced, "From now on, everyone has to do their homework in their rooms. You're not studying around the dining room table anymore, because from now on, the only one who's allowed to put her books here is Mom! And you," he addressed me, "sit down and finish your paper. I'll take care of the rest."

I sat. The topic of my paper was "Parental Involvement in School." The draft pages I had written four years earlier had disappeared inside our Subaru when it was stolen, but I remembered the chapter titles, and Eliezer stood over me like a hawk and made sure that I sat down and wrote something every day. He took care of the kids, did the shopping, and paid the bills. The only thing

I did was cook, and he did the dishes. Even on Election Day, a national holiday, he asked me to stay home and write. "I'm taking the kids out of the house," he informed me, "and you're not budging from the table." Thanks to Eliezer's stubbornness, love, and support, I finished my paper within a month.

The next step was typing. I heard that one of the mothers was having financial troubles, and I thought of helping her by asking her to type my paper. I asked an intermediary to give this woman my paper, as if it were hers, and the intermediary also delivered the payment. Later, when the mother came to speak with me about her son, she used examples from my paper to define the distinction between involvement and interference. I was so pleased that she had used the opportunity to learn. I was also pleased that she never sensed the true identity of the writer.

After I turned in the paper, I was given a date for an oral exam – another hurdle! Every day I got out of bed at four a.m. and walked around the garden, going over my summaries on notecards. Eliezer acted the role of an excellent teacher: not only did he make sure I was studying, but he also encouraged me. I got a 98 on the test, and he was in seventh heaven. We celebrated at a restaurant with the whole family. During the meal, Eliezer praised me in front of the children, and each time he said, "Follow your mother's example," I insisted, "Follow your special father's example."

It wasn't easy to be head of a school in the community where I lived. My students were also my neighbors and would see me going out to the yard in my sweats and taking out the trash. But my relationship with the parents was excellent. I took with me from Ofira the atmosphere of informal communication, freedom, and intimacy. There was only one thing I was strict about: I never went grocery shopping in Givat Ze'ev. I didn't want parents asking me about their children while I was buying laundry detergent, nor did I want them peeking into my grocery cart to see what I was cooking for my family.

As part of the preparations for transforming the school from the secular to the TALI framework with its emphasis on Judaic studies, I began to study educational leadership at the Schechter Institute of Jerusalem. There I was exposed to the multifaceted nature of Torah interpretation. I became acquainted with the many streams of Judaism, opened a new window on my study of Talmud and Mishnah, and was exposed to a more pluralistic, moderate approach. I shared my experience with Eliezer and the children, who protested, "Hey, what's with these new commentaries? Calm down!" I often spoke at home about women's role in society and equal rights for women. I related that I had even seen women who read from the Torah during the prayer service. This put off Eliezer and the children. "That's not our way," they protested. "Women in our community don't read from the Torah, and they never will!"

Our vociferous arguments on this issue disrupted our family discussions at the Shabbat table. Eliezer would point to my shoulder pads, fashionable in those days, and remark, "You women already dominate us. You even stick on those pads that make you taller than us. Enough already, we got the picture." On the other hand, he pushed me to study, and was pleased that I brought home new readings of the texts that expanded our points of view.

Finally, my vision was achieved: the school year began, and my school held morning prayer services and Rosh Chodesh ceremonies, as well as study sessions on the weekly Torah portion and Pirkei Avot. The emphasis was on study through experience, and the joyous sounds of the students' singing and dancing rang through the corridors and from the windows. There were two ceremonies that Eliezer particularly enjoyed: the celebration for first-graders receiving their first *siddurim*, and the one for second-graders receiving their first Bible.

On these occasions, Eliezer made sure that the synagogue was sparkling clean. One of the teachers, Miri Ben-Avi, suggested that after handing out the prayer books, the children should sing "*Ani Nishba*" (I pledge) by Chaim Moshe, while standing beside the ark, books in hand. My husband said to me, "You've earned your place in the Garden of Eden."

Ironically, during the TALI school's first year, it was members of the religious community who tried to stop me. They argued that I was moving too close to the Conservative movement. But Eliezer encouraged me to continue, and I felt that Uriel was also supportive. "No one else does what you do in that school," my husband said. "You're bringing them closer to their heritage. There's nothing wrong with that." I knew very well why Eliezer was saying that – as *gabbai* (beadle) of our synagogue, he also encouraged the youth to come to services, and gave them *aliyot* (calling them up to the Torah) without asking too many questions, so they, too, would feel closer to their heritage.

Slowly the TALI atmosphere moved from the confines of the school and enveloped the entire Givat Ze'ev community. The values of giving and helping others became cornerstones of the teaching staff. We transmitted these values to our students through hands-on experiences, such as the used clothing bazaar, Tessa's Shop, founded by community resident Tessa Lishansky, with the aim of aiding needy families. The students sorted the clothes and even donated some of their own clothing. In addition, every Rosh Chodesh, one class was responsible for donating food for the needy. The parents also joined in the excitement and volunteered to operate the shop in the evening hours. After Eliraz was killed, the name of the shop was changed to Hasdei Eliraz (Eliraz's Thrift Shop), and it is still operating today.

We also held a monthly *seudah shlishit* (third Shabbat meal) in the school gymnasium, together with town residents, school parents, and members of the *garin torani* – a group of youths who came to live in the town to encourage Jewish learning, under the leadership of Rabbi Lior Engelman. We sang songs and studied the weekly Torah portion together. At each event we asked two families, one secular and one religious, to introduce themselves to the participants and relate their stories. This activity, a communal meeting centered around Jewish sources and social issues, continues today. Without the dedicated, excellent teaching staff, and the cooperation of the parents and the educational administration, such initiatives would not be possible.

The school was full of vibrant activities. We held ceremonies for Rosh Chodesh – monthly award ceremonies where students received certificates of excellence (not only for academic achievements but also for social service and volunteer initiatives) – and holidays. We also organized joint prayer services for the entire student body, which were led by the students themselves. We read the Scroll of Esther on Purim, and invited town residents and youth group members to the reading. And of course, we planned bar and bat mitzvah ceremonies. I studied the Torah portions together with the students, and then they wrote a sermon, assisted by their homeroom teacher, on the values they learned from their portion. These activities enhanced the atmosphere of the school, and turned it into an ethical institution that educated the students toward love of humanity and of Israel.

Six years after our school joined the TALI network, I received the Genger prize for "inspirational leadership and exceptional involvement in community, grounded in faith in humanity." The ceremony was held at the Bible Lands Museum in Jerusalem on the eve of Chanukah, just after the memorial ceremony for Uriel, whose absence I felt deeply. I was so pleased that Eliraz, wearing his uniform, was able to attend. He was proud of me.

When Uriel was killed – and my world fell apart – I feared that this educational project of which I had dreamed would disintegrate. But despite it all, I found comfort in the TALI network.

Eliezer pushed me to continue. For the first time in my life, I flew to the United States, to learn about the Schechter school network, and out of crisis, my spirit grew. This was my place of sanity. As Hillel the Elder said, "My feet lead me to the place I love." I didn't know how to go to any other place besides the school that Uriel and Eliraz both attended in their early years, until they switched to the religious school system. I felt an obligation to the process that I had begun, and the doing and giving helped me regain my strength. The students, the wonderful teaching staff, and the supportive community of parents were a source of inspiration.

I felt that Uriel, watching from above, was proud of me for leading this process of change, because he had gone through a similar process. When he reached the elite reconnaissance unit, after studying at Or Etzion officers' academy, there were only two religious youngsters in his corps. Like me, he was exposed to all sorts of people, from backgrounds that were new to him, people from *kibbutzim*, *moshavim*, and all over Israel.

After the shivah for Uriel was over, I announced that I would return to the school, but gradually. I walked through the gate and went directly to my office, avoiding contact with the students. In each one of them, I recognized something of my blonde, curly-haired boy, my Uriel. I didn't want the students to see me cry. I knew that as principal, I had to instill in them faith and hope for a positive future.

I had never asked for special consideration, and when others tried to offer me special treatment, I rebuffed their attempts. I told my students that life was full of crises, and that we had to face them and overcome them, not just give in. Before Yom Hazikaron and Yom Hashoah I would cry at home while practicing my speeches, but at the ceremonies, I stood proud and tall.

The gradual return to contact with the children intensified my desire to protect them and strengthen their religious roots and faith, as Uriel had wanted, and as I believed. Slowly I began to venture from the principal's office into the teachers' room, and then I allowed myself to go out into the hallway. When one of the students greeted me by saying, "Miriam, I haven't seen you in such a long time! I missed you so much," it infused me with strength.

PART TWO
Uriel

CHAPTER 8

The Magician – Uriel Is Drafted

Uriel, my oldest son, began first grade in the Beit Horon school. A special minibus was sent to our out-of-the-way settlement of Givon to take him there. On his first day, he carried a huge, bulky schoolbag on his back. I had no idea how much it looked like the kitbag used by Golani soldiers. The backpack contained new notebooks, a pencil case, and two books, a *siddur* and a Tanach. The *siddur* was a relic from my brother's bar mitzvah. It had a wooden cover, and it was heavy.

I accompanied Uriel to the minibus. On his skinny little legs, he tried to climb up the first step, clutching the side rails for support, but he couldn't do it. I watched as he tried again, but the schoolbag pulled him backwards and sideways. Again I watched as he almost slipped. What does a mother do when she sees her child struggle? I felt like grabbing him and lifting him into that bus, straight into the seat.

"Mommy!" Uriel called, "Mommy, I can do it!"

Such a simple sentence, and so powerful. It would accompany him throughout his life, and it became a motto for my own life. Uriel recognized that the step was high and difficult for him to climb, but he knew that he had inner strength, and that he could put that strength to use. Over the years, I came to view that step as a symbol. Life presents us with so many steps. I've often faced steps I thought I wouldn't be able to climb. But then I remember my little boy's words – "Mommy, I can do it!"

In third grade, Uriel went to my school. Then he transferred to a religious elementary school in Ramot. In ninth grade, he entered the Youth Village School in Jerusalem. One fine day he informed us that he had decided to switch tracks. He wanted to transfer to the Or Etzion religious army preparation academy, a boarding school directed by Rabbi Chaim Druckman.

We were in shock. What did he mean, a military preparation academy? What would the neighbors say? We were under the impression that boarding schools were only for problem kids. We asked Uriel, "Why do you want to go to a boarding school? Aren't you happy at home?" His reply: "I know what I want to do with my life. I want to be a military man."

Just like that. In ninth grade he read and learned everything he could about military academies, and at age sixteen, he committed himself to the uniform.

I packed a suitcase with a blanket, sheets, and pillow – all new – and clothes for two weeks, enough to last him till he returned for Shabbat. We drove with him to the dorm. When we saw the other teenagers in uniform, tall and strong, we were sure they would throw him out. Our Uriel was a scrawny four-eyes, a leaf blown away by the wind. He led me to the room he was to occupy with three other boys, and as soon as I stepped inside, I recoiled. What a mess! I went to look for a rag and bucket, and began to wash the floor and wipe the dust from the window.

"Mom, what are you doing?" Uriel interrupted me. "Stop that!"

"But how can you sleep here?" I protested. "If you insist on sleeping away from home, you should at least have decent conditions! How can you put your new sheets on such a dusty mattress?

"Mom," he laughed, "You're afraid of a few specks of dust? Do you know what I'll be sleeping on for the rest of my life? Sand! I'll be eating tons of sand!"

He introduced me to his roommates and they also laughed at his mother as she cleaned.

There were two bunk beds in the room. "Uriel," I pulled him aside, "you should grab the bed next to the window, so you can breathe some fresh air."

"Never mind," he shrugged, "we'll be switching around anyway."

"What do you mean, switching around?" I said in shock. "You won't be sleeping in the bed I made for you, with the new sheets and blanket and pillow?"

"No, Mom," he said, turning serious. "This is my new life. I'm starting a new life."

I asked to see the bathroom. It was my right. I was his mother, and I was worried.

"The bathroom isn't in the room, it's down the hall." He took me to see the bathroom and showers.

I peeked inside, and my face fell. I knew what a boys' bathroom was like, but what was that stink? And why was the faucet dripping and the sink black?

"Where's the toilet paper?" I asked.

"It's probably all gone," he said. "So what? Who cares if there's no paper!"

"You can't live like this," I protested.

"Mom, don't move a muscle," Uriel ordered. He realized that if he didn't give me an order, I would start cleaning. So I stood in the doorway, staring at the narrow stream dripping from the faucet, and I couldn't understand how my fragile, sensitive son could leave the cushy conditions of home and go to live in a military dorm.

Two weeks later, when he came home for Shabbat, he had turned into a soldier. He didn't have a rank, but he was wearing a uniform, and all the neighbors gazed at him admiringly. "Uriel Peretz is a soldier – who would believe it?"

No one believed that he would manage in the dormitory. I saw his roommates. They were big, strong guys, while Uriel was scrawny. Eliezer called him "Smurf" because, like the characters on the TV show that was popular then, he was short, thin, and bow-legged. What would he do in that place? How would he survive?

"Don't worry," Eliezer reassured me. "Let him try it. In three months they'll call us and say, 'Take the Smurf home, he doesn't fit in.'"

But each time Uriel came home, he was beaming with joy. He sat with us and told us about life in the dorm, academics along with military training.

"Training?!" I jumped up from my chair in shock. "You're already holding a weapon?"

"Not yet," he smiled, "but I'm doing navigation."

Three months later we were invited to the first parents' meeting. We went in quietly and stood along the edge of the room, trying not to attract attention. We were certain that the moment they saw us, they would tell us that he was being kicked out. A boy from Uriel's class stopped us. "Excuse me, who are you?" he asked.

Heads lowered, we admitted, "We're Uriel Peretz's parents."

"Ah!" he exclaimed. "The king!"

Eliezer and I looked at each other in amazement. He must be mistaken, confused.

"We're the parents of Uriel Peretz," Eliezer repeated. "Uriel Peretz, the little guy," I added.

"Yeah, the king!" the kid affirmed.

"You must be mistaken," I insisted. "We're the parents of Uriel Peretz from Givat Ze'ev."

"Yes, the king!" he repeated, for the third time.

That was the nickname that stuck to Uriel from the time he was still in his first month in the premilitary academy. Our Smurf had become a king. "You're the king?" we asked, hugging him, and he just smiled. But the stories I began to hear from his classmates proved that the nickname was justified. Who would the boys call a "king"? The leader, the one who unified the group, the one who looked out for the others. That was him. Uriel never placed himself in the center; he always had the group as a whole in mind. He was even happy to carry out a lowly job such as cleaning the toilets. "I'm doing it for my buddies, my brothers," he would say. These days some might call him a "sucker," but this word was not part of his vocabulary. He performed any job without complaining, from cleaning the bathroom to carrying a jerry can of water on a training exercise. He never asked, "Why do I always have to do it?" As he saw it, his classmates were like brothers, and this led to the attitude that a deed on behalf of country and people was a deed on behalf of family and brothers.

Uriel was the one who organized the group for an outing to the Ashkelon beach. When one of them was stuck without equipment, it was Uriel who provided the missing items. When other students got into a fight, he was the one who went to the rabbi in charge and in his mannerly way, helped make peace. Later, in the army, they called him "the magician" and also "the diver." The second nickname came as no surprise to me, because as a child he swam like a fish in the ocean at Sharm.

From one month to the next, I watched as he grew stronger. He flourished in the atmosphere of the academy. Each year he earned another shoulder badge, but I knew nothing about the ranks, nor was I interested in learning. "Mom, look!" he said proudly. "You'll see, I'll earn the chief of staff badge! I'll be the first Moroccan chief of staff, and you'll be so proud!"

"I'm proud of you already," I said, hugging him lovingly. I was no longer upset by the conditions of the dorm, nor was I upset later when I saw the conditions at his guard post. How could I complain, when my son was so happy?

Uriel was no more than an average student, but in the military field he excelled. "The most important thing is for him to earn a matriculation certificate," Eliezer said to me. Although I realized that academic studies were not his top priority, I didn't believe that the military would become his life's goal. The mothers of his classmates related that their sons came home and immediately stripped off their uniforms and removed their boots. But Uriel walked down the street like a peacock, wearing his uniform and boots, puffed up with pride. At the high school graduation ceremony, Rabbi Druckman came up to us, shook hands, and wished Uriel good luck in his military service.

Following high school, Uriel applied for the Golani *sayeret* reconnaissance unit, the elite special forces unit that he had heard so much about at the academy. But he was not accepted. Why? In my opinion, it was for physical reasons. The soldiers in the special forces were big, strong guys, real fighters, while my Uriel was the antithesis of the combat image. His small stature simply didn't meet their standards. But he didn't give up. He said, "Mom, I only want Golani and I'll get there. I can do it!"

In the end, he was accepted into the reconnaissance unit – as a cook. He was thrilled. "So what if I'm only a cook?" he said. "I'm in the special forces!" For two months, he chopped onions and peeled potatoes in the most professional way he could. He learned how to cook from me, although in our home I was the only one who cooked and served. When he came home for breaks, I saw knife cuts on his fingers. I felt sorry for him, but I understood that if you want to be a leader, you have to know how to chop onions, and along the way, you have to shed tears. In order to reach others' hearts, you have to know how to remove the peels, one by one. Week after week he stood in the kitchen, watching the soldiers returning from action in Lebanon, and said to himself, "One day I'll be there with them."

When he came home, he continued to prepare for that day. Every Shabbat evening after dinner, he would hold a regular ceremony at home. He pushed back the table, spread mattresses on the floor, and asked Eliezer and me to watch. Then he said to Eliraz, "Come punch me, come toughen me up." After the punching round, Uriel would take a measuring tape and measure himself, checking to see whether his shoulders had broadened or his biceps expanded a bit. It was hard for me to watch my sons hitting each other with all their might, but I realized that this was Uriel's way of reaching the goal he had set for himself.

After two months of potatoes and onions, the kitchen officer recommended Uriel to the reconnaissance unit commander, and he joined the training course, which he passed successfully. When he entered the special forces unit, his new goal was to become an outstanding soldier. In one of the navigation exercises, he and his friend Uzza broke a record, navigating over 25 kilometers (15 miles) in less than four and a half hours! Eventually, that same Golani reconnaissance unit that had initially refused to accept Uriel into its ranks decided to name one of its major endurance exercises after him: the concluding northern exercise, which begins at the top of Mount Meron.

For Uriel, the twenty-month training period was pure happiness. Unlike most Israeli soldiers, who go home every other weekend, the soldiers in this elite unit come home only once a month. He would arrive exhausted from the activities and training sessions. I didn't ask any questions, as I knew he wasn't allowed to talk about what he was doing. I made his favorite foods, spicy Moroccan fish and onion-stewed chicken. Eliezer would wait by the door for him. Sometimes he would wait hours until Uriel walked in, sweaty and filthy, just as Shabbat began.

When he came home, I washed his uniform. But instead of putting it in the dryer, I hung it out on the line, so that the whole world would see and know that my son had come home. When

I hung up his socks to dry, I prayed, "God, keep giving me socks with thorns." Each thorn symbolized Uriel's steps on this land. The socks told me Uriel's story. They revealed exactly where he had walked. I would sit and pull out thorn after thorn from inside each sock. They stuck in the socks up to knee height, and I admonished them, "Cheeky thorns, how dare you stick yourselves inside my son's foot?" I took out my wrath on the grains of sand that fell out of his boots: "Why did you get into his boot? Why did you hurt him?" In the same breath, I would turn toward the slice of sky beyond the kitchen window and ask the Master of the Universe to send me as many thorns as possible. As long as my son would continue to come home.

On Shabbat, I would sit with Uriel and stroke his hands, which were also filled with thorns and swollen with pus. I pulled out the thorns, cleaned his wounds, and bandaged them, and massaged his feet. I felt that my son's young body needed stroking and love, although I never heard him say "It hurts" or "It's hard." Such expressions never passed his lips. After Uriel was killed, we found a sheet of paper in his room that contained lines written in his hand. He wrote, "With all the thorns and barbs that have scratched my body, you could put together a three-foot hedge. But these aren't just ordinary thorns – they're thorns from the Land of Israel." Indeed, the saying goes that the Land of Israel is earned through suffering, and whoever lives here must know how to accept its thorns with love.

One Friday afternoon, Uriel thumbed a ride home. By candle-lighting time, he had gotten as far as Nabi Samuel, still a ten-minute drive from our house. He got out of the car and with only a minute to go before Shabbat started, he called me and announced, "I'm close to home, I'll walk the rest of the way." It just so happened that on that Friday, our hot water heater short-circuited. How would he be able to take a hot shower, I worried. I boiled water in the tea kettle, filled up the bathtub, took seven rolls of aluminum foil and sealed it on all sides, leaving no holes, to keep in the heat. The second Uriel walked in, I pounced on him. "You must get in the bathtub!" I led him over to it. He took a look at the silver cover and couldn't believe his eyes.

"Mom, I can't believe you did this!" he laughed. But I believed it, and I was the happiest mother in the world. How wonderful that I could spoil him, make his life a little easier.

When he came home, I watched over him like a prince. I permitted no one to disturb him, so that he could rest a bit and sleep. But Shabbat morning, he woke up early to go to synagogue with his father. They welcomed him with great respect – the first special forces soldier from Givat Ze'ev. When he came home from synagogue, he would sit and read a book. Eliezer and I pinched each other. We couldn't believe our eyes. Was this the boy who had never shown much interest in books? The moment he began to serve in the special forces, he became a bookworm. He even forced us to read certain books, like *The Alchemist, Jonathan Livingston Seagull*, and *The Little Prince*. He asked me to read *Military Leadership* by Chaim Laskov.

His friends would come to visit on Shabbat, and they would sit and play backgammon. I don't know where he got the dice from, but the sight reminded me of the days when my father used to play checkers with my brother Charly under the balcony. After lunch on Shabbat, they spread the mattresses out on the floor once more, and were at it again. "Eliraz, harder! Give me all you've got!" Uriel would shout, and Eliraz would give it to him. Uriel's eyes were shining with tears, and I intervened; how could I stand by and not separate them? But Uriel said, "Mom, stop, I'm preparing for an anti-terrorism course." When they finished hitting each other, Eliraz took the measuring tape and checked whether Uriel's shoulders had broadened. Yes, they did expand during the special forces training, but not by much. Sometimes, when Shabbat came around, I would see that he had lost five kilos (eleven pounds) in one week, and I wanted to put back all five in one day. I would run after him with meatballs and cake.

Before the concluding ceremony of the special forces training course, Uriel warned me, "Mom, most of the guys here are Ashkenazi, so I'd like to ask you to behave respectfully and with restraint." In other words, no Moroccan-style ululating. "All right," I agreed, "we'll be happy even without the *kululu*." Uriel told me that he would be given the flying tiger pin, and I responded, "With or without the pin, the main thing is that you completed the course."

The ceremony began. The soldiers demonstrated many skills, but I barely understood what was going on. At the Shabbat table, when Uriel tried to explain battalions and the tripartite division, I asked why they had to divide. Such was the extent of my ignorance regarding the army. But there was my Uriel walking up onto the platform, and I saw his commander, Assi Levi, present him with the tiger pin and land a punch on his chest. My boy swayed. Luckily Eliezer was holding me tightly so that I wouldn't leap from my chair. Hey, what do you think you're doing? I wanted to ask. Why are you hitting my son? Can't you see that he's small, that he's about to fall down? Afterward I found out that this was a standard demonstration of the unit's team spirit. But at the time, I felt like slapping the commander.

The ceremony ended and Uriel came down from the platform, standing straight and proud, and we all rushed up to him and hugged and kissed him. I said, "You wore yourself out for a year and eight months for that pin? For the flying tiger? My precious, if you'd only told me, I would've bought you a pin just like that without all the effort!"

All the guys from the course came to our house for a celebratory meal. That's what happened after Uriel finished the military preparation academy, and ever since then, it has become a tradition for our family – we invite everyone. Uriel rushed around, helping me with the preparations. He ran to the store to buy meat, insisting, "Mom, we have to serve large quantities, because the guys haven't eaten in a while." I promised him that we wouldn't lack for food. I made fish, meatballs, couscous, and many kinds of salads.

"Your son is going to be great," they told me. "Your son is going to be a real someone," and I wiped away a tear. The most important thing was for him to be healthy and happy. You should all come home safely.

For a moment I thought it was over, that the training course was behind us, finished. Maybe I hoped it would be that way. But I admit that I was proud of Uriel when he and a few other guys from the reconnaissance unit decided to join an officers' training course. The only part that worried me was that he had to travel to the Bahad 1 base in the south. It was such a long way for him to go. Sometimes he had to return to the base on *motzaei Shabbat*, right after Shabbat was over, and I couldn't sleep. How would he manage those trips in the dark? I was so naïve.

For the ceremony marking the completion of the officers' training course, we wanted to avoid the mistake we had made at Uriel's first military ceremony (when he received his beret) – we'd already failed once. Then Uriel had asked us not to bring any-thing. At the last minute I stuffed a few packets of Bamba snacks into my purse. But when I saw the other parents carrying their pots, I was filled with shame. "Uriel, why didn't you tell me to bring food?" I asked. "It's not necessary, Mom, never mind." So at the officers' ceremony, held in Mitzpe Ramon, we arrived like the family of Sallah Shabati: the five other children stood beside the gate with baskets and coolers, and Eliezer and I carried a box on our shoulders.

"Excuse me, what's this all about?" asked the surprised guard, stopping us.

"We're here for Uriel Peretz!" we answered in chorus.

"This is a military base, not a restaurant," he protested.

"That's all right," Eliezer replied. He took out a folding picnic table, opened it, and we began to set out the food. We invited everyone to join us. Eat and be merry! The soldiers filled their bellies and I gobbled them up with my eyes. Let them enjoy the feast.

Uriel took me to see his room. I entered, and for a second I turned pale, just as I had on the first day at the academy. Bunk beds, a mess. Then I noticed something strange. The sheet I had bought for Uriel was on one bed, the blanket I had bought him on another, and I found his towel on a third bed. "Who's using this towel?" I asked.

His answer: "Everyone."

"What do you mean, everyone? That's the towel I bought you!"

"Mom," Uriel said, hugging me, "don't you get it that in the army, everything belongs to everyone?"

No, I hadn't gotten it yet, but I was learning. I was beginning to understand that it was like a home, with the atmosphere of a family. The ceremony began, and Uriel was only one of four hundred. But he was the only one I was looking at, the only one I saw. He looked so handsome in his officer's uniform. Eliezer gazed at his oldest son with pride, and his brother Eliraz looked on in admiration. From that moment on, Uriel was not just the older brother, he was "the commander." When the ceremony was over, I watched as the other graduates surrounded Uriel, and the officers told me about "King Uriel"; it was like a repeat performance of the graduation ceremony at the premilitary academy.

At home, I lit candles and prayed. I still didn't understand anything about the IDF, but I wasn't blind to the reactions of those around me. Every time I said, "My son's in the *sayeret*," people's eyes widened in admiration.

After the officers' training course, Uriel was sent to Hebron to serve as commander of the backup company for the Golani Brigade's 51st Battalion. We didn't see him much, as visits home were rare. When he finally did come, he barely spoke.

"Uriel, what are you doing there?"

"Stuff."

"Is everything okay?"

"*Yihiyeh beseder* – It will be okay."

I bit my lip. "God willing."

I learned from others that even during his tour of duty in Hebron, he found time in his busy schedule to give Torah lessons to the soldiers who were former *yeshivah* boys. He spoke to them about *moreshet hakrav*, IDF military history and legacy. Hebron was also where he met a couple who became our good friends, Rivka and Ze'ev (Zembish) Hever. They met under amusing circumstances. When Uriel was in the *sayeret*, he wanted to save some money so he could travel to Sharm to look for our old house. He was offered a job as a waiter at a bar mitzvah on a Shabbat in Ramat Aviv Gimel. The bar mitzvah boy was Zembish's nephew, the son of his sister Tzipi. As Uriel was carrying a tray of food to the table where the Hever family was sitting, it swayed under the weight of the dishes. Rivka remarked, "Excuse me, waiter, it looks like you don't know how to hold that tray."

After Uriel apologized, she asked, "What do you do aside from being a waiter?"

"I'm in the Golani special forces," came the reply.

Rivka stood up and exclaimed, "You're in the *sayeret*? And on your free Shabbat you're working? You sit down and my daughters will serve you instead!"

Of course Uriel refused to sit down. He continued working so he could earn the extra cash, and never told me about this encounter with the guest.

Later, as an officer in Hebron, Uriel gave an order to close Hashuhada Street. At that moment, Rivka Hever and her daughters were coming down the street. The Hever family lived in the Givat Hacharsina neighborhood of Hebron, and Rivka regularly brought cheesecake to the regiment commanders. She was like a mother to all the soldiers who served there.

"The road's closed," declared the soldier on duty. "Commander's orders."

"Can you call your commander, please?" Rivka asked.

The soldier contacted the commander on the radio, and he came.

One of Rivka's daughters said, "Mother, look at him, don't you recognize him?" Rivka shook her head, but her daughter reminded her, "That's the waiter from the bar mitzvah."

Uriel came closer. "*Shalom*, what's going on?"

"Commander, don't you remember me?" Rivka asked. Uriel demurred.

"You were that waiter with the swaying tray at that meal...."

"Oh, yeah," Uriel mumbled in embarrassment.

"So can I go see the regiment commander?" Rivka asked. Uriel replied that this was impossible, but she begged, "At that meal I did you a favor, by not reporting you about the tray you couldn't handle. Now it's your turn to do me a favor. Let me go through. I've brought cheesecake for the regiment commander."

"Cheesecake?" Uriel smiled. "I love cheesecake, too!"

"Tomorrow I'll bring you some," she promised, once he permitted her to pass. After that, Rivka Hever adopted Uriel as her son. She spoiled him with her cheesecake, invited him to her home, and asked him to speak to the youth in the local Jewish community. Of course, Uriel agreed. But I had no idea. I never imagined that somewhere in Kiryat Arba, he had a second mother.

After Uriel was killed, a synagogue in Givat Ze'ev was built in his name. The regional council chairman told me that Rivka Hever wanted to come to the dedication ceremony. "Who's that?" I asked. "I don't know anyone by that name."

Rivka came to the ceremony, and when she spoke to me about Uriel, I was astonished. "How do you know my son so well?" She knew everything about him – where he served and what he had done, his favorite foods. On that day she became like a sister to me. The first Passover after Uriel's death, we went to Rivka and Zembish for the Seder. We felt like family with them. When we entered their home, I saw a large photo of Uriel hanging in the entryway. Eliraz also felt close to them, and never did anything significant in his life without consulting with Rivka. To this day, the Hever family is an important source of encouragement, support, and help for us.

During his service in Kiryat Arba, Uriel built his backup company based on the vision statement he had written during his officers' training course, in which he had outlined five values and principles of his command:

1. History of Eretz Yisrael, the Land of Israel – Uriel wanted each soldier to know the history of Israel, so he would know why he was serving in the IDF, what his ancestors had fought for, and what he was fighting for.

2. Love of the Land of Israel – For Uriel, it was not enough for the soldiers to know history. He took them on navigation exercises because he wanted them to know each stone and plant, every hill and valley. He wanted them to know the story of each place, and to fall in love with the land through the soles of their feet. To him, this connection was both physical and emotional.

3. Professionalism – Uriel aspired to transform his platoon into the best one in the battalion. He told his soldiers, "We're going to be the elite unit of the battalion." From his point of view, professionalism meant intensive training with constant daily improvement.

4. Unity – He explained that team spirit was the key to success. When the entire platoon was unified into one body, attacking as one block, then every soldier could be 100 percent certain that his friends would carry him on their backs for enormous distances when needed.

5. Excellence – Uriel inculcated the platoon with this spirit. "We're the best platoon in the division!" he repeated to them. "We have to prove it every day." When his soldiers earned first place in a brigade exercise, his pride was boundless. He was proud of them, and they were proud of him.

But the beginning of his command was not easy. The soldiers in the platoon had been in the army longer than him. Some were also older than him, others were about to be released. They had done their homework and found out two important things about him. First, he came from the special forces. They considered this a minus, as they would have preferred having a commander who had moved up in the ranks of their battalion, not someone from outside. Second, he didn't like Mizrachi-style Israeli music. "How can you be a Golani commander without liking Zohar Argov, Margalit Tzan'ani, and Sarit Haddad?" they asked Uriel, who preferred Israeli folk rock singers like Rita, Shlomo Artzi, and Ehud Banai.

So Uriel taught himself to like Mizrachi music. He knew that in order to reach hearts, you have to peel away many layers and weep many tears. Eventually, when Eliraz would come home from the army, he would also sit at the Shabbat table and start singing Mizrachi songs. "What's that?" I asked him, and he answered, "How can I be a Golani combat soldier without these songs flowing in my blood?"

Slowly Uriel earned the soldiers' trust. In letters that his soldiers wrote us after he was killed, they described why Uriel was a good commander. They wrote about his concern for each soldier, his ability to listen, and his sensitivity, and the way he spoke to them on their level. He knew who had a toothache, who had problems at home, and who was most in need of that job as a guard in Givat Ze'ev during his days off, so that he could help his family. Every soldier was like a son to Uriel, and the platoon was like his family. His soldiers wrote that they weren't afraid to go to Lebanon with him, because they had been prepared physically and also because they knew the commander marching in front of them. Uriel gave them a feeling of safety.

From Hebron, Uriel went with his soldiers to the Tzivoni outpost in Lebanon. This was Lebanon in the late 1990s, when every day you would turn on the radio and hear about fallen soldiers. The day he went into Lebanon signaled the beginning of a different kind of worry – existential fear. When he was on the training course, I worried about how he would travel at night in the dark. Now I realized that every single second, he was fighting for his life. I felt that death was approaching me, that battle history wasn't just a slogan. I couldn't relax, because I knew that my son had to be first.

At night in bed, sleep evaded me. I lay there and envisioned Uriel's death in detail. I saw them bringing his body to me. I wasn't dreaming or hallucinating, I simply saw it – the funeral procession leaving the door of my house, and Uriel, my oldest son, in the casket.

Eliezer got angry at me. "Push those thoughts away," he said, and went off to the synagogue to light more candles, give more *tzedakah*.

But I protested, quietly. "Go on, go to synagogue, light candles, pray… I know it won't do any good."

CHAPTER 9

For Every Descent There's an Ascent – Uriel's Last Summer

In the summer of 1998, Uriel had a week's leave, and he offered to take us on a trip up north.

Eliezer and I were thrilled. We hadn't been on a week-long trip with him for years. Since he had entered the military preparation academy, we had seen him only on weekends. Eliraz couldn't join us since he was already in the army. Avichai didn't come because he was in summer camp. So Hadas, Bat-El, and Elyasaf came with us.

"Where will we sleep?" I asked.

"Mom, don't worry," he answered. "I've arranged everything. I reserved rooms for us in the Hermon Field School."

I crowded into the back seat of our car with the kids, while Eliezer sat beside Uriel. The whole way, I watched the restrained movements of my oldest son as he held the steering wheel. We were driving on the Jordan Valley road, traveling toward Beit She'an, when suddenly a policeman popped out in front of us and signaled for Uriel to stop.

I was gripped with fear. "What happened?" I asked from the back seat.

The policeman ordered Uriel to get out and bring him the car registration and insurance papers. Uriel got out and went over to the police car. From the back seat, I could see them talking – and talking. I have no idea how long the conversation lasted, maybe

116

five minutes, or fifteen minutes. But when it was over, the image I recall is of the policeman hugging Uriel.

"What happened?" I demanded as soon as Uriel came back to the car.

"Nothing, everything's fine."

"So why did he stop you?" I protested.

"Mom, what do you want from me?" he grumbled. "The policeman was just doing his job. Everyone has to do his job as best he can."

"So why did he hug you?" I demanded, dissatisfied.

Then Uriel smiled. "The policeman asked me what I did and I said I was in *sayeret* Golani, and he hugged me."

I smiled, too. If I had thought that the policeman had caused our trip to begin on the wrong foot, our luck had turned. If the policeman hugged Uriel, that was a sign that our journey would turn out all right. I never dreamed that this would be our last trip together.

The first site we went to was the Keshet Cave. Uriel began to explain to us how the cave was formed, and Elyasaf, not the most well-behaved child, interrupted him. "Come here, kid," Uriel said, hugging Elyasaf and holding him at his side. He continued with his explanations, while Eliezer and I swallowed every word. We melted. When I saw how he was able to magnetize all of us, including Elyasaf, I understood how he captivated the soldiers. The knowledge he displayed was thorough and broad.

The second stop was a cave at the lookout named after Lieutenant Colonel Amir Meital, commander of Battalion 13 of the Golani Brigade, who was killed in a military operation. Uriel told us about the battalion commander's personality, and we felt that he was slowly imbuing us with the Golani legacy. Until then, I hadn't understood what Golani was all about, or what Battalion 13 was. I was impressed when I saw the depth of love and respect he had for it. Uriel said, "This is Amir's Lebanon. This is my Lebanon." I didn't fully understand what he was saying. I never imagined that Lebanon would take them both.

From there we drove to Mount Bental, where we learned about the Yom Kippur War, Avigdor Kahalani, and the battles of Emek Habacha (the Valley of Tears). I began to feel uncomfortable. Would our entire family trip become a military tour? But apparently Uriel read my thoughts, because next he drove to the Hermon and suggested we go up on the cable car.

"Cable car?" I yelped in fright.

"Mom, what are you afraid of? I'm behind you!" Uriel exclaimed. We have a video clip that documents that moment for posterity: I'm going up in the cable car, and Uriel's sitting behind me, holding little Bat-El. A moment of joy.

That was my first visit to Mount Hermon. "Dad," Uriel said to Eliezer, "do you remember that when I was twelve, you took me to ski here in the snow? You didn't take Eliraz."

Eliezer smiled. He recalled that his workplace, the Ministry of Health, had organized the trip and allowed him to bring just one child. Eliraz had told him, "Take Uriel. You'll have another opportunity to take me."

They laughed, my two men, until Eliezer had tears in his eyes. "I brought you here as a little boy," he said to Uriel, "and now you're bringing me here. We're coming full circle."

The next stop on the trip was Tel Faher, also called Golani Lookout, a former Syrian outpost in the Golan Heights. In 1967, during the Six-Day War, it was the site of a fierce battle between the Golani Brigade and the Syrians, which ended with Israel conquering the outpost. At this point in our tour, we were dragging, dreaming of air conditioning and somewhere to sit down. Uriel, by contrast, was every bit the professional tour guide. "At this site, I would like to ask for your full attention," he said. He explained the Syrian attack formation, the Golani response, and who was killed. He had us stand beside the names and described the battle in picturesque language. This was the first time that I really felt like I understood IDF battle history. I didn't feel like he was putting us into a military film – instead, I felt like he was taking us on a Golani training course.

After his explanations, Uriel noticed that we needed to cool off, so he took us to the Banias waterfall. I have another wonderful video of that moment. It shows Uriel swimming in long, gentle strokes, like a fish. Then he sat on a rock, and I remember the point at which I said to myself, God, he's so beautiful.

I didn't go into the water; I was scared. I love the beach, but here the water was frothing and foaming. I sat on the side, hugging little Bat-El. Uriel called to us. "Come in! Come in!" Just then, a park ranger arrived.

"What's wrong?" I jumped.

"You're not allowed to swim here," he said. Without blinking an eye, Uriel got out of the water and apologized. As he realized, the ranger was only doing his job to the best of his ability, as everyone must. I saluted Uriel silently for that as well, for his discipline. Only a person who knew how to obey orders could demand obedience from his soldiers – and receive it. "Look at him," Eliezer whispered to me. "What a man. Would you ever have believed it?" Our hearts melted with pride. We felt that we had been given a great privilege to raise such a child.

When evening fell, Uriel drove us to the Hermon Field School and announced, "I won't be here at night."

I tensed. "Where are you going?"

"Don't worry about me," he reassured me. "I'm just going to pay a visit to my battalion, in the Odem Forest."

My body shook. In bed that night, I whispered to Eliezer, "How's he going to get to the forest by himself? In the dark? It's deathly scary."

But come morning, Uriel was back, wearing a wide grin. "Mom, why were you worried again? This is my territory. My base."

I lowered my head in shame. Wasn't it normal for a mother to be afraid of a forest in the dark?

He sat with us for breakfast. "Eat quickly," he urged. "We'll continue our trip."

"How will you drive?" I asked. "You didn't sleep a wink all night."

"So what?" He burst out laughing. "I'm used to not sleeping."

"You can continue traveling with us?" I asked. "What a question," he replied. "Today we'll go somewhere special," he promised, and was as good as his word. He took us to Yehudiya waterfall.

"Why did you say it was a hard hike?" I teased him on the descent. "Getting to the waterfall is easy."

"Mom," he said, growing serious, "Don't forget that for every descent in life, there's an ascent. Remember that you can't stay down. You always have to go up."

At that moment, I didn't understand what he meant. But looking back, I think that Uriel was saying that in moments of crisis, you have to stand on your own two feet. When you descend to the very lowest point in life, you feel like your strength has been used up and you have no more resources to tap. Back then, Uriel was telling me that descents are easy and quick, while ascents are slow and difficult – but not impossible.

We reached the waterfall, and Uriel swam with Elyasaf, Bat-El, and Hadas. Swam? He rough-housed with them, grabbing them and tossing them in the air, and they screeched with delight. I felt that our family story with Uriel was being rewritten. This trip – we never dreamed it would be our last together – was reinforcing sibling ties, which had loosened ever since Uriel had gone off to the premilitary academy and then the army.

We finished our dip in the waterfall. What next? The ascent. I couldn't climb it. The path was windy, it was suffocatingly hot, and in front of me, Uriel was bounding like a deer.

"I can't do it," I groaned. Uriel stopped and encouraged me. "One more step, two more. You're doing great, Mom. Remember that you have to gather a lot of strength and faith in order to go up."

I nodded, gathered my strength, and moved forward, slowly. Thanks to him.

We continued on to Manara. At the lookout over the Jordan Valley, Uriel pointed out the sights and told us about the helicopter disaster of 1997, in which seventy-three IDF soldiers were killed when two helicopters collided. Then he took us to his outpost – Tzivoni, right on the Lebanese border. There I really gasped.

"Uriel!" I gripped his hand. "You're not posted near Lebanon, you're right inside it!"

He replied with the usual, "Mom, calm down."

When he showed me the border fence, Uriel told me about Avraham (Avi) Limoi, a soldier who had been killed a few months earlier by a Hezbollah explosive device. My chills intensified. A few months later, Uriel became Avi's neighbor – at Mount Herzl cemetery.

At certain times, I had the feeling that Uriel was deceiving me. On one hand, he radiated euphoria and gave me the feeling that he was confident and safe. On the other hand, the entire trip – which had become a military training exercise – had been strewn with the names of fallen soldiers. We picnicked outside, surrounded by nature, and I asked him, "Uriel, how can it be that soldiers get killed in this pastoral place, in such a peaceful setting?"

"Don't trust the quiet," he replied. "There's another side to Lebanon. At night, this land takes off its mask. It's another world, a world of hidden explosives. It's not what you see now."

I discovered the other Lebanon one month after Uriel was killed, when Chief of Staff Shaul Mofaz asked us to light Chanukah candles at Tzivoni outpost. The presence of the chief of staff gave us a secure feeling during the helicopter flight, and Elyasaf even fell asleep in Mofaz's lap. But when we landed, I saw the fog. I heard the sound of shooting, and I breathed the Lebanon that had taken my son.

On the third day of our trip, Uriel led us up the summit path of Mount Meron. He marched up front, while we straggled behind. At the first lookout, over Zefat, we stopped. We looked at Zefat, and Uriel pointed out Nahal Amud and the grave of Rabbi Shimon bar Yochai. Then he showed us where Lebanon was. "Let's go on to the next one, the Lebanon Lookout," he proposed. But something stopped us, as if our feet had been obstructed by a higher power.

"Enough. We're exhausted, it's too hot," we mumbled.

"Too bad," Uriel said. "We made it up to here– when will you have a chance to visit here again?"

But we plodders kept complaining. "It's boiling out. We've seen enough, we've heard enough."

We never dreamed that the Lebanon lookout would be the site of Uriel's memorial.

Since his death, I can't stand to hear the song "This is my last summer with you / With the first rain, I'll disappear." I have the feeling that this song was written about Uriel. We didn't know that this would be our last summer with Uriel. We didn't know this would be our last trip with him, but when the first rain fell, he was no longer with us.

CHAPTER 10

I Knew Uriel Would Die

I had a feeling that Uriel would die in the army.

I know it sounds awful, but a mother knows, a mother feels. For days, weeks, months, the feeling gnawed at me that it was only a matter of time. I didn't dream it, I didn't have visions. But I knew that every day our soldiers were being killed in Lebanon. I pictured his funeral, step by step. Eliezer berated me, "Stop it!" He would rush to the synagogue and buy more tea and sugar for the congregants who came to Selichot, the dawn penitential prayers before the High Holidays. I would tease him, "What are you buying that for? Do you think it will help? That it will change his fate?"

Uriel's death was born along with him. In essence, it was determined even before that, during the pregnancy, when Eliezer had hepatitis, and the doctors recommended an abortion, although the Baba Sali blessed me and promised that the baby would be fine.

A feeling of helplessness before death hovered over me during the first few months of his life, when he lost consciousness, lolled his head backwards and rolled his eyes. "He's dead! He's dead!" I would scream, running to fetch the elderly Moroccan women in the neighborhood. The childhood image of Uriel that remains burned into my memory is of a little boy with eyeglasses and a frog-like gait, his hand grasping my dress – a child who needed his mother's total protection.

123

Three months before he was killed, on Yom Kippur eve, at the final meal before the fast, Uriel hugged us and said, "Mom, Dad, please forgive me."

"Forgive you?" I was astonished. "For what?"

"Forgive me that in Lebanon, we can't always see everything."

Eliezer asked him to explain, and he mumbled, "Hezbollah lays explosives." He didn't give any further details.

I began the fast with these words burned into my brain.

On Yom Kippur Eve, after the prayer service in synagogue, Jews usually rush home, so as to avoid the possibility of entering into an inappropriate conversation with someone along the way, which might lead us to speak unkind words on the Day of Judgment. That was our intention that year as well. But Uriel, who was wearing white, pure as an angel, wanted to visit a neighbor who usually spent many hours maintaining the synagogue, but couldn't go out that evening because he had fallen from a ladder and was confined to his bed.

We went to visit the man, and after we came home, Uriel said, "Mom, Dad, did you see how he has enlarged his house? Maybe you should also think about fixing up our house. It's time to renovate."

Eliezer and I exchanged surprised looks. What was up with him? Yom Kippur Eve was hardly an appropriate time to suggest redecorating.

Yes, Uriel knew that he was going to die. At the beginning of the Jewish New Year, he was suggesting that we should continue our lives. We should rebuild.

Three months after his death, we found a diskette with a file in which he described the twenty-two years of his life. With spelling mistakes due to inexperience in typing on the computer – in those days, it was still a novelty – he reconstructed his memories until age four, including incidents he had heard from me. He began the file with a description of his death:

A Dream

The packs filled with gear made walking in the mud of Lebanon nearly impossible. It was foggy, and there was an annoying drizzle. Suddenly, a big black form jumped out of the bush in front of me and ran north. I placed the night vision gear on my left eye, quietly removed the safety catch, and aimed at the black form.

I saw an enormous wild pig coming toward me from about sixty meters (two hundred feet) away. I recognized those big eyes, shining at me from behind the lens. He looked at me, then looked westward, and back at me. Then he continued running north. It seemed as if he was trying to tell me something. I informed the troops behind me, and we continued.

After advancing 120 meters (400 feet), I saw a flash and heard the sound of shooting. The bullet flew toward me at 900 meters per second (60 miles per hour). The Angel of Death was on that bullet. Actually, he was riding it like an experienced surfer rides his surfboard, surfing between the air currents and the thick underbrush.

Before the bullet entered my body, the angel got down off it and grabbed me with two hands, like Superman hanging on to a spacecraft. The bullet hit the shoulder of my vest and tore the left pocket of my shirt. It pierced the first layer of flesh and entered my chest through the ribs. The angel left the bullet and entered the right-hand chamber, sat on the edge and began to laugh.

That's it, I thought. I'm dead…

Then a feather pillow hit my face. My annoying brother woke me up.

I tried to understand the meaning of this awareness of death, of moving toward it in a fully conscious way. I found the answer in Uriel's wallet. Inside it was a small folded slip of paper, with a quotation from Zionist philosopher Rabbi Avraham Yitzchak Hacohen Kook's *Orot Hateshuva*. "As the answer deepens, so does the fear of death subside, until it completely fades and is replaced by an attitude of 'She laughs at the very last day' (Proverbs 31:25)." In other words, when you have an answer to the question of why you are fighting and why you live in Israel, you have no fear of death, because it is death out of belief in your actions.

The newspaper was another one of the early, almost prophetic signs that took on special significance only after they were realized. *Yediot Aharonot*'s Yom Kippur supplement for 1998 bore the headline "Leadership." We usually don't read anything except the prayer book on Yom Kippur, but when we returned from synagogue after the Musaf service, I pulled out the supplement and began to read.

"Mom, what are you reading?" asked Uriel.

I answered that I had flipped through the supplement and saw that there was an interview with Tamir Yadai, who at that time was the commander of the Golani Brigade's 13th Battalion.

Uriel said something strange, unrelated to my answer: "What's decreed for someone is decreed."

I didn't understand where that sentence came from. Was my son preparing me for his departure? I kept the newspaper. I didn't think his death would come so quickly, or that I, out of the desire to continue his life, would work in the field of leadership education.

It was time for Ne'ilah, the concluding service of Yom Kippur. At this time, the Holy One, blessed be He, was about to lock the gates of heaven and seal our judgment – who would live, and who would die. One of our good friends, Eli Abuzedaka, who admired Uriel and his service in the special forces, paid a premium price to buy the aliyah for this service, and gave Uriel the honor of opening the ark. But at that very moment, Uriel got up and walked out.

I watched from the women's balcony on the second floor as my oldest son walked out.

My eyes searched for Eliezer's, and when I found them, I saw astonishment and worry reflected in them. Worry because some of the terrible thoughts haunting me were being realized. My husband looked at me, I looked at him, and each of us said wordlessly, "The heavenly gates are locked, and Uriel is outside." We did not speak, but we each felt with a powerful force that this was it, it was over. On Eliezer's face I saw his supplication: "Wait a little bit, have mercy on the boy, he's not there yet."

Later, we asked Uriel why he had left the synagogue, but he avoided us and didn't answer. We never spoke of it again. For me, it was yet another link in the chain of signs. I knew this would be the last Yom Kippur of his life.

Yom Kippur was followed by Sukkot. That year, the Golani Brigade was celebrating the fiftieth anniversary of its founding. The radio had been trying to interview Uriel for some time, but he always refused. On that day, however, the Jerusalem radio station managed to get him on the air. "What does Golani mean to you?" asked the interviewer. Uriel replied that Golani was family, friendship, roots, history, and future.

"We heard you have a brother who is also in Golani," the interviewer commented, and Uriel crowed, "My brother Eliraz is a champ! He's better than me." That's how he spoke of Eliraz, with pride and love. Ready to end the conversation, the interviewer said, "Good luck to you," and Uriel added, "I have just one small request. I would like to wish my mother the best year ever."

I listened to the radio, and turned pale. Another strange utterance. Why was he wishing me the best year ever? Did Uriel know that this year would be difficult for us, and so he was wishing us the best year ever?

On the last day of the shivah for Uriel, we were supposed to have celebrated the marriage of Yair, my sister Zehava's oldest son. I ordered my family: "Don't come to the shivah. Go to the wedding, go to rejoice with the bride and groom." As I said this, I recalled another sign, something that had occurred two weeks earlier on Erev Shabbat, Friday night. During the meal, I had told Uriel about Yair's upcoming wedding, and then I said, "I want to show you what I'll look like at the wedding." I don't know what inspired me to put on my new dress and jewelry for him.

"See?" I stood before him. "This is what I'm going to wear at the wedding."

As usual, Uriel was sitting at the head of the table, and he smiled at me and said, "Mother, you're so beautiful. You should dress like that all the time."

Later I tortured myself with guilt. Why did I get dressed up? Why did I wear that beautiful necklace? Did I know he wouldn't see me at the wedding? Did I want his last image of me to be one in which I was elegantly dressed?

Another sign. On Wednesday, at one p.m. – one week before Uriel fell in action – he called the school. Sima, the secretary, who is also no longer with us, told him that I was in a meeting.

"Tell Mother to turn on the radio," he requested.

"Why?" asked the secretary. Uriel spoke curtly. "Tell Mother to turn on the radio and she'll understand everything."

The secretary interrupted the meeting. We turned on the radio and heard the beautiful song by Chaim Moshe: "When you come home for another Shabbat, we'll wait in the doorway…. Just come home."

I looked at her, and she looked at me, and we were both confused. The song was very moving, but I didn't understand the message Uriel was trying to give me. He wasn't scheduled to come home that Shabbat.

Several hours later, Uriel called again. I didn't ask him about the song on the radio; I acted as if it hadn't happened. I merely said, "How are you, Uriel? I've already bought you a gift for your birthday. I want to send it to you."

He answered, "Don't send it, Mom, I'm coming home."

"But I want to send it," I insisted.

"I'm coming home," he repeated. "But if you want to prepare a package, send as much stuff as you can for the soldiers. I don't need anything."

Before we ended the conversation, Uriel repeated: "Turn on the radio, and you'll understand everything.... Today it's them – tomorrow it's me."

I shivered. What was he trying to say? I felt that Uriel was preparing me for something.

That evening, I understood. Three soldiers from the communications company were killed in the Tel Ka'aba region. One of them, Sergeant Nahum Elah, is buried next to Uriel. The "tomorrow" arrived exactly one week later, when Uriel went out on an ambush from which he never returned.

The signs chased me and wouldn't leave me in peace.

Two days later I noticed that the other school secretary, Yisraela, looked upset. I asked her what had happened, and she answered, "I don't want to talk about it." I pressured her, but she avoided me. After I begged her to explain why she looked so distraught, she came into my room, sat down in front of me, and said in a choked voice, "I had a dream."

"Good," I smiled. Dreams were a sign of blessing.

"No," she shook her head. "I dreamed that your son Uriel was killed."

She said it in just those words, "Your son, Uriel," as if trying to be precise.

I replied, "A good dream, a peaceful dream," the Sephardi response when one hears about a dream, meaning, "Everything will be okay."

"But I dreamed about Uriel." Tears shone in her eyes.

"Uriel is fine," I declared. "I just spoke to him."

I spoke to Uriel in the afternoon on the day he was killed, a Wednesday. He sounded happy. There was nothing in his voice that indicated that in a few hours, he would no longer be among the living. It was his birthday, and I wished him *mazal tov*. After he died, I was told that on his last day, at one p.m., Uriel had given a training session to commanders who were visiting the outpost. The topic was how to prepare an ambush. In his explanations, he used two marking tapes. When he was asked why he was using two tapes, he replied, "The second one is for my replacement."

"Why do you say that?" they asked. "How old are you?"

He replied, "I'm twenty-two, today's my birthday."

Before he left on his last mission, Uriel did not fill in the date on the record. Instead he wrote "Happy birthday."

In hindsight, I see this as his last will and testament. I believe that Uriel wanted us to remember that day with joy, despite the constant pain. He wanted that date, which became the date of his death, to live on in our memory as a day of happiness.

That Wednesday, I had a teachers' meeting, and something inside me made me distressed and agitated. Ostensibly I had no reason to worry, but the teachers felt that I was not my usual relaxed self. I sat on tenterhooks, feeling helpless and empty. On the one hand I had a sense of acceptance of what would happen; on the other, I protested and fought against the world, a last-ditch attempt to prevent the inevitable. The meeting began in the afternoon and continued into the evening, and as the hours slipped by, I felt as if something was closing in on me. I saw that it was something dark and heavy.

Then, at eleven p.m., the hour when Uriel was killed, I did something inexplicable. I took my personal planner out of my handbag and pulled out a photo of Eliraz at Atzmona waving the Israeli flag, and announced to the teachers, "Here's my son, Eliraz." As if an inner voice was telling me that Uriel was no longer, and that I had to put the next child on the stage.

Stop it, I chided myself on the way home, be happy! It's Uriel's birthday, the birthday of your oldest son whom you brought into the world twenty-two years ago!

I opened the door and saw Eliezer sitting by himself in the living room. The entire house was dark; only one light was on.

"What happened?" I pounced on him, and began to turn on the lights. I was frightened, the house already felt like disaster.

Eliezer didn't protest. He remained where he was, in his easy chair.

"What are you reading?" I asked, approaching. My face fell. He was holding a pamphlet entitled "Memorial Sites." The school had received it a few days earlier, and I had brought it home to read when I had time. I placed the pamphlet on the table. Why had he picked that up? Why was he reading that particular thing?

Again I told myself to calm down. Everything's fine, I told myself: Eliraz was in the army in the special forces, and all the other children were at home. Hadas was in ninth grade, Avichai in seventh, Elyasaf in sixth, and Bat-El in third. But I wasn't placated. I couldn't calm down. November is a sad, cold month, and the image of the quiet, dark house made me feel awful.

"Listen," I told Eliezer, "I'm uneasy. I have a bad feeling. Tonight I want to sleep with the radio on, but I don't want to disturb you."

I added, "I'll sleep in another room," and Eliezer nodded.

The midnight news broadcast announced that Hezbollah had fired on IDF positions. At that very moment, I knew that Uriel had been killed.

They still hadn't said anything about soldiers being injured, they just said that positions had been fired on. But I knew. I lay in bed and waited for the announcement. I lay there and waited.

A minute passed, a quarter of an hour, another half hour, another hour.

At two thirty a.m. I heard knocking on the door. I was upstairs on the second floor. I opened the window and saw three soldiers.

Two thirty a.m. Stillness and silence, the whole town was asleep, and the soldiers hadn't said anything yet. I looked out over the mute houses on the street, and although Eliraz was also serving in the special forces at the time, I cried out from the open window, "Urieeeeeel!"

I wanted everyone to wake up, for everyone to be shocked, everyone to get out of bed. My oldest son had fallen!

From the upstairs window I shouted down to the messengers: "I know, Uriel's been killed!"

They were silent.

I ran down the corridor, between the rooms. "Get up, get up! Uriel!"

Two kids come out of one room, one comes out of another, and I'm screaming at the top of my lungs, "Uriel!"

The children stared at me, wide-eyed. What sweet dreams had I interrupted? I ran to Eliezer and wept.

"What happened?" he hugged me, and I sobbed, "Uriel... Uriel..." I still couldn't say the word. Finally I shouted, "Dead! Dead!"

I had to spit those words out of my mouth again and again, over and over, until I got downstairs and opened the door to the three messengers. But then I grabbed one of them, I pushed him up against the wall and begged, "Tell me he was wounded."

"No," he said, avoiding my eyes. "Your son Uriel was killed."

The big birthday package was sitting on the table, wrapped and decorated with birthday greetings, symbolizing the stark contrast between life and death.

I collapsed onto the sofa in the living room. My son Uriel, Uriel my son.

Why was I so surprised? After all, I had seen the writing on the wall. There had been countless signs.

From that point on, my memories are cloudy. They gave me injections and pills. I held little Bat-El and wavered between reality and illusion.

At five a.m., I called my sister Zehava and whispered, "Uriel."

"What happened? Is everything all right?" she asked. I was no longer capable of uttering the word "dead." Zehava figured it out by herself. One thought kept going around and around in my head: how do we get word to Eliraz, our other soldier? Who would tell him, who would say to him, "Your brother..."?

I remember when Eliraz arrived. "My brother! My own brother!" he cried, and every syllable exploded in my head like lightning.

To me, Eliraz's "my own brother" was more painful than "my own son." I couldn't listen to his pain, his longing.

Years later, that image would be repeated at Eliraz's death, when Bat-El, then a soldier, came home. The same scene. When they informed me that Eliraz had been killed, again I would ask: Who will tell her? Again I would wait, this time for Bat-El's arrival.

At Uriel's funeral, the sun was shining. They drove him to the front of the house in a command car. I saw the command car and I understood that Uriel was right when he said, "I'll come home." He didn't walk down the stairs to the door, but he came.

We climbed up the stairs leading to the street. One step after another, we climbed to meet Uriel, our Uriel, who was lying there in silence in the military command car. I couldn't believe that those were my feet walking up those stairs.

Years later, the same feeling would return after Eliraz fell in combat. Again, as in an instant replay, I would have to climb up that staircase, step by step. I wanted the funerals to start from there; I wanted my children to say goodbye to their home. The home in which they had grown up and from which they went off to the army.

I reached the sidewalk. There were hundreds of people waiting there, and still I couldn't believe that it was my son Uriel in that command car. After Eliraz died, the trip to Mount Herzl was even more difficult, because Eliezer was no longer at my side. I had to make the return trip alone.

I don't remember anything about the funeral. It was completely erased from my mind. I only wanted one thing with my whole heart and soul – I wanted them to let me get into the hole gaping in the ground, to let me be there with him. After all, I was his mother. Why were they covering him up with mounds of dirt, why were they choking him? My boy loved air and wide open spaces. Even then, at that very moment, I wondered what would happen when the first rain fell. Wouldn't he get soaked, down to his bones? I shouted and screamed that I wanted to take Uriel's place. Not to die with him, but to lie beside him there, inside the pit.

On Wednesday, November 25, 1998, First Lieutenant Uriel Peretz – patrol squad commander in the Golani Brigade's 51st Battalion – led an ambush in southern Lebanon. He said to his soldiers, "We're going out on a little hike," and led them into an ambush in Wadi Karush, near Markaba village.

At one point, his sergeant, Tomer Reichman, moved close to him, and Uriel said, "If you get near me, you'll blow up together with me." Then Uriel saw a flash from the direction of the village. He ordered the soldiers to move away from each other and to lie down. Then he climbed up a rock. Six explosive devices were hidden underneath it, and Hezbollah blew them up with a remote control detonator. Uriel was killed on the spot. His navigator, Staff Sergeant Nitzan Baldran of Kibbutz Lotem, was killed as well.

Sergeant Tomer took over the command, led the soldiers away from the site, and returned to the booby-trapped rock in order to recover Uriel's body. Ever since then, for the past twelve years, Tomer calls every Friday to wish me *Shabbat shalom*, a peaceful Sabbath.

CHAPTER 11

Uriel's Lookout –
Life in One Sentence

On the path at the peak of Mount Meron there is a lookout point. It stands at the exact spot where we stopped on our hike, and it bears Uriel's name.

Uriel knew that he would be killed. Maybe he didn't know exactly when it would happen, maybe it was just conjecture, but I'm certain that he knew it was only a matter of time. The Talmud says that forty days before a man's death, his soul knows it is about to depart from this world. After his last Shabbat at home, Eliraz accompanied Uriel to the Egged station in Jerusalem. Uriel hugged Eliraz and said, "Brother, if something happens to me, dedicate a lookout in my name, a place with a view of Israel. That's all I want." Two weeks later, he fell in action.

I hadn't known that Uriel had said these words to Eliraz. I heard about their last conversation only after the shivah. Eliraz said, "If we want to commemorate Uriel, we already have his last request. He asked for a lookout."

We consulted with Uriel's friends and they recommended places visited by Golani special forces patrols. One of them was the Elah (terebinth or pistacia tree) Lookout, located above Moshav Menahemiah. It has a view of Tiberias, the Jordan River, and all of northern Israel.

Four months after Uriel's death, we met with the Israel Nature and Parks Authority and asked for permission to establish a lookout point at Elah Lookout. While we were at the meeting, a Parks Authority representative from Mount Meron Field School came in and said, "I have a proposal for you. On Mount Meron there is a trail called the summit path, and there's a lookout on that path that's not named after anyone yet."

"So what's this lookout called?" I asked, and he replied, "The temporary name is 'Lebanon Lookout'...." I recalled that this was what Uriel had called it, and then I answered, "Okay." Until that day, I had never set foot on that site, or seen it. But the word "Lebanon" won me over, because Uriel had lived and breathed Lebanon, and it was where he died.

After an agreement was reached, we drove there with Uriel's friends. We saw that it was a delightful trail, nature in all its splendor. The route was thick with vegetation, and when we climbed it, I felt as if I was walking the path of Uriel's life. We reached the lookout, and my head spun. I saw two sights before me: on one side, southern Lebanon, the place where Uriel was killed, and on the other, the grave of Rabbi Shimon bar Yochai, who had served as an inspiration for Uriel's faith. From his example, Uriel had drawn the courage to go into Lebanon, with the story of bar Yochai's battle against the Romans echoing in his mind. It was a battle over Jewish identity and spirit, a battle that has not yet ended.

Then they asked me to write an epitaph, one sentence.

One sentence? I couldn't think of just one sentence that would express Uriel in a nutshell. To this day, I can't summarize him in one phrase. How can you encapsulate a child's life in a few words? But that was the request. I mulled it over for an entire year, until I found the words that were later inscribed on the lookout:

Uriel Peretz – fighter, scout, Torah scholar, lover of the Land of Israel

Why did I decide to begin with "fighter"? Because that's what he was, long before he went to the army. A fighter in the battle of life. As a little boy, short and weak, he had to fight in order to board the bus. Bigger and tougher kids pushed him. Then he had to fight to get into the premilitary academy and into the Golani elite reconnaissance unit, his highest aspiration.

"Scout" because he was connected to the Land of Israel. He walked on its soil, he absorbed its thorns, and he left the imprint of his boots on it.

"Torah scholar" because the Torah was the wellspring of his life, the inspiration for his belief in the integrity of his path. Beyond studying Torah, his everyday conduct revealed the extent to which he internalized its values.

"Lover of the Land of Israel" because loving the land means loving it to the death. It means giving your life and soul for it.

So the dedication comes full circle, beginning with "fighter" and ending with "lover of the Land of Israel."

Many tourists visit the lookout, including some who discovered it in David Grossman's book *To the End of the Land* (Hebrew title: *A Woman Flees Bad News*). Often they call me from the site and ask me to tell them about the place and about Uriel. "Open your eyes," I say. "Take a look around. Lebanon on one side, and on the other, down below, Rabbi Shimon's tomb, the Gush Halav and Dalton area, and the settlements on the Lebanese border. The people who live in those settlements, my children included, are protected by IDF soldiers. They are protecting the people who get up in the morning and go to work in the fields, and the children walking to kindergarten. The soldiers are the ones who make it possible for them to live a calm, quiet life."

But mainly I tell them about my son, Uriel. I say that Uriel was small in stature, but that his spirit was very big. I tell them how we chose the place, explain the background behind the dedication, connect them to Uriel, and bring him closer to them. That way he lives on in the travelers' minds. With every visit, every story, I feel that Uriel lives on – and that I live with him and feel his presence.

I also say, "They tried to break his spirit in Lebanon. But when you continue traveling in Israel, when you stand here at the lookout and look toward Lebanon, your very presence announces that our spirit has not been broken. Each one of you is a continuation of Uriel. Uriel died, but you are his next generation."

Later on, something interesting happened in connection with the lookout. The Golani reconnaissance unit decided to name one of their final endurance exercises – the concluding northern exercise – after Uriel. This meant that every soldier who entered the unit would study the life story of Uriel Peretz in preparation for this final training exercise. And who was the first soldier to complete the Uriel Peretz Concluding Northern Exercise? His brother Eliraz.

When Uriel was killed, Eliraz was in the final stage of this endurance course, which started at the top of Mount Meron, on the summit path.

After the lookout point was authorized, Eliezer decided to organize a march, the Lebanon Lookout March. Since then, we have held the march every year on the first day of Chol Hamo'ed Sukkot (the intermediate days of Sukkot).

Every year we rent three buses that leave from Givat Ze'ev. We invite anyone and everyone to join us: soldiers, Uriel's friends, young people. Whoever shows up is welcome. And many do come. It was important to Eliezer that this be a volunteer project for the entire family, so everyone can come, free of charge.

Every year we choose a different site in Israel to visit. After touring the site, we go to Mount Meron, hike up to the lookout, and, while facing Lebanon, hold a small ceremony, which includes explanations about the scenery, mostly given by Eliraz, before he was killed. We conclude by singing "Hatikvah" and then go down to the tomb of Rabbi Shimon bar Yochai to pray.

Our entire family participates in the organization of this project. After the first day of Sukkot is over, we all report to the

Berman Bakery in Jerusalem, which donates rolls. We bring them home and set up a long table in the living room. We do the work in pairs, conveyor belt style: the first person slices open the roll; the second spreads white cheese, yellow cheese, hummus, or *matbucha* – Moroccan roasted tomato and pepper salad. When the roll reaches the end of the assembly line, we wrap it in plastic wrap and pack it in a crate.

Throughout the night we prepare boxes of sliced vegetables, pour hot water in thermoses that we collect from neighbors, pack cakes. I add sets of black coffee, instant coffee, sugar, and sugar substitute. Nothing is forgotten. Bags of sweets await the little kids, and of course, we also bring along a portable *sukkah*.

I have a special notebook that says "Commemoration Notebook" on the cover. I use it to record the exact quantities we need for every event, trip, or memorial ceremony, so that everything is organized and efficient. We have T-shirts with "Lebanon Lookout March" printed on them, and signs for the buses. We have clear operating procedures for each family member. They're not combat procedures – call them memorial procedures.

Eliezer died in Elul 5765 (September 2005), a month before the annual march. Despite the fact that we were still within the year-long period of mourning for him, the rest of the family kept the tradition that he had begun. Following Eliraz's death in 2010, the march was particularly difficult for me. It was the first time we organized a condensed version of the Lebanon Lookout March, with family only, and Eliraz did not stand beside me on top of the mountain. Still, many people showed up. We concluded the ceremony with a powerful rendition of "Hatikvah," and a prayer that God should give us the strength to return to the site next year and to our tradition of a big, happy march, as Eliezer had wanted.

PART THREE

Eliezer

CHAPTER 12

Covenant of Disaster – A Marriage in Grief

There are many tests in a marriage. The hardest of all is losing a child – which is the product of love. Our child fell in combat, but the disaster we shared led to questions that could cause disagreement, because each of us stood alone in our mourning. Each of us dealt with the tragedy in a different way. The announcement of Uriel's death led to questions on issues that Eliezer and I had never processed. We knew how to live together, but we didn't know how to mourn a son together.

People asked whether we wanted to see his body, and if so, who would go. I couldn't bear the thought that Uriel would be buried without me saying goodbye to him. Yet I feared that until my dying day, that image would haunt me – my oldest son, dead.

Because we entered the disaster from a relationship that was loving, accepting, and supportive, we didn't slide into arguments or criticism. Each of us had full faith in the other. We walked on eggshells, trying to be as considerate as possible of the other's feelings. We were not dealing with questions of logic, because it was not logical for parents to bury a son. These were questions of emotion, for which there is no right or wrong answer. But we knew that every decision we made would come from love.

After some deliberation, I agreed with my husband, and neither of us went to see the body. We parted from Uriel as we see him in our memories, beautiful and whole. During the shivah as well, conflicts arose between us. I didn't want the whole dynamic that surrounded it. Our mourning customs, which obligate eating and drinking, triggered deep resistance within me. Yet Eliezer, in his gentle way, explained how important it was to continue our ancestral traditions.

In many instances, we were forced to make immediate decisions, and because we were in shock, we relied on the dear, close people who surrounded and supported us. We were spared some of these decisions, such as the details of the ceremony and the site of the burial, and this made it easier for us.

During the shivah, Eliezer sat in silence, while I talked. Sometimes I felt that this was unfair. Why did I have to bear the burden of talking, while he was quiet? Later, when we processed the grief, I understood that each person reacts in the way that helps him to survive, to hold on. I remember that I wanted to gather everyone, the entire family, so that we could mourn together in a unified way. But I had to accept the fact that everyone develops his own way of mourning and wants to be allowed to mourn as he sees fit. At night, Eliezer paced the living room, between the walls that were filled with photos of Uriel, and I heard his silent cry, "My son, my son, Uriel. Would that I had died instead of you."

We participated in a support group for bereaved parents, sponsored by the Ministry of Defense. We came as a couple, although Eliezer objected to the idea. If at home he was uncommunicative with me, how would he speak to strangers? But he agreed to come with me to the group meetings. At first he just listened, and I didn't pressure him to open up. It was enough for me that we talked on the way home; together we processed what was said.

Over time, Eliezer developed warm ties with people in the group, which also showed us the power of marriage and how difficult it was to be isolated. Grief cracks everything apart – questions of faith, the family unit, marriage. Some of the couples in the group got divorced, or one of the partners died, and they acknowledged that after the meetings ended, they had no one with whom to share their insights and pain. We felt that on that score at least, we were lucky. We had each other.

Disaster is a fire that nothing can extinguish. It's an inferno that cannot be contained by one person alone. When Uriel was killed, I felt there was no one who understood my pain better than my Eliezer. I couldn't even share it with my children, at least not on the same level. But at night in bed, I could cry alongside my husband. The most devastating sentence I ever heard him say was, "Ay, my son Uriel." Only at my side could he utter such a sentence.

Being in a marriage makes it easier – it's a kind of consolation. We both knew we had each other to live for. Our world was narrowed, and our presence with each other suddenly took on greater importance. He encouraged me to go out, to buy new clothes. I didn't go to family celebrations. I just couldn't do it. So Eliezer went without me. He came back from the weddings of Uriel's friends, where he put on a happy face, but at home he removed the mask. We accepted the reality that we wouldn't be attending Uriel's wedding.

My husband Eliezer devoted his life to commemorating Uriel. He founded charitable funds and a synagogue, and even had two Torah scrolls dedicated in Uriel's memory, one in Givat Ze'ev, the other in Atzmona. Eliezer also had the second scroll dedicated in memory of Nitzan Baldran, son of Jacky and Tzipi, who was killed alongside Uriel. Eliezer also made sure that every time the mourner's prayer, Kaddish, was recited for Uriel, someone recited it for Nitzan as well.

I began to teach classes to soldiers on the topic of leadership. I pieced together an image of Uriel out of letters from his soldiers, commanders, and friends – an image of him as commander, as seen through their eyes. Uriel loved the Land of Israel and the military, and he considered a leader to be first and foremost a man with a vision.

Even then, I was afraid that the weight of the disaster would break my husband, and I felt that if something happened to him, I couldn't bear the burden alone. His existence was part of my strength, and my dependence on him grew. "He's the minister of foreign affairs. He takes care of the accounts and the errands," I thought. "I couldn't do all that by myself."

Sorrow registered in his every movement. He met Uriel three times a day – at synagogue, in the Torah scroll that bore Uriel's name, which he took from the ark, and in Uriel's empty chair. But I had no photographs of Uriel at my school. I didn't want the students to feel that I had only one child in my thoughts. Every day, my gaze fell on the face of a boy who reminded me of my eldest son. They kept on living, I thought, and I have to show them that it's possible, and that they should continue to see only hopeful things in front of them.

Eliezer hung the mourning notice in his office, next to photos of Uriel. They remained there until he died, a tortured testimony of the death of his eldest son.

Sorrow and loss transformed our relationship into something beyond love. We were like smoking brands that ignited sparks in each other. A covenant of disaster linked us and transformed our marriage into something deeper.

After such a disaster, there is a tendency to bring a new child into the world, a natural reflex of the continuity of life. Eliezer wanted another child to bring joy into our home, and in the first months I also entertained the thought that only when I held a baby would I be able to smile again. But in time, reason overcame emotion.

I realized that I was searching for a replacement for Uriel, and we both knew that we would never have another Uriel, because he was one and only, unique. We left the decision up to God. If He gave us another child, we would raise him in love. If not, we would wait for grandchildren. After all, I had kept my older children's clothes in order to hand them down to Uriel's children.

When Eliezer relaxed, our marriage was enriched on the emotional plane. I felt that my husband had only to glance at me, and he could feel what was going on inside me. I knew that my husband, my beloved, was also my partner in pain.

Every year, on the anniversary of Uriel's death, Eliezer became ill and was even hospitalized. Nevertheless, when he was able, he insisted on saying a few words at the gravesite.

Here are two of the eulogies he gave at Uriel's grave:

> *It's hard for me to stand here beside you, Uriel, and not touch you. It's hard for me to stand here and not hold your hand. It's even harder for me to talk to you when you don't answer me. Today, a year after the date of your death, I've come here, Uriel, to tell you about things we managed to do this year, things we did without you and for you.*

> *Did you know that the synagogue – where you prayed, which you helped build and were so proud of, where you brought your friends from the special forces unit when you organized a meal for them at our home, and which had no name for two years – was named after you? I'm sure that this pleases you. You're not actually inside it, but your spirit, Uriel my son, is present there.*

> *It's important for you to know that we're having a Torah scroll written in your memory. When the scroll is ready, I'll miss you again, because I feel your absence deeply. You, who so often raised the Torah scroll with your small but strong hands, will not stand to raise it up high for all to see. Another Torah scroll in your name*

was donated to the Atzmona premilitary academy by a certain benefactor. You became deeply attached to the academy late in your short life, and you loved to go there to study together with Eliraz.

You will be proud to hear that the Nature and Parks Authority has authorized the establishment of a lookout in your name at the Mount Meron Nature Reserve. There, on the path at the peak of the tall mountain, we can see Lebanon and the place where you fell. You won't believe it, you didn't order the name, but the lookout is now called "Lebanon Lookout." It's where we hiked together last summer, two months before you died.

It's important for you to know, Uriel, that your many friends are the ones who bring light into our home, and you should be proud of them. Your friends from the academy, from the special forces unit, the battalion, the neighborhood, and the synagogue embrace us with deep love. Don't worry – they've eaten.

Because you were a skilled navigator, we thought it would be appropriate to honor your memory with a navigation exercise in your name. So a week ago, we held one in Canada Park. A thousand people participated. You were the only one missing, Uriel, but we felt you everywhere. At the sight of five hundred soldiers who came from all the elite units, our hearts were wrenched by your absence. Your good friends from the special forces were privileged to run the navigation course in your memory, and I'm certain that while they were running, you spurred them on from above, encouraging them to keep going, to break a record. That's what you would have wanted.

I hope you would have approved of everything we've done, and if there are things you would like us to do that we haven't done yet, please find a suitable way to get the message to us.

I wanted to tell you Uriel, about things that are happening at home right now, events in which your absence is felt deeply. Did you know that Eliraz will soon be finishing his reconnaissance course? He's now doing the concluding exercises. He has no one to share these experiences with, but I know that you're encouraging him from above, because you admired him, you always said he was better than you. You were so modest and kind.

Did you know that Elyasaf's bar mitzvah is in two weeks? Can you imagine how we will be able to have such an event without you? You, the driving force behind Avichai's bar mitzvah, who gave us so much help, are suddenly gone. We know you already gave Elyasaf his gift, as if you knew you would no longer be with us here. Last year, you sent your brothers and sisters on an airplane flight over Jerusalem; that was a special parting gift they will never forget.

I have many more things to tell you. Know that our hearts are constantly focused on you alone. Our life at home has changed in every respect. It's hard for me to tell you this, because you won't like hearing it, but Uriel my son, I'm waiting impatiently to see you. I'm looking forward to the day we meet. No, it's not a weakness of belief, I simply can't go on any longer. I'm dying of longing for you, please understand me!

Pray, Uriel, for us, and for all the Jewish people.

Pray up there, that this burial plot here will not grow.

Dad

* * *

Today is the third anniversary of your death, but I'm keeping a different count. Every year I say to myself, "There, you've grown a year." This year you're already twenty-five. I imagine you at that age, perhaps married, perhaps with children, perhaps a battalion commander. I picture this, and then I go back to the real count, the count that means one more year of sorrow, one more year of missing you. A year of life in suffering.

But I also see your brothers and sisters learning, growing, and developing. I see them blossoming, and in them, I see your death. I see how they hurt for their oldest brother, my oldest son who is gone. Your brother Eliraz is already a deputy company commander. Hadas will soon finish high school. Bat-El's entering junior high. Avichai is making great strides and thriving in the national youth council. Elyasaf continues to visit you often. He goes to see you in secret, without telling us.

Mom says, "If only you would come visit for just a moment. If only you could see us for just one minute, your brothers and sister, and me. To see and not believe your eyes, to be amazed at them, to laugh at us a bit. To see my new project – commemoration."

I don't know what you think about it, but my life is constantly busy with you, with preserving your memory.

Mom does this with IDF officers, and as you know, she knows how to talk and teach them about the concept of the leader as presented in the letters your soldiers and friends wrote. I'm doing it in my own way, by dedicating a Torah scroll to the school. Your brother Eliraz brought his platoon to the ceremony. Not only would you have seen him, you would have been very proud of him.

We fulfilled your wishes and established a lookout in your name at the top of Mount Meron, from which we look out on the place where you fell. You would have been very happy to be there with all the friends and acquaintances who came to the dedication ceremony, including friends and neighbors from your childhood in Sharm. My cousin Avi said to me, "Eliezer, look what Uriel has done. Look how many people are surrounding him, how thanks to him, people are touring Israel and seeing another beautiful part of this country."

You have also been memorialized by three of our friends: three babies in various places around Israel bear your name with pride and humility. Uriel Shalom, son of Shlomo and Tzipi Berniker; although Tzipi never knew you, she chose to give her son your name. Uriel Avizered, grandson of Granddad Claude of Givat Ze'ev, who loved you so much. And Uriel Eleazar, son of Patricia and Zion Zozotte of Ashkelon, who knew you as a child in Ofira.

Despite all these things, I can tell you, Uriel my son, that I am not comforted, nor will I ever be. I've been condemned to bear this disaster and to come here every year and continue our special count, the count of your death.

CHAPTER 13

"Hang On" – Parting from Eliezer

When Eliezer fell ill, we all became sick along with him. I hadn't looked for proof of the unity of our family, but I found it during the period of his illness. Of course, I never needed any such proof. I knew that Eliezer and I were one being.

I felt it during our lives in Sharm, and the feeling grew when we moved to Givat Ze'ev and he was appointed *gabbai* of the Sephardi congregation. Our two older sons, Uriel and Eliraz, helped him, but the only problem was that the congregation did not yet have a building. So where would we pray? In my school, the secular school.

On Friday, after school was over, my three men arrived and began to set up the chairs. On Sunday morning, if I came to school and saw that all the chairs had not been put back in place, I wrote a harsh letter to the *gabbai*, and Eliezer would reply in a formal letter: "To the school principal. RE: Care of property. We very much appreciate your assistance and are grateful to you for hosting us. I am making every effort to take good care of the school property, and if something has been inadvertently damaged, I will be happy to fix it."

When Uriel went to the premilitary academy for tenth grade, Eliezer began to complain of stomachaches. At first he tried to ignore it, but when he began to writhe in pain, I convinced him to see a doctor. The doctor checked and said that the pain was psychological, and there was no physical reason for his complaints. Eliezer was pleased. "You see?" he said when he came home. "There's nothing wrong with me."

But the pain intensified and I didn't accept the diagnosis of psychosomatic pain. I knew Eliezer, I knew what a hard worker he was. It didn't make sense to me that such an energetic person would be lying in bed for no reason. I went with him to the doctor and demanded a thorough checkup. We received a referral for a colonoscopy. I was pleased. I thought, finally they'll check him out and find the source of the pain. I never imagined that the test results would lead to bad news.

After the test, the doctor called us into the room and said he saw a growth in the intestine, and that Eliezer had to be hospitalized immediately. "Right now?" I still didn't accept it. It was a Thursday, and I protested, "But we haven't done our shopping for Shabbat!"

"No shopping. No time for that," the doctor ruled. "Your husband has to be admitted." Only then did I realize the severity of the situation, and the first thought that went through my head was of Bat-El. She was still a baby; she deserved to have her father raise her and spoil her and lead her to the *chuppah*. I was so dependent on Eliezer. How would I manage with his absences from home?

The next day, Friday morning, Eliezer had an operation. Uriel was given special leave for the weekend, and he remained by his father's side in the hospital. He cared for him devotedly, bathing him and helping him put on his *tallit* and *tefillin*. When Eliezer came home, we all pitched in to help. Eliraz bought his father a walking stick, as he had difficulty walking. On Shabbat morning, Eliraz helped Eliezer get dressed and supported him as he walked, step by step, to the Sephardi congregation. Eliezer had initiated a building project for the synagogue, and it was in the early stages of construction.

Eliezer underwent chemotherapy treatments. At first I went with him to the hospital, and later his good friends from the Ministry of Health in Jerusalem accompanied him. Even when his hair fell out, he lost weight, and he had violent reactions to the treatments, Eliezer continued his routine. He gritted his teeth, went for a few hours every day to the job that he loved, and continued working on the synagogue construction project.

Eventually Eliezer recovered and got stronger, but a cloud continued to hang over us. We constantly feared that the disease would return, and the children couldn't shake that fear. Eliezer went back to work full-time. He was careful to have a colonoscopy every year. One month before Uriel was killed, the test showed something abnormal, and again our fears resurfaced. This time, although he didn't complain of pain, he underwent a full battery of tests. A week before Uriel's death, we received the welcome news that everything was fine.

"Uriel, you can relax," I reported to him by phone. "Dad is fine. The cancer hasn't returned." On the other side of the line, Uriel shouted with joy.

When Uriel fell, I was comforted by the thought that his last moments were calm, because he knew that his father was okay.

Slowly the work on the synagogue building progressed. Two special people helped Eliezer with the project: Shaul Mizrachi, the chairman of the regional council, and Asher Kadosh, who invested a large portion of his time and money in this undertaking. Asher continues to aid our family today and is like a second father to my children. They consult with him about any question or decision, according to Eliezer's request.

For five years, the synagogue had no name, despite the fact that Asher Kadosh, the principal donor, could have named it in honor of his parents. Numerous people from the congregation contacted Eliezer and offered to donate large sums in return for naming the synagogue after their relatives, but Eliezer refused.

He repeatedly asserted that this synagogue would be named after someone special. One month after Uriel's death, the congregation decided to name the synagogue after him – Darchei Noam Synagogue in memory of First Lieutenant Uriel Peretz, may God avenge his death. From the women's gallery up above, I watched as Eliezer sat in his regular place, beside the empty chair, the one in which his eldest son no longer sat.

One month after Uriel's death, Eliezer developed diabetes. A year later, he had his first heart attack, and from then on, his health continued to decline. I believed that he would get stronger, so that he could strengthen me as well. Several weeks before his sudden death on 4 Elul 5765 (September 8, 2005), Eliezer began to renovate our house. He said that the house was crowded, and that we didn't have enough room to host Uriel's friends from the premilitary academy, the special forces unit, and the battalion, who came to visit us with their families. In retrospect, I had to ask myself whether Eliezer knew that his time was limited and that we would need a larger house when we sat shivah again.

During the first month of the renovations, I made no complaints, which didn't tally with my usual pedantic character. Although we didn't have a kitchen and were living among piles of sand, I envisioned the spacious home we would enjoy when the work was finished, so I didn't complain to Eliezer about the noise and dust. That month, he had his annual routine colonoscopy, and the results showed that the cancer had returned. His physicians set a date for an operation. But the evening before Eliezer was to be hospitalized, something happened that changed my attitude: the water pipes burst in the house, and with them, my anger. I was unwilling to accept a lack of proper sanitary conditions in the house. I called Eliezer to tell him about the burst pipes, and he said he was on his way home. But it took him about two hours. Every so often I called again and asked, "Where are you?" The first time he answered, "I'm with Uriel." Half an hour later, "I'm with my father." It was the eve of Rosh Chodesh Elul, and he was visiting their graves. When he finally arrived home, I exploded: "You're going for a rest and I'm at home with the problems!"

"If that's how you feel," he responded, "I won't go in for the operation until we finish the construction."

But this was not an option, as the cancer had returned and he had to be operated on again.

On the day of the operation, at six a.m., Hadas and I went to the hospital with Eliezer. His face was pale, as it had been for some time. I tried to encourage him, but it seemed he felt this was the end.

Eliraz surprised us, arriving from Gaza at four a.m., in time to pray Shacharit, the morning service, with his father. When the nurse came to take Eliezer to the operating room, he seemed like a different person, gripped with fear. Did he know?

The nurse asked him to take off his wedding ring. Eliezer pointed to me and said, "I'm not saying goodbye to her." When she insisted, he removed the ring, and I saw tears in the corners of his eyes. To me, removing the ring from his finger became our farewell ceremony.

I placed the cellphone next to his ear and played a recording of Or-Chadash Uriel, then six months old, shouting "Grandpa!" For a moment, he was the happiest man in the world. Eliraz, Hadas, and I escorted him to the door of the operating room.

"Eliraz, you can go back to your soldiers," I said. "The operation will take a while. I'll let you know when it's over." Eliraz remained with us for another hour. Bat-El joined us after visiting Uriel's grave on Mount Herzl. Elyasaf was at the premilitary academy in Yatir, and Avichai was at home with the construction workers.

The hours dragged on and on. All the patients who had gone into the operating room after Eliezer came out, but he remained inside. After five hours, the doctor came out and announced that the operation had been successful, that it had taken longer due to adhesions from the previous operation, and that in a few minutes the nurse would call me into the room to see my husband. I informed the children that the operation was a success, and repeated that there was no reason for them to come, everything was fine.

I went back to sit on the bench and waited for the nurse to call me in, but when the minutes passed and she didn't come out, I opened the door of the recovery room and asked if I could see Eliezer Peretz. The nurse said, "Wait another two minutes," but my eyes searched for his bed. The moment I saw him, I felt that Eliezer was no longer there. I can't explain this feeling. I decided to approach without permission. I stood beside him, and he asked me to moisten his lips with a cotton swab. I have no explanation for what happened afterward. I ran out into the corridor, grabbed my two girls by their arms, and exclaimed, "Dad is about to die, come with me!"

Hadas and Bat-El couldn't understand my strange behavior. Just a minute ago, the doctor had informed us that the operation was a success. When I entered the recovery room with them, I saw the doctor running to Eliezer's bed. He said, "Your husband had a heart attack this very second."

Eliezer managed a smile to the girls before he was rushed to the intensive care unit, where the staff fought for his life. Every so often, the doctors came out to update me, sometimes giving hope, sometimes instilling fear, until finally a doctor came out and announced, "We failed."

I asked them to let us say goodbye to him. We said goodbye.

The funeral was held at eleven p.m., and thousands came to escort Eliezer on his last journey. Before he was buried, Hadas made a special request to all those present, to sing a song that her father loved: "May this hour be a time of mercy before You."

Eliezer used to sing this song whenever he was overcome with longing for Uriel.

Within the silence of night, the singing burst forth and rose ever higher. "A time of mercy"? There was no mercy.

This is what we wrote on Eliezer's headstone:

> *Did good works, loved others and taught them Torah, loved his people and homeland; forever mourned the death of his oldest son, First Lieutenant Uriel, may God avenge his death.*

My husband died of a broken heart, and because the house was a wreck, we sat shivah in the Givat Ze'ev synagogue, which bore Uriel's name.

It was a strange and difficult situation. I sat shivah for my husband outside our home, outside my own home. What did I do after the seven days of mourning were over? I returned to the shell of my house, which was filled with construction workers. I had no alternative but to face the details of construction: Belgian windows, number seven nails, number ten iron profiles, Italian tiles, plaster and paint. What did I know of such things? Today, when I'm asked to strengthen others and offer my life story as an example of the verse "A righteous man may fall seven times, yet rise again" (Proverbs 24:16), I try to explain that I didn't rise – reality forced me to rise. I was busy with the physical construction of my home, and there was so much work, I didn't have time to become addicted to longing and pain.

Five months after his death, when the renovations were finished, I finally understood how alone I was. To his last day, Eliezer was our family's secretary of state. He was the one responsible for shopping, bills, and errands, and suddenly I had to learn to do all the tasks he had done. A new notebook joined the commemoration notebook – a home management journal. In it, I recorded all the tasks, contacts, and various maintenance and repair people.

I felt that this job was above my head, that I couldn't do it all. But as the days went by, I realized that my moments of greatest crisis came when small, everyday things went wrong, when there was a power outage, or when the drains were blocked. Eventually, I discovered something else: in those moments, when I broke down and shouted, "Eliezer!" he would come.

It happened during the first winter without him. There was a torrential rain, and the gutters were blocked. Eliezer had been responsible for cleaning the gutters. The entire house filled with water. "Eliezer!" I shouted, trying to mop up the water with towels. "Eliezer!" I shouted, running up the stairs to the street level. When I reached the top, who did I see in front of me? The plumber, who was a friend of Eliezer's. Was it just a coincidence? Perhaps. But I feel that it wasn't. I hear Eliezer's voice telling me, "I went, because I can count on you. You'll manage, you'll bear up."

When Eliezer died, I felt that in addition to the loneliness and aching, he left the memorial project on my shoulders, and it was a heavy burden. I was torn. What should I do first? Prepare for Uriel's annual memorial ceremony, or Eliezer's first memorial ceremony? More than once, I found myself standing in front of the photo of Eliezer that hangs in the entrance to my home, asking in a tone of complaint: Who decided that this would be the division of labor between us? You go off to the world of the dead, while I remain in the world of the living and commemorate the dead. Did he really think this was fair? Was it my purpose in life to organize memorial ceremonies and write eulogies? I was tired of it. I had no more to say, no more words in my mouth.

Luckily, Eliezer's friends from work at the Ministry of Health's district office in Jerusalem became like family, and aside from their constant support, helped me with the memorial project. Each year they organize a study day in his memory, and attend the memorial ceremonies, the ones for Eliezer and Uriel, and then Eliraz. Thanks to them, I feel that I have others on whom I can rely.

But I feel Eliezer's absence all the time, hour by hour. We missed him at Hadas's wedding, at the signing of IDF enlistment papers for Avichai and Elyasaf, the births of Eliraz's children, Bat-El's enlistment. They say that time dulls the pain. But as the children grew older, left home, and began to build their own lives, my longing for Eliezer only grew. When I play with Aluma, Hadas's daughter, my heart aches. I think of how Eliezer would have loved to listen to her and play with her, how much he was missing, how much happiness he didn't enjoy.

At Eliezer's funeral, I was unable to say a word. I translated my feelings into words at the first memorial ceremony for him:

Uriel took half of my heart, and the other half died on the day you went. You are the joy of my life, the light that lit my path. Now the house is ready, Eliezer! Your dream house. Spacious and beautiful, but sad and painful. Or-Chadash runs around as you had wanted, but there's no one to see his laughter or what he does, no one to sing to him, "My hat, it has three corners."

Our children – the children you always took care of – are now fatherless. They refuse to accept the fact that their father is no longer alive.

And Uriel.… You left me alone to cope with his memory. You joined him so quickly. Give him a big hug for me, kiss him on the forehead and the top of his head, and say, "That's from Mom." Ask his forgiveness for my complete dedication to you, my love – my entire soul, all my thoughts.

I've been condemned to live, and on behalf of what we built together, I'll try to continue to build our home and raise our children. I'll do it alone, but I ask you to stay at my side. You know that I don't know how to do anything without you. So help me, be with me.

I have no thoughts about marrying again. I never did. No man can ever take Eliezer's place. He was unique in his sensitivity, his love for other people, his ability to give to others. He was the closest person to me, ever, and I thank God for the good years we had together.

Now I have three memorial ceremonies every year, for Uriel, Eliezer, and Eliraz. That's the order. I live from one memorial to the next. My diary is filled with dates of cemetery visits, and I have to divide myself in half – one half of me lives with the living, the other half lives with the dead. Ever since Eliraz joined his father and brother, I don't know which one I should miss first, and I'm horrified – perhaps I'm too busy missing Uriel and Eliraz, and neglecting Eliezer? Perhaps I don't give him enough room in my thoughts, my memories, and tears?

At the Shabbat table, I torture myself. Sometimes I glance at Eliezer's photo and tell him, "See, we have children and grandchildren, a Peretz dynasty." But I cringe inside. We've shrunk.

Ze'ev Fish, Eliezer's colleague and friend, wrote this about him:

> One July day, in the early morning hours, sometime during the nineties, the staff of the Health Ministry's Jerusalem district branch organized an inspection tour of youth group summer camp sites in the district forests. This was a very sensitive topic from the public health point of view, as it involved the welfare of tens of thousands of kids. Like many other similar trips, this one was organized by Eliezer Peretz, the seasoned senior district inspector.
>
> I knew that in those days, my friend Eliezer was at the height of an aggressive program of chemotherapy treatment. So in the morning, I went to the district office and gently offered to take his place and lead the team until he felt better. I'll never forget the look on his face. It was a look that said, "What are you talking about? Nothing in the world will stop me. I'll get it done – only me, by myself!"

I stuck around and joined Peretz's team. The inspection included several campsites. It was boiling hot outside, and every so often Eliezer stopped the car, moved a few steps off to the side, and vomited his guts out. Then he got back in the car as if nothing had happened and declared, "Yalla, let's move on!" We didn't skip even one site on our inspection tour. We kept going.

He missed no detail, and as always, he was able to see both sides of an issue: to some he gave polite, professional explanations, while others he criticized and rebuked. Late in the day we returned to the Health Ministry, after completing all our tasks. That's how Eliezer was: district supervisor, friend, father of a family that has become a household name in Israel.

Eliezer began his professional career in Sinai. He held various positions before joining the Jerusalem district. After several years, he was appointed district supervisor. This was his official title, but in his practical, everyday work, Eliezer was much more than that. He was the person everyone turned to about words or actions that seemed unfair, and he fought like a lion over every injustice. His thunderous voice still echoes in the ears of the other district and sub-district supervisors, at every monthly meeting. I called him our "soul trouper" – our office psychologist.

Even as national supervisor of environmental health, I was also subjected to his criticism when necessary. Yet he voiced even the harshest admonitions with nobility, responsibility, and a sense of natural leadership that cannot be learned in any institution or formal framework. He would put his arm around your shoulders and whisper sage advice. Here and there, I would hear rumors about anonymous, unrestricted giving, even to complete strangers. After his death, I heard fascinating stories from the recipients themselves.

Eliezer was very proud of his family. His wife Miriam – an amazing woman, noble, gentle, strong, an educator – and his children, each one a special breed. After his oldest son was killed – First Lieutenant Uriel Peretz, of blessed memory, a Golani soldier of whom Eliezer was so proud – Eliezer and Miriam began the project of commemoration that engaged us all, a project that was 100 percent Zionism and love for the Land of Israel, a project of giving. To this day, I can see his energetic figure before me, with his penetrating, direct gaze, as he displayed Uriel's memorial album. Eliezer spoke of Uriel and commemorated him openly, but his generous heart could not withstand his grief.

We continue to support Miriam and his wonderful family, this time by remembering Eliezer, our hearts heavy, shattered. We have established a yearly study session dedicated to Eliezer's memory and legacy, the Peretz legacy. Miriam and Eliezer needed great courage, Zionism, love of Israel, and an inconceivably endless capacity for giving when they agreed to their second son's request to continue in Uriel's path, in the exact same military course and unit. After Eliezer died, Major Eliraz Peretz, of blessed memory, his second son, fell in action as well, and the entire country came to a standstill in recognition of the resilience of Miriam and the family. Her words tore at our heartstrings and were carved deep within our consciousness. Eliezer no longer stood at her side, but his spirit was present there. Eliezer Peretz was a human being, a personality, a legacy.

CHAPTER 14

Mama *Diali* –
My Younger Brother Charly

When I was three years old, Charly, the third child in our family, was born. From the very first, he was different. In Morocco of the 1950s, the term Down's syndrome was unknown, and even if some were aware of it, they never mentioned it to our family. But we all knew that Charly, our beloved brother, was developing differently, as he didn't walk or talk at the expected age.

The minute he was born, my mother realized that he was different from me and my sister Zehava. Something about his facial features aroused her suspicions, and she felt uneasy. Since he was her first son, according to custom, he was named Shalom after my paternal grandfather. Mother attributed his delayed development to the high fever he had suffered in the first few days of his life, or to an incident when he fell off the bed. But deep inside, she knew that something was not right. Distressed, she went to pray at the graves of *tzaddikim* (revered for their righteousness) in Casablanca and visited rabbis to ask for advice. One rabbi recommended that she put baby Shalom, whom we always called Charly, in a basket, tie his arms together, then place the basket in the street so that passersby would release his bonds, symbolically releasing him from his difficulties. It was believed that this gesture would lead to his recovery.

Mother was a believer, and she did what the rabbi told her. She put Charly in a basket, tied his arms together, and set the basket in the street. She stood a few steps to the side, watching to make sure he would come to no harm. A policeman passing by saw what she was doing, and because Charly was blonde, blue-eyed, and rosy-cheeked, he suspected that she had kidnapped a Christian baby. Her protestations were to no avail. The policeman grabbed her and threw her in jail.

On that particular day, a Muslim holiday was being celebrated in Casablanca, so when Father went to the jailhouse waving Charly's birth certificate, there was no one around to pay any attention. The prison gates remained locked. Only after the holiday ended three days later did the policemen bother to check the documents, which proved that blonde Charly was indeed the son of Ito and Ya'akov. They released Mother.

As I was only three, they didn't share the details with me. I only knew that Mother went away for a while and then came back. But over the years, I heard the story of her imprisonment over and over. In retrospect, I think there was something in this story that led us to develop powerful bonds of love toward Charly. I realized that just as Mother had sacrificed herself for him, so would I.

Father continued visiting the tombs of *tzaddikim*, searching for a cure for Charly. In one of these visits, he fell asleep with his head resting on a tombstone. In a dream, he saw the *tzaddik* bringing him an envelope with a letter for the *tzaddik*'s sister, who had the cure. Father awoke from the dream astonished, and went to his rabbi to ask for an explanation. The rabbi listened and deciphered the dream: he told my father that he had to make aliyah to Eretz Israel and visit his sister, our aunt who lived in the north on Moshav Mishmar Hayarden; near her house he would find a cure for Charly. We had no idea where this *moshav* was, nor that our aunt lived close to Mount Meron, site of the tomb of Rabbi

Shimon bar Yochai. But we did know we had to follow the rabbi's advice.

We immigrated to the Holy Land in late 1963, when I was ten. Charly was seven, and until then, he had never stood up, nor said a word. At the immigrant camp in Hatzerim, we witnessed a miracle: he began to walk and talk. In gratitude, Father vowed that every year on 7 Tammuz, he would visit the grave of Rabbi Shimon bar Yochai at Meron. He kept the vow faithfully, and I remember the trip to Meron as an amazing experience, our annual family vacation.

Preparations began weeks in advance, in the month of Sivan. A row of plastic baskets stood in the entrance to our home: one held almonds, another dates, and a third was full of candies for the special meal. We were a welfare family – we barely had enough food in the house – but Father saved every penny he could for an entire year so that we could make the trip to Meron that would heal Charly.

We spent a whole day dragging around on buses with our baskets and blankets; from Be'er Sheva to Tel Aviv, and from there to Tiberias. I glued my nose to the window, drinking in the beautiful scenery. We spent the night at the *tzaddik's* grave, while the adults prayed and my little brothers slept. The air was filled with excitement and love, because we knew that everything was being done to honor Rabbi Shimon bar Yochai and Charly, the special guest. Because in our family a mitzvah is always accompanied by a festive meal, the next morning we continued by bus to the town of Hatzor Haglilit and from there to Mishmar Hayarden, to the home of Aunt Freha Buskila, Father's sister. She welcomed us with hugs and kisses, and a delicious meal of couscous. Father sat next to her and they chatted in Moroccan Arabic, reminiscing, while we children looked on. Their reunion taught us about family ties and longing.

Only one thing marred our joy – the fact that Mother didn't join us. Mother almost never left our house. She went out to clean houses and stairwells, but she did not come to my sister Zehava's wedding, or mine. When she finally agreed to attend the wedding of Elisheva, the youngest of the family, she said she didn't like going out in public because she was a reserved person who kept to herself, and she felt embarrassed. But I am certain that Mother acted this way because her life was interwoven with a thread of sorrow, and she felt the need and obligation to protect Charly from society. On the rare occasions when she went out with him, she would grasp his arm, and if she saw someone staring at him, she would pull him aside so he wouldn't notice or hear any comments. She worried that if he went out in public, he might drool, and someone might make fun of him, and she feared she might not be able to control his reactions.

Until he was eighteen, Charly attended the Magen School for special-needs children in Be'er Sheva. He took music lessons and loved to play the drums. Once, at a party, he put on a drum show that impressed our entire family. After he finished school, he went to work at the Center for Occupational Rehabilitation in the Old City, where he made laundry pins, receipt booklets, and stickers for spice bottles. But during that time he became aggressive, bordering on violent. I saw how my parents cared for him devotedly, though they were already advanced in years, and never allowed strangers to touch their son, the prince.

Charly was no longer a child. When Mother would implore, "Charly, don't go there, it's dangerous," he would shout at her and go anyway. But at other times, he would kiss her, sob, and beg for her forgiveness. He was physically strong, and sometimes he might push us, but we never got angry at him. When he didn't obey, Mother would say, "Charly, my son, come and eat." Food calmed him down. Father taught him to play checkers, and they would sit for hours at the checker board. When he was finished playing, he would help Mother in the kitchen. Because of Charly, I discovered the close connection between love and sacrifice at a very young age. Mother sacrificed her life for him. She would not allow the word *institution* to be mentioned in her presence, and we children promised that we would continue to care for him.

Eventually, that time arrived.

In March 1997, three days before the ceremony that marked the completion of Uriel's officer training course, Mother was admitted into Soroka Hospital in Be'er Sheva with pneumonia. After the ceremony, we all went to visit her in the hospital. Uriel was not given leave from the army, and he told us, "Tell Grandma that I'll come visit her tomorrow at nine a.m." My father was no longer alive; he had died in 1983, leaving Mother alone in her home. Who sat beside her bed in the hospital? Charly. He was the one who cared for her, day and night. Not only did Charly nurse her, he also followed Mother's custom: when one of her children was hospitalized, she didn't go home, but slept on the floor. Now it was Charly who moistened her lips during the day and slept beside her bed at night.

I approached Mother's bed and said in Moroccan Arabic, "Mother, we've just come from Uriel's ceremony." At the sound of his name, her eyes flickered, and she murmured, "*Mazal tov, mazal tov.*" But something in her voice sounded strange and sad. Her soul seemed to sense danger. I stroked her hand and said, "Uriel's an officer!" She asked what an officer was, and I explained: "He'll be leading the soldiers!"

Mother nodded her head, let out a deep sigh, and said, "*Ya binti*, may God give you strength."

That night, Charly wanted to sleep next to Mother again, but we insisted that he get a good night's sleep and we took him home. Charly cried, "*Mama diali* [my mother], I want to sleep beside you." But Mother also pushed him to go home. This was the first time Charly had ever been separated from her, and Eliraz stayed with him in Be'er Sheva.

The next day, at eight a.m., Eliraz called her and said, "Grandma, you're about to be released from the hospital. I'm cleaning the house." Mother protested, "No, no, don't clean." She asked about Charly. Eliraz told her that Charly had slept well, and added that they were preparing the house so it would be clean and organized when she returned. At nine a.m., Uriel arrived from Mitzpe Ramon. He walked into the hospital, went up to the ward, and asked the nurse, "Excuse me, which room is Ito Ohayon in?"

The nurse looked up at the uniformed soldier and said, "She died one minute ago."

Uriel did not make it in time to part from my mother, who closed her eyes for the last time at the age of seventy-eight. Even then, I had the feeling that it was no coincidence, that there was a reason. They had a special relationship; their souls were strongly bound to one another. Each morning my mother stood beside the mezuzah, grasped it between the palms of her hands, bent her head, and prayed for many long minutes. From the time we were little and as we got older, we children heard only one sentence escape her lips: "God, don't let me witness the deaths of my children or grandchildren." It was a sacred moment, a moment of godliness that awed us into silence. I knew that Mother knew. Her soul sensed that the moment Uriel became a commander and marched in front of his soldiers, he would not live – and she could not face this.

Mother died on 7 Adar. On 7 Kislev, before the year-long period of mourning for her was over, Uriel was killed and went to join her. Later, I tortured myself, asking where I had gone wrong, why I hadn't succeeded in protecting Uriel and Eliraz, as Mother had protected my brother Charly. But I couldn't shut myself up at home, as she had done, and disconnect myself from life. I chose to live, even through the pain of grief.

During the shivah for my mother, Eliezer proposed to Charly that he come live with us, and that's what happened. Charly couldn't understand where Mother had disappeared to. He sat and wailed for days and nights on end: "Where's my mother? Where's my mother?" We answered him over and over, "We're here, and Mother's here with you."

The separation was very difficult for him. The minute Mother passed away, something within Charly died. But over time, we observed something new beginning to blossom. Mother had protected him from the world, while we wanted to open him to the world. We bought him new clothes, took him out, and planned to build him a separate living unit attached to our house. But then Uriel was killed, and our plans were sidetracked. When the command car arrived at our house with the casket, Charly refused to heed the officers who surrounded it. He lay across the casket and cried bitterly, "Uriel! Ur-i-ellll!"

When we got up from the shivah for Uriel, I called my siblings to discuss what to do with Charly. It was clear that we would continue Mother's path and keep him out of an institution. We decided that Charly would take turns living with us, and we arranged a rotation.

At first, Charly went to live with Elisheva, my younger sister, in Netivot. Eliezer bought him a mobile home that was set up in her yard. But Charly refused to live in it, and asked to live inside her house. She and her husband Avraham treated him like a son. He played with their children and watched films he liked on their computer. Every Thursday he would bring Elisheva a pen and paper, and she would write down a shopping list for Shabbat. If the list was too short, he would add items. The next day, at six a.m., he would go to the grocery store and do the shopping, wandering the aisles, chatting with the employees and the customers. He also bought cans of cola and sweets for *oneg Shabbat*, a Shabbat treat for his nieces and nephews. He loved to fold the laundry, pull weeds in the garden, and help Elisheva clean the house. During the Shabbat service, he would go up to the ark before it was opened, and sing the traditional *Yimloch* song, along with the children of the community.

On weekdays, Charly spent most of his time at the tomb of the Baba Sali in Netivot. He asked Avraham, Elisheva's husband, to buy him a supply of auspicious *chamsa* charms and red strings, and he sold them there. The pilgrims who flocked to the *tzaddik's* tomb invited him to join them in their ceremonial meals and asked for his blessing. Charly stayed at the tomb until late in the evening, and he gave the money he earned with his own two hands to Elisheva, to help support the family.

Before the holidays, he would visit the homes of the holy rabbis of Netivot. At Rabbi Abergil's home, he received a 100 shekel note and three *matzot* for the Seder plate. Rabbi Bokobza gave him vegetables. At the home of Rabbi Ya'akov Ifargan, known as the "X-ray rabbi," he received a crate full of food. Charly was pleased that he was able to thank Elisheva and her husband in this way. He felt that he was accepted as a son in their home on the merit of his own deeds.

Charly's second rotation was at Zehava's home in the Gush Katif settlement of Netzer Hazani. He didn't have any qualms about hitching rides to there from Netivot, and whoever picked him up would always drive him straight to Zehava's door. He wasn't afraid of the Arab neighbors, either. When a terrorist alert was sounded in the settlement, Charly would reassure everyone, telling them that nothing would happen. He would often wander around the settlement, going into greenhouses and talking with the farmers about their crops, and returning with fresh produce. During one of the holidays, Charly asked Zehava to arrange a job for him. She asked the synagogue *gabbai*, who said that Charly could clean the pew boxes in preparation for Passover. On Sunday at four a.m., Charly woke Zehava and asked her to prepare a bag of food and a bottled drink. She explained that the synagogue was close by, and that he had plenty of time, but to no avail. "I'm going to work!" he exclaimed proudly.

Charly's third stop was the home of our brother Machluf in Be'er Sheva. Each time he went there, he was particularly excited, because it meant returning to his childhood haunts in the north Dalet neighborhood. He loved seeing the synagogue congregants and listening to Rabbi Bazari's classes. He always paid a visit to Mother's neighbors, and told them about the delicacies that Machluf's wife, Tzipi, prepared. All week long he waited for Shabbat, for her special *chamin* (stew).

After staying with Machluf, Charly would return to our home in Givat Ze'ev, where we had prepared a private bedroom for him, with a shower and toilet. He used to sit at the head of the table, and even when guests came, he insisted on keeping his place of honor. In his simple language, a combination of Hebrew and Moroccan Arabic, he was able to calm me, especially during periods of military operations in Gaza and Lebanon. "The boys are okay, I'm praying for Eliraz, Avichai, and Elyasaf. Don't worry," he used to say.

We did all we could so that he would enjoy his stays with us. One summer, Eliezer and I took him to the beach for the first time in his life. We couldn't find an inflatable tube that was big enough to fit him, as by that time he was a large, bearded man, nor did we have a bathing suit his size. But he wore short pants, and urged us impatiently to get organized for the trip. He went into the water wearing his black *kippah*, and crowed like a baby in the waves.

Charly's first visit to the beach was followed by his first trip to a water park. As he was a big man, it was difficult for him to slide down the water slide, and he was also quite scared. A friend of Eliezer's supported him from behind and slid down with him.

Then there was his first visit to a restaurant. The waitress presented him with the menu, and although he couldn't read, he was impressed by the photographs of the dishes. When she asked him what he would like to order, he answered, "Everything!" After the meal, he was the only one who went up to the waitress and thanked her profusely, as if she herself had labored over the stove. Eliezer said to him in jest, "I'm the one you need to thank – I paid for it." But Charly wasn't satisfied. He asked to see the manager, and thanked him as well for the food and for the waitress's kind service.

We took him on a vacation to a hotel, to visit the Western Wall, and to the tomb of Samuel the Prophet. He loved the rare occurrences of snow in Jerusalem, when he would go out to the park and throw snowballs with my children. He knew that on a snow day, I wouldn't go to work at the school but instead stay home with him, and so he prayed for the snow to continue. Sometimes, when I was at work, he would surprise me by cleaning the house and folding the laundry, while listening to recordings of Moroccan *piyyutim*, liturgical songs. He had a large collection of numbered recordings, and he knew which songs each one contained.

He would often call the school and say to the secretary, "Good morning, I'd like to speak with my sister Miriam. I want her to come home to put on a film for me." He loved to watch action films, but only if they were somehow related to Morocco. When I came home from school to a sparkling clean house, he would say, "My sister, everything is ready for you." He would ask me not to bother making lunch especially for him, but to sit with him and chat.

He became an active participant at Darchei Noam synagogue, named in memory of Uriel. He regularly attended services, where he would have an aliyah and bless our local council chairman, Shaul Mizrachi, who was like a member of our family. Even after

Shaul completed his term as chairman, Charly continued wearing the shirt that bore his name, a keepsake from the election campaign, and kept on blessing him.

Charly came to stay with us for a short period every winter and in summer, during the long school vacations. When he came into the house, he would ask me to take a piece of paper and sit down. Then he would dictate a list: "I want you to buy an electric hot pot, a tape player, socks, undershirts, games…" He didn't want to return to Netivot empty-handed, without gifts for Elisheva's children.

Charly loved Eliezer dearly. Eliezer would buy him the fruit that he loved, especially bananas. Because we kept them in a bowl on the table, he would eat them all during the night, and in the morning we would wake up to an empty bowl. Eliezer decided to do something about this. He numbered the bananas, and in the morning he would ask, "Who knows where banana number two has disappeared to?"

When Eliezer died, Charly felt the loss of another parent. He fell atop the grave and beat himself. He realized that Eliezer was like a father to him. When Uriel was killed, he comforted me, saying, "Don't worry, my sister, Uriel's alive and Grandma Ito is caring for him." When my husband died, Charly said that Eliezer and Uriel were next to Rabbi Shimon bar Yochai, and so I was forbidden to mourn and cry all day. He thought I should be happy, or at least continue living, because both my dear ones were in good company.

After Eliraz was married and had children, he offered to adopt my brother Charly. He spoke about it with his wife Shlomit, but before they had time to consider the logistics, Charly contracted pneumonia and was hospitalized in the intensive care unit. Each night, Eliraz came home from the army to care for him. Although his health continued to deteriorate, Charly asked me about Meron, as he knew we had to fulfill our vow to visit each year. I promised him, "Everything will be fine. We'll go there when you get out of the hospital." I arranged for an ambulance equipped with oxygen bottles to transport him.

One week before Charly lost consciousness, Eliraz went to visit him. He bathed him and dressed him in clean clothes. Charly, forever grateful, said, "I'm going to be fine. You… you look out for yourself."

PART FOUR
Eliraz

CHAPTER 15

"Mother, What Are You Worried About?" Eliraz Enters the Army

Eliraz grew up with Uriel in the wadi behind our home in Sharm, and they played together for hours, climbing trees and investigating snakes and scorpions. As soon as they came home from school, they would run down an unpaved path to the wadi. Outside in the yard stood a green wire mesh fence, and they climbed it and jumped down into the dirt, while I stood beside the window and watched them in trepidation. What if they fell? What if they tumbled down? They both fell, then got up, stuck full of thorns, and waved at me, smiling their mischievous kids' smiles as if to say, "Mom, what are you worried about? It's only a wadi." They also badgered me: "Mom, why are you staying inside? Come with us! You're missing out; try it at least."

From a very young age, Eliraz exhibited the personality of a leader. When he was ten years old, he invited his friends to a traditional Lag b'Omer bonfire in the wadi. For weeks, they collected boards and brought them home, blocking the entrance to the house. I wrung my hands. Why did they have to build a bonfire in the wadi? It was dark and dangerous there.

"What's the problem?" asked Eliraz. He had a solution for everything. Light-footed, he climbed the rocks, hung up an electrical wire, and set up a lamp on the fence, aiming it downward so that it illuminated the wadi.

"How will I bring you food?" I pressed. I thought I would have to go around the entire length of the street in order to carry the trays down to the wadi.

Eliraz, with his genius for invention, was undeterred. He took the trays, placed them in a plastic basket, tied a rope to it and had me stand at the highest point. "This is like a well, and you're lowering a bucket into it," he explained. Slowly I let out the rope until the basket landed in his arms, and when he had finished unloading its contents, he shouted at me from below: "Mother, pull!" and the empty basket returned to me. I delivered pita, hummus, and meat. But the fire intensified and the bonfire spread, scorching the weeds around.

"Eliezer!" I shouted, "He'll burn down the whole house!"

From down in the wadi, Eliraz laughed. "Mom, it's not even a bonfire yet, it's barely a little flame. Look how happy everyone is."

Two hours passed, and Eliezer was pacing the house as if walking on coals. "I'm worried," he complained. "I have to go down to see Eliraz. What's he doing down there? He has a big group of friends, and it's a big responsibility."

Eliezer climbed the fence. But when he lifted his leg to place it on the ground, he slipped down the rocky incline, and slid all the way down on his backside. "Eliezer!" I shouted, my heart pounding, while my playful son Eliraz stood at the bottom, splitting his sides with laughter.

"Eliraz, what's so funny?" I demanded, my voice ringing in accusation.

"Dad rolled a bit!" he replied, as thirty pals from his class hooted in the background.

Eliezer walked back home on the road. At night we couldn't fall asleep, because of the smell from the bonfires in the wadi, but mainly out of worry. At two a.m., we heard suspicious sounds. Eliraz had told all of them to climb the rocks, jump the fence, and catch some sleep on the grass behind our house. He didn't want them to go inside, for fear they would wake us up. At the break of dawn, he slipped into the house on tiptoe and brought out breakfast supplies to the lawn: cookies, a thermos with hot water, chocolate powder, sugar, tea, and milk.

Eliraz drank tea with milk, not instant coffee, and definitely not black Turkish coffee. Eventually, when he joined the elite special forces unit, everyone made fun of him. "What kind of a soldier are you, Moroccan or British?"

Then it was morning, and the kids wanted to go home to get some sleep. They were exhausted. Eliraz was the only one who acted like an endlessly rechargeable battery. He was never tired, not even for a moment. If it was a vacation day, he had to go on an outing. Years later, he came home after the final southern exercise of the special forces, after days of extremely challenging field navigation, and within minutes he was showered, dressed, and off to the wedding of his pal Shlomo Berniker, where he danced until dawn as if he had just woken up from a good night's sleep.

An apricot tree grew in our yard, and Eliraz was in charge of picking the fruit at the top. Uriel tried to reach the highest branches, and when he couldn't, he brought over a ladder. But Eliraz put a hand on his shoulder and said, "Come, I'll show you another way." He led his older brother to the other side of the tree and shook the closest branch vigorously, until the top branches broke and the fruit fell into the wadi, giving him another excuse to jump the fence.

One day, Eliraz climbed a branch that couldn't bear his weight, and it broke. Both branch and Eliraz fell straight into the neighbor's yard. We were frightened, but Eliraz stood up, flashed a bright, toothy smile, looked at us in astonishment, and asked, "What's the big deal? All I did was fall into the neighbor's yard."

I never heard Eliraz say "It hurts" or "I don't have time." From the minute he opened his eyes, he was off on a daily search for adventure. I often asked myself, What's driving him? How does he manage to get up every time he falls?

Fragile Uriel was a model of restraint. Once he fell on Shabbat on the way to synagogue, and on the way home, I saw that his face was pale. But he never said a word; he just lay in bed silently. On *motzaei Shabbat* he said to me, "Take me to the hospital." The X-ray showed not just one but four fractures in his hand. Eliraz, by contrast, was an initiator, even as a child. He would always say, "*Yalla, let's do it!*" He would carry his younger siblings, Elyasaf, Avichai, and Bat-El, on his shoulders, and take them on adventures that ended well only by virtue of a miracle. Even if his escapades led to scrapes and scratches, he would never complain. At school he was known as a serious mischief maker. When a ball got stuck on top of a building, Eliraz was the one who would climb up the drainpipe to the roof, where he would stand up straight, spread out his arms, and call out, "Hey, guys, awesome view up here! What are you doing down there?"

It was a rare occasion when Eliraz entered the house by the front door. He couldn't even understand why it was put there, and almost always crawled in through the kitchen window. Recently, I was surprised to get a phone call from Or-Chadash, his oldest child, who announced, "Grandma, we're here at your place." I apologized that I wasn't home and promised to return quickly. Or-Chadash laughed at me just like his father used to, and said, "Grandma, didn't you hear what I said? We're already inside the house! I went in like Dad, through the window."

In elementary school, Eliraz was a good student. At Himmelfarb High School in Jerusalem, his favorite subjects were sports, and literature with teacher Tamar Krieger-Armoni. But at the end of tenth grade, we were called in for a conference. Eliraz was about to be expelled from school. When Eliezer and I entered the guidance counselor's office, our legs were shaking. What would be the fate of our mischievous son? If the school gave up, how would we be able to control him?

We sat down, and the guidance counselor said that Eliraz wasn't meeting the standards of the school. She described his pranks, one by one. With a serious expression and severe tone of voice, she told us how he had entered the classroom with a supermarket cart loaded with wooden boards and his friend Shlomo. The teacher was so shocked, he didn't even shout. He simply couldn't understand what the cart was doing there, or fathom the reason for the spectacle. "His attitude to his studies is inappropriate for a religious boy," she added. "In Talmud class he sleeps like a log."

Eliraz, who was sitting beside us, listened to her and grumbled, "True, I fell asleep. The class was boring." To the estimable counselor, he said, "Let's see you sit in a class like that. You would fall asleep, too."

"Shhh," I restrained him. As an educator myself, I wouldn't permit him to mock the counselor. In refined language, I appealed to her on behalf of my son. I reminded her that he was very much interested in his history, literature, and Israel studies classes, and that he was an outstanding student in sports. Eliezer also begged for the decision to be retracted. After a long conversation, the counselor sent us to the class coordinator, Jeremy Stavitzky, who also defined Eliraz's behavior as problematic, to put it mildly.

"He'll improve," we promised him. "He'll change. We'll take responsibility for Eliraz changing his behavior."

The class coordinator listened, and decided that he would give Eliraz a second chance, on condition that he turn in a Talmud paper by Sunday, and come to school at seven a.m. for a whole week. I breathed a sigh of relief, but Eliezer – rascal father of the rascal student – had to ask, "Can we please have an extension? We're going to Eilat next week...."

I stared at Eliezer in astonishment. What are you doing? Your kid is being threatened with expulsion. Just one minute ago we were pardoned, and instead of jumping at the opportunity, you argue with the class coordinator and say that our family is about to go on vacation to Eilat for the first time? Why should he care about that?

Luckily, the class coordinator laughed. "Okay, we'll put it off by one week."

When we returned from our vacation, we paid a private teacher a lot of money, and Eliraz wrote the paper. Who would ever have believed that this kid would grow up to study Talmud intensively as a young man? Later, he studied with a different attitude, willingly, out of interest and love for Talmud, and it was an inspiration to him till his dying day. Even more surprisingly, Jeremy became Eliraz's favorite homeroom teacher. Until his death, Eliraz remained in contact with him and consulted him on many issues. During his undergraduate studies in education, Eliraz did his training under Jeremy, who had in the meantime become a school principal.

In high school, Eliraz grew his hair long. It was black as a raven, but the sun bleached the ends golden, and it made for a unique combination. He was handsome, with big eyes, long eyelashes, and that black-gold hair. I eventually found out that girls were chasing him, but I never saw them with my own eyes, for a simple reason: if he brought them home, I'm sure he snuck them in through the window. Even Ezer Weizmann, then president of Israel, noticed him, during a condolence visit to the home of First Lieutenant Alon Babian, of blessed memory, who grew up in Givat Ze'ev and was killed in the helicopter disaster. "Is it real?" he asked, pulling Eliraz's locks. "Or is it a wig?"

I laughed when Eliraz told me about his encounter with the president, but Eliezer was not amused. The long-haired look upset him. Once I heard them arguing. "I can't bear the sight of your hair!" Eliezer protested. Eliraz responded, "Dad, I know my hair bothers you. You're the *gabbai* of a Moroccan synagogue and it's awkward. But I want you to know that my God doesn't look at hair length. My God allows me to grow my hair long. He allows me to wear ripped jeans, and to pray whenever I want."

"Leave the kid alone," I begged Eliezer, but he wasn't mollified. When Eliraz finished eleventh grade, Eliezer took him to consult with a rabbi. When they got there, Eliraz went in alone. After the meeting, the rabbi said, "Leave the kid alone. Let him continue on his own path. He needs freedom. Don't worry, his faith is pure."

Only then was Eliezer placated. Eliraz – with his long hair and ripped jeans – took advantage of the summer vacation to work in construction. He could have found other, easier jobs in Givat Ze'ev. "But Mom, it's building the country," he asserted, and he went off to lift sacks of cement. Even the Arabs who worked at the building sites in our town were afraid of him; they called him *majnoun*, or "crazy." They had never seen a Jewish boy who could lift the heaviest sacks so quickly and efficiently.

Eliraz also worked in agriculture, because he loved the land. At Uriel's funeral, his younger siblings picked up clods of earth that covered the grave and hurled them to the ground. This was painful for Eliraz to watch. After the shivah week was over, the first thing he did was to take his brothers and sisters to the wadi behind our home, where they planted trees. He told them, "The land that took our brother Uriel is good, fertile land."

Every time I look at the wadi and see how those trees have grown, I know how old they are. They are as old as the years that Uriel has been gone.

When Shlomit finished sitting shivah for Eliraz and returned to her home in Eli, the first thing she did with her little children was to plant trees in the yard. She also told her children that this land is precious, beloved, and fertile.

When the school year began, Eliraz found another job, in a women's hat shop on Agrippas Street in Jerusalem owned by our neighbors, Adele and Eli Vaknin. He would place a hat on his long, abundant hair and model, showing the women how beautiful they would be – and he made sales. We observed the contrasts in his personality with wonder: at the construction site he was strong and powerful, while in the hat shop, he was delicate and light as a feather. He knew how to adapt himself to any situation, like a chameleon.

Before Passover, Eliraz found another job cleaning houses. "I'm an expert at windows and gas ranges," he informed me proudly. From the money he earned in these odd jobs, he paid for a diving course in Eilat, and Uriel dove along with him. When his friend Ezri Lerba traveled to Australia, Eliraz gave him money to buy a top model surfboard for him. Of course, Ezri refused to take money for the surfboard. Eliraz used this board during his stay at the Atzmona premilitary academy in Gush Katif, and during his army leaves. We felt that the world was created so that Eliraz could enjoy it to the maximum, and he feasted on it in huge bites – between the waves and on the land.

In twelfth grade, he went to Poland on a class trip, and this was the journey that changed his life. When he came home, I saw a different Eliraz in front of me. I had given him a camera so that he could take photographs to show me, as I had never been to Poland. He photographed the abandoned shoes that the Nazis removed from the feet of their victims, and four hundred images of flowers growing in the earth that was soaked with their blood. He took only one photo of himself, wrapped in the Israeli flag, sitting on the grass together with Jeremy the class coordinator, his arm around Eliraz's shoulders.

After I developed the film, which cost quite a bit of money, I was angry with him. In my hands I held four hundred photos of flowers of all colors – red, yellow, pink. When he got home from school that day, I demanded, "What is this?"

Eliraz answered, "What do you see, Mom?"

I recall that I got even angrier, and said, "Now you sound like the story of Jeremiah the Prophet, when God asks him, 'What do you see?'" (Jeremiah 1:11).

Eliraz took the first photo of a flower from my hand and explained. "Mom, that's not a flower. That's little Mendel. This next flower is Rachel. This one is Sarah, this one is Shimon. These are Jewish children who were incinerated, butchered, whose heads were sliced open, whose blood was spilled. And why, Mom, why? Because they were Jews, because there was no one to protect them."

He swore that he would never again set foot in that place. "As long as I live, I will never let such a thing happen to my people," he vowed. I realized that the trip had strengthened not only his Jewish faith, but also his belief in our land and our people.

He served as a counselor in the Bnei Akiva youth movement. When he decided to leave Bnei Akiva to be a counselor in the Scouts in Kfar Adumim, he sent the Bnei Akiva kids a letter, which documents the rich, complex nature of his spiritual life. This is what he wrote:

Hey, guys,

What's up? How are you? How was your trip? I really hope that you managed it and were able to get to know yourselves a little bit better. Yes, this is my last activity with you, and I've thought long and hard about the choice of topic. Finally, I realized that I've taught you lessons about everything, and all of them are relevant to you, but I've never done an activity about you. So I've chosen a journey, an activity to help you understand yourselves better and do a better job at listening to yourselves.

Now, as I write these lines, my eyes are tearing up. I'm sad, I'm not crying, but tears are trickling. What can I do? I love you so much, if you could only understand how much I love all of you, then maybe...

You're probably asking yourselves, if I really love you that much, then why am I leaving you? So, know that I'm leaving you out of love, because it's important to me that you have another counselor, a counselor who's different from me, maybe the exact opposite of me. Actually, you need someone you might not love so much. Why all this? So that you'll learn.

I've taught you out of a worldview and way of thinking that is my own, and only mine. But in order for you to be wiser, you need someone else. You come to Bnei Akiva and you have fun, learn about morals, ideas, and a certain way of thinking – so you need to relate to Bnei Akiva as a place where you go to learn, not like in school, but in a fun way. At Bnei Akiva you learn about life, and I don't want you to learn from only one person.

Now you're probably thinking, "Okay, Eliraz left, and now he's not our counselor any more, and he probably won't listen to us anymore" – but you're wrong. I'll speak to you whenever you want, on any topic in the world, and I'll try to answer you – even if it's a question about God, people, girls, sex, the world, space. Anything you want to ask. I won't ignore you, I'll always take you seriously.

You're welcome to call me and visit, any day, anytime. If you want, we'll go on hikes together, and if you invite me to your activities, I'll come. Please know that I'll be part of you for your whole life, and even forever, and you're part of me for my whole life, even forever. I've planted my feelings within you, and my thoughts are buried in your heads – I'm you, and you are me – together we are a whole.

So goodbye for now. I'll see you soon.

Yours, I love you so very, very much,

Eliraz Peretz

At the end of twelfth grade, after taking his matriculation exams, Eliraz decided to attend the premilitary academy at Atzmona in Gush Katif. He went there wearing his patched jeans, white T-shirt with the torn neck, and sandals. We feared that the academy director, Rabbi Rafi Peretz, wouldn't accept him because of his unkempt appearance, but when we arrived at the academy, we relaxed. His entire group, the academy's fourth graduating class, looked like him. They all had long hair, and for once our kid looked like everyone else.

Five months later, we were invited to Parents' Day, and to our surprise, most of Eliraz's friends had already changed their look. They had cut their hair, and from under their shirts peeked the fringes of their *tzitzit* (four-cornered garment worn by religious Jewish males). Our son was the only one who looked the same as before.

Toward the end of the school year, we visited the academy again. By this time, all the classmates looked like proper *yeshivah* students, except for our Eliraz, who looked exactly like he had on the day he left home. "Tell me," Eliezer asked Rabbi Rafi Peretz, head of the academy, "what am I paying you for? He looks exactly like he did on the day I brought him here. He could at least get a haircut."

Rabbi Rafi Peretz and Rabbi Lifschitz took us aside and said, "Your kid is exhausting us at night. The boy asks questions, he analyzes and examines, he addresses the question of faith at its deepest point – the question of the meaning of life and of his own existence. I warn you," the Rabbi Rafi added, "that the day Eliraz finds an answer to his questions, things won't be easy for you. Eliraz will reach a very high spiritual level."

When Eliraz went to Atzmona, he adopted a dog, which he named Joker. His caravan became the gathering place for the guys and he organized a little garden outside. Each morning, he rose early, before the others got up for prayers, and ran to the beach with his friend Naftali and with Joker. No surprise, as he was born in Sharm and the waves called out to him. One day, when little Joker had trouble keeping up, Eliraz took pity on him. He pulled off his undershirt, stuffed Joker inside, tied the dog on his back, and they continued the run together. Every day, after his daily run, swim, and surf, he would arrive at synagogue. There as well, he didn't behave like the others. While his friends prayed, Eliraz sat and read books of sacred literature that he chose. Slowly, perhaps because the rabbis never pushed him, he became deeply immersed in his studying, pursuing the basic questions of the meaning of life and the creation of humanity.

When he came home once every two weeks, we couldn't see any difference. But at the end of his first year at Atzmona, we welcomed a new Eliraz – sporting short hair, a white shirt, gleaming *tzitzit*, and an expansive faith. I was astonished, and my astonishment grew when he asked me, "Mom, where did you immerse these dishes?" He wanted to know if I had taken the dishes to a *mikveh*, in accordance with the laws of *kashrut*.

"Watch it," I replied. "You've been eating off these dishes your whole life. Don't you start checking up on me."

On Shabbat, around the table, he wanted us all to learn a Torah lesson together. He searched for friends in Givat Ze'ev who would study with him on Shabbat, and he found some. From that day on, not one Shabbat passed without Talmud study. The boy who had fallen asleep during Talmud class began to collect Passover Haggadahs. He searched for commentaries on the Haggadah and filled his room with sacred books. I felt as if the whole house was being filled with his light and faith, and we followed him happily. We walked in Eliraz's light.

The connection between Eliraz and Rabbi Rafi Peretz grew deeper and stronger. Eliraz studied Mishnah with his young son and even slept over at his home on occasion. Michal, the rabbi's wife, was very fond of Eliraz, and when he visited them, she prepared vegetarian dishes that he loved. Eliraz invited Uriel to visit him in Atzmona. When Uriel came out of Lebanon or had a long weekend of leave from the army, he would come home for a day to visit, and then go to see Eliraz at Atzmona, where they spent Shabbat in the rabbi's home.

The last holiday that the two brothers spent together in Atzmona was Simchat Torah. My sons insisted on celebrating the holiday there. They danced fervently in circles as their singing reached the heavens, and Eliraz rode on his friends' shoulders with the Israeli flag waving in his hand. After the retreat and evacuation of Gush Katif, a booklet was published about Atzmona that contained a photo of that dance. When I saw the picture of Eliraz waving the flag, I could almost hear him singing the song. It was his favorite, "*Shuru, habitu u're'u*": "Behold, watch, and see / How great is this day, this day / Fire burns in our breasts / The plow slices the field." It symbolized his grip, our grip, on our homeland. At Rabbi Rafi's initiative, this became the unofficial hymn of the premilitary academies. Later on at Eli, the residents would refuse to celebrate Simchat Torah without Eliraz. Everyone knew that this was his holiday, the holiday of the Torah, the holiday of joy.

In Atzmona, even before he donned a uniform, Eliraz's spiritual and military character was formed. The letters he wrote during that period, in his almost indecipherable handwriting, revealed to us the fundamental questions that occupied him, as well as his great love for the IDF, the State of Israel, and the Jewish people. In a seemingly casual manner, he would jot down sentences randomly on bus tickets or slips of paper, while he was traveling. His writing obviously stemmed from his own thoughts and feelings, and not from any formal study. But for us, this collection of scribbled notes is a record of Eliraz's soul during that period.

When we sat shivah for him, many people brought letters he had written them. One of them was his friend Yonatan, who brought a stamped letter from 1997. They had met during the exceptionally challenging trial course for the exclusive naval officers' track. When the course was over, Yonatan gave his address to the friends he had made there, and invited them to keep in touch and visit.

"The others all threw away the address," said Yonatan. "Eliraz was the only one who wrote to me." He didn't begin his letter with, "How are you? What's doing?" Rather, he began with a lesson on biblical battle history.

This is what Eliraz wrote:

> *I Samuel, chapter 14, describes King Saul's first war. In this battle, the people had no arms. In their time, they had only two swords – one belonged to Saul, the other to his son Yonatan [Jonathan]. The rest of the people grabbed anything at hand, and that's how they went out to fight.*
>
> *The battle began. Saul [sic] gave an order, and the people followed him. He took his boy, his arms bearer, and together they went to outflank the enormous forces of the Philistines (from the same root as "Palestinians"). He went around them by way of a rocky crag, a great sharp rock, and moved behind them. He and his arms bearer began to attack them from behind. In his first fiery attack, Saul killed dozens, sowing fear and panic among the enemy, and that's how he defeated them.*
>
> *There are many lessons we can learn from this story. With our entire enormous army, we still need a few*

special forces – small, strong, and skilled. Naval officers are one of the forces that lead in battle and in defense of the state, and so I very much hope that you'll succeed, enlist in the IDF, and become a commander in the navy. We need good people in all fields – in the army, education, and the economy. Naval officers are the bearers of the flag, and the leaders, the driving force in the sea. You have the privilege of belonging to the group that will begin the naval commanders' course. It will be very difficult. They'll break you, they'll beat you down, but always remember who you are, what you are, and why you are fighting.

An eighteen-year-old boy wrote this, a youth who had not yet enlisted in the IDF. Eliraz continued:

The answer to these questions is very clear, but still, we must study them in depth. This is what I have been doing for the past year in Atzmona, and I'll be continuing my studies for another eight months. Maybe to you, the answers are simple.

Who are you? Yonatan! This is the personal side of your life. What are you? A Jew! Part of the whole that forms the Jewish people.

And why are you fighting? For the security and safety of the State of Israel!

Because we have enemies who hate us, who want to erase our Jewish identity and blur our identity. If we forget and abandon our identity, there will be no reason for us to remain in our land, and it will no longer be called "our homeland." Use your remaining time to study (if you want, about your roots) in order to strengthen the understanding that this is indeed our land. I'm not worried, because I know that love for the People of Israel and the Land of Israel is part of you, rooted within you.

If you have difficulties along the way with the philo-sophical-conceptual questions, or if the path is unclear and you can't find an answer to "why" and it really bothers you, then this is my address.

Good luck in the army and the rest of the way –

Eliraz Peretz

I had no idea that at age eighteen, my son had reached such a level of understanding.

Still, Eliraz had a compelling *joie de vivre.* After he was killed, we found a note he had written at age sixteen: "Things I want to do, and that I will do!!!" He listed sixteen activities (although in the original he wrote seventeen, he accidentally skipped a number). The list is written in pen and also pencil, and shows additions, erasures, and editing marks. On the back, he wrote, "Personal, confidential. Do not open without permission."

Here is the list:

1. Trip to the Far East
2. Trip across Israel
3. License for motor scooter and motorcycle
4. Trip from Rosh Ha'ayin [*sic* – meaning Rosh Hanikra] seashore to area near Gaza
5. Rappelling
6. Parachuting
7. Bungee jumping from cliffs
8. Acceptance to very elite unit
9. Live near the beach

10. In the summer, build a shelter on the beach and live there for a month
11. Become a karate instructor
12. Motorcycle trip from Metulla to Eilat
13. Surf
14. Fight in a master's judo tournament
15. Diving course
16. Die having fun

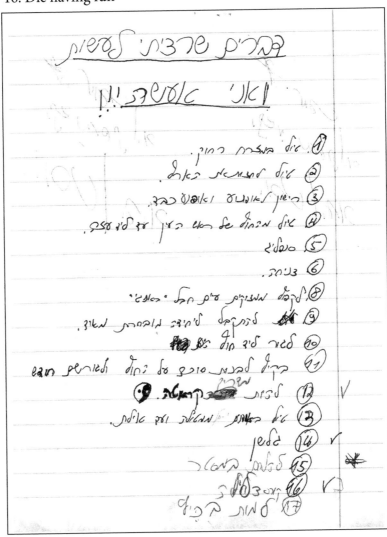

Is there such a thing? To die having fun?

Shortly after he turned nineteen, Eliezer and I accompanied Eliraz to the army enlistment office in Jerusalem. When he climbed up the stairs of the bus, and we waved goodbye to him. Eliezer recited some prayers, but my own mouth was dry from so many supplications. In my heart I begged, "God, please watch over him." He wanted to be a naval officer, but he didn't pass the trial course, as at the time he wore eyeglasses with a high prescription. But as was his nature, he didn't take it badly. We didn't observe any disappointment. Love of life sharpened his understanding that everything was for the best. He accepted reality without complaint, and followed Uriel into the Golani reconnaissance unit.

Eliraz's commander, Oded Bashan, was Uriel's best friend. Uriel was the one who established the rules. He never spoke with Oded about Eliraz, and Eliraz asked Uriel not to talk about him to his friend. Every time he came home, I saw that he was blossoming, that he was truly happy. Eliraz didn't know the meaning of the word *tired*. The harder his training exercises were, the happier he was.

Uriel was killed when Eliraz was seven months into the reconnaissance course. Oded told me that when they received the news, they were in the middle of a navigation exercise, and he was the one who had to inform Eliraz, but he couldn't get the words out. He didn't know what to say first. Should he say, "My friend, my companion, my soul mate Uriel is dead"? Or "Your brother is dead"?

Eliraz told me how he found out. He said that in the middle of the navigation course, he was called over to the road. He didn't understand what was happening, but suddenly he saw Oded's car from far off, and the realization hit him: We never stop navigation in the middle of the course! It must be Uriel!!

On the night between Wednesday and Thursday, 6 Kislev 5759 (November 25, 1998), at two thirty a.m., the military officers knocked on the door of our home. Eliraz arrived home at ten a.m. the next day. He came in wearing his uniform, covered with dust, but didn't utter a word. His silence was thunderous. He hugged me, and then his father, and one sentence escaped his lips: "My brother, brother of mine."

When a long tear was made in his army shirt, according to the traditional sign of mourning, I wept. Eliraz wept quietly and with restraint, and then fell silent. He only spoke when he was spoken to. He had never been one to chat without a purpose. After the shivah, his commander came to visit us, and said, "I'm not burying two brothers. The special forces unit operates in Lebanon, so Eliraz can't continue. I can't lose another brother."

Eliraz stood up from the corner of the room and announced, "I'm continuing. I want to keep going. I got to the special forces when Uriel was alive, and I know that if Uriel were still alive, he would want me to continue. This is the path I've chosen."

The commander turned to look at us, his parents. He explained that Eliraz's continued service in the elite unit depended on our agreement and signature on an official document.

Eliraz traveled to Atzmona to consult with Rabbi Rafi Peretz. For a week he sat there, studying Torah. Then he consulted with Major General Doron Almog, chief of the southern command, who had also lost a brother in battle. Eliraz had met Almog earlier, during the general's visit to Atzmona to speak with the cadets, and he decided to call his office. Later, Almog told me that when he was informed that a new recruit was on the line asking to speak with him, he refused, as this was not accepted procedure. But when he found out that it was a bereaved brother, he ordered his subordinates to set up a meeting immediately.

Major General Almog said to Eliraz, "If it's what you want, then don't give it up."

Years later, when Eliraz went to Gush Katif as an officer, Almog visited his base as head of the southern command. The battalion commander said, "This is Eliraz Peretz, brother of Uriel Peretz," and Doron Almog embraced Eliraz. When he got up to speak to the soldiers, he spoke about Uriel and Eliraz Peretz, and when he completed his tour of duty, he invited Eliraz to the ceremony.

We were very moved by the major general's support and warmth. One day, Eliezer and I met him by chance at the Kiriya central army headquarters, and were also given that same warm attention. Who would ever believe that one of the first visitors to come to my home after the news of Eliraz's death would be Major General Doron Almog and his wife?

When the IDF withdrew from Gaza in 2005, *Yediot Aharonot* asked Doron Almog to write about "his Gaza." He wrote that "his Gaza" was Uriel and Eliraz Peretz.

This is what he wrote, under the headline "Coming Full Circle":

> One story remains engraved in my memory from my days in the Gaza Strip. It sounds imaginary, but it's all true. It happened in 1998. I was then head of military doctrine and instruction for the General Staff.
>
> One day, a soldier from the Golani special forces unit called my office. His name was Eliraz Peretz, and he asked to speak with me. He told me about his brother, Uriel Peretz, of blessed memory, and said, "My parents and commanders are refusing to allow me to go out on combat operations. I know that you're also a son of a bereaved family, and I want to ask for your advice."
>
> I invited him to my office and explained to him that danger was present everywhere. "This is your life," I told him. "Decide how important it is to you, and if you make the decision, insist that your officers accept it." We said goodbye, and I didn't follow what became of him after that.
>
> Three years passed, and in April 2001, I was chief of the southern command. I visited the Golani 51st Battalion at Netzarim. The battalion commander pulled

*me aside and said, "Doron, I have a surprise for you."
Suddenly I saw that same soldier before me. In the
meantime, he had become a platoon commander. He
told me that as a result of our conversation, he had
decided to remain in combat service. He had finished
his training course, joined an officers' training course,
and now he was a platoon commander.*

*Almost one year later was the terrible month of March
in which 135 Israelis were killed in terrorist attacks. In
that awful month, a terrorist penetrated the yeshivah
at Atzmona and killed five students. I went to the site
and saw the room where the terrorist had committed
the murders. It was used as a synagogue, and it was
full of holy books, bookcases, tables, and blood. Lots of
blood. On the way out, I saw a sign on one of the walls:
"This room is dedicated to the memory of First Lieutenant Uriel Peretz, who was killed in combat in Lebanon."*

*I immediately connected that name with the story I
had heard four years earlier from the bereaved brother.
I take this story with me everywhere, and to me, it represents my personal Gaza – a place where circles are
closed, a place of deep, deep pain.*

Eliezer and I had difficulty deciding about Eliraz's return to
the elite unit as a fighter. Eliezer gave donations to charity, went to
synagogue, and prayed to God to help him make a wise decision.
Each day, the awareness grew within us that despite our pain, we
could not stand in Eliraz's way. We wouldn't prevent him from
fulfilling his ambitions, and we wouldn't extinguish his dreams.

"Mom, I've decided. I'm continuing," said Eliraz. "I'm not
willing to accept a non-combat position. Do you think I'm capable of sitting at a desk, being responsible for maps? I want to be a
fighter, leading in combat."

"What if something happens to you?" I couldn't utter the end of the sentence. "What will we do?"

"Mom," he answered, "this is what I want to do with my life. I want to serve in a meaningful position. I feel protected."

The night before we signed the document, Eliezer and I couldn't sleep a wink. I lit candles in the house. Eliezer went to synagogue, stood against the sacred ark, and his tears fell onto the Torah scroll. We opened the Rosh Hashanah prayer book to "Et Sha'arei Ratzon," Eliezer's favorite *piyyut*, which describes in detail the biblical story of the binding of Isaac. Every time we came to this part of the service, I felt it was written for us, for all the bereaved families. This was the point at which Eliezer wept every Rosh Hashanah. Years later, the congregants decided that my son Avichai would sing a few verses of this song. When he sings, "Woe to the mother who cries and wails / the binder, the bound, and the altar," the synagogue fills with quiet weeping, and everyone knows that the words are intended for one woman – me.

This song contains a unique expression that is appropriate for our situation, an expression that we have adopted in our family – "The eye weeps in bitterness, but the heart rejoices."

Yes, we wept. But still, something within us said, "Go with the decision, joyfully."

In the morning we got up, dressed, and drove with Eliraz to a notary public in Jerusalem. When he gave us the pen and paper, we froze. We couldn't move our fingers to sign. We were struck with the feeling that perhaps at that very moment, we were signing over Eliraz's life.

The notary studied us out of the corner of his eye, and silence filled the room.

Then Eliezer cried out, "Blessings and success!" and he signed. I followed suit.

We left the room as different people.

Letter written by Eliraz in first grade, as a religious student in a secular school, to school principal Avi Harari.

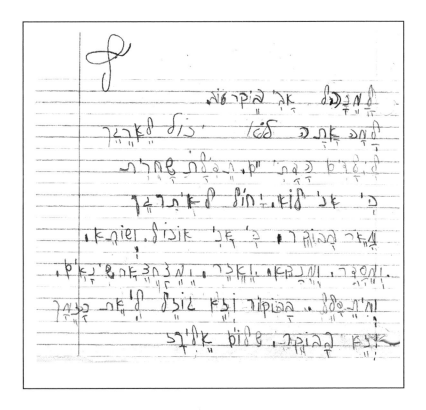

Dear Principal Avi, Good morning.

Why can't you organize morning prayer services for the religious kids? Because I kan't get organized early in the morning, because I eet, drinck, straighten, cleen, help, brush my teeth and pray in the morning. It takes up all my time, and its in the morning.

Goodbye
Eliraz

List of teaching topics prepared by Eliraz as a Bnei Akiva counselor:

Lessons to be taught in activities before I leave:
Before instruction
After instruction

I think I finished everything but I was able to add more things.
√ 1. Friends
√ 2. Unity
√ 3. Community origin
√ 4. The Land of Israel
√ 5. National unity
√ 6. Israel's uniqueness
√ 7. Love your neighbor as yourself
√ 8. Don't take advantage
√ 9. Holocaust
√ 10. Yom Ha'atzma'ut [Israel Independence Day]

√ 11. Political situations
√ 12. Israel vs. other countries
√ 13. Why Israel is persecuted
√ 14. The individual in society
√ 15. Personality and talents of each individual
√ 16. Death=life
√ 17. More
√ 18. Teacher
√ 19. Responsibility and maturity
√ 20. Individual, group
√ 21. Values
√ 22. Where there's a will, there's a way
   23.
   24.
   25.
   26.
√ 27. Prayer
√ 28. Bnei Akiva

CHAPTER 16

"Israel, My Land" – Eliraz Is Wounded

The Golani special forces unit operated in Lebanon, and the commander informed Eliraz that in the near future, he would not be going into action there.

This was hardly what Eliraz had in mind. He had been waiting impatiently to go out on combat operations with his team.

On a Thursday evening, Eliraz returned home from the final southern endurance exercise. This was no easy trial. The course was exhausting, and at the time he was light as a feather, as weeks of going hungry had made him skinnier than ever. His arms were full of scratches and cuts, bruises and thorns, but his feet were dancing and he had a smile on his face. That evening, in another hour, one of his friends was getting married. "How about resting a bit," Eliezer suggested. But Eliraz, ever lively, ran to shower and freshen up. He put on a white shirt, *tzitzit*, and sandals, and that was it. He flew out of the house. Other times he would go to friends' weddings straight from the base, black from head to toe, his cheeks smudged with camouflage colors. He would jump and dance just as he was, rejoicing and bringing joy to others.

In the officers' training course, Eliraz met German Roshkov from the Nachal Brigade. His parents were divorced and lived in the Ukraine, so on every leave Eliraz brought German to our home, and he became like another son to us. On Shabbat he would go to synagogue with Eliezer and Eliraz. Sometimes the congregants would ask Eliezer, "How is it that you, the *gabbai*, don't arrange an aliyah to the Torah for your guest?" Eliezer would offer them all kinds of evasive answers in order to avoid revealing the fact that German was not Jewish.

On Shavuot, German deviated from his usual custom and didn't join Eliezer and Eliraz in synagogue. He decided to stay home with me, asking if we could study the book of Ruth together. When we finished studying, I asked him, "Why are you fighting for me? My son Uriel was a Jew, but why you? You could die. Uriel fought for his people, for Jerusalem, which his grandfather Ya'akov had dreamed of in the Sahara Desert in Morocco. But you, German, why are you endangering yourself?"

With deep emotion, German cited a verse from the book we had just studied (Ruth 1:16). "For wherever you go, I will go, and wherever you live, I will live. Your people shall be my people..." Then he added, "This is my people!"

During the course, German demonstrated broad knowledge of Jewish history, and when I tested him and Eliraz in preparation for the final course exams, he even surpassed my son. Our relationship continued after they completed the course, when German was made a commander in the Nachal Brigade. On occasion he would call to ask my advice on leadership issues, and of course he maintained his strong friendship with Eliraz. His mother Ludmilla came to live in Israel, and settled in Kiryat Shemona.

In March 2002, First Lieutenant German Roshkov was killed in a battle with terrorists near Kibbutz Matzuva. Eliraz consulted with Rabbi Rafi Peretz, and fought for German to be buried in the military cemetery, like all soldiers. I, who knew German as well as the pain of loss, eulogized him in place of his own mother, who did not know Hebrew. I had my eulogy translated into Russian for her as well. Since then, our souls are bound together in blood. Eliraz continued to maintain ties with Ludmilla, who faithfully knit a garment for each of his children as if for her own grandchildren.

When he went up to the northern border with his soldiers, he sent
them into Kiryat Shemona to visit his "second mother."

On the day Eliraz was killed, IDF representatives visited Ludmilla's house as well. In her home, a picture of Eliraz hangs beside
a photo of German.

Thankfully, the concluding ceremony of Eliraz's officers' training course took place at Latrun. In this, the Holy One, blessed be
He, did us a great kindness, because I was incapable of returning
to Mitzpe Ramon. Had I stood there in the shadow of memories,
searching the grounds for Uriel, how would I have room in my heart
for Eliraz? We went to Latrun with a folding table, coolers filled
with food and treats, and enormous cheerleading signs. The verse
from the *piyyut* echoed in my head – "The eye weeps in bitterness,
but the heart rejoices"; but inside, I barely knew what I was feeling.
Joy? Sadness? As an officer, would he be exposed to greater dan-
gers? Mainly, I felt fear. But when Eliraz marched, we all got up and
shouted, "Eliraz the champ!" Through the shouts, a tear escaped.
Eliraz was thrilled, and I saw how his chest filled with pride.

Afterward, Eliezer and I exchanged a look. We spoke with our
eyes, as there was no need for words. He knew that I knew, and I
knew that he knew, and we both knew that we couldn't stand in
Eliraz's way.

After the ceremony was over, Eliezer hugged his son, and
began to say something, but the sentence froze on his tongue.
"Uriel…," he said, and stopped. "Uriel…," he repeated, and again
fell silent. It took a third try for him to finish: "Uriel…would have
been proud of you."

Eliraz, wearing a big smile, replied, "I know."

He was given the position of officer at the Golani Brigade
training base, and we had no idea what was going on or what he
was doing. He was like a secret underground bunker. He never let
out a word, and when pressed, he would merely say, "It's great." He
never complained, never grumbled, never broke down. Only after

Eliezer and Miriam with Eliraz on the day of his wedding to Shlomit

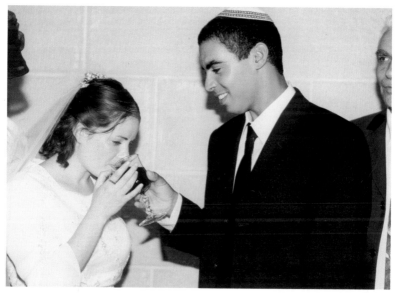

"Voices of joy and gladness" – Shlomit and Eliraz under their chuppah

On Eliraz's wedding day. Back row, left to right: *Hadas, Miriam (with photo of Uriel above her), Eliraz, Eliezer, Avichai, Elyasaf.* Front: *Bat-El.*

With Dad. Hadas, Elyasaf, Eliezer, Avichai, Bat-El. In background: *photo of Uriel.*

Avichai and Elyasaf (during high school) with their dad

Avichai and Elyasaf in Golani reconnaissance unit

"Her" Golani. Back row: *Bat-El, Avichai.* Front row: *Eliraz, Miriam holding photo of Uriel, Elyasaf.* (Photographed by Elad Gershgoren)

Yom Hazikaron 2009. Avichai, Elyasaf, Miriam, Eliraz.

Hadas' wedding day. Eliraz, Shlomit holding Hallel Miriam, Hadas, Miriam with arm around Or-Chadash, Bat-El, Elyasaf, Avichai.

Hadas as a bride, with Miriam. In background: *photo of her father, Eliezer.*

At Hadas' wedding. Miriam, Eliraz, Elyasaf, Avichai.

Elyasaf with Rivka Hever, close friend of the Peretz family

Eliraz and Shlomit with Or-Chadash and Hallel Miriam

The Eitam family: Hadas and Avichai with Aluma

Eliraz – "And you shall be especially happy"

Elyasaf on Mount Evyatar, during training course for Golani reconnaissance unit

Bat-El at Chavat
Hashomer base

"Team Uriel" with Commander Bat-El at Chavat Hashomer base.

Bat-El at home, on leave for the weekend, with Miriam

Bat-El at beret ceremony for Matan Issachar, her future husband

At Bat-El's engagement party. Avichai, Bat-El, Miriam, Elyasaf, Hadas.

On Bat-El's wedding day, two months after Eliraz's death. Back row: *Elyasaf, Miriam, Shlomit holding Gili Bat-Ami, Bat-El, Avichai, Hadas, Avichai Eitam.* Front row: *Hallel Miriam, Or-Chadash, Shir Zion, Aluma.*

Bat-El on her wedding day. Back row, from left: *Miriam, Shlomit holding Gili Bat-Ami, Bat-El.* Front row: *Hallel Miriam, Aluma Eitam, Or-Chadash, Shir Zion.*

Bat-El with Avichai (left) *and Elyasaf*

From left: *Hallel Miriam, Shlomit holding Gili Bat-Ami, Bat-El, Or-Chadash, Shir Zion*

Charly (Miriam's brother) in intimate conversation with Asher Kadosh

Charly Ohayon with Or-Chadash

Eliraz Peretz, deputy commander Battalion 12, in the Philadelphia Corridor. (Photographed by Reuven Castro)

Miriam buries Eliraz. (Photographed by Alex Kolomoisky)

Prime Minister Benjamin Netanyahu paying a condolence call after Eliraz's death. Left to right: *Elyasaf, Hadas, Shlomit holding Gili Bat-Ami, Miriam.*

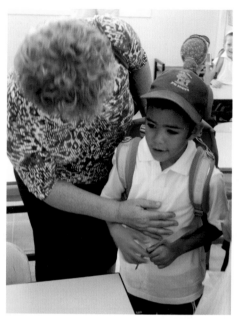

Or-Chadash begins first grade at the Talmud Torah in Eli. (Photographed by Eliana Passentin)

Miriam and Shlomit accompany Or-Chadash to first grade.
(Photographed by Eliana Passentin)

he died, stories began to leak out that bore witness as to what kind of officer he had been.

A soldier named Uriel came to the shivah. He told us that Eliraz, his officer, was not able to pronounce his name. "I was a problematic soldier," he revealed to me. "When I got to the induction center, I announced that I was going to be released within three days, because the army wasn't for me. On the first day, I did everything possible to get kicked out. On the second day, I did the same thing again. I failed on the third day as well, but they still didn't kick me out. On the fourth day, I met Officer Eliraz, and something about his behavior convinced me to stay. I don't know what it was.

"The first week was over, and I couldn't believe I had survived. The second week began, and again I tried to do everything to be disqualified, anything in order to be kicked out. There was a problem with the APCs [armored personnel carriers], and Eliraz sat us all in a U and announced, 'This Shabbat, one of us is going to be grounded. One of us made a terrible mistake.' I was thrilled. Here it was, this was my chance to run away from the IDF. But when Friday came around, Eliraz called us together again and said, 'This week one of us made a mistake, and mistakes have a price.' That's it, I said to myself, it's me, I fell asleep a bit while on guard duty. When Eliraz grounds me, the IDF will forget about me. This is my chance to get out of it. Everyone was tense to find out who had bit the dust, and I knew he meant me. Then, all of a sudden, Eliraz announced, 'I'm grounding Eliraz Peretz. I left my weapon in the APC for two minutes.'

"We were astonished. Eliraz added, 'Me and you – we're one. We're a family. I won't ask you to do something that I can't handle myself. Go home. *Shabbat shalom*.' I listened to him openmouthed, as if hypnotized. That's how an officer talked? He was apologizing for two minutes? He was grounding himself for that silly mistake? I had never encountered such honesty. I had never met with such a high level of personal example. At that moment I decided: for Eliraz Peretz, I'll serve for three years, three years of quality."

Another visitor during the shivah was Wanda, a soldier of Ethiopian origin, who related how Eliraz had watched him carefully, supporting him so that he wouldn't break down. "You'll break the Golani record, and when you reach the end of the course, I'll give you a special flag!" Eliraz promised. He fulfilled that promise. When Wanda completed the course, Eliraz presented him with a victory flag bearing the quote about "all the thorns," and he explained that this saying had been written by his brother Uriel. Wanda said, "Whatever I am, it's thanks to Eliraz. Without him, I would be someone else."

More and more soldiers came to the shivah and recounted how much Eliraz had cared for them. How on Thursdays, he would make sure they took food with them, in case there wasn't any at home. How he went to visit a soldier whose house had burned down, collected supplies for him and helped to paint and plaster. We learned so many things about Eliraz the commander, and I admit that these testimonials caused me pain. I had known so little about him, because he didn't talk. He only said one thing: that he dreamed of becoming a unit commander in the 51st Battalion, in which Uriel had served.

One day, Eliraz and I had a private conversation. I told him that I had adopted the expression "For whenever I speak of him, I do remember him still" (Jeremiah 31:19). Eliraz said, "Mom, I remember Uriel in silence."

I asked, "How? How do you remember?"

Eliraz related that a myriad of details reminded him of Uriel: "A song by Rita [the well-known singer], the smell of the ocean, sounds of breathing while diving." I noticed that since his brother's death, Eliraz had strengthened his religious faith. He understood that death had meaning, but in contrast to me, he was silent. On Yom Hazikaron, Israel's memorial day for fallen soldiers, he brought soldiers to Givat Ze'ev so that I could talk to them about leadership and faith. After the lesson, one of the soldiers came up to me and asked naïvely, "Tell me, is there a connection between Uriel Peretz and our commander?"

"He was his brother," I answered.

Eliraz had never even told them that he had a brother who was killed in action.

Eliraz rarely spoke at the yearly memorial ceremonies for Uriel. When we begged him, he said a few words that touched us deeply. Here is the eulogy he gave at the second annual memorial ceremony:

> My oldest brother Uriel, who today is younger than me by four months, one week, and twenty-one days.
>
> My brother, the smell of touching you,
>
> The fistfights we got into,
>
> The sharing of thoughts,
>
> The questions we haven't yet answered,
>
> Our trips together,
>
> Skinny-dipping in Nachal Arugot,
>
> Diving together with the same balloon.
>
> To be a brother means being with a person when his nation is being attacked,
>
> And feeling that his body is suffering the injury.
>
> My brother, time has indeed passed…
>
> And time is only a matter of time
>
> For we'll all get to the place where you went
>
> Some by old age, some by car, some by war, some by illness
>
> But in the meantime, I'm here and you're there…

Eliraz advanced in the ranks of the military. During Operation Defensive Shield in 2002, he served as deputy commander for a superior he particularly admired, Avihu Ya'akov, of blessed memory. Eliraz didn't tell me that he went into combat. He just said, "Don't worry, Mom, I'm at Mount Dov."

I never imagined that my son was actually fighting alongside his soldiers in the alleyways of Jenin, and that his life was in real danger. Staff Sergeant Gad Ezra of the 51st Battalion was killed, and the media published his last letter to his girlfriend, Galit, in which he said that should he not return, he wanted her to continue with her life and marry someone else. The phone rang, and an unknown woman on the other end of the line identified herself as Gad's mother. She asked if she could speak with Eliraz.

"Eliraz is at Mount Dov!" I answered. She realized right away that he hadn't told me the truth, and that I had no idea my son was fighting in the battle that was going on in Jenin.

"I only ask," she said, "that when Eliraz gets home, he should bring the gun to us."

I didn't understand her request. I had no idea what she was talking about.

Two weeks later, Eliraz came home, cheerful and happy as usual. He came bouncing through the door as if nothing had happened. There was no visible sign that he had been in combat. But on Shabbat, he went up to the Torah and recited the Hagomel blessing for one who has been saved from serious danger.

"Why is he reciting this blessing?" his father asked. "What happened?"

"I'll tell you at home, Dad," Eliraz answered.

At home he pulled down his pants, and I turned pale. His legs were black, full of shrapnel. "I wasn't really at Mount Dov. I was in Jenin," he admitted. "And some of my soldiers were killed."

We heard about the battle of Jenin only after his death, from the family of Nissim Ben David, of blessed memory. Nissim had attended the Atzmona premilitary academy, and he wasn't even a Golani soldier – he was serving in Givati. But when he heard about the fighting in Jenin, he asked to join Eliraz's battalion.

Eliraz Peretz was the only name Nissim knew in the battalion. They fought together, shoulder to shoulder, until Nissim was hit by a sniper's bullet. Eliraz laid him on the ground and lay on top of him as a living shield against the continuous gunfire. He noticed that Nissim's breathing was becoming labored, and he began to give him mouth-to-mouth resuscitation.

In the commemorative video clip that Nissim's family put together, Eliraz was asked, "Didn't you hesitate to place your mouth on top of his, when he was covered with blood?"

"Nissim's blood flowed through my veins," he replied. "When my mouth was inside his, I had only one thing in mind – how I kiss Shlomit. So nothing held me back."

Eliraz asked Gad Ezra to help him lift Nissim's body. At that moment, a sniper shot at them and killed Gad. Eliraz was able to recite Shema Yisrael with Gad before his soul departed from his body. Eliraz aimed at the sniper, but his gun was locked, so he took Gad Ezra's gun and continued the battle.

Eliraz was wounded and had shrapnel inside his legs, so he was evacuated to Rambam Hospital. When asked his name, he replied, "Yisrael Artzi," which means "Israel, my land." Later, Eliraz explained that he hadn't wanted to give his real name so that we wouldn't hear that he'd been wounded, and that was the first name that came to mind. Yisrael Artzi, a name that aptly fit his character.

In the emergency room, the staff cut off his boots and pulled out the shrapnel. They found a big piece in the sole of his foot, and ordered him to lie in bed for a week. "What do you mean, a week?" Eliraz protested. "My soldiers are fighting in Jenin! I'm going back to them." He got out of bed and began to totter down the hospital corridor – barefoot, but wearing his army shirt and insignia. He peeked into the rooms, looking for a soldier who would lend him some army boots. To this day, when I imagine this surrealistic image – an officer in uniform, barefoot, hobbling down the corridor – I can't help but burst out laughing.

That's how he got to the room where Ro'i Greenwald, a soldier from Mitzpe Yericho, lay wounded. Eliraz told him what had happened, and asked if he could borrow some money to buy shoes. Ro'i asked his father, who was standing next to his bed, and the father gave Eliraz three hundred shekels with which he bought some sport shoes. So, with shrapnel in his legs, Eliraz returned to the outskirts of Jenin, where he held up a flashlight and stopped an APC. "Where to?" Eliraz asked. The soldier replied, "Jenin," and Eliraz jumped in. "I'm coming with you," he announced. Bewildered, the soldier tried to protest, but Eliraz insisted: "You have two options. Either you get out of this APC, or else you take me along."

He returned to Jenin and continued the battle.

Eliezer and I sat listening to him, and suddenly I remembered. "Eliraz," I jumped, "Gad's mother called and asked you to take the gun to them."

When he returned from visiting Gad's family, he was white as a sheet. Eliraz related that Gad's mother took the gun strap, but refused to take the weapon.

"But that was Gad's gun," he reminded her.

"No," the bereaved mother corrected him, "look at the number."

"I looked," Eliraz told me, "and it was the number of Uriel's gun."

Uriel had been an officer of the backup company for the 51st Battalion. When a platoon commander is killed, the weapon is transferred to the sergeant, in this case, Gad Ezra, of blessed memory.

Later, Eliraz introduced Galit, Gad's girlfriend, to his wife Shlomit's brother, and they were married. Eliraz saw this as much more than coming full circle: it was the fulfillment of the last request of his brother-in-arms. New life had begun.

CHAPTER 17

At First Sight –
Eliraz and Shlomit

One day, I opened the door and there, standing before me, was Shlomit – pretty, gentle, and calm. I knew she was supposed to arrive, but I never imagined that this would be a fateful visit.

Shlomit Gilboa of Kiryat Arba had completed her stint in the National Service and was working in a school with my friend Rivka Hever, Uriel's "second mother." For Yom Hazikaron, she planned to create a memorial display at the school that would focus on one soldier, based on her understanding that kids can't process endless names and large numbers of fallen soldiers. Rivka recommended that she choose Uriel Peretz.

So Shlomit came to Givat Ze'ev, and Eliezer picked her up at the gate and took her directly to the synagogue that was named in memory of Uriel. The synagogue was his pride and joy, and every guest who visited our home was taken there first. Then Eliezer brought her to our house. Shlomit charmed me from the very first with her kind, sweet personality. Eliezer and I sat with her in the living room, and he was also impressed by her, although at first he said nothing. I showed her the album we had made for Uriel. I flipped through it, showing her the photos. She looked, and finally she asked, "Who's that standing next to Uriel?"

"That's Eliraz," I replied.

"How old is he?" asked Shlomit. "What's he doing now?"

I told her that he was her age, twenty-four, and that he was a deputy commander in the army. I could tell that her interest was sparked. She took the items documenting Uriel's life, and after she left the house, Eliezer announced, "That's your son Eliraz's bride."

That evening, we called Eliraz and informed him, "We've found a bride for you!"

"What's wrong with you?" he laughed on the other side of the line. "Are you off your rockers?"

"We've found you a bride," I repeated, in a slightly more aggressive tone.

"Are you nuts?" he said, pouncing on us. "I just got out of Jenin, and that's what you're worried about? Finding me a bride?"

A few days passed. Shlomit kept calling, and Eliezer had deep conversations with her. He had already fallen in love with her himself. There was only one problem: she hadn't yet met Eliraz. Each day, the connection between Shlomit and Eliezer grew stronger. He began to worry.

"Listen," he told her, "my son Eliraz isn't serious. I'll introduce you to his friend, he's more serious." So he sent one of Uriel's friends to meet her. But two weeks later, Shlomit said it wasn't right. She continued her conversations with Eliezer, who by this time had become quite fond of her.

When Shlomit's students returned after Passover vacation, the memorial display was ready. She invited us to the school. When I arrived at the gate, I was moved when one of the students identified my face from the photos, and asked, "Are you Uriel's mother?"

I had given Shlomit a video to use in her display, which had been filmed while Uriel was stationed in Hebron. He was shown helping a little preschool-age girl cross the road. As Shlomit had done her National Service in Hebron, I thought I would give her a challenge. I asked her, "Perhaps you recognize this girl?" In fact, she did. The girl was in third grade by then, and she introduced her to us.

I had to choke back my tears. I couldn't help thinking that this girl could have been Uriel's own daughter.

I told the students about Uriel's childhood, how things had been difficult for him, and how he had worked hard and overcome the challenges. They listened to me, their eyes wide. I felt that Shlomit, as a new teacher, had taken an important step by focusing on one soldier, one individual, who was an entire world unto himself.

A few months later, the date of Uriel's memorial ceremony arrived, and there on Mount Herzl, Shlomit and Eliraz met for the first time.

Hundreds of people came to the ceremony, and when Eliezer saw Shlomit standing to the side, at a distance, on the staircase, he called her over. She stood beside me, and I felt her presence up close. "You see?" I said. "This is what's left of the boy. After all the stories – this is what's left. The grave, and the wind."

We asked Eliraz to say something about Uriel, his oldest brother. Eliraz studied the tombstone, and said, paraphrasing the words of the popular Naomi Shemer song "*Shiro shel Abba (Yibane Hamikdash)*": "God, if You carved a rock from the mountain – as You carved out part of the Peretz family and took my brother Uriel – You didn't carve it in vain, God, because from these stones, the Temple will be rebuilt."

When the ceremony was over, Eliezer said to Shlomit, "I'd like you to meet Eliraz."

Later, Shlomit told me that she was surprised. She had thought that Eliraz was very religious and wouldn't even look at her. She was amazed that he did look at her, and not just a passing glance. I think that there, on Mount Herzl, is where love began to blossom.

After the memorial ceremony, everyone came to our house for the required meal, and Shlomit gave me a surprise, a photo of Uriel helping the girl from Beit Hadassah in Hebron cross the street. That picture hangs on our wall, among all the other photos of him. Every time I look at it, I think about Uriel's never-born children, about his deep sensitivity, and I imagine what a wonderful father he would have been.

I had prepared a big meal, and Shlomit came to our house after the ceremony to help me set the table. I suspected that she had really come to see Eliraz, and I was thrilled. I wanted him to be happy. Shlomit should have left early so as to catch the last bus to Kiryat Arba. To this day, I'm not sure whether she missed that bus on purpose. Someone had to drive her to the central bus station in Jerusalem, and Eliraz volunteered. When he returned, at a very late hour, he said he had driven her all the way home.

They become officially engaged on the eve of the Passover Seder. Eliraz was still in the army full-time, and I have no idea how many times they actually met before they decided to get married, but Eliraz told me that he asked her some important questions to see if they would be compatible. He told Shlomit that he intended to remain in the army, and he wanted to know what she thought about it. Shlomit knew that marrying a career officer would require her to pay a heavy price, but she agreed. Eliraz was of the same mind as his father, who had wanted twelve children, and informed Shlomit that he also wanted a large family. He wanted her to know what the most important things in his life were: the army, and family.

One day, Shlomit came to visit us. She said she had been to the Hermon with Eliraz, and I realized that things were serious. When he announced, "We've decided," we were thrilled. We were excited to hear that he had proposed to her at the Western Wall.

The engagement ceremony was held in her parents' home in Kiryat Arba, the evening before the Seder. Shlomit sang and played the piano, and her siblings and other relatives played the accordion and sang on and on. When Shlomit placed a memorial candle for Uriel on the table, I felt that she was already connected to our family to the depths of her soul, and that the hand of Divine Providence was guiding us. She lit the candle, standing beside her future husband, and recounted that she had felt a connection to Uriel long before meeting Eliraz. She said that Uriel gave her much strength and joy, and that on that evening, he was giving her the most precious gift of all – his brother.

Right after the Seder, we began to plan for the wedding, which was set for 29 Sivan (June 9, 2002), two and a half months later. But where was Eliraz? In the army. I bought him clothes for the wedding on my own. I wanted him to wear a suit, because he still looked like a little boy and I hoped that a suit would make him look grown-up. On the phone, I asked him for his size, and he said "40," but on Friday afternoon, when he came home and tried on the pants, I saw that he was swimming in them. They fell off his body onto the floor. What to do? Shabbat began at six thirty p.m., and the wedding was on Sunday, leaving almost no time for alterations.

I took the suit and ran to Shuli Cohen, Givat Ze'ev's legendary seamstress and a family friend. I found her in the middle of Shabbat preparations. "Shuli," I begged, "drop everything. We have no choice, the wedding's on Sunday." She grabbed her measuring tape, pinned up the pants with Eliraz in them, and took them in by at least four sizes. "Mom," he muttered, "I'm only wearing this suit under the *chuppah*." And that's what he did.

We handled all the preparations for the wedding without any involvement on Eliraz's part. Eliezer was the one who chose the Nof wedding hall in Jerusalem, because it overlooked Mount Herzl. Eliezer wanted Uriel to be with us at the wedding: he visited the grave and placed an invitation on the gravestone. When he came home, he found a letter from Eliraz.

Dear Dad!

After years of living under your roof, under your wings – it's time to leave.

Father, you gave me my life, and you gave it meaning, resolve, and patience. You painted my life in color, and taught me how to walk in your path. You taught me to use all the exceptional strengths that I inherited from you, my parents.

Now I, like you, am going to build a nest, a house, a home among the Jewish people. I pray that my children will at least be like your children, loving their people and all of humanity, and connected to the land.

I'm sure you've also given me many things that I have yet to discover.

You've shown spiritual resilience for me, and although you sacrificed your oldest son, you signed for the second one. I put you through a trial that even our forefather Abraham didn't have to go through – and you passed it with flying colors.

Thank you, Father, for giving me the strength to continue.

Please know, Father, that throughout all the battles, I knew I wouldn't die.

Even when the bullets flew past my neck, even when I was wounded, I never lost hope. On the contrary – I sang, sang a song of life.

And then we were at the hall. We gathered together all our emotional strength so we could rejoice. Eliezer wanted to place a photo of Uriel beside the *chuppah* with a lit memorial candle. My strength faltered. What was he thinking, a photo of Uriel? This was a wedding, I argued, Shlomit and Eliraz's wedding! I managed to convince Eliezer to give up the idea.

I knew that when he stood under the *chuppah*, Eliraz would mention Uriel. I didn't ask or hint, but Eliezer and I knew that especially on this, the happiest day of his life, Uriel would be with Eliraz. Indeed, Eliraz was a bit late for the wedding because he had gone to visit his brother's grave first. Rabbi Rafi Peretz, Eliraz's rabbi and teacher, performed the wedding ceremony. The ceremony began, but Eliraz had still not mentioned Uriel, not one word.

Eliezer glanced at me, asking wordlessly, "What's going on?"

I nodded to him. I had no doubt that Eliraz would say something.

The final moment came, and Rabbi Peretz instructed Eliraz to recite the traditional verse from Psalms, "If I forget you, O Jerusalem…" and break the cup. Silence filled the room. Eliraz announced, "If I forget you, my brother Uriel, may my right hand forget its skill; may my tongue cleave to the roof of my mouth." Rabbi Rafi repeated, "If I forget you, O Jerusalem" – but Eliraz, in his usual intense manner, continued with his own pronouncement, vowing to remember Uriel.

They began their life together in Gush Katif, because Eliraz was studying in Atzmona in the program for soldiers who had completed their compulsory service. They lived in a small mobile home on a dune by the sea, in a calm, peaceful environment. Eight months later, Eliraz returned to the army and began a company commanders' course. He was often called to the field, and Shlomit had to stay behind by herself. So they moved near her parents, to the settlement of Ma'ale Hever, where their oldest child, Or-Chadash, was born. The *brit milah* ceremony was held in Ma'arat Hamachpelah, the Tomb of the Patriarchs, in Kiryat Arba. Eliezer was the *sandak*, honored with holding the baby. His hands trembled with emotion as he held his first grandchild. He and all those present were overcome with joy, and with memories of Uriel.

Then Eliraz announced the name: Or-Chadash Uriel. This unique name was Eliraz's idea. When Shlomit was pregnant, he had danced with the Torah scroll at the Simchat Torah celebration in Atzmona, and sang a song from the morning prayer service: "*Or chadash al Tziyon ta'ir*" (Shine a new light on Zion, and may we all soon be worthy of its light). When he returned home from synagogue that day, he said to his wife, "If we have a son, we'll call him Or-Chadash."

Eliezer very much wanted his first grandson to be named after Uriel. He wasn't afraid that naming the new baby after a dead person would bring disaster to the child. On the contrary, in his family, it was considered a meritorious practice that brought good luck and long life. The first time we heard the name Or-Chadash, it sounded strange to us. But the more we got used to the sound, the more we identified with its meaning. *Or* means light, which symbolizes joy, freedom, faith, redemption. In addition, the initials of Or Chadash, *aleph* and *chet*, combine to form the word *ach*, "brother." For us, his arrival into the world symbolized a new beginning.

Eliraz and Shlomit chose unique names for their next three children, as well: Hallel Miriam (Hallel, "praise," because she was born a few days after the end of the Second Lebanon War, and Miriam after Miriam the Prophetess and myself); Shir-Tzion; and Gili Bat-Ami Ito (named after my mother, Grandma Étoile, whom Eliraz admired).

From Ma'ale Hever, they moved to Eli, because Eliraz wanted to study Torah there, in the program for IDF graduates. They and their three kids lived in a crowded mobile home that shook in the wind. After three years on the waiting list, a house became available, and they moved in; it was as if they had moved to a palace. In 2009, the Israel High Court of Justice ruled that their home, along with ten other houses in Eli, had to be demolished due to the contention that they had been built on Arab land. But to this day, ownership has not been proven. In 2014, the government decided to cancel the demolition order.

Eliraz was a crazy father. The moment he entered the world of fatherhood, he became addicted to kids. On Fridays, while the children were in preschool, he helped Shlomit get the house ready for Shabbat. Sometimes he baked fish in the oven, or made a stew with vegetables and cracked wheat. Then they would go out for coffee and talk, trying to make up for what they had missed during the two weeks of his absence. They often came to visit me. Eliraz always said that he wouldn't miss any opportunity to see his mother. After collecting the kids from preschool, he would jump and roll around on the floor with them, horsing around. He also took them on nature hikes.

On these outings, he would take along Gilad and Yo'av, the sons of Ro'i Klein, of blessed memory, former deputy commander of the Golani Brigade's 51st Battalion. Klein was killed in the Second Lebanon War, in 2006, after jumping on a grenade in order to save the lives of his soldiers. As he jumped, his soldiers reported, he cried out, "*Shema Yisrael!*" The Kleins were their neighbors. Eliraz's leave from the army, once a week or once every two weeks, always seemed too short and compressed, because he tried to work in as much as possible, even at the expense of sleep time.

Despite being far away for much of the time, Eliraz was a very involved father. Every time he phoned, he would ask what was going on at home, and the kids felt very close to him. Once, when Or-Chadash was upset, Shlomit called Eliraz, and he spent fifteen minutes calming him down. Afterwards, Eliraz told her that he had been on the phone during a dangerous combat operation, when he was responsible for his own safety as well as that of his soldiers. When Shlomit expressed regret that she had bothered him, he declared, "I cannot bear the idea of being unavailable to my kids when they need me."

Another time, Hallel was in a panic about having dental work. Shlomit told Eliraz, and he tried to determine the source of her anxiety. Thinking that she was afraid of the dentist's gloves, he walked in the door wearing a pair of gloves himself. He stroked her and hugged her until she got used to the sensation, and her fear subsided.

His last Shabbat was a happy one. His brother Avichai went to visit him after a long trip abroad, and Eliraz took him and Shlomit to see the place where they would build their house, after they received the necessary permits. It was in the Hayovel neighborhood, at the highest point in Eli. He chose a plot at the top of the hill, with an expansive view: on one side, the ocean and the towers of Tel Aviv, north to the smokestacks of Hadera's power plant, and on the other side, the Hermon. It had a feeling of freedom and open spaces.

He didn't have time to submit the papers for a construction permit. Today, anyone who visits Eli can see Eliraz's house. At the entrance to their home, the Israeli flag flies high on a tall pole.

CHAPTER 18

I Knew Eliraz Would Live

Just as I knew that Uriel would die, I knew that Eliraz would live. A mother knows, she feels it.

From the moment he came into the world, Eliraz radiated vitality. Because he was born on 8 Av, the day before Tisha b'Av, I would say to him, "Maybe you'll be the Messiah," because Jewish tradition holds that the Messiah will be born on that day. Eliraz laughed and said, "That can't be. I'm dark-skinned, and the Messiah won't be dark."

He burst into the world after an easy birth – as opposed to Uriel's, which was difficult and painful – and let out a loud cry right away. Raising him was also simple. He slurped from the bottle easily. In preschool he was joyful and impish, constantly gathering other kids and proposing schemes like climbing trees, jumping on rocks, and other activities that seemed hazardous to their parents. And then there was the time when he was five that he slipped away from me and we found him on one of Sharm's cliffs, legs dangling, staring at the ocean. He knew no fear.

Eliraz was a kid who fell down and got up. He would get bruised, or get in trouble, but he always got out of it. He had dark hair with curls bleached by the sun and eyes that shone with tremendous *joie de vivre*. He even safely navigated the crises of adolescence and the deep inquiry into questions of faith. In his first few months at Atzmona, he would start his day by running, swimming, and surfing, all before his morning prayers. The endless vitality he exuded led all of us to view him as protected. This feeling intensified during his military service, when he participated in combat operations in which his soldiers were killed, and death brushed close by. Each time he came home safely, I felt that God was watching over him, and would continue to do so.

One of the few operations that Eliraz shared with me was the exchange of fire in which Staff Sergeant Yehuda Bassel was killed. They were both standing by the window of a house in the al-Attara refugee camp, when something prompted Eliraz to turn his head away from the window. At that very moment, Yehuda was killed. Eliraz told me, "Mom, that bullet might have been aimed at me. Death is always around me. I feel it, I practically breathe it, but it never touches me."

I believed him. I wanted to believe that death would never touch him.

Ever since he was killed, I wonder about the source of that confidence. Why did I think Eliraz would live? Why did I think he was protected? I have no answer.

Actually, I do know why. It's what every mother wants for her children – for them to live.

During the Second Lebanon War in July 2006, after I became a widow, something inside me began to doubt. My complete faith that nothing would happen to Eliraz began to crack. My fear grew. I saw the war on television, and this time I felt the great danger that Eliraz was in. I didn't want to worry, but how could I not? I battled with myself. I hung signs at the entrance to the house: "Only good news allowed"; "Announce only happy news here." I wanted to do everything possible to keep the Angel of Death from our house. I was overcome with a feeling of helplessness: what could I do besides write another sign to hang up, light candles, pray, visit Eliezer's grave, pray again, and plead?

At night, I slept with one ear cocked. I prayed I wouldn't hear footsteps or knocks on the door. When a neighbor walked down the sidewalk, I jumped out of bed. I discovered that despite my best intentions, fear seeped into me. It crept under my skin and inhabited each and every cell.

At the height of that war, on the eve of Tisha b'Av, Eliraz's birthday, I dreamed that something terrible happened to him. This was the one and only time that I had a bad dream about him. After the war, when he came home, I asked him, just by the by, if anything had happened to him on that day. His face grew dark. "Yes, Mom. I lost two soldiers. Death was near me."

I had always felt connected to my sons, and this incident only served to intensify my feelings.

When Eliraz returned from the war, I didn't wait for him beside the door. I went out into the street to welcome him home, and I clasped him to me with hugs and kisses. I wanted to kiss every part of his body, inhale his scent. Because he hadn't seen Shlomit for a month, I booked a room for them in a hotel on Mount Zion, overlooking the Western Wall, and I asked the staff to pamper them with all the available comforts. I wanted only for them to be happy. I took Or-Chadash to stay with me, while Hallel Miriam, who was still nursing, remained with her parents. Eliraz arrived in uniform, dusty and filthy, surprised and pleased. Two days of calm.

My qualms did not fade away. Instead, they grew, especially when the Gaza War, or Operation Cast Lead, began in 2008. Eliraz and his younger brother Elyasaf both participated in this war, and my fears doubled. I didn't know who to worry about first. May God protect them, I prayed, trying to be calm. I also thought, Eliraz no longer belongs to me. This time, his wife was the one who had to agree for him to continue his military service.

During this operation, with both of them in Gaza and the images on television too terrible to bear, friends called and asked me why I didn't ask for Elyasaf to be pulled out of Gaza. In their question, I heard a kind of forewarning: "Don't say we didn't warn you." I read about the battles, about the Golani Brigade commander who was wounded, about the soldiers who were killed, and I felt death coming closer to my house. This time, I feared, the signs wouldn't help. At that moment, I needed just one person. I needed to hear his sage advice. I needed Eliezer to help me decide what to do about Elyasaf.

But Eliezer wasn't there.

While I deliberated, I received a phone call from Liat, the officer in charge of wounded soldiers for the Golani Brigade. She reported that the brigade commander was asking whether I wanted to pull Elyasaf out of Gaza, and I felt that the decision over his life was placed in my hands. Once again, I felt helpless. I had to deal with the question all alone. I desperately wanted to hear Eliraz's opinion, but I wasn't able to contact him. What should I do?

That same day, I also received a call from the mother of a friend on Elyasaf's team. She reported that a bomb had fallen next to them, and a few soldiers were wounded. Elyasaf was fine, she said. This information should have pushed me to take Elyasaf away from the horrors, but I knew that had I done so, he would never have forgiven me. I called one of his friends who was wounded in the incident and hospitalized, and simply asked him the fateful question. "What do you think about the possibility of pulling Elyasaf out?" I queried.

The friend answered, "When we see Elyasaf fighting even though he lost his father and his brother, it strengthens us."

At that moment, I decided: my sons would always be in places where they can strengthen others. Still, scenes flashed through my head. What if I asked for Elyasaf to be pulled out from Gaza, and he was wounded while leaving? I would never forgive myself. If something happened to him during the battles, I wouldn't forgive myself either. So I lit a candle, gave *tzedakah*, asked the neighbor to say a blessing for him when he was called up to the Torah, and informed the officer that he could continue fighting.

When Eliraz had a free moment, he sent me a calming message: "Mom, everything's going to be fine." Eliraz and Elyasaf both returned safely from Operation Cast Lead, and we continued our daily routine. Eliraz advanced in rank and became the deputy commander of the 12th Battalion. Again I had the feeling that he was protected and safe. But every once in a while, things happened that put a crack in my sense of security, such as the last Purim he celebrated.

Purim is a merry holiday. As the saying goes, "*Mishenichnas Adar, marbim b'simchah*" (When the month of Adar begins, joy multiplies). I had planned to celebrate in the Golan Heights, at the home of Effi and Illit Eitam, the parents of Avichai, my daughter Hadas's husband. But at the last minute, Eliraz announced he was coming home, and invited us to go to his house. I packed a basket of food and we were on our way. It was pouring rain.

We stopped in Ofra at the home of Hadas and Avichai. Although it was just fifteen minutes away from where Eliraz lived, I called to say we were almost there. As mothers do, I asked, "Is everything ready?" I knew he would invite lots of friends, even though Shlomit had given birth to Gili just two months earlier. I imagined that Eliraz was already home, helping her with the preparations.

"So you're at home?" I asked.

"Close," he replied.

"How close?"

"I'm here, in Gaza."

"What do you mean, in Gaza? You've invited guests, your wife just gave birth, and you're in Gaza? What's going on?"

"Mom, what are you worried about?" he responded. "Everything will be fine. Everything's ready."

We got to their home, I spread out a tablecloth, their friends arrived, but no Eliraz. Some ninety minutes later, he burst into the house like a windstorm, jumping around exuberantly. His arms were loaded with bags, one filled with bottles of wine, the other holding dozens of small containers of salads. In a moment, the table was loaded with all sorts of treats. We sat down to our Purim feast, with Eliraz at the head of the table, while I sat across from him at the other end. We ate and sang, and all of a sudden – in the midst of our raucous joy – he burst into tears. "My brother Uriel! Dad!" he wept.

I broke into chills. I had never seen Eliraz in such a state. I saw that he had sipped a little wine, but he wasn't drunk. His Purim joy turned into a lament for his father and Uriel.

After several long minutes, he calmed down, and then he began to speak. He said something special to each person at the table. He took his *kippah* from his head, placed it on the table, and said to an officer friend, who wasn't religious, "See? This *kippah* can't separate me from you. We are the children of one people. We are brothers, and I love you, my brother, even without a *kippah* on your head."

When he came around to me, Eliraz asked me to sing him his favorite childhood lullaby. I was shocked. My son was thirty-two years old and a father of four. What was going on? I couldn't remember which song he meant. I used to sing lots of lullabies to him and Uriel.

From the head of the table, Eliraz began to sing a tune.

I felt as if he was flying me backwards in a time machine, to a long-ago place. I tried to remember. I began to sing, "The light has been gone for a while / Don't you leave now as well / Come, Mother, come, Mother / Sit with me until I grow up."

I choked on my tears. I realized that he was feeling like a grown-up boy, a father of four who wanted his mother beside him for a while. He wanted me to be with him just a bit longer.

Surprisingly, Eliraz asked me to stop. "What song are you singing?" he demanded. "That's a sad song. 'The light has been gone for a while.' What does that mean? The light's not gone. What a depressing song."

We continued with the meal, and then he focused his big eyes on me and said, "Mom, you know how much I love Dad. Oh, my Dad! And I love you so much. But I'm allowing you to build a new life."

"Enough!" I hushed him. "Stop it!"

But Eliraz insisted on continuing. "Mom, you have to live. You have to be happy."

I couldn't understand where this was coming from. Since his father's death, Eliraz had taken on the role of head of the family. What did he mean by speaking to me about a new life? At that moment, for just a second, a terrible thought flashed in my head: there was something about this occasion that reminded me of a farewell and a dying wish – to keep on living, to rejoice, as the light was not extinguished.

Immediately I repressed that thought, and I told no one about what I had sensed.

"Eliraz," said my daughter Hadas, "you've already spoken to each of us. What do you have to say to Shlomit?"

Eliraz gazed lovingly at his wife. "Between Shlomit and me is a Garden of Eden," he said, without explanation. Shlomit looked at him with love and admiration.

I knew that he was right, it was a Garden of Eden between him and his wife. But that sentence that sounded like a last will continued to gnaw at me.

At that moment, the door opened, and in walked Ro'i Klein's parents. They stared at Eliraz in surprise. They couldn't understand why he was crying or what had happened. At first they thought that maybe he'd been drinking. But Eliraz called to them from the head of the table: "For your brokenness is vast as the sea; who can heal you?"

A drunk would never say such a thing – it's a quotation from the book of Lamentations (2:13) that I adopted as a personal statement when Uriel was killed. But I didn't understand why Eliraz chose to recite it to them. Why had he picked that particular verse? Was he preparing us for another disaster?

I returned home with a heavy feeling. As much as the festive meal had been full of joy, it had left me full of doubts. Had Eliraz been telling me something?

Today, in retrospect, I know that God never surprises us, and He never brings punishment without preparation. The Purim feast, one month before Passover, prepared me to part from Eliraz. As with Uriel, I recalled that the Talmud says that forty days before a person's death, his soul knows that it is about to leave this world. Purim and the Passover Seder are separated by only one month. Was Eliraz's soul already aware?

It was no coincidence that the joy of the holiday was diluted with Eliraz's weeping. That Purim, around the table, was his goodbye to us. The clues he gave us contained clear messages. We'll never know exactly what he meant to say, but I think that when Eliraz told me, "I'm permitting you to build a new life," he may really have been intending this for Shlomit.

Passover approached, and already I felt that I wasn't myself. Usually I'm energetic, cleaning and sorting with a vengeance. Since my days in the immigrant camp and in high school, when I worked as a cleaner, I've been a fanatic cleaner in my own home. I have to get to all the corners. But this time, a heavy sadness had invaded my limbs, and my movements were slow. I caught myself ignoring things, working sloppily. What was wrong with me?

Two weeks before Passover, when Elyasaf and Bat-El were at home, I decided to do something drastic: to open Uriel's boxes. After he was killed, the army had sent me boxes with his personal items. I had opened one box, and pulled out his toothbrush. I had sniffed it, and smelled my son's mouth. I closed the box. I couldn't go on. Now, for some reason, I had the urge to take down those boxes.

This time as well, I opened a box and closed it right away. I couldn't help asking myself why it was suddenly so urgent to open those boxes. Maybe it was an inner voice telling me that I had to make room, because I was about to receive new ones?

"Keep on cleaning. Stop fiddling around with nonsense," I ordered myself, but my hands were heavy, and I felt overcome with melancholy.

On the Friday that Eliraz was killed, Elyasaf woke up and came to me in the kitchen, shaking with fear. "Mom, I want to tell you something," he said.

"What is it, Elyasaf?"

"I had a strange dream," he answered. "I dreamed that you were sitting down in a strange way, sitting down and getting up."

He continued to tell me that over the past few days, all of his dreams had been odd. In one, a Torah scroll fell down in the synagogue.

I was filled with sudden strength. "A good dream, a peaceful dream," I announced, following Moroccan custom. "All will be well. We've booked places for Seder night at Eshel Hashomron Hotel, and Eliraz will come, too." I dropped some coins into the *tzedakah* box that stood on the windowsill.

I asked Elyasaf to help me pack up the year-round *chametz* dishes so they wouldn't get mixed up with the special Passover dishes, and continued to clean and organize. In an attempt to annul Elyasaf's dream, I made extra work for myself, convincing myself that disaster couldn't happen on Passover eve, and that the dream contained no hint about Eliraz. I explained to Elyasaf that his dream might have been related to our dear friend Moshe Elah, the father of Nachum, who had fallen in Lebanon and was buried next to Uriel. At that time, Moshe was fighting for his life, and he died a few weeks after Eliraz was killed.

That day, at three p.m., Eliraz was killed.

I remember the exact time. Bat-El called from the army, we wished each other *Shabbat shalom*, and with the phone in my hand, I banged my head on the door of the kitchen cabinet.

I shouted to Bat-El on the phone: "God, I just hit my head really hard!" and hung up at once.

I clutched my head in my hands and continued to shout, "God, what a bruise! What a bruise!"

I sat down, hands holding my head, and burst into tears.

Avichai and Elyasaf checked my head and said, astonished, "Mom, we can't see any bruise. We don't know what bruise you're talking about."

But I kept wailing. I sat in the corner of the living room on the easy chair, under the photos of Uriel, grasping my head.

Then I calmed down. I was sitting in the same chair in which I had sat when they came to tell me about Uriel. Suddenly, my neighbor Eti walked in. In a few minutes Shabbat would begin, Shabbat Hagadol, the Shabbat before Passover. Why was she coming to my house?

I looked at her, and she looked at me, and we were both silent. Inside, my mind was churning: Why in the world was the neighbor coming to see me on this Friday afternoon? Didn't she have last-minute preparations to do before Shabbat Hagadol began?

She told me about a certain problem, and I calmed her and said that everything would work out fine. Then, in a shocking outburst, without a word from her, I screamed at her: "Have you come to tell me something? Did you want to tell me something about Eliraz?"

I have no idea why I said that to her. Mother's intuition, I guess.

"Eliraz is wounded," she said.

"Thank God!" I said. "Wounded." Like one possessed, I rose from the easy chair to get dressed and go to the hospital. I never imagined that at the top of the stairs outside, just a few yards away, the street was already full of people.

"I know," I said, without being asked. "Eliraz is wounded. I'm getting dressed. Do you by chance know which hospital he's in?"

No one answered. Instead, everyone gave me strange looks.

I tried calling Liat, the contact officer for wounded soldiers, but she didn't answer.

I tried calling Eliraz, but he didn't answer.

I called a few other people in my cellphone contact list, but no one answered. Hadas was the only one who answered, and she said she was checking into what had happened to Eliraz. But Hadas already knew, and she was on her way to tell Shlomit.

Something was tearing at my heart. Why wouldn't anyone answer me?

"What's wrong with everyone!" I shouted.

Then Avichai came in. He had gone to immerse himself in the *mikveh* before Shabbat, and someone had called him. Apparently he already knew.

"Sit down, Mom," he said. "Sit down. They're checking into what's happened to Eliraz."

At that moment, my legs turned into stone. I kept repeating, "Eliraz is wounded, Eliraz is wounded." I repeated this out loud, even though deep inside, I knew that he was dead. It was like I had two minds. One knew the truth, while the other tried to hold on to hope, to illusion.

I prayed to the Holy One, blessed be He, to take me to him.

"My Eliraz is alive. My Eliraz can't die. Eliraz..."

Out of the corner of my eye, I noticed one of our friends, who was then inside the house, peeking outside. I realized he was waiting for the military representatives to come to inform me. Then, like a crazy woman, I ran to the front door, locked it, ran to the back door, and locked it securely as well. I closed all the blinds, and shrieked, "No one's coming inside this house, and no one's leaving, either!"

I stood before the photo of Eliezer that hangs in the entranceway, and wailed, "What have you done to Eliraz! You went up there in order to protect him! I'm here, down here, to watch over all the rest!" I kicked the wall with all my might.

Then I went back to the easy chair and collapsed into it. I knew, and I didn't know. I didn't know, and I knew.

At five thirty, after Shabbat had already begun, when the military representatives arrived, they found the table set for Shabbat, down to the white tablecloth, and the house ready and kosher for Passover. "This is an ordinary house!" I shouted. "A normal house! One family can't lose two sons! Why, God?! Why me?!"

They stood before me, and I closed their lips with my fingers. I begged, "Don't tell me. As long as you haven't said anything, my son is still alive."

They tried to speak. After all, it's their job. I knew that the three angels had visited Abraham to announce that his wife Sarah would give birth to a son, while my three angels had come to inform me once again that I no longer had a son.

"Maybe you've got the wrong address?" I suggested. "Or the wrong last name? It doesn't make sense for two sons from the same home, from the same family, to be killed." Not that I wanted another mother to receive the terrible news; I simply couldn't believe that such a disaster could take place.

I wouldn't let them speak.

"Miriam," one of them said, trying to pull my hand away from his mouth. "I have to do this."

"Please, tell me he's wounded," I wailed. "Gravely wounded…"

Even when they read me the prepared text that they have to say, I screamed, "I don't believe it!"

Then I called Shlomit, Eliraz's wife.

"Shlomit," I said, "There are people here saying that something's happened to Eliraz. What's happened to him?"

Shlomit replied with words that I'll never forget: "Now I'm like you."

"No!" I cried. "You won't be like me! You won't be a widow!"

Then I understood. My son Eliraz was no more.

From that point on, I don't remember who came in or what they said. Only one memory remains in my mind: the announcement. When Uriel was killed, I wondered how they had informed Eliraz. Now Bat-El had to be told. She was a soldier in the education corps. Who would tell her? How would she receive the news? Who would be the one to rip a hole in her life once again? The same story, the same announcement, once again. Was I hallucinating?

On Friday, March 26, 2010, [female] combat lookout soldiers stationed with the Kisufim Battalion observed two terrorists planting an explosive device alongside the border fence, south of the main road to Gush Katif. Major Eliraz Peretz, deputy commander of the Golani Brigade's 12th Battalion, rushed forces to the site, sent out tanks that fired at the terrorists, and moved the medical and mortar teams to the hill that controlled the area from above. These teams fired at the terrorists and stopped them in their tracks.

Eliraz identified the explosive, took a team from one of the companies, and outflanked the terrorists from the northwest, intending to make contact and neutralize them. When the team approached the terrorists, heavy fire was directed at them from the houses in Gaza. They did not stop. The force continued to advance, hitting and killing one terrorist. As Eliraz reported on the radio, "Contact," the second terrorist stood up and fired a round that hit a grenade in Eliraz's bulletproof vest. The grenade blew up. Eliraz and Staff Sergeant Ilan Sviatkovsky (21, from Rishon LeZion), were killed on the spot.

CHAPTER 19

Forgive Me, My Sons

On the eve of Yom Hazikaron 5770 (2010), less than a month after Eliraz died, I was asked to write a piece about my feelings:

Uriel and Eliraz, my life's joy, and my heart's grief.
Forgive me, my beloved children.
Forgive me that I am here, continuing without you.
Life grasps onto me, it grips me by force and doesn't release me.
I don't know why. Why me?
I'm a mother like all other mothers,
Hoping for her children's success, health, and safety.
Like all mothers – afraid, worried, hurting.
Forgive me, Uriel, my oldest son.
This year, I won't stand before your grave on Yom Hazikaron.
I've done it for twelve years, half of them with Dad beside me,
Along with Eliraz,
Who salutes you, and silently shouts:
My brother, my beloved!
I'm sure you already know that Eliraz, your brother
Whom you so loved and admired,
Whom you called "champ,"

The one you always told me was better than you –
Your brother Eliraz has joined you.
This year I'll stand beside him, because he needs me.
He's new in your section.
He has to get used to the dark, the earth.
You know, I never played favorites with you.
I always sat between the two of you.
With my right hand, I stroked your golden locks,
While with the left hand, I smoothed Eliraz's kinky curls.
A hug on the right, a hug on the left
Always together, with one mother.
Now I'll stand at a distance. Four yards separate you from Eliraz.
I'll gaze at you from behind Eliraz's grave.
I know you'll allow me.
I hear your voice saying,
"Mom, my younger brother Eliraz needs you now. I'll be fine.
I permit you, Mother,
Permit you to be with Eliraz for more time.
And when you're finished, when you've poured out your heart, your pain, Mother,
Come to me for a little while, because I need you, too.
Because a mother's embrace is never forgotten.
Maybe with me, you'll find some small comfort.
I'll give you a big hug and say,
'Don't worry, Mom, I'm here,
I showed him the way, I paved the road for him.'
Mom, I'm here for him, with Dad.
Dad's waiting with the tallit, his two hands stretched out toward our heads to bless us:

'May the Lord bless you and keep you...and grant you
peace.'
And you, dear Mother, you must continue
The life of a mother
For yourself, for Avichai, Elyasaf, Hadas, and Bat-El,
For Shlomit and Eliraz's children whom I did not know,
For me, and for Eliraz."
And I, your mother, will forever hear the voice bursting
from your tiny cradle, from your grave.
I'll always hear the lullaby you loved to hear before bed:
"The light has been gone for a while;
Don't you leave now as well.
Come, Mother, come, Mother,
Sit with me until I grow up."
Hugging, kissing, loving
and continuing,
Mom
On another occasion, inspired by Seder night, I wrote:
Two sons
One military plot
And one mother
Standing before them
In silence.
Two sons
One military plot
One people
And one precious, beloved land
One God and one prayer
If only comfort would arrive.

PART FIVE

My Family Tells Their Story

CHAPTER 20

Hadas Peretz Eitam

I remember both of them together and each one separately, but whenever I feel that I'm giving one of them less room in my memory, I direct my thoughts to Dad. Because Dad is the essence, he's the heart. He unites them both up there, and us down here.

I remember both of them, miss both of them, and talk to both of them. But when I talk to them, there's a difference. I didn't have the opportunity to live with Uriel. There's a gap of eight years between us, and when I grew up and wanted my oldest brother, he was studying away from home, in the premilitary academy. So I mainly remember the excitement we felt when we went to see him for a ceremony or a visit. But with Eliraz, I lived a full life. I fought with him and laughed with him. I see him before me with his long hair and *sharwal* pants, searching for himself along the paths of Judaism, and I see him becoming more religious. If I had the opportunity to get angry at him, that means I had the opportunity to live with him. I didn't have a chance to get angry at Uriel; I only had a small taste of him.

Unlike Uriel and Eliraz, who breathed the dunes and the ocean of Sharm from birth, I was born in Givon. My two older brothers were bosom buddies, the two oldest kids in the family. Avichai and Elyasaf also grew up together. Bat-El got the position of the baby in the family. I was third in the birth order, so I was always somewhere in the middle. We all resemble each other, and we're all different from one another. That's the strongest characteristic of our family: a hundred and one contrasts that together make up the whole.

With Mom it's very clear. She's black and white in the same dosage – she laughs and cries in the same breath, talks about life and death with the same love. Dad was also a rare combination – on the one hand, a decisive, opinionated man, and on the other, gentle and loved by all. He was the *gabbai* of the synagogue, while his wife was the principal of a secular school.

Uriel, my eldest brother, was a complex person. He knew how to lead, but he also knew how to speak to each individual in his own language. I learned from Uriel that each person has different sides that can exist together, without contradiction. That knowledge enabled me to grow boundlessly. On the surface, things seemed simpler with Eliraz: he was a person of black or white, with no middle or compromise. But at the same time, he had a sensitivity and softness that deepened during the years when he became a husband and father. This is the "unification of opposites" that Rabbi Kook writes of, that is clearly expressed in each and every member of the Peretz family.

On the day Uriel was killed, I remember the moment we climbed the steps outside the house that lead up to the street. Uriel was waiting beside the house in the casket, in the military jeep, and the trip to Mount Herzl was long and slow. In a way, that endless trip was even harder than the funeral. The soldiers rode in front of us and my brother was being taken to be buried. How was it that life continued to flow, the stoplights continued to change, cars stopped at the checkpoint, people walked on the sidewalks, and the doors of the shops opened and closed? These were the questions that passed through my head.

Even before Uriel was buried, I realized I'd have to cross all of Jerusalem and follow this road every time I wanted to visit my oldest brother. The same questions hammered at me when Eliraz was killed. Once again, the military jeep would pull up? Once again, we'd ride behind it? Once again, we'd sit shivah? Where would we find the strength? We had the strength, period. Strength is something internal that you're not aware exists inside you until the moment you have to use it. We didn't overcome, because we were never defeated.

That's the characteristic of this home. That's the greatness of this nation. You can't really fall, because there's something much bigger than you that drives you and carries you with it. I live in the knowledge that even if suffering comes, this strength will always be an available resource that will enable me to survive it. Death becomes an expression of a personal worldview that helps you to live, not just go through the motions.

I believe that if Uriel hadn't been killed, I wouldn't have reached this understanding at such a young age. Most people reach it at a much later stage in life, but I guess I had to grow up early.

Uriel was killed, Eliraz went back to the army, and I, the oldest daughter, stayed at home. My brothers Avichai and Elyasaf bounced around and searched for themselves, while I was the sister who worried and watched over them, a kind of extension of the parental unit. I constantly had my eyes on them to see how they were doing and what they were up to.

I was then in ninth grade at Or Torah in the Ramot neighborhood of Jerusalem, but after Uriel was killed, I decided to switch to the *ulpana* (girls' religious high school) in Ofra, which had a dormitory living arrangement. I felt that I needed to make a change. In fact the best period of my life was spent there.

After Uriel was killed, I asked why – because everyone was asking why, because we had to ask, not because I understood the significance of the question. Still, after Uriel died, and years later, even after I buried Dad and Eliraz, I always had thoughts about faith, about life. I love God very much, and believe in Him strongly and trust in Him.

Because of this attitude, I didn't become bitter or angry. God has also done many good things for me in life. What I see in front of me are only portions of reality – physical, material parts – and I believe that reality includes many other parts that will never be revealed to human beings. Every time something good happens to me, I still look for Dad. It's a habit that comes from love, and now I try to get used to the fact that I see him only in my thoughts. My mental powers seem to be much more real than my reality, which is lacking. I don't mean that questions are futile. They are natural and logical. But if they don't take you anywhere, then they are empty and hollow.

As a believing person, I accept God's decisions even when they seem hard to understand. Instead of torturing myself with questions that will never be solved, I have to focus my mental energy on how to live with them in the best possible manner. After you've buried three loved ones, the survival effect is intensified. The true battle is to transform survival into development, which is much more than just how to get through the day. This is our true battle, and each one of us struggles with it, every single day, in his own way and with his own resources.

I did my National Service as a youth counselor at Yemin Orde Youth Village, on Mount Carmel in the north. I felt energetic and positive. The new landscape, the mountains and the sea, had a positive effect on me. I fell in love with the kids, new immigrants and children from difficult family backgrounds. I was particularly entranced by the ideology of the place, which focuses on repairing the soul as the key to repairing the world.

After National Service, I went to Bar-Ilan University to study educational counseling and Hebrew literature. I lived in the dorms and tried to adapt to the student lifestyle, but it wasn't really me. Looking for a new direction, I filled out an application for a position as a counselor at Ahuzat Sarah, a home for children, some of whom have been removed from their homes by court order. I turned in the forms, but reality forced me to forget this idea.

Dad died.

Then, toward the end of the *shloshim*, the thirty-day mourning period, I received a letter asking me to come in for an interview. I went, but after the interview, I began to have doubts. On one hand, I very much wanted to move into the children's home – both because of the important, challenging work, and also because I had told Dad that I wanted to work there, and he had been supportive. On the other hand, how could I leave home? It was Mom who encouraged me to continue with my plans. She knew that for me, it would be the fulfillment of a dream. I decided to take the job. I went to live at Ahuzat Sarah as a counselor for the ninth-grade girls, while continuing my studies at Bar-Ilan.

At the end of my third year at the university, I went back home to live, and it was not an easy adjustment. I think any person who has experienced two years of independence feels strange when he comes home, but for me it was particularly difficult. To return home and not to see Dad standing in the doorway, with a smile and a hug, was to return to a different home.

Noa, my soul sister, called and said, "There's someone I want you to meet. You know his father, he's easy to talk to, and he has the same name as your brother." I agreed, and that's how I met Avichai, who was an officer in the Egoz special forces unit of Golani at the time.

After Uriel was killed, I asked myself how I could marry a boy who hadn't known him, and after Dad died, I wondered how I could marry someone who had never known my father. But my father-in-law, Effi Eitam (former government minister and IDF division commander) knew them both: he had been Uriel's division commander, and he had been sitting in the war room when

Uriel went out on his last mission. Effi had been with us during the shivah. He knew my father, and helped us bring the first Torah scroll dedicated in Uriel's memory to the synagogue in Atzmona.

I viewed this is as the hand of fate. I felt that my father, up above, had arranged to send me Avichai, whose family knew ours.

The first time Mom heard about my boyfriend, she couldn't believe it. When belief finally settled in, she radiated joy.

We were married one week before Uriel's memorial ceremony, and one year later, our first child, a girl, was born. After the birth we went to Mom's house, and the joy of the *zeved habat* naming ceremony for our daughter was intermingled with the memorial for Uriel. We decided to name her Aluma, which means "beam of light," because she was born on the eve of Chanukah, the Festival of Lights. Her name also means "sheaf," which binds together and unites the family.

As of this writing, Avichai is studying at Har Hamor Yeshivah in Jerusalem, and I work as an educational counselor at a school in Kfar Adumim.

In my opinion, Mom is larger than life. When she speaks, there's not a dry eye in the room, and people – from youth and soldiers to bereaved families – draw strength and inspiration from her. In the endless talks she gives, at a frequency that sometimes seems extreme to me as I worry that it might ruin her health, she is shaping the next generation of Israel's youth. But we are the only ones who know that in addition to all her qualities, she is the best grandma in the world. The grandchildren are like a beam of light for her, as they give her the strength to continue.

CHAPTER 21

Avichai Peretz

Sometimes I look back and ask myself, how did we get to this point? Never in my wildest dreams did I ever imagine that at my age I would have buried two brothers and a father. In those moments when reality explodes with a series of disasters that seems so illogical, an illusory thought crosses my mind – maybe it didn't really happen? Maybe it's just a bad film? Maybe tomorrow morning I'll wake up and see Dad drinking coffee in the kitchen, Uriel will ask me about my army reserve duty, and Eliraz will ask if I'm working hard in my studies?

I yearn for these images. It's not longing, because longing comes from an absence. Rather, I yearn for what still exists in my imagination. I get carried away, and I imagine how life could have been different. I see Uriel accompanying me to the induction center. Eliraz flips through my schoolbooks, punches me on the shoulder, and says, "Great, bro', I knew you would study." And Dad hugs all three of us in a wide embrace.

Imagination is deceptive, and coming down to earth is painful. These are things that won't happen, because it happened. I put aside the question of why, because there's no answer to it. Even faith and Judaism have no explanation for this, and so I have to move forward, look ahead. Until the next time my imagination overcomes me and tries to sell me an illusion.

Twelve years ago, when I was thirteen and a half, I encountered death for the first time. I remember my bar mitzvah as a happy occasion. Uriel came to the synagogue, head bald underneath his *kippah* – he had shaved his head so that his hair wouldn't get in the way of wearing a helmet. Eliraz, who was about to be inducted, still had long curls. Golden curls.

Our family is divided into pairs: Uriel and Eliraz, Elyasaf and me. Mom says that Elyasaf is like Eliraz, because he is gentle and sensitive, while I resemble Uriel, a bit more severe and harsh. But in my opinion, that's not accurate. Uriel was a pillar of support. He was an impressive presence everywhere he went. Despite the difference in ages between the first pair of boys and the second, we always followed them to the wadis and the springs. On Shabbat, we would hike together from Givat Ze'ev to Nabi Samuel. Uriel was far more than an older brother to me. He was a myth, a model to be admired. The fact that he went off to boarding school at a young age didn't undermine his authority at home.

Once, when I was disrespectful to our parents, he took me into his room, closed the door, and said, "Avichai, you can't talk like that. You have to listen." Although he was angry at me, I was grateful, because his rebuke helped me understand that I wasn't listening to others enough. To this day, on certain occasions I still hear his voice encouraging me to listen.

We had endless conversations about the army. I would tease him: "Hey, Uriel, don't those thorns hurt? Don't your legs hurt?" The silly questions of a curious child. He wouldn't answer, he would just smile. His smile said everything. Eventually, when I went out on dangerous missions and someone would come and slap me on the shoulder, I wouldn't speak either, I would only smile. Not because I wanted to imitate Uriel, but because I had nothing to say. When your ideology is clear, there's no need for words, and a smile is a kind of answer – naïve, perhaps, but one that comes from inside.

The night Uriel was killed, Elyasaf and I were sleeping beside each other on mattresses on the floor. I don't know what possessed us to sleep that way on that specific night, but we were close, and it was fun. Out of a deep sleep, I heard Mom screaming, "Wake up! Wake up! Uriel's been killed!" I rubbed my eyes, I didn't understand what was going on. Was it a horror film? Could I return to the mattress and to my dreams?

I went down to the first floor and saw Mom sitting in the easy chair. Dad was sitting in a side room with the military officer. Even before I got downstairs, my eyes focused on a package standing on the table in the dining area. The package we hadn't yet sent, with Uriel's birthday present inside. I didn't want to speak with anyone. I didn't want reality to get too close to me. I wanted to stay inside the dream I had been dreaming seconds earlier. Why wake up?

During the shivah and the time that followed, my parents were attentive to me and encouraged me to talk, but I wasn't able to express myself. As a boy of thirteen and a half, it seemed to me that they were living with Uriel too deeply. I saw Mom crying, I saw Dad walking back and forth by the walls with the photos, and I felt out of touch. The pain of a bereaved brother is very isolating. The parents and the widow are the ones at the center of attention, and you're pushed to the side. You learn to live at the side. But what do you do there? I felt that I was just marking time, not really living life.

Uriel's death created a serious conflict for me with God. I talked to Him like a child. "Listen," I said to Him, "I don't deserve this punishment. Maybe I haven't done anything special and deserving of reward, but I also haven't done anything so terrible to deserve such a punishment." At the time I was studying in a religious high school in Ramot. I felt that I had to rebel, because if I didn't act out, I wouldn't be able to continue functioning.

I asked to switch to a secular school, "Tel Aviv" High School in Jerusalem. My parents agreed to my request, but there as well, I wasn't a great student. I couldn't sit still. I had my own car, and I used it to skip out to the beach, where I would sit and read. I swallowed tons of books. Or else I would just drive around.

A few times, I ran into my father in the streets of Jerusalem. Maybe he came to look for me, maybe it was just coincidence. Dad knew that I was skipping school, but he never got angry at me. Mom was the one who disciplined us. She has the personality of a principal, while Dad was much gentler. Even when he caught me in the act, he would say, "Come, let's go have lunch," and he'd take me out to a restaurant. He knew that I was bit wild, and that shouting and punishments wouldn't help; I needed time in order to mature.

Somehow I got through high school, although I didn't finish all the coursework. I knew that in other circumstances, I would have put more into it. Then I went to the premilitary academy in Atzmona – to fight my own fight, to search, hoping that I would learn to understand myself better. I knew that my attitude was hurtful to Dad, but I couldn't lie to myself. I went there saying to myself, "I'm here by mistake. I'm on my way to becoming an atheist. To me, all is vanity of vanities. Prove me wrong." I was also different from everyone else in my outward appearance: the others dressed like religious guys, while I looked like a secular kid, in faded jeans.

Eliraz bought me sandals that were suitable for the sand in Atzmona, and we drove down to the academy together. When I went in for my interview with Rabbi Rafi Peretz, and heard the conversations among the boys, I felt like even more of an outsider. Each guy went in for his interview and tried to convince the rabbi to accept him. I went in and announced with complete straightforwardness: "I don't know why I'm here. If you want me to come study here, convince me." I didn't try to ingratiate myself or play a role. In retrospect, I discovered that it was my honesty that impressed him. I was accepted.

I spent one year at Atzmona, which was an amazing place: the sands of Gush Katif; the long, gorgeous sunsets; the palm trees waving in the breeze beside the ocean; the quiet and the calm broken by the sounds of mortars and Kassam rockets. I'm deeply attached to the ocean. Every morning I went down to the beach, surfed, and swam with the fish. When I went to class, I mainly studied about King Solomon and read the Song of Songs. It talks a lot about love, and that's what I was looking for during that time – love for Judaism, love for the reality of Israel.

My searches were difficult and exhausting, but every spark of love that I found helped me to connect to myself, to my existence within this reality. It enabled me to better understand Uriel's death. I told God that I was closing the account between us, and that from then on, I would accept everything He gave me with gratitude and love. The academy motivated me to move from indifference to action, and I decided I wanted to enlist. But first came the evacuation.

I call it "evacuation," not "uprooting." You can't uproot the Land of Israel from my heart, and no one can uproot Gush Katif from inside me. I still live it, and it still lives within me. I hear the waves, I see the foam on their crests, and the landscape is implanted deep within me. I believe that the evacuation is a stage in our history, and that in the end it will lead us to a better place, a place where the most popular prayer in Judaism will be fulfilled: *oseh shalom bimromav* – "May He who makes peace in His heights make peace upon us and all of Israel." This is what every person wants: peace.

At that time, Eliraz was on the battlefield, with Golani forces guarding a line in Gaza and securing the evacuation. I knew he was near the academy. Every once in a while, he would pop over to Atzmona, and we would study together, or else he would take me for a ride around the settlement of Neve Dekalim, or we would go diving. We had many wonderful moments together there. Once

I rode a bicycle to his outpost, despite the danger, and brought him something tasty to eat. I knew that as long as my brother was commander of the region, no one could touch us. We were safe.

When the time came, there was no need to evacuate me by force. I left of my own free will. The entire academy left willingly, accepting the government's decision. The soldier who gave me his hand and led me outside was one of my best friends, a combat soldier in the Duvdevan elite unit, a religious boy. We both wept, and our weeping was unrestrainable, the kind of weeping that is most similar to mourning.

I returned home knowing that an important chapter in my life had ended, and I was broken, shattered. Mom led me to bed so I could lie down and sleep, and I saw the pain in her eyes and in Dad's. To them, it was a grim replay of the evacuation from Sharm. What do all parents wish for their children? To avoid the troubles they have experienced. "They evacuated us from Sharm so that you would have a better life" – this was the hope deep in their hearts, and this was the source of their disappointment.

The tragic journey worsened when I took Dad for a checkup in the hospital, and they discovered that his cancer had returned. On the drive home, I wore sunglasses so that Dad wouldn't see me crying, but I'm sure he noticed anyway. Dad was a soul mate to me, a friend and a brother, and to this day I can't understand how he did it – how he was able to remain my authority figure and mentor, and also play the part of my best friend in the whole world. It's amazing to me how these two contrasting roles could exist in one person, but that's how he was.

When we arrived home, I got out of the car before him so I would be the one to tell Mom that he was sick again. She was silent, and her silence echoed in my ears. We were already well acquainted with that frightening quiet that comes from helplessness. I had heard it before, when Uriel was killed. So what did this mean? Was another disaster coming our way? Was death looking for our family again?

The day before the operation, I told Dad that I wanted to sleep over at the hospital with him. But fifteen minutes later, Mom called and said she was afraid to stay in the house alone. This was during the renovations, and doors and windows hadn't yet been installed. Dad said, "Go home and help your mother. She's afraid to be alone with the construction workers." I didn't like this, as I preferred to remain with him, but Dad insisted. The next day, around twelve noon, Mom called and told me that the operation had been successful. Fifteen minutes later, she called again. "Come quick, Dad's in critical condition."

I didn't understand. What had happened during that quarter of an hour? I didn't have a car, so I went out of the house and began to run. I reached the gates of Givat Ze'ev, and a neighbor stopped for me. In retrospect, I assume Mom had called her and asked her to pick me up. She drove me to Jerusalem, and on Begin Boulevard, we got stuck in a traffic jam. Every second that passed rattled my nerves: How could I sit in the car when my dad was fighting for his life? I decided to get out. I crossed the street like a madman, and was hit by a car coming in the opposite direction. I stood up in terrible pain and massaged my leg. Later we discovered that the car had hit my right leg and cracked my femur. I kept running.

I got to the gate of Shaare Zedek Hospital and began to climb over it. The guard ran over to me. He quickly realized I wasn't a terrorist, and that every second of delay might keep me from being with my father in his last moment. Finally, I entered the hospital, but the elevator was in use. So I ran up the stairs, to the tenth floor. Only then did I stop to take a breath. I couldn't enjoy breathing, as Mom rushed toward me crying, and said that Dad was in critical condition. His life was in danger.

I saw my uncle sitting on a bench, reciting Psalms. Dad's room was full of people, doctors rushed in and out. One of them came out to us and reported that his status was fatal. A few minutes later another doctor came out and said, "He has a problem with a muscle in the heart, it's torn." "What does that mean?" Mom asked. Only then did the doctor admit that Dad was dead. I understand the doctor's way, as he had treated Dad for many years, and he had also known Uriel. He was trying to deliver the news in a roundabout manner, because he didn't know how to say it directly.

Again there was a moment of silence. I actually felt my breath taken away. "Please, no," I begged God. In the space of a moment, I once again became that little boy asking Him not to take his oldest brother.

Then we all went into Dad's room. His eyes were already closed. I held his hand, and my sister Hadas slipped her hand into Dad's armpit, which was still warm, and we both absorbed his warmth. When I had a moment alone with him, I asked him to forgive me for all the bad things I had done, and told him how much I loved him.

The funeral was enormous. He was brought to the synagogue he had built, that was named after Uriel. I saw hundreds of people I didn't know who came to pay their last respects, because he was a man of good deeds and anonymous giving. I gave a eulogy for him in the synagogue, and said that I had lost not only a father, but a dear friend, a person who encompassed all the characteristics that express human intimacy.

We recited Kaddish – Eliraz, Elyasaf, and I – and then the funeral began. We stayed in the synagogue, because this is the custom in Jerusalem – the sons don't follow their father. The explanation for this is that when a son follows his father's funeral bier, it's as if the son is demanding his portion of the inheritance. But if the sons absolve the father on earth, he will be absolved in heaven as well. I accepted this with understanding, as part of my agreement with God. Dad was no longer; he was buried.

We sat shivah in the synagogue hall. The three of us – Eliraz, Elyasaf, and I – wept like little kids. I didn't ask myself why God had struck me again or whether He was testing me once more. For three days I was silent, I didn't say a word. Mom pushed me: "Talk, let it out." But I couldn't. I wrapped myself in a wall of silence, and with that silence, I continued onward, and I'm still continuing. Six weeks later, I was inducted into the army.

I decided to join the Golani special forces unit, because Golani is courage; it's a combination of simplicity and power. I knew that Golani was for the bad boys in school, not the outstanding students, but the ones with a youthful innocence that pushed them to attack with all their might and protect the state. The symbol for Golani is a tree and earth, roots that connect us to this place.

Mom didn't try to stop me. Dad had signed his permission before he died, and she didn't retract it. "I won't prevent you from doing what you want," she said, and I heard the worry in her voice. After burying a son and a husband, she couldn't tell me directly that she was encouraging me to endanger my life. But in between the lines, I could also hear her pride.

I went to Golani hiding my pain. I didn't want people pointing at me, saying that I was "the brother of…" and "the son of." I wanted to be ordinary Avichai, to achieve things honestly, on my own merits. I passed basic training and the special forces unit tryout course. I began the course, and after four months, I was wounded. I had a nerve problem, and my medical profile was lowered to 64, a non-combatant ranking. I was the most miserable soldier in the IDF. I was heartbroken. Me, with a profile of 64?

They sent me to serve as intelligence NCO at the Golani Brigade training base. The commander of the special forces training school, who had been a friend of Uriel's in the premilitary academy, assigned me to be his signal operator. I spent five months there, all the while trying to raise my medical profile. During that time, I completed all the requirements to become a combat soldier, and when my commanding officer was appointed deputy commander of the Golani Brigade's 13th battalion, we blurred the military classifications a bit. On paper I was his signal operator, but in practice, I was a combat soldier in every way, despite the 64.

During training on the Golan Heights, I climbed Mount Hermon, just as Uriel had done, and reached Adi Lookout, where his soldiers had placed a rock from the place where he had been killed – Tzivoni outpost, which Israel had returned to Lebanon. This is a custom of "Golanchikim," Golani soldiers – to take a big rock from the site of a soldier's death. From Adi Lookout, I climbed up to Tziporen outpost, where I had a view of the exact place where my oldest brother's life had been cut off.

After countless medical committee hearings and visits to private specialists, as well as putting pressure on the decision makers, I succeeded in pushing my profile back up. It was very important to me to raise it, so that no one could say that since I had a profile of 64, I couldn't be a combat soldier. After maneuvers in the northern part of the country, I went down to Gaza. Lieutenant Colonel Rassan Elian, who was deputy commander of the Golani Brigade, was then given command of the Golani special forces unit, and after observing my performance in several operations, he asked me to return to the unit with him as signal operator.

On the eve of Tisha b'Av, Mom and Eliraz came to the Gaza border to bring me some home-cooked food. Mom was Mom – she worried I wouldn't have anything to eat after the fast. I was then serving in Kisufim Outpost, the post from which Eliraz went out on his last mission. He and I sat and talked: "What's going on, bro'? What's up?" Eliraz was studying at the time, as part of his army training, and I allowed myself to have a bit of fun at his expense. "You're just a 'jobnik' – a desk jockey," I ribbed him, "while I'm the signal operator for the deputy battalion commander." All in the spirit of fun, of course.

A day later, eight terrorists approached the fence. We were waiting for them; we knew they were coming. I hit two of them and neutralized them. When I went home for Hadas's engagement party, the groom's father, Effi Eitam, came up to me. He had already heard what had happened. He hugged me and said that the encounter was a kind of test, and that no combat soldier could know how he would perform until the moment of truth arrived. I didn't smile as Uriel used to do when I was a kid, but deep inside I was pleased, as I had succeeded in foiling the terrorists' plan to harm civilians. I was very sorry to have spilled blood, but I was happy to be protecting my country, my homeland, and that the moment I was put to the test, I performed honorably.

I served in that area for a long time, with many good people. The commander of the 13th battalion asked me to remain with him as signal operator until my release from the army. But I decided to follow in my brothers' footsteps: I returned to the special forces unit, which was then stationed at Mishmar Hanegev, and went on dozens of missions in the Gaza Strip.

On the mission before my last one in Gaza, I met up with Elyasaf, who had finished the training course just a few weeks earlier. I helped him organize his gear in preparation for his first mission in Gaza, and then the question arose of whether two brothers should or could go on the same mission. We both thought of Mom, and we decided that I should be the one to go out, since I was more experienced. But because he had arrived by bus and I had come in a different vehicle, luck was on our side and the commanders didn't notice that we were both at the staging ground, the place from which the soldiers go out on missions.

When we got off the bus, I put the gear on Elyasaf, attached the straps of his helmet, and did a meticulous job on his camouflage paint, smearing his face thoroughly. Then I stuffed a handful of candies in his pocket and gave him a kiss. "Good luck, bro,'" I said. "Good luck, bro,'" he replied.

I began to march. In the Golani special forces, the fighters don't wear rank insignias, to give everyone the feeling that we're all equal. But I knew that I was in front and Elyasaf was walking behind me, with the younger members of the team. It was a crazy scene. We had grown up together, matured together, and now we were fighting together. How lucky we were that Mom was already in bed sleeping. She had no idea what we were doing.

In June 2008, I flew to Toronto, Canada, as part of a mission of IDF fighters sent to strengthen the ties of Jewish youth with their Jewish heritage and the Land of Israel. When I returned to Israel two months later, I participated in a major operation up north. Afterwards, I went to Givat Haviva, to study for the matriculation exam in mathematics.

When I realized that the exam would be on the date of Uriel's memorial ceremony, I decided not to miss it, because to me, all of life is a test. I took the exam while the rest of the family was with Uriel on Mount Herzl. I felt that my oldest brother was part of my life, and that he was beside me during the test.

I was discharged from the army on December 8, 2009, and began to integrate into ordinary civilian life. But six weeks later, one of my best friends, Dvir Emanuelof, also from Givat Ze'ev, was killed. The well-known Israeli song "We're from the Same Village" wasn't written specifically about us, but it certainly expresses what we had together. Dvir was about to be released from the army when he was sent on Operation Cast Lead. I was completely shattered. I didn't know how I could go on.

During the shivah for Dvir, I gathered all our buddies in our home and said that we had to do something in his memory. We decided to establish a library and study hall in his name at the Bnei Akiva branch in Givat Ze'ev. We collected tens of thousands of shekels, and on Jerusalem Day, five months after Dvir was killed, we held the opening ceremony. I felt that I had done something with my own hands to memorialize Dvir, who in life had given me more than I had given him.

When this task was finished, I decided that I needed a vacation, a kind of escape. I announced that I was going to travel in South America for ten months. Mom didn't tell me no, but she did ask me to try to make my trip a bit shorter. She gave me a letter that I kept in my wallet, and every time I read it, I cried. This is what she wrote:

My precious son Avichai,

You're already on the plane. A long period of preparation has come to an end. There were tensions, there was pressure, but it's all over and the time has come. I won't lie – it's not easy for me. The house is empty without you. You breathe life into our home. Even when we have our disagreements, I never forget and I'll never deny the wonderful position you occupy in our home, as my right hand. Always offering help, always active, a true leader. Sometimes we have our differences about the right way of doing things, but we've never disagreed on the goal.

You set yourself a special goal, the room for Dvir. You showed initiative, leadership, organizational skills, and that's not all. Some may think that you're rough around the edges like me, but you have a very sensitive heart. When you thanked everyone, you didn't forget to mention Mother. I see you, and I see myself. We're both focused on the goal.

Now you've set yourself a new goal. Go in peace, enjoy the wide world and the adventures you'll have on the way. Collect experiences, landscapes, impressions.

Do what I didn't have the opportunity to do, but am privileged to have my son do. Just as you told me "I'm releasing you," I'm also releasing you – setting you free to a life of happiness and enjoyment. Enough of memorial ceremonies, funerals, and grief. It's time for fun and joy, for new learning.

I'm certain that you'll return a different Avichai, because your journey isn't to South America. Your journey is to yourself. South America isn't the destination. The important thing is the path. All of our life is one long journey – to Canada, to South America, to Gaza. Especially on foreign soil, you must be proud of your roots, the roots you acquired at home, from me, from Dad, and from your brothers.

Look after yourself. Don't believe everything you're told. Be careful, don't be a wise guy. Remember, we're waiting for you at home. We're waiting for you to recite Kiddush and the Havdalah blessings when Shabbat is over, for your presence. Don't put me to another test. Take good care of your body and your soul. I'll pray from afar for your safe return, but the responsibility is all yours.

You're going off to freedom and fun, but there's no meaning in any freedom if you don't have anyone to share it with. I'm here for you, the family's here for you. You're flying away from us, and you'll come back to us.

There's one thread that connects us, the thread of love. The thread is very long now – sixteen hours by plane and many days in South America. Every time you miss us, pull that thread toward you, and we'll be with you. And every time I miss you, and it's already happening, I'll pull it toward me.

Go in peace, my dear beloved son. I'm pleased for you, but your temporary absence is painful. Go, breathe the air, fill yourself with the joy of the world, and come home to our family nest in order to build your own family nest.

Waiting for you, missing you, and already looking forward to your return,

Mom

I answered her in a letter that she saved:

What's up, Mom? How are you feeling?

I'm halfway through the trip, and I thought it would be nice to write you something. Just so you'll know that I'm the same. I'm returning the same as when I left. There's no change in my outlook on life – the trivial remains trivial and the significant remains significant. The values of nation and homeland, giving, and the family remain in their unshakeable place, just as you taught me, you and Dad. You are both so precious to me, very precious. You are always in my heart, in the special place that belongs to you, and only you. A place that no one can ever occupy, a gentle place that is the source of all my emotional strength.

Dear Mother, I love you so much. More than that – I don't love you with an ordinary, simple love as a son loves his mother. I love you much more. All this is because I know your greatness and your strengths. I love you from my heart, but more importantly, I love you with my head.

You are the one in whose womb I swam, who nourished me with your blood, whose breath was mine. You are the one who gave birth to me, who nursed me. You watched my first steps and heard my first words. You held me safe in your arms, you were with me through daycare and preschool, when I started first grade and graduated from high school, and when I completed my studies at the Atzmona academy. You were with me in the army, at Mount Dov and Adi Lookout, in Lebanon, Shechem, and Gaza.

You were there as I initiated my first project, the library in memory of our beloved Dvir. Now you're with me here in these foreign lands, which are beautiful, but have no soul. (I picture you crying now.)

I was with you as well. I was with you when Uriel was killed, I was with you when Dad died, I was at your side when you were sick, weak from always being strong, and I was beside you when you stood up again on your sturdy, resolute feet.

You are my mother, Miriam Ohayon Peretz, the Moroccan. You made aliyah to Israel without a penny, during a period of ugly, baseless ethnic prejudice that made things even more difficult, yet you didn't give up. You worked as a cleaner, you supported your family, you took care of your parents and siblings, and in addition to all that, you also earned a university degree. You met Dad, got married, and gave birth to a little boy named Uriel, about whom much more remains to be said. After him came Eliraz, Hadas, me, and little Elyasaf and Bat-El.

You and Dad raised and educated us in simplicity. You raised us within Judaism, with all it entails: love of God, love for other human beings, love for the Land of Israel, its inhabitants, and landscapes, giving, and doing good deeds. You instilled in us characteristics that shouldn't be taken for granted, like ambition and the drive for excellence. Above all, you always encouraged us to broaden and deepen our internal and spiritual world. All this came from your merits, and understanding of reality and the tools that would help us become ethical, courageous individuals.

The day soon came when the first one was put to the test, Uriel. At first, he was put to the test of life, the test of determination, of humaneness toward his soldiers, of personal example and excellence. In the second stage, he was put to the test of death, which also put you and us to the test of life.

You, whose "brokenness is vast as the sea, who can heal you?" – you who are so special, more courageous than all of us – sent another son to the battlefield, Eliraz. You did so knowing that his fate might be the same as that of his brother, although you could have decided otherwise.

You gave me your blessing and sent me off, too.

But Satan accused you, and said to the Holy One, "This woman doesn't really believe. One more blow and she'll collapse and lose her faith." The blow was not delayed. Your husband, our beloved father, died. This was a harsh and agonizing blow, which put you to the test of all the values you taught us, and above all – the test of faith.

In pain and tears, I sing you a song whose meaning only you understand, and I sing it only to you:

Speak to my mother, for her joy has departed,

The son whom she bore at ninety years,

Consumed by flame, condemned by knife

Where may I find comfort for her?

I ache for my mother who cries and wails

The binder and the bound, on the altar of the Lord.[1]

While his death was set before us, great joy reigned in Heaven above, for vile Satan was thwarted.

All this due to a brave woman who showed everyone that faith has a face in this world.

Words cannot describe my love and admiration for you. Endless days and sheets of paper are not enough to describe the works of your simple life, filled with so much substance and meaning. Mother, you know I'm terrible at talking and expressing myself, maybe even a bit deficient in that area. The point of this whole letter is to tell you that I love you and to explain a little bit, just a tiny bit, why.

I want you to know that I love you in all your amazing hues, love you with my heart and my head, love you with both of these at the same time. That's the other love that I wanted to express at the beginning of this letter. I still read the letter you wrote me sometimes, and when I do, I hear your voice, as if you're reading it to me. I love you and miss you, and all of my brothers and sisters.

---

[1] From the *piyyut* titled "Et Sha'arei Ratzon," which is chanted in Sephardi synagogues on Rosh Hashanah when the ark is opened and before the shofar is blown.

"'For the mountains shall depart and the hills falter, but My kindness shall not depart from you, neither shall the covenant of My peace falter,' says the Lord, Who has compassion on you" (Isaiah 54:10).

It was an amazing trip. I began in Brazil, went surfing in Panama and Costa Rica, and then wandered to far-flung places like Nicaragua, El Salvador, and Honduras, where I went diving in the second-largest reef in the world and hiked through forests. In the capital of Tegucigalpa, the civil war was raging, there was shooting in the streets, and the state attorney was killed just a few steps away from me. I was forced to take shelter in the entrance-way of a building. What a crazy world. I called Eliraz from almost every location. I told him that in Bocas del Toro, I went into the water to surf with a friend, and all of a sudden, an enormous shark swam in front of us. I knew he would be thrilled. I told him about the mountain peaks I hiked up, and the wonders of nature I saw. In one of our phone conversations, he told me something that gave me a new outlook on life.

Eliraz said, "Look, in the country where you're traveling right now, there are Muslims who believe that everything is predetermined, and man has no ability to change his fate. Everything's written in advance. Man's life is determined by nature, and he has no control over the results of a *hamsin* or a storm. On the other hand, you have the Christians, who act like they're above nature. With them, a person can commit a crime and then go to the priest and ask for forgiveness. The priest, as God's representative, forgives him, and that's it, presto, it's all over. We Jews are right in between the Christians and the Muslims. The laws of nature apply to us, we know that we're limited, but we still believe that we have the ability to change certain things and bring good into the world."

This conversation told me not to get carried away into extremism, but rather to choose the middle path. To understand that in

certain areas of life, we are limited and subordinate to the laws of
nature, while in others, we can oppose and change things. Our
talk gave me renewed strength. I recall another amazing conversation we had while I was there. I told him that I was going around
from one country to the next and spending all my savings on
handouts. I felt sorry for all the people living in poverty, especially
hungry kids, and darn it, soon my own pockets would be empty,
too. Eliraz told me that it was the role of every Jew to give, both
in Israel and when I went to a foreign country. He encouraged me
to give happily.

Sometimes I traveled with other Israelis, but often I preferred
to be alone. I would pack a bag with food for a week and go off into
the unknown. I breathed in the nature and hummed "Jerusalem
of Gold" to myself. I let my thoughts rage, and I thought about the
things Homer said in the *Odyssey* – that the whole purpose of the
human journey is to return to the place from which we came. I
thought about the words in Song of Songs that gave me the desire
to live for others, not for myself. The moment I understood that
this was my purpose, I knew it was only a matter of time before I
went home.

But before I did, I went on my last trek in Ushuaia, the south-
ernmost city in the world. I crossed the border from Argentina
into Chile on foot, chose a mountain that looked impressive, and
started to climb. For three days I climbed by myself, with fourteen
ounces (four hundred grams) of raisins as provisions, because
my pots had been swept out to sea, and I didn't have anything
in which to cook my pasta. When I got to the snowy peak, I let
out an enormous roar. I felt as if Uriel and Dad were standing
there with me. Throughout my travels, I had felt their presence,
as if they were accompanying me. But on that last trek, on that
mountain with no other people around, their presence was more
tangible than ever.

When I returned to Israel, Elyasaf was the only person to whom I divulged the time of my arrival. I wanted to surprise Mom. He came to the airport and covered me with hugs, and right away we began to hit and punch each other. People stood by and stared at us, probably thinking we were about to kill each other. "This is my brother, I haven't seen him for ten months!" I explained. Elyasaf took me from Ben-Gurion Airport to a mall to buy clothes, because I was wearing a short-sleeved shirt and it was cold out. Then we went to an army base, where Mom was giving a talk to officers.

Elyasaf had planned everything, including an entry permit for the car. He knocked on the door of the auditorium where Mom was speaking, and when she saw him, I'm sure her heart must have skipped a beat. "Excuse me," Elyasaf interrupted, "there's someone here who hasn't seen you for a long time." Then I stuck my head in, and Mom began to laugh and cry, laugh and cry. It was an amazing feeling. We talked for a few minutes outside, and I said, "*Yalla*, go back to the lecture, I'll see you at home."

I don't know how Mom continued her talk. She said it was a test of her leadership.

Elyasaf and I went back to the car and I told him I had to go see Eliraz. We called him. "What's up?" Elyasaf asked. He said he was on Highway 6, on the way home. We knew he would get off the highway at Kesem Junction, so we stopped the car on the side of the road and waited. Just as his car was parallel to ours, I honked the horn. He glanced over, saw me behind the wheel, and couldn't believe his eyes. He got out of the car and gave me the biggest hug I've ever had in my life. It was divine.

Then we went to surprise Hadas. It was her birthday, and she was at a meeting in her school. We had some giant costumes in the trunk of the car. I put on the tiger costume and Elyasaf dressed up as a lion, and we both went in during the middle of the meeting and hugged her. Until I took off the mask, she was sure it was her husband. When I finally got home, Bat-El was still awake, waiting for me. Mom was so excited, she couldn't wait, and had told her that I was home.

After returning to Israel, I talked to Eliraz about my future. He was the only one I could consult with. I told him that I was considering two options: to study, or to work in something related to security. We thought about it together and raised all kinds of questions about the future. And then it was Purim. Mom always said that she knew Uriel would die, but I never considered the possibility that Eliraz would die. No one did.

On that last Purim, in his home in Eli, I sat beside him with a bottle of vodka. We both drank, sang, and munched olives, took another swig and another olive, and suddenly we burst out crying. "I know why you're crying," Eliraz said. "And I know why you're crying," I answered him, and we continued singing and crying. Mom was shocked. After all, the verse says, "When the month of Adar begins, joy multiplies," but we were behaving exactly the opposite. As the Hebrew saying goes, "*Nichnas yayin, yatza sod*" (When wine slips in, secrets slip out), and our secret was our deep sadness. We cried over Uriel, over Dad, and over everything that would no longer be. I didn't know that this would be my last Purim with Eliraz, but I did know that I would never forget that Purim feast.

On the last Shabbat before Eliraz was killed, I was at home, and at the last minute I felt like seeing him again. So I called him before Shabbat began. "Hey, bro," I said, "I haven't had time to see you." At once he answered, "Come to us for Shabbat." So I went. After Shabbat was over, Elyasaf came to pick me up in Eli and drove me to Hadas's house in Ofra. Later, Eliraz surprised us and came to Hadas's place as well. So that's how it ended up that the four of us – Eliraz, Elyasaf, Hadas, and I – had a moment together. What fun! We talked about the Torah scroll we dreamed of dedicating in Dad's memory, we laughed about me still recovering from the trip to South America, and we kissed Hadas's daughter, Aluma.

I left Ofra with Eliraz, planning to drive him home to Eli. He was going back to the army early the next morning, and I would take his car to be fixed in Jerusalem. But he said, "Never mind, there's no reason for you to drive to Eli and then leave again for Jerusalem. Just leave me at the hitchhiking stop, and I'll find a ride home." I said I wasn't having any of that. Still, when we got to the exit from Ofra, Eliraz tried to open the door and get out of the car, so as not to bother me. "Don't go! Don't go!" I shouted, and I grabbed him with all my might. In retrospect, that, too, was a sign.

Eliraz gave in, and on the way to Eli, we talked about the individual's role in the world, and about the army. Eliraz said that if I had questions, I had to consider them carefully, "Because if you don't, they'll take you away from this world." That was his expression. Then he hugged me and said, "Don't worry, everything will be all right. We're made of the same stuff, we're the same thing."

When I arrived at Eliraz's house before that last Shabbat, his kids jumped all over me in joy. I brought the food that Mom had prepared – chicken, meatballs, and rice – and found him standing outside with Or-Chadash. We walked together to synagogue, the kids hanging off him, Or-Chadash on his back, Hallel Miriam holding his right hand, Shir-Tzion holding the left. At the Shabbat table, we sang songs, danced, and talked at length. Shlomit also danced. The atmosphere in their house was always calm and happy. After the meal, I was exhausted, and I fell asleep on the couch in the living room, wearing my clothes. When I felt someone covering me with a blanket, I half-opened my eyes and saw that it was Eliraz.

In the morning we went to synagogue together. Eliraz called me up to the Torah, and when we went back to his house, I did something that still makes me happy, even today: I took the three older kids to the playground, to give Eliraz and Shlomit some privacy and a chance to rest. Tiny Gili was the only one who stayed behind.

I led the kids to the wadi, just as Eliraz and I used to do when we were kids, and we played on the swings. Toward sunset, Eliraz took me to the piece of land near his home, showed me the view, and said, "Here's where I want to build my home." Today I think of that sentence as a kind of will.

After Shabbat was over, after our meeting at Hadas's house, he returned to Kisufim. I know that place like the back of my hand – I've traveled every hill and road around there. We talked on the phone every day, and on his last day, he sent me a text message: "I'm fine, don't worry." That was the last sign of life I had from him.

Then the accursed Friday arrived. It was pouring outside, and I was with a friend at the spring in Givat Ze'ev that had been named after Dvir the previous year. We had spent much of our childhood together at that spring. Suddenly I got a phone call from Elyasaf: "Eliraz has been fatally wounded. Come home quick." I began to drive like a wild man, the car skidding in the rain. I uttered just one sentence. "God, I'm begging you, not Eliraz."

I arrived home and saw people gathering out front. I began to realize that something had happened. I called a contact in the military, and for the first few moments, he tried to avoid the question. I told him, "I know. Eliraz was killed."

He confirmed my suspicions.

I went to Mom. She was packing a bag to go to the hospital.

"Mom, there's nowhere to go," I told her.

"What do you mean?" she protested.

"Mom, there's nowhere to go," I repeated.

"What are you saying?" she repeated.

"Mom, listen to me," I said for the third time. "No. No."

Just as that accursed Shabbat began, the military representatives arrived. The funeral was held on Sunday, and I eulogized

Miriam hosts soldiers at TALI Public Secular School A in Givat Ze'ev

Inauguration of Torah scroll in memory of Eliraz at TALI A school, Givat Ze'ev. On left: Avi Lebsky, TALI Fund.

Principal of TALI A Public Secular School in Givat Ze'ev

Eliezer at brit milah ceremony for Or-Chadash Uriel, at the Tomb of the Patriarchs (Ma'arat ha-Machpelah)

Or-Chadash visits Grandpa Eliezer in his office

Eliezer and Or-Chadash

Eliraz and Or-Chadash

Shlomit and Or-Chadash

Eliraz and Or-Chadash at a spring in Eli

Eliraz and Or-Chadash

At Mount Meron nature reserve. Eliraz holding Hallel Miriam on his back and Shir Zion in an infant carrier, Shlomit.

Hallel Miriam, Or-Chadash, and Shir Zion

Gili Bat-Ami

Aluma Eitam, daughter of Hadas and Avichai

Shir Zion with Shlomit in the background

Uriel completes his officer training course. Back row: *Hadas, Avichai.*
Front row: *Eliraz, Miriam, Elyasaf, Uriel, Bat-El, Eliezer.*

*Eliraz completes his officer training course. Hadas, Elyasaf, Miriam, Eliraz,
Bat-El, Eliezer, Avichai.*

Uriel studying for the final exams of the Golani reconnaissance unit

Major Eliraz of Golani Brigade's 51st Battalion, in the town of Rajar

Eliezer Peretz – also Golani

Eliezer in Golani Brigade's Re'em Battalion

Eliraz and Uriel at home in Givat Ze'ev

Miriam and Eliezer on the day Eliraz was drafted

They were all his sons. Elyasaf (left) *and Avichai with Chief of Staff Gabi Ashkenazi.*

Eliezer and Miriam on the Lebanon Lookout Walk in memory of Uriel

*Eliraz and Eliezer choose a lookout in
memory of Uriel*

Uriel returns to Sharm el-Sheikh to dive

Uriel returns to Sharm for a visit, 1998

Darchei Noam Synagogue in Givat Ze'ev in memory of Uriel Peretz, may God avenge his death

Synagogue in memory of Uriel. Effi Eitam, commander of the 36th division, with Eliezer.

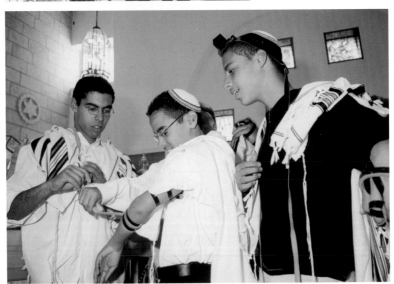

Elyasaf (center) *at his bar mitzvah ceremony.* Left: *Eliraz,* right: *Avichai.*

*Shlomit and Miriam with Chief of Staff Gabi
Ashkenazi.* (Photographed by Alex Kolomoisky)

*Ceremony for placing flag on Eliraz's grave. Front row: Shlomit, Miriam,
then-Chief of Staff Gabi Ashkenazi.* (Photographed by Alex Kolomoisky)

Ceremony for granting ribbon of commendation to Eliraz. Bat-El, Hadas, Shlomit holding Hallel Miriam, Commander of Golani Brigade Ofek Buchris, Miriam holding Gili Bat-Ami, Commander of the Northern Command Gadi Eizenkot, Avichai.

With Shimon Peres, Israel's ninth president

Eliraz with the same words he had used for Uriel, our oldest brother: "If You carved a rock from the mountain to build a new dwelling, You didn't carve it in vain, God, because from these stones, the Temple will be rebuilt." I said the words, but I couldn't absorb that it was real. I couldn't believe that I was burying my brother. I couldn't believe believe that for the third time in my life, I was sitting shivah. There's no logical explanation for it. I have no answer.

All of Israel came to the shivah: the prime minister, the president, the minister of defense, the chief of staff, Uriel's friends, everyone. Each time someone important showed up whom we didn't know, I was surprised, and yet, I wasn't surprised at all. Our mourning for Eliraz became the mourning of the entire State of Israel, the entire Jewish people. They viewed us as an ordinary family, not as battle-hungry soldiers, but as people who believe in ideals and basic values, who only dream of peace and love.

I know the exact spot where Eliraz was killed. I walked that sand with my feet during operations in Gaza. I remembered the place, and marching briskly toward the goal, I asked myself why I wasn't there during that operation. Maybe I could have warned him about the terrorist. Maybe I could have helped him after he was wounded.

But I no longer ask God why. I chose to accept His actions, although it's not an easy choice. People ask me how it is that I, who have all the reasons in the world to be sad, am able to be happy and make others happy. I answer that my strength comes from the fact that I accept all of God's actions, and instead of questioning them, I say thank you. I believe with full faith that the day will come when the Messiah will arrive, and then I'll see the three of them – Uriel, Dad, and Eliraz.

Until that dream is fulfilled, I don't live surrounded by death; I live with them. I take them with me to work, they go with me to my studies (law and business) and to synagogue. On Friday night, when I welcome Shabbat by singing, "*Shalom aleichem malachei hashalom*" (Peace unto you, angels of peace), I mean them – the three people who continue to live in my heart and in the hearts of tens of thousands of other people.

To me, visiting Mount Herzl is not a punishment, it's a family outing. More than a quarter of my family is there. When they were buried, something of me was buried along with them, and when I go to the cemetery, I'm going to visit myself as well.

It wasn't easy for me to get accepted to college, but before Eliraz died, he told me, "Forget everything else, bro'. Go to college." I wanted to fulfill his dream. He suggested that I write to the dean, tell him about Uriel and Dad, and about Dvir, who was killed the day after I started studying for the psychometric exam (college aptitude test). He made me promise that I would also complete the matriculation exam in literature, which I hadn't yet done. Although I hated pulling out the bereaved brother card, I followed his suggestion, so that I could fulfill his wish.

Now I'm in my first year of college, and I've no doubt that this is the hardest of my twenty-five years of life. I think about the three of them in my law class. Suddenly they pop up while I'm writing a paper, or in the library. In these moments, I tell myself that I'm still at war, and that every person's aspiration is to keep moving forward, not to stop, and certainly not to go backward. My battle is to have a normal life.

I put on the song "Sad Roses" by Idan Reichel, and I think about Shlomit. I hear the *piyyut* sung on Friday night, "*Yedid nefesh... nafshi cholat ahavatecha*" (My soul's Beloved …my soul pines with love for You), and I think about Dad. Then I hear "Forever Young," and I'm reminded of Uriel. The song "*Ani v'atah neshaneh et ha'olam*" (You and I will change the world) also reminds me of Uriel. At the concluding ceremony of the officers' training course, held in the Ramon Crater, Uriel said, in the spirit of that song, "We have been chosen to be officers for a good reason. We were chosen to educate, and we are worthy of it. We will change this country, whether we want to or not." Surrounded by the songs and memories, I'm able to write the paper I'm supposed to hand in the next morning.

Some days I sweat blood, but I try not to look too far ahead. I take it one step at a time, moving slowly and carefully toward the goal. On Shabbat I go to Mom's; during the week I also stop by to visit her, and I speak to her every day. She continues to push me forward gently. Her forehead caresses my back.

Maybe one day I'll write a book. Life has left impressions and scars on me. It has swung me from one extreme to another: from joy to sadness, from peaks to abysses, and I would like to write about what happens between these extremes. Perhaps I'll write about love. I'm waiting for it. I think it can sweeten my reality. Maybe I'll write about my dream – to live life in a way that will justify what I've gone through. To be a good person. To be a small light that pushes back the darkness, in the hopes that we'll all become a big, bright light. To see the fulfillment of our dream of peace, not just between nations, but between people.

No one knows yet how universal peace will be obtained. Rabbi Yehoshua Zuckerman, head of Har Hamor Yeshivah in Jerusalem, a man who is very dear to me, explained to me that peace, *shalom*, doesn't mean making peace with one another, it means making each other *shalem*, completing one another. Peace is the knowledge that you aren't perfect, and that I, although I'm missing something myself, am destined to complete you. We are all halves that can complete the other half, and out of this recognition, each one of us can relate to the other. A religious person can embrace a secular person, a left-wing activist can embrace a right-winger. In this way, we can complete each other, and then we truly will be a light unto the nations.

CHAPTER 22

Elyasaf Peretz

The first time a kid runs, falls, and gets hurt, he is shocked. Why does it hurt so much to fall? Why is the bruise so painful? Why did he stumble? Could it be that someone pushed him? "Mommy! Mommy!" he screams, and cries in pain. When his mother comes and hugs and kisses him, the child, who has calmed down in the meantime, can't possibly imagine how many bruises are awaiting him down the road. Nor does he realize that after the next fall, he'll cry less, because he won't be so surprised.

Physically, it won't be any less painful. The second time around, he might fall just as hard, but something inside him will have changed. He won't get used to falling – no one can ever reach that level of completely blocking sensation – but he will be tougher. That's my situation right now. I'm tough. I try to peel away those outside layers of sandpaper and protective screens, in order to return to myself, to what I was before. But it's not easy.

I'm twenty-four years old, Jewish and Israeli, the fifth child in the family. Just as Uriel and Eliraz grew up together with a gap of just eighteen months between them, so I grew up with Avichai. Mom thought she would have only four kids. When I was born, she said that God had added another child, and that's how I got my name – Elyasaf, meaning "God has added."

I was born on 25 Kislev, the night when the first candle of Chanukah is kindled. From a young age, I was taught that this is one of the most important dates in Jewish history: the Maccabees defeated the Greeks, and the high priest lit the menorah, which symbolizes heroism. I grew up in the knowledge that I was joining a chain of Jewish history that stretched from then until now. But when I was in sixth grade, Uriel was killed.

I didn't have the opportunity to get to know Uriel well, because when I was little, he left home to go off to boarding school. I have one powerful memory of him: when I was a little kid, all of five years old, I decided to run away from kindergarten. As soon as the teacher's head was turned, I climbed the fence and ran home. I didn't even know if Mom was at home. I pushed open the door, and there was Uriel, right in front of me. I don't know which of us was more astonished. I was afraid he would tell the teacher, and he was shocked when he considered the distance I had gone on my own. Uriel was angry at me: that I remember. He told me I shouldn't run away from kindergarten, and he took me back. I realized that if Uriel was angry, he must be right, because I admired him and his uniform. He was almost a soldier then.

A kid of twelve can't comprehend death. I, at least, didn't understand what it meant to have a brother who was killed in action. But I understood what death caused: I saw my parents broken. I felt that everything was broken. I knew I had to maneuver between the pieces, cover myself with them, and ponder them. Out of these pieces, I had to build a new life for myself, one that would always be lived in the shadow of the one who had been, and the thing that had happened.

My bar mitzvah ceremony was a traumatic crisis point: we didn't have a big celebration in a hall, and I couldn't enjoy it, because I saw Mom sitting in the women's balcony of the synagogue, crying. Mom cried and the whole synagogue cried along with her. Although it was the custom in our family for the bar mitzvah boy to read the entire Torah portion and the Haftarah from the Prophets, I read only half. Why? Maybe because I was the kind of kid who didn't like to follow the crowd, or maybe because I took advantage of my parents' pain to wring concessions from them. Maybe because I was angry at God. I knew that was ridiculous, that really I should be angry at the terrorist who had killed Uriel, or at the army that had sent him on the mission. My anger was illogical. It came from pain. So without noticing it, I began to toughen up.

I remember telling myself that death, as opposed to all the other punishments I knew, was a double whammy: not only did they take away your brother, they also took away your basic right to react, to protest, to defend yourself. Even the biggest troublemaker in school gets a hearing before he is expelled. They give him a chance to state his case before he is punished. But in death, it doesn't work that way: your brother is dead, and you can't talk about how wonderful he was and how it's not fair for him or your family to be punished. It's a fact. If you want, you accept it; if you don't want to, then don't accept it – but even if you don't accept it, it doesn't matter. That was the hardest thing for me to swallow. In those days, when the entire family was falling apart, I sat on the sidelines, at a distance, disconnected, and I asked myself what else could happen to me in life, as the worst thing had already happened – Uriel was gone.

Dad's death, when I was eighteen, was another story. I didn't deal with Dad's death, because our house was destroyed physically, as it was under renovation, and we had to rebuild it. I didn't deal with Dad's death because after the *shloshim*, the thirty-day mourning period, I went back to the premilitary academy in Yatir where I was studying. After high school I went to the army, which is the ultimate place where everyone has to suppress his feelings. The army is the place where you disconnect your feelings from your brain, and you have to do it, even if you're a bereaved brother and also fatherless.

In the army you have to be tough all the way. You go into the Gaza Strip, get to the house of a wanted terrorist, and you know that guys will come out wounded. You know that the terrorist who comes out of that house might be the one who killed your brother, or the killer's cousin. You know that Kassam rockets are being fired from that house onto Sderot and Ashkelon. But when you open the door of that house, you don't wrench it open or rip it off the hinges. You open that door slowly and quietly, you don't kick it in, because there might be little kids in that house. While you search that house, you try not to make too much of a mess, and when you go in to use the bathroom, you clean up after yourself. You act like a human being, even when you stand in front of the owner of the house who might love to kill you, who might actually try to kill you a minute after you leave.

Sometimes emotion eggs you on, and says, "What do you owe this guy? He's a terrorist." But then a miracle happens: your brain wakes up and orders you to behave like a human being. In the army there's no room for lots of emotion; you have to operate with your brain. I learned this the hard way. Until I got to the army, I wavered on the borderline between emotion and reason.

I went through the preliminary military call-up twice. I was drafted only after extensive back-and-forth discussions about my case, because during high school – when I couldn't manage the lows – I had acted up, and this complicated the draft process. In retrospect, maybe it's a good thing that I got into all that nonsense. It led me to attend the premilitary academy for a year of thorough self-examination, and in the end I understood why we really do have to serve in the military and defend our country. When I got the placement I wanted, and also accepted the fact that certain questions would never be answered, I decided that I would serve and give it all I had.

I went to the test day for the special forces, was invited to the tryouts for the navy commando unit, and then I twisted my ankle. In September 2006 I went to the second tryout, and someone died right next to me. We did an exercise that tests how you function with a snorkel under the water, and a guy from another premilitary academy had cardiac failure. The tryout was stopped. I think I was the only one who wasn't affected by this reminder that life is intertwined with death.

During the third tryout session, like the others, I had to speak to a psychologist who asked me why I really wanted to join the navy special forces. I could tell that the answers I was giving him weren't convincing enough. I couldn't say that I had always dreamed of the navy commandos, like the ones who were dying to get in. When the navy plan got scratched, I decided to join Golani, like Dad, and my three older brothers, Uriel, Eliraz, and Avichai. I wanted to continue the tradition, although I did feel that it put pressure on me. What would happen if I failed in the very place where my three brothers had succeeded? How embarrassing. They had set high standards, and it wasn't easy for me to live up to them.

Throughout this process, Mom stood by me with her usual love and pride. She hadn't brought us up to be fighters; rather, she taught us to continue the path that our family had forged. If I hadn't gone into the army, I'm sure Mom would have been disappointed. If I had joined but not gone into Golani, she wouldn't have been disappointed, and of course not angry. But at home, they definitely would have made fun of me: What do you mean, you're in Nachal or the artillery corps?

In the tryout course, I already felt the burden of having to prove myself. I'm not the kind of person who looks for the easy way in life, or uses even legitimate justifications that could help me achieve goals or give me an advantage. This was the understanding that I developed at age eighteen: that these things are always within me, in my inner self, and I can't set them apart as a separate entity. I decided to do everything in my power so that I would be treated like Elyasaf Peretz – not "the brother of" – without any title, just an ordinary "Golanchik," a rank-and-file Golani soldier.

I could have been accepted into Egoz, a highly respected unit, without passing another tryout course, as the one I had completed for the elite naval unit entitled me to do so. But I decided that I wanted the Golani reconnaissance unit, although I wasn't sure I would pass the tryouts and be accepted. I weighed these two possibilities – certain acceptance into Egoz against the prospect that I might not be accepted into the Golani special forces – and I chose the Golani unit, because I believed in myself. I believed I would succeed.

The day of the tryout for the special forces fell on Uriel's annual memorial day. I told Mom I wouldn't come to the memorial ceremony, as I couldn't be in two places at the same time. I refused to put off the course by a day, because I wanted to prove that I was entering on my own merit, not on the basis of special considerations. I wanted to go with everyone else and earn my own way honorably, so that no one could point at me and say that they made exceptions for me because of Uriel. Mom tried to convince me to come to the memorial ceremony, but I refused. The battalion commander called me in for a talk; he wanted to release me, but I refused. In the end they ordered me to go to the memorial ceremony.

The tryout course began at twelve noon, and the memorial ceremony started at three p.m. By four thirty p.m., I was on my way north to the base. It wasn't easy to leave the cemetery and go straight to the tryout. It was yet another trial. It meant not being with the guys during the opening pep talk, not making those first connections. It meant arriving at the base and being thrown straight into an environment devoid of emotion. A tryout is the most straightforward thing in the world: if you're strong, you'll be accepted; if you're not strong, you won't. What happened a week ago or a year ago is of no interest to anyone. It's three days in which you have to demonstrate all your physical and mental powers. When I passed, Mom was happy. She also told me that she had no doubt that I'd be accepted.

During the sixteen-month training course, I was exposed to the entire range of Israeli society – people who came from *kibbutzim*, *moshavim*, Tel Aviv; religious and secular. It was a unique melting pot. I actually felt less comfortable among the religious guys in the team: when everyone else was praying, I felt uncomfortable standing on the sidelines. During the course I also began to understand the artificiality of the separation between religious and secular. I saw how similar we were, how simple it was to talk about the divisive topics, and how we were unified by the basic desire inside each one of us – to be a good person.

Toward the end of the training course, I completed the process that I had begun in high school: I learned to accept myself, to understand that I didn't have to be the most unique or the most outstanding. It was okay that there were others who were more outstanding than me. I understood that by trial and error, I would get to places where I felt comfortable, and that the most important thing was for me to be myself. It's hard to reach this understanding in the special forces, which is a competitive environment, but I have the army to thank for it.

After I went into the army, my connection with Eliraz deepened. Even when he didn't have time for conversations, I knew that he was watching over me, that he was there for me. Before Operation Cast Lead, we sat together to prepare our gear for combat. It was Friday afternoon before Shabbat, and Eliraz called me and asked, "What's up, bro'?" To tell the truth, I was quite surprised. Shabbat was about to begin and our gear wasn't yet ready – why was he talking in an everyday tone of voice? Was that the most important thing for him to ask me at that moment – what's up? "Eliraz, Shabbat!" I said, and he replied, "Saving a life supersedes Shabbat. Come talk to me, tell me what's going on with you."

That was Eliraz's charm. He looked like a serious religious guy, a "*dos*," but actually he wasn't so fanatic. He came to the base, checked my equipment, picked up my bulletproof vest, and gave me advice. Because he was then serving as battalion operations commander, he was more than aware of where I was going and what I was about to do. We both fought in the Gaza Strip, and I tried to completely disconnect emotion from reason, but it was impossible.

On the first day of combat, I met up with Dvir Emanuelof from Givat Ze'ev, Avichai's best friend. Before we went into the combat zone, we hugged each other and said, "It'll be okay; don't worry." This brief memory returned to me when I heard on the communications network that he had been killed. I imagined that Mom must be trembling in fear, but I never imagined that they were running a war room in our house, with phones ringing off the hook and the entire family council debating whether or not to pull me out of Gaza.

I continued doing what had to be done, and suddenly Eliraz appeared before me. I was thrilled. After the initial hug, we began to punch, hit, and kick each other. He shouted, "Brother!" and I shouted "Brother!" All the soldiers around us were astonished. How did I have the courage to punch the operations officer? Meanwhile Eliraz was about to choke me with hugs. In our outward appearance, Eliraz and I are very similar. We're also similar in the strength and joy that erupts from within us.

After a month or so I went home, and that's when I heard that Mom had wanted to pull me out of there. I was grateful that I hadn't known about this. If I had known, it definitely would have affected my fighting. Who am I to judge Mom, who had already buried her eldest son? Had Mom come to Gaza and ordered me to leave, I couldn't have refused her. She deserves it all, and she has the right to demand and to give me orders. She's my mom. I'm dust at her feet. I'm her son and her pupil. A certain reality was forced on her, but in her own special way, Mom knows how to accept the most tragic things and give them significance. I can't even begin to approach her level of insight, which was earned in suffering. Maybe I'm only just starting.

When I hear about Grandma Ito's modesty and strength, it sounds a bit clichéd to me. But now I'm beginning to understand that Mom's strength didn't come from nowhere. She got it from her mother, who was a deep believer. Our generation asks questions. In my grandmother's generation, they accepted. My grandfather never asked why he was a Jew or why he was religious; he simply was that way. My mother was given the privilege of experiencing two generations, the accepting and the questioning, and thus she is able to accept the greatest suffering with love. And I? I'm nothing beside her.

I see myself in the most crucial position. I'm constantly inquiring and exploring. There are answers that are very difficult to accept, and there are things that must be set aside until the right time comes. Sometimes I feel like shouting, "Doctor, don't tell me to just drink water! Give me some medicine, it hurts!" At these times, faith is the only thing that helps and strengthens me, faith in the right path.

Three days before Eliraz was killed, I spoke on the phone with a good friend. We got into a long, deep conversation about facing challenges, and I told her that sometimes in life, there are things that you're aware of, but don't deal with because you don't have the strength to do it. You know they're there, but you push them aside with full awareness, until the time when you have enough strength to face them.

When I said this, I was referring to Dad's death, which I'll face in the future – maybe when I get married, maybe when I have kids. I never imagined that three days later, reality would slap me in the face with the death of my second brother.

I cannot understand Eliraz's death, and I can't deal with it. I can't dismiss the disturbing thoughts that it forces into my soul. I think that death is trying to say something, to me or to everyone, because death is not random. It has to be making some kind of a statement. So my goal is to understand what Eliraz's death teaches me about life, and in general.

If I weren't a believer, if I thought it was fate or luck – or more precisely, bad luck – I would live my entire life differently. I would think that death was a random matter, that there was no purpose, that it was a matter of one second, a stray bullet that could have killed another soldier just as easily. But after seeing how thousands of people, religious and secular, left and right, connected with Eliraz's image and mourned his death because he touched them to the depths of their soul, I believe that he had a purpose, a mission. If not for Eliraz, our nation would not have united.

Of course I would have preferred it if my brother hadn't been the messenger who united the nation, but I often get insights through other people. Someone told me that due to Eliraz's death, he was able put his life into the right perspective. Another told me that reading Eliraz's life story illustrated for him the importance of serving in the army and protecting the country. A secular youth who was raised only on love of homeland but not tradition, told me that thanks to Eliraz, he was exposed to the values of our faith. I don't care what each individual takes from Eliraz's character or how exactly Eliraz influenced him or her. The main thing is that as many Israelis and Jews as possible take something from him and are influenced by him, because each person who is inspired by him deepens the recognition that his death was not in vain.

But all this does not relate to my personal pain. It remains the same pain, and the feeling remains the same feeling. You feel like you've lost something, that something inside you was lost, and it's not an ordinary lost object. Forgot your wallet, it fell out of your pocket? Tomorrow you'll find it, or you'll get a new one.

Even losing a wallet can have several levels. If the wallet fell out of your pocket while you were attending to people wounded in a terrorist attack, you can comfort yourself with the thought that your action justified the price. If the wallet was stolen from inside your towel at the beach, you think of it as a meaningless loss. But losing a brother is different. It's a constant feeling of loss. Eliraz is with me and not with me to the same extent. When do I think about him? It would be better to ask me when do I not miss him. I think about Eliraz when I'm studying, sleeping, dreaming. He's a constant presence in my life. It's not a rare occurrence when he appears – it's the breaks between appearances that are rare.

I believe that God appears in our world through private individuals and events, mostly during crises – as in the verse in Ezekiel, "and I passed by you...and said, with your blood, live" (16:6). You can't build on top of a house without harming the integrity of the existing roof. Some plants have to rot in order for new growth to begin from within. So what do you do? Avoid breaking the roof of the second floor and thus prevent the construction of another floor above it? Stop the plant from decaying and thus prevent the appearance of a new fruit? No, because the pain of destruction leads to growth.

These are processes that I think we all go through. Only through crisis can we grow. This concept appears in the Torah: in Egypt, the word for the place where the Israelite women sat during childbirth was called *mashber*, which also means "crisis." The purest thing, bringing new life into the world, emerged from crisis. Why is the new mother described as *niddah*, impure? Because the moment she brings new life into the world, she also mourns. As long as she doesn't give birth to the fetus, she has another person inside her. The moment the infant comes out, something inside her breaks, and she becomes a different person.

I'm not sanctifying death, I'm sanctifying life – which is the highest value. King David didn't build the Temple, because he had too much blood on his hands. Instead, Solomon was given the privilege of building it. The Torah also says that no iron implements or destructive tools can be used to construct the altar in the Temple; it must be built only from whole stones. I hate wars and love to protect my country. I believe, I try to believe, that we have to go through these crises in order to discover a new reality, one that is much better than the present one.

In my everyday life, I try to follow the regular lifestyle of a guy my age. I rented a little apartment in the Nachlaot neighborhood of Jerusalem so I would have a place of my own; and the other half of the week I'm at Mom's. I took a tour guide course sponsored by the Ministry of Education for the Masa Israel Journey program, which takes young people on a week-long trip throughout Israel. It teaches them to connect with the land through their feet while learning about their Jewish and Zionist past. I'm studying for the psychometric exam, and I hope to be accepted to the department of plant studies at the Hebrew University's Agriculture Faculty in Rehovot. My dream is to find a little place in southern Israel and do organic farming, make olive oil, and grow spices.

Of course I would prefer it if my life were much easier, but as I've learned, easy come, easy go. So I'm not looking for a way to escape the pain. Sometimes I write. Some poetry, some thoughts. I try. The muse comes to me in sadness, in autumn, in grayness, in uncertainty and fragility.

During the morning recitation of the Shema prayer, we say "*emet v'yatziv*" (true and constant), but when we recite it in the evening we say "*emet v'emunah*" (true and faithful). This prompts us to ask, why the difference? In the daytime, by the light of the sun, things are clear and unwavering. But at night, when you can't see, you need truth and faith. Hope. And words from the heart.

* * *

Two poems by Elyasaf:

The black night that always comes without warning
Without asking or stating, requesting or declaring
Conquers the morning.

The lovely morning that wanted to go on for one more
minute of grace,
One more minute of fragments of certainty, melts.

The noble, bright morning doesn't open its mouth,
doesn't say goodbye
As it melts slowly into the kingdom of blackness and
fear...

How goodly are the stars, the moons of blessed memory.
They haven't forgotten my covenant, haven't protested
my words:
May the light never end,
May darkness never remain,
May the good slowly be revealed,
May the darkness melt and diminish.

You know what else, child? Stars aren't only in the
heavens.

At our house, next to our yard,
Hiding behind the fence,
Stars shine under a pillow carved in stone –
Stars with a spark of a distant life.

They compel us not to forget;
They force us to continue to rejoice.

For time can't remember what it will never forget, and
People don't fall in a place where strength is gone.

We're standing on the edge here
At the beginning of the race.

Just one step separates
Between tomorrow and the remnant.

Morning again reigns.
Again you sit and need
The words that come out in the wee hours,
The release of creation written without letters.

Letters in yellow carved on my heart,
Letters that fly from the depths of my soul.

1:3
Small shards
Begin as a vast whole.
People pick up
Things that are supposed to fall,
Like a leaf resting on the railroad tracks,
Waiting for the day when autumn is back.

CHAPTER 23

Bat-El Peretz Issachar

In fifth grade I wrote a story, "The Smile Comes Back." I typed, printed, and illustrated it, and bound it in a folder with a transparent plastic cover. It's about a girl. Now when I leaf through it, I feel embarrassed. It's a story written by a girl whose life forced her to mature.

The plot centers around Michal, whose brother was killed in combat in Lebanon. At university, Michal meets Yair, and they go out together until they decide to get engaged. But when Yair sees the photo of her dead brother, he's put off. "He looks a lot like me," said Yair, and he runs out of Michal's house, slamming the door behind him.

I had to write a happy ending for this story. On the last page, I wrote, "After the engagement, everything was fine. The whole family celebrated, but it was still hard for Michal because her brother wasn't there to celebrate with her."

No one asked me why a girl in fifth grade would write a story with such ideas. Everyone knew that I had taken them from home, from my life. I was nine years old when Uriel, my oldest brother, was killed in an ambush in southern Lebanon. At fifteen, I sat shivah for the second time – for my father, Eliezer. At twenty, when I was a soldier, my second brother Eliraz was killed.

Matan, my husband, doesn't resemble the hero of "The Smile Comes Back," but he continues the Golani tradition of our family.

Under the *chuppah*, I thought about all three of them – Uriel, Dad, and Eliraz. Each of them was a unique personality.

I'm the baby of the family, the sixth and last. I was born six years after Hadas, and Dad called me Princess. Everyone knew he was crazy about me. I would come home from preschool, and he would blow up an inflatable pool in the backyard and get inside with me. I would call him at work and say, "Dad, I can't work the TV," or "Dad, I'm hungry," and he would drop everything and come home.

But my two older brothers, Avichai and Elyasaf, had no intention of spoiling me. When Mom and Dad went out for the evening, they would say, "No problem, we'll watch Bat-El. We'll watch a movie together." The minute the door closed, they would turn off all the lights and run after me with forks, making ghost noises. In the morning, when I squealed on them to Dad, they put on innocent faces and said, "What are you talking about? We took great care of her."

At one point, I refused to stay with them anymore, and I wouldn't let Mom and Dad go out at night, not even to a wedding. Once, when Mom was already dressed to go out, she couldn't find one of her blue high heels. She ran around the house looking for the shoe, which had disappeared as if swallowed by a mouse, while I played the innocent. I had thrown the shoe down into the wadi so that Mom wouldn't go out. I helped her look for it, but it was nowhere to be found. A few weeks later, we went out for a walk in the wadi on Shabbat, and we found the blue shoe. That's when Mom suspected that I had played a trick on her. She explained that even when my brothers drove me crazy, they did it out of love.

When I started kindergarten in Givat Ze'ev, Uriel went off to Or Etzion premilitary academy. He came home only once every two or three weeks, and we became distant from one another. He wasn't the classic older brother who helps his little sister do her homework.

I remember that he used to come home from the academy exhausted, desperate for sleep. On Shabbat morning I would sneak into his room and pull off his blanket, but even that didn't wake him up. At the Friday night meal, though, I would sit on Uriel's lap. He would play with my hair, while I drew letters on his back. Most of all, I loved it when he would come home and discover he had forgotten his key. Then he would come to my kindergarten classroom with his uniform and weapon, and everyone would gaze at him in admiration.

I'll never forget the night of 7 Kislev. It was a Wednesday night, and I came home late after a class activity. It was after ten p.m. when I finally fell asleep. All of a sudden, Mom's shouts woke me up. She ran around in the hallway screaming, "Get up! Get up! He's been killed!" I jumped out of bed and ran to the stairs, my eyes quickly scanning everyone's faces. I saw Mom, Dad, Avichai, Elyasaf, and Hadas. So who could it be? Either Uriel or Eliraz.

Then I saw Mom holding the book *Bnei Keshet*, Uriel's book, and I realized it must be him. Mom hugged me tightly, and then they took her into another room and gave her a shot to sedate her. The door of the house was open, every minute more and more people came in. I don't think I fully understood what had happened.

As a little girl, you aren't able to absorb that death is a final, irreversible thing. At six a.m. I went to the home of a friend who lived on our street. I said, "Did you hear? My brother was killed." I saw that everyone else was crying, so I cried, too, but I didn't absorb it. Recently I traveled to the United States as a counselor for a group of bereaved brothers and sisters, and I met other kids who were going through what I had gone through years ago. It takes time for the penny to drop, to start to realize, that's it – you had a brother, and he's gone. Was.

Mom wondered whether to take me to the funeral, but I said: "Yes, I want to go." After the burial, the family sat on a bench at the entrance to Mount Herzl, and everyone came up to us, hugged me and kissed me – literally crushed me – and I remember that I couldn't understand what they wanted from me. I just wanted to get out of there. During the shivah, I sat with my friends in my room and we talked. It was a kids' shivah, kind of laid-back, because kids aren't really supposed to sit shivah.

Uriel was killed in November, and a few months later we went to Mount Herzl for Yom Hazikaron. The entire hill was crowded with people. There was no room to move, a lot of commotion, and it was terribly hot, and then we heard the siren. It's a shocking sound, abnormally intense, ear-splitting. It's not like the school bell. It rips your soul apart. I was unable to stand during the moment of silence that follows the siren. Someone standing next to Mom screamed, and people fainted. When we finally got out of there, I announced to Mom that I was never going back to Mount Herzl for that ceremony.

Mom understood me and she didn't pressure me to return, but in ninth grade I worked up my courage and made the trip to Mount Herzl. We stood beside Uriel's grave, Dad and Mom on one side, Eliraz and I on the other. The siren was the same, no less strident, and the gun salute was also terribly frightening, but I stood close to Eliraz. He hugged me and covered my ears. Standing beside him, I could be brave.

On Yom Hazikaron in 2010, I had to choose where to stand during the siren: beside Uriel, or Eliraz, who had died less than a month before. I was very scared. Who would give me strength? Who would support me? We decided to divide up. Avichai, Matan, and I stood beside Uriel; Mom, Hadas, and Elyasaf stood next to Eliraz. Suddenly I felt a miracle happening: this year, the siren wasn't loud at all, and there was no gun salute. When the siren echoed through the cemetery, I found myself smiling. I felt as if Eliraz was hugging me and covering my ears, proving that he was still there, even though he wasn't standing next to me.

My mom saves every note we ever write to her, and she saved the poems I wrote to Uriel in a special folder. In red pen, with spelling mistakes, I mimicked the rhyme scheme of a poem by Miriam Yellen-Steklis:

> *I waited and waited, cried and cried, but who didn't come? Uriel.*

> *He promised me twice that he would come for my twenty-second birthday. And who didn't come? Who didn't come? Uriel.*

> *We prepared candies and letters, and all sorts of good-ies. And who didn't come? Uriel.*

> *But why, God? Why charming Uriel, with the broad smile on his face?*

> *Uriel, I love you so much. I hope we'll see each other at fifty or a hundred, mainly so you'll give me a hug, just one...*

In another poem, I wrote:

> *Most of the times when he came home from the army*

> *He would fall straight into bed.*

> *It made me mad*

> *Because I wanted to talk and chat, and simply missed him.*

> *But Uriel would fall asleep right away*

> *and never noticed me waiting there.*

> *Now that he's been killed,*

> *I'm willing for him to come home and crash on the couch.*

> *I don't care anymore if he doesn't talk to me, even for an hour.*

Let him just come home

Because I'm waiting...

Mom also kept "The Smile Comes Back." Although there's no similarity between me and the main character of the story, we do have one thing in common: after Uriel was killed, I felt like everyone was feeling sorry for me. Girls who had never looked at me before tried to be my friend. Even the teachers refrained from criticizing me for talking in class or neglecting my homework. That really annoyed me.

I was silent for a long time, until I couldn't hold back any longer. In fifth grade, I asked the teacher for permission to speak to my classmates. I stood up in front of the class and said: "I would like to ask you to stop feeling sorry for me. I'm not terminally ill. The fact that my brother was killed doesn't mean that you can't argue with me or get angry at me. If you really want to help me, then get angry at me! Treat me like an ordinary girl."

I don't walk around the streets wearing a sign saying, "I'm the daughter of a bereaved family. Two of my brothers were killed." It's the last thing I talked about when I went through the military induction process, the last detail I mention when I go for a job interview. It's very important to me for everyone to know that both my brothers were heroes and rare young men. But it's also important for me to be myself – Bat-El – and to know that I got to where I did on my own merits.

At age fifteen, in my first week of tenth grade, Dad died. Ever since I remember myself, I knew that Dad wasn't healthy. The year I was born he got cancer, and he got better after the chemotherapy treatments. But the year after Uriel was killed, Dad had a heart attack, and I was very worried, as I was so close to him. I made him promise: "I want you to be at my wedding" – and he promised. Even when the cancer returned, I convinced myself that he would get over it, because he was strong.

When Dad went in for the operation, Mom said, "Don't come. It will be a long wait, and we'll call you when he gets into the recovery room." But that morning, I decided I had to go to the hospital. First I went to Mount Herzl, I sat with Uriel for a bit, and then I went on to Shaare Zedek hospital. Luckily I arrived the second they brought him out of the operating room. One more minute and I wouldn't have seen him. The doctors said everything was okay, that he was recovering. Then suddenly Mom saw that behind the glass door, they had begun to run around. She gripped my hands and Hadas's tightly, and pulled us in there. "Dad's about to die!" she cried.

I tried to calm her down, but it was too late.

I couldn't understand how the One on High could take Dad, who was such a *tzaddik*.

I'm not a big fan of clichés like "You have to accept everything with love." I have strong faith in the Holy One, but it's my right not to accept the chain of disasters as a given. I would like to ask the Master of the Universe, "Why?" But on the other hand, I don't spend all day looking for answers, because I know I won't find them, and because the search itself won't get me anywhere. I put all my strength into the question of how to go on from here.

My connection with Eliraz was much stronger than my bond with Uriel, who went away to boarding school. Eliraz knew every-thing about me, when I was angry, who I liked, what made me laugh, what I cried about. His presence was very strong, both at home and in my life in particular. After Dad died, he took Dad's roles on himself. Even when he was serving as deputy battalion commander, and came home to his wife and kids only once every two weeks, he found time for quick visits to us, and he would talk to me and encourage me with a friendly word.

When I graduated from high school, I knew I wanted to serve in the army – not National Service, but the army. My first thought was to go into Golani like my brothers, but I didn't find a posi-tion that was meaningful enough for me there. That's how I got into the education corps. I did a course that prepared me to be an educator and a commander, and served at Chavat Hashomer base.

At first, I commanded three classes of new recruits at the Center for the Advancement of Special Populations, soldiers who had dropped out of other frameworks because they were unable to adjust. My challenge as a commander was to encourage them and prepare them for meaningful military service, despite their problems and limitations. I said to myself, "I won't be serving in Golani, but I'll send them lots of soldiers."

Every team at Chavat Hashomer is named after a fallen soldier. My soldiers were called "Team Uriel," and Mom came to speak to them. It was at Chavat Hashomer that I began to get to know Uriel. He was a commander in the full sense of the word: stern and exacting, but sensitive, a listener who showed concern for the slightest personal problems of every last soldier.

Eleven years after his death, we gathered at the cemetery. The eulogy I gave there expresses the process of maturity I underwent:

Uriel:

I can't believe it's been eleven years. I still remember the letter I wrote you for your birthday, a happy letter. Now, instead of a happy letter for your birthday, I have to write you a eulogy. I was only nine and a half when you were killed, and since then I've graduated from high school, gone into the army...

In the army I got to know you again. I met you again, and I meet you at all sorts of levels and all kinds of places at Chavat Hashomer through my team, which is named after you. Every morning while it's still dark and cold outside, I hear your name reverberating in the air when they greet me. Next week I'll come here to tour Mount Herzl with the new team, and I'll tell them about my personal national hero.

Uriel, I know that your army wasn't the same as mine. You were a fighter, you defended our country. I'm doing something totally different. I train commanders, but you remain my best model of a commander, one who is above all a human being.

I feel your presence in everything I do. I look at our photos and think about what a great brother you were to me. I read the letters that your soldiers wrote you, I read your vision statement and the things that were important to you, and I get to know the commander that you were.

Out of that point and that place, I grow and take with me the things that are important to me. I read about how you took care of each soldier – the one who had a toothache, the one who needed to supplement his income – and I learn from you. I feel as if you're talking inside me, empowering me in what I'm doing. From you I learn not to give up, even when things get tough. I learn to do everything in the faith that this is our land and this is what has to be done, and if I want something, I have to do everything in my power to achieve it.

Today I'm almost twenty. In a little over six months, I'll be discharged. I have to think about big decisions, like what to do after the army, what to study, what to do about Matan. I'm happy because even if you and Dad aren't here physically, I know that you'll support me in every decision I make, and you'll find a way to guide me to the right places from above.

I'm happy, brother, that I had the privilege of knowing you for nine years physically, and another eleven years through a somewhat different type of relationship. The only thing I have left to say is how much I love you, how much you add meaning to my life. Thank you for the privilege of discovering you each time anew.

Now give Dad a big hug and tell him that we love you both. Tell him that we don't forget.

From the moment I began my army service, the connection between Eliraz and me grew stronger. I often called him to ask about a certain weapon or to seek advice about enrichment materials. I often said to him, "It's hard, I can't go on," and he, in his calm voice, would answer, "You have to do it, and you can."

When I was practicing on the firing range at the Golani training base, I went to visit him. I was a young soldier with a broad-brimmed hat and battered M16, looking for the commander. They asked me, "Who do think you are, looking for him?" I answered proudly, "I'm his little sister." Once I was in the field for a week of training, and every time we wanted to start shooting practice, we were ordered to cease fire. I would get my soldiers raring and ready to go, magazines properly prepared, and then I would have to stop them again. I called Eliraz, annoyed: "Who's doing this to me?" He replied, "I am, but I'm not doing it on purpose."

Another time when we were at the range, Eliraz came to my soldiers' tent and asked them for Bat-El. They couldn't see his insignia in the dark, and one of the soldiers advised, "Bro', I suggest you call her 'Commander.' If not, you'll pay for it by running all night long." Eliraz replied, "It's okay. Just tell me where I can find her." The soldiers pointed him in the direction of the staff tent.

He came up behind me, tapped me on the back, and said, "Grab a helmet, we're going to fly." I froze in my shoes. What did he mean, fly? He held my hand and said, "Walk behind me and don't say you're my sister. Don't open your mouth!" The helicopter landed next to us, and Eliraz continued to organize things. He hoisted me up, and when the doors closed and I got excited, he said, "Mazal tov, sis." It was a surprise he had organized for my nineteenth birthday.

There were no seats inside the helicopter. Everyone was standing, and when one of the soldiers put his hand on me by mistake, Eliraz gave him a sharp look that said, "Don't you dare touch my little sister." He didn't say a word, but his look had a powerful effect. We flew for fifteen minutes, while he showed me the territory and pointed things out. When we landed he helped me get down, gave me a hug, said "Yalla, bye," and just like that, he was gone.

When I was in tenth grade, a neighbor introduced me to Matan Issachar from Givat Ye'arim. He studied at the Atzmona premilitary academy, and had just completed the training course for the Egoz elite unit. At first we were good friends who just met and talked. As a good friend he also came to the shivah for my father, and after a year of friendship, we decided to take our relationship in a more serious direction.

Today when I look at the walls of my room, which are covered with photos of us together, I can see what a long road we've traveled together: adolescence, the matriculation exams, all of it. We have photos of us carrying schoolbags, when we skipped school to meet in Jerusalem; in driving class – we bet on which one of us would pass the driving test the first time (I won); in uniform; hiking on our days off.

As we matured, our relationship grew stronger. He is a very special young man, simple and modest. He truly completes me, and I don't mean that as a cliché. Everything that I'm missing, I find in him. Although Matan is a year older than me, I never felt that he was more mature than me, because the circumstances of my life forced me to grow up early. But I knew that he knew how to listen to me. I also knew that even when he couldn't fully understand what I was going through – things that a person who hasn't known grief will never understand – he at least tried, and I realize how much maturity and patience that takes.

Eliraz, who acted like a second father to me, didn't accept Matan so quickly. He was worried for me. His opinion was that if it was serious, then it was serious all the way, and if not, then it should end. When Matan got to Golani, Eliraz emphasized that one shouldn't mix army and family. But we heard that he watched out for Matan from a distance.

A few months before Eliraz was killed, in one of our endless heart-to-heart conversations, I told him that I was thinking about my future. I said that after I was released from the army I wanted to go travel, and that Matan might start officers' training and stay in the army for a long time, so why get married young? What was the rush? Eliraz said, "Batya" – his pet name for me – "if you've found the one you're looking for, don't put it off." He suggested we get married during Sukkot, after my discharge. He said to Matan, "If you're a real man, then give Bat-El a ring."

In my second year in the army, I switched to Sha'arei Avraham training base to serve as a commander in an officers' training course for women. It was there that I received the news that Eliraz had been killed.

I had stayed at the base for Shabbat, because we had just begun a new course three days earlier. Shabbat began, and I put on my dress uniform to prepare for Friday night services and the meal. Suddenly someone called one of the staff officers who shared my room. They said I had to go to the adjutancy immediately. All kinds of scenes ran through my head. I thought maybe something had happened to Mom, but I told myself, "No, if something had happened to Mom, they wouldn't have let me know in this way."

I preferred to think that maybe they were calling me to an urgent staff meeting, or that something had happened to one of my soldiers. I never imagined that something had happened to

Eliraz. Later on, I found out that the local military officers (the people charged with making these announcements) had forgotten all about me. When Mom asked them, "Who will tell Bat-El?" they replied, "Who's Bat-El?" Then a race against time began, as they were afraid I'd hear it on the news.

I got to the adjutancy area and saw my commanding officer. The door of the company commander's headquarters was open, and inside sat a senior officer and my training course commander. I grew more and more confused. I went up to my commander and asked her what had happened. She looked at me, placed her hand on my shoulder, and asked me to come into the room. "I don't want to," I replied, and burst into tears. I begged her not to take me in there. I understood that if everyone was waiting for me, it must mean disaster. Another one.

They put me through the routine identification procedure – name, dog tag number, address – and I begged them, "It's me, just tell me what happened." Then the officer said, "I'm sorry to inform you that your brother Eliraz was killed in an incident in Gaza." He said it in a dry tone of voice, according to protocol, but his eyes were red. I mumbled, "My mom's going to die. She won't be able to stand it." That's the only thing I could say, and I continued to mumble it all the way from Sha'arei Avraham to Givat Ze'ev.

I got out at the steps leading down to the house, and Avichai and Matan came up to meet me. I got to the door and couldn't believe what I was seeing. There was Mom, sitting in that same brown easy chair, surrounded by neighbors and friends. As soon as I crossed the threshold, silence fell, and everyone moved aside. I felt like I was in a replay – I'd already been through this scene. At that moment, I said to myself, "Bat-El, you'll get your chance to break down. But now you have to be strong for Mom." To be strong, in my definition, is to cry without completely losing control.

This is how I eulogized Eliraz:

When Uriel was killed, I was nine years old, and I didn't understand a thing. But now, Eliraz, I understand, and it's tearing my soul apart with deep pain, profound pain. I had so many experiences with you. You always took care of me, spoiled me, took an interest in me, protected me.

Eliraz, after Dad died, you became my father. I consulted with you about everything – home, army, life, and especially Matan. How it hurts me to think that after all the discussions and decisions we made, you won't be there when it actually happens. You won't escort me to the chuppah like Dad promised he would do, and like you promised, because you both died.

I want to say to both of you that this is pain that can't be explained, pain I still haven't internalized and don't understand. But you should know that I have a brother who is a hero, the salt of the earth, a tzaddik who followed his own path unhesitatingly. I'm proud of you, Eliraz, proud of you for continuing in this path, for continuing to love this land and this nation, to your death. Thanks to you, Eliraz, and thanks to Uriel, we can stand here, our heads held high, cry out to God in heaven and ask for mercy for the Jewish people.

There's only one thing I want to ask you, God in heaven: this is the third time that You have tested us as a family. Over the twenty years of my life, I've buried my father, my brother, and another brother, and I beg You and ask You to stop. We've already proved to You that we've stood the previous trials, and we'll stand this one as well. From now on, I want You to give us only happy

*occasions. No more funerals, no more memorial cer-
emonies. Give us the strength to support Eliraz's wife,
a tzaddikah. Give us the strength to raise Eliraz's children and the privilege of telling them who their father
was – such a hero, such a tzaddik.*

*Shlomit, I'm talking to you, the person and soul whom
Eliraz loved and admired most in the world. You're a
hero, and we're with you. I promise you that we'll walk
this path together. We'll walk Eliraz's path, and we'll
give you strength, because we have experience.*

*Eliraz, my dear, beloved brother, finally you are at rest.
You're returning to the bosom of our family up there.
You are my hero, you are my example of the meaningful life that I want to live. I swear to you down here that
I'll raise my children to walk in your path. They will
know you, they'll talk about you, and they'll fight for
this land, just like you.*

*I know we'll meet up, I know that one day I'll join you,
Dad, and Uriel. But until then, I'll continue what you
started here.*

When I got up from the shivah, my commanders proposed
that I switch to a less demanding position, and I considered it.
There was a certain logic to the idea. I had only three months left
until I finished my service, and I knew that my position included
weekends, firing range practice, weeks out in the field, and endurance courses. But I heard Eliraz's voice echoing in my ears.

Eliraz had been in the sixth month of the reconnaissance unit
course when Uriel was killed in an ambush in southern Lebanon,
and he decided to continue. I told myself that if he was able to
complete the course for the Golani elite unit after his brother was

killed, how could I break down? I understood that I, too, had to set my sights straight ahead.

After the shivah, I went to the base and in my first talk, I said to my soldiers, "Hi, I'm Bat-El. I'm going to be your commander. You know where I just came from. I decided to return to this position because I believe in the army and I want to complete a meaningful service. So I'm asking you to help me by drawing a line between my personal life and my professional role. If you run into problems and crises, don't keep them from me. I'm here for you."

That was one of the hardest things I ever did in life, a kind of performance. I felt that I was cloaking myself in camouflage, putting on the poker face of the stern commander. I demanded discipline and taught classes, while at night I let out everything that stayed bottled inside me all day, crying into my pillow. Luckily, I had only four hours to sleep, so I didn't have time to think.

I'm glad that I finished my service in a position where I could make a difference, give from my experience, learn from my mistakes, and learn about myself. I gained from each soldier under my command. Every day I had the opportunity to fix what wasn't so good the day before, and to become a better person. When I stood on the parade grounds at the ceremony where rank insignias are handed out, I looked up to the heavens and said to Eliraz, "Look, I went through with it to the end."

In my final talk with my soldiers, I read them a letter that expressed everything I had wanted to say during the course, but couldn't:

> *My dear Team 2 members,*
>
> *I've been trying to write to you for a while, but I simply haven't been able to. So I'll go back a bit to my decision to return to serve as a commander here at the training*

base. During the shivah for Eliraz, the option of going back and continuing with this team wasn't a question, but every day it became clearer to me that this was what I wanted to do: finish my service in a meaningful way, return to one of my great loves – being a commander – return to my home here, receive a team of fourteen women soldiers and lead them through professional training, and much more.

I was very scared, but I knew that this was what I needed and wanted to do. I recall my introductory talk with you. My throat was choked with tears, and I'm almost sure you noticed. After that talk, I couldn't look at you, as it had drained all my energy. But in that same breath and those same tears, I knew I had made the right decision.

This time around wasn't simple, not for me, and not for you either. It's not easy for you to be on a team in which the commander is not always 100 percent there, doesn't always share in your experiences and difficulties. I assume you felt that you missed out a bit, and I want to ask your forgiveness for that. I wasn't always able to cut off completely and be here for you, seven days a week, twenty-four hours a day. But I hope that I did succeed in bringing a drop of myself or added value that sometimes made up for that.

It's important for me to say how much you have been a part of enabling me to cope, to get out of bed each morning and keep on living. After a thing like this happens, the last thing you feel like doing is getting up in the morning and continuing your routine. You just don't feel like doing anything. You want to stay inside the pain and hope it's a nightmare that will soon be over. You don't find meaning in anything. But you enabled me to find meaning during this period.

I quickly fell in love with your ability to hold on to yourselves even when no one was there for you, to be true friends, to laugh, get wild, and be exactly the team that I needed. You filled me with a sense of responsibility, and the moment I realized that there was a team out there that was mine, waiting to give me the morning salute, I couldn't disappoint you and just not show up. I understood that I had a responsibility, I was the commander, and so I had to get up and go out there.

Anywhere you go, in any corps you join, I'm sure you'll leave your mark. Maybe this mark will be visible, maybe it will be expressed only later on, but know that your efforts were not in vain. When you receive soldiers under your command, they are your entire world. You think about them when you go to sleep, when you get up with them in the morning, and the whole time in between. The soldiers will cause you to become more professional, sensitive, and patient. They will make you want to improve constantly, just like you did for me.

Be sensitive and modest. Don't behave arrogantly just because you grew up in a certain place, or finished the education course, and you think you know the right way to live life. There are no shortcuts in being a commander. You have to take the hardest road, think about the entire team as well as each individual within it, know each of their stories, what background they come from, what makes them tick, what makes them smile.

Song

This is where my military service ends, and I had the privilege of having you as my last class. Thank you for the honor of being part of the process you underwent, of sharing the hard times and the experiences, of learning from you and about you, and also about myself. Thank you for sharing the deep questions and the true inquiry into what it means to be a commander. I wish you the best of everything in this world. I trust that you'll be amazing, just as you're capable of being, and most importantly, that you'll always have smiles on your faces.

Two months after Eliraz fell, I turned twenty, and I told everyone to forget the parties. I asked that no one even wish me *mazal tov*. On the day of my birthday, Matan was on his army base, but on the weekend, after Shabbat was over, he pleaded with me to go out with him for half an hour, just the two of us. I almost cancelled on him. I said I didn't want to go, that I didn't feel like seeing anyone. Matan promised that we would go somewhere quiet. He took me to Ein Hatayasim (pilot's spring) near his house, a lookout next to a spring. I got out of the car and saw a long row of roses. I started walking along the row, and never imagined for a moment that he was planning to propose. At the end of the row stood two fancy boxes, and only then did I realize what was going on. I said, "No, you're not proposing to me. I'll kill you if you propose to me!" He said, "No way, why should I propose to you? Open them."

I opened the first box and found a necklace inside. In the second box, I found a note wrapped in a ribbon. I went to the car to read it. Matan was all smiles, and he said, "No, read it here, right now." I argued like a child. I said I'd rather read it in the car because it was dark on the path, but Matan insisted, saying it was a short note. I opened it and read, "Batush, will you marry me?" By then I couldn't refuse.

It takes a lot of courage to propose to a girl two months after her brother was killed. With this act, Matan was saying, "I want to put some happiness into your life and your family." He didn't say, "I want you to stop crying and not be sad," but rather, "I want you to have a reason to get busy with the hall and invitations and a wedding dress."

When we announced that we were getting married, lots of people asked me why I didn't wait a bit longer. The answer was simple: we had planned to get married before Eliraz was killed, and I had learned that in Jewish tradition, we don't put off celebrations. Besides, there is something symbolic about the family dynasty. Three years after Uriel was killed, Eliraz married Shlomit, and this built up our family somewhat; it began a new chapter for us. Two years after Dad died, my sister Hadas got married. And when I saw Mom running around to buy white flower girl dresses for Eliraz's three girls, who would escort me to the *chuppah*, I hoped that our joy would send a ray of light to her world as well.

Brigadier General Rafi Peretz, the chief rabbi of the IDF, performed the ceremony. He's not a blood relative of ours, but he's definitely part of the family. He taught Eliraz and Avichai at the Atzmona academy, and later, my Matan. I had always dreamed that Dad would escort me to the *chuppah*, and after he died, I made a deal with Eliraz that he would escort me. It was a powerful, difficult moment, but when Matan and I stood under the *chuppah*, I couldn't help but feel happy. This was the moment I had awaited for so long. I felt my three angels – Dad, Uriel, and Eliraz – standing in front of me, giving me their blessings and rejoicing with me. They were there with me.

Matan went back to the army. He has another year left of service, and I'm getting used to our new way of life. Soon I'll start studying for the psychometric exam. I'm looking for a job, I pop in to visit Mom, the usual routine. Of course Matan is keenly aware of the family he has joined. But I want to live my life, not just the lives that are no longer.

I feel like I've already lived a hundred years. In the past, I thought: here, we've had our blow, and from now on, everything will be fine. But again and yet again, the illusion was broken, and we were brought back to a reality in which there are no answers, only two paths: the first is to refuse to accept, refuse to cope, throw away life, decay, and finally die. The second option is to cope. Coping sounds like something big, but actually it's expressed in the smallest ways. To cope means to get up in the morning, go back to school, feel that it's okay to be happy, let yourself cry when needed, stare reality in the eye, and choose.

I choose the second path. I choose to keep believing in the One Who sits up there making the decisions. I choose to keep believing in life, in happiness, and in love.

CHAPTER 24

Shlomit Gilboa Peretz –
Parting from Eliraz

The following words were spoken by Shlomit on the *shloshim*, the end of the thirty-day mourning period for Eliraz.

Razush!

You knew much pain and sorrow in the life you lived. Yet you continued to live and be happy. Still, you always warned me not to dare die before you, because you wouldn't be able to stand it.

You never liked for us to use the word fear, to say the word doubt. But when you thought about something happening to me, you would say right away that you were scared to death, without a second thought.

But now you've gone and left me here.

I'm the one who has to deal with it.

I'm the one who cannot die of fear, pain, and longing.

Eliraz, it's very important for us to do everything possible, as much as possible, to commemorate you, to continue who you are forever: your great spirit, your refined truth, your spiritual strength, joy, goodness, and enthusiasm for life. May they endure and find their way into every heart.

I promise you, Eliraz, that I will continue what was always more important to you than anything else, what took precedence over everything. I promise you that my greatest commemoration of you will be to continue to raise our children – Or-Chadash Uriel, Hallel Miriam, Shir-Tzion, and Gili Bat-Ami – according to your path.

I'm only begging you, Razush, and before God, to help me, to continue guiding me on this road, every step of the way, in every decision I'll have to make. Be with me every minute and give me strength, power, and joy.

Please, God, make me an instrument of your mission...

Shlomit

CHAPTER 25

Where's Dad? Or-Chadash Begins First Grade

The day before I was to accompany my oldest grandchild, Or-Chadash Peretz, to his first day of school, I was informed that the IDF had killed one of the members of the terrorist cell that had slain his father, Eliraz. Was this the hand of God, or merely a coincidence?

At eleven p.m., the wounded soldiers' contact officer for Golani called to convey the message officially, but the rumors had reached me several hours earlier, through friends of Uriel and Eliraz. The officer asked whether she could come to visit with me, and I answered that there was no need. Even without the official announcement, the last few nights had been crazy.

In our family, there's never just one event. Things always come in series, and that was the case now as well. I was preparing for Eliezer's memorial ceremony. Five years had passed since he had died of a broken heart over Uriel's death, and I was trying not to imagine the scene. It would be the first time that Eliraz would not be standing in front of his father's grave to recite Kaddish, and I wondered what I would say at the ceremony. Sometimes I feel that I've had enough of memorial ceremonies, and that my lips can't express any more pain. At the same time, I was also excited about Or-Chadash entering into the world of learning. The contact officer's phone call came right in the middle of that boiling cauldron of endings and beginnings.

On the phone, I was silent. In the first few moments, I didn't know what to say or how to react. What's for sure is that I didn't feel any joy or satisfaction of payback. Neither do I feel that way today. Five months after Major Eliraz was killed in a terrorist incident in the Gaza Strip, the army completed its mission and eliminated the perpetrator. But Eliraz isn't here. He won't be taking his firstborn son to his first day of school. I can only think and believe that the combination of events isn't coincidental, but rather that something symbolic is going on here.

Or-Chadash is starting a new path. At school he'll learn not just to read and write, he'll begin the long process of getting to know his people, his roots, the source from which his father drew his faith and strength. The terrorist who was killed the night before didn't intend just to kill Eliraz. He wanted to destroy the spirit of Judaism and Zionism. I believe that with the proximity of these events, Eliraz was saying to his eldest son: "When they killed me, they thought they were destroying the spirit that nourished me. But you, Or-Chadash, are starting a new road. Trust in the State of Israel, trust in the army. They will do their job so that our spirit will never die. Don't worry, son, there's someone here who will protect you and your spirit."

I sat at home, mumbling these words, until it seemed that I was hearing them uttered in Eliraz's voice. I knew that words didn't have the power to compensate Or-Chadash for the fact that his father wasn't standing beside him, or dancing with him, or protecting him with his body. But over and over I heard Eliraz say, "Don't worry, we have a state and we have an army, and our army knows how to reach every individual who wants to harm us. The person who killed me wanted to harm my spirit, not just my body, and you, my eldest son, are starting your studies today to continue our spirit – the spirit of the Jewish people."

I have to reiterate and stress that I didn't rejoice over the death of the terrorist; I wouldn't rejoice even over the death of a leading terrorist whose hands are covered in blood. When Uriel was killed, I didn't ask who placed the explosives or how exactly the fight took place. When Eliraz was killed, I didn't ask who the sniper was. I refused to occupy myself with these questions, because I knew they wouldn't lead me to a place of growth. I knew that the little strength I still possessed had to be dedicated to my daily existence – getting up every morning, functioning, taking care of my own children, and Shlomit and Eliraz's children. Sometimes I find myself wanting to know, to investigate, but I thrust the feeling aside. It's not the lack of knowledge that bothers me, it's my longing for him.

When they told me that Uriel had been killed, the first thought that went through my head was, "Too bad I wasn't there."

In my imagination, I saw myself going out on the ambush mission, standing in the line of soldiers. I'm a mom, I have good instincts. I would have shouted to Uriel, "Be careful of that rock! There are explosives under there!" I also imagined Uriel turning around and asking, "Mom, what are you doing here?" and me answering, "Listen, Uriel, I don't know anything about the army, but I do know how to be a mother."

I imagined myself leaping onto the rock and blocking Uriel's path, and absorbing all the bullets and shrapnel with my own body. Uriel would have remained alive.

When I was told about Eliraz, I reacted differently. I wanted to know whether in that moment he had thought of his children, if he had held their image in his mind. I wanted to know the last thought that went through his head when he saw the flash, when his last breath left his body.

I'll never have the answers to those questions, but I have a feeling that Eliraz's last thought was of the Jewish people, that even in the last moment of his life, he was occupied with the great mission that stood before him, not with private thoughts. That's my feeling, but in his pants pocket we found drawings that his children had made for him. He had taken them with him on the mission. In another pocket was a book of Psalms.

When they brought me Eliraz's *tallit*, I sniffed it. It smelled of the army, of the grease they use on the rifles. I pictured Eliraz at the height of his holiness. That grease symbolized the struggle for our spirit and faith; the *tallit* that belonged to a combat soldier enfolded a book of Psalms and a rifle.

On September 1, Bat-El and I ordered a taxi and traveled to Eli at six a.m., to Or-Chadash's school. We knew that with that act, we were perpetuating Eliraz. While Eliraz himself had gone to first grade in the secular school where I was principal, he had dreamed of putting his eldest son into the religious framework of a Talmud Torah school. We arrived at the school and saw all the little boys dressed in white, singing and dancing in a circle to Chassidic tunes. Or-Chadash was standing off to one side by himself, watching the other boys, because he didn't have a daddy to hold his hand and lead him into the circle.

That wasn't how I had imagined the happy day when my oldest grandchild would start first grade. In my imagination, I pictured Eliraz bouncing Or-Chadash on his shoulders, throwing him up to the ceiling, dancing with him in boisterous song. He wasn't one of those stern fathers. Just the opposite: he was a dad with a kid's soul, who climbed trees with them and came into the house through the window. He was a crazy father, simply nuts. I'm sure that on his son's first day of school, Eliraz would have entered the classroom with a roar, firing up everyone's kids.

I watched Or-Chadash and saw that something in his eyes was dark and covered by a screen. That pained me deeply.

When I stuck my hand in my purse to take out a tissue, I discovered that in all the excitement, I had forgotten to bring my camera. Luckily – or unfortunately – there were plenty of cameras and photographers around. The media already knew about the death of the terrorist who had killed Eliraz. But only a few them knew that Shlomit was accompanying Or-Chadash to first grade just two days after their lives had been miraculously saved when a stone was thrown at their car on the way from Kiryat Arba to Eli.

The journalists approached Shlomit, and she told them that for her, this was a very important day. She said, "If I had been told on an ordinary day that a terrorist from that cell was killed, I wouldn't have been excited. I'm not looking for revenge. But on Sunday a stone was thrown at us on our way home. The car was damaged, but miraculously, we weren't hurt. Yesterday a terrorist from the cell that killed Eliraz was eliminated, and today Or-Chadash is starting first grade. When you look at life from the perspective of more than just coincidence, the combination of events is very significant. There are still people who don't want us to be here, but we'll keep on living and rejoicing."

The journalists asked Shlomit how Or-Chadash reacted to the news of the terrorist's death, and Shlomit related that he hadn't yet heard the news. "I heard about it late last night," she replied. "Or-Chadash was already asleep, and this morning we were busy with the excitement of starting first grade. I'll tell him, but not from a place of revenge, rather from the place of 'Am Yisrael chai', the Jewish people lives and will continue to live – a place where children continue to go to first grade, a place where the IDF and the General Security Services do their job in the best way possible."

The next day I went to visit the graves of Eliezer, Uriel, and Eliraz, to tell them about Or-Chadash starting first grade.

I told Eliraz that his son hadn't participated in the dancing, because it was a circle of fathers and sons. I told him that all the first-graders at the Talmud Torah had been wearing new, colorful kippot, but his son was the only one who entered the classroom with the beret of Golani's 12th Battalion on his head. He hasn't taken it off since the day his father was killed. I think the beret helps him feel that his father is still with him, always with him.

After the ceremony at school, I went to Ofra for a meeting with the leaders of the Ezra youth group, who had asked to hear about my sources of strength during times of crisis. It's strange that people come to me with this question, and that I'm the one who's asked to talk about this. Who says I have strength? Who decided I'm the strong one?

As usual, I spoke to them from the heart, about my life. I told them that I had just come from seeing my grandson off to first grade. I told them about the beret that never leaves Or-Chadash's head. I told them that I couldn't be happy about the death of any human being, even when a terrorist was liquidated, because he also had a mother and family, and other people who will mourn his death. At the same time, it's clear as day that everyone who wants to harm us must be aware that we will defend ourselves.

Eliraz wasn't a warmonger. He never bought his kids toy guns or little plastic tanks. Even on Purim, he wouldn't allow them to shoot cap guns, like many Israeli kids do when Haman's name is mentioned during the recitation of the Scroll of Esther. Eliraz had no desire to kill or be killed. But he was first in line for every defensive action. When he went into Gaza, he thought about the children of Kibbutz Ein Hashloshah who only wanted to play in safety, and whom he wanted to protect.

I told them that I trusted the IDF to protect us everywhere in the Land of Israel, and that we had to protect the IDF from all harm, and encourage its soldiers when they stood up against the enemy. "The eternal people does not fear, doesn't fear the long road..." That's what Eliraz used to sing.

PART SIX

And Now

CHAPTER 26

Dancing with God – Faith in the Shadow of Death

My sons wanted to serve in the Israel Defense Forces. They wanted it to be a service of life. They didn't want to die. They viewed military service as a mitzvah and a privilege, not an obligation.

I didn't feed them Zionism for breakfast, but every single day they saw how happy we were here in Israel. We gave our children values: love for fellow human beings, kindness, giving and doing for others. We taught them through personal example, not words.

They saw their father working as a volunteer to establish the synagogue in Givat Ze'ev. They saw me, a religious mother, sending her children to study in religious schools, but choosing to serve as principal of a special secular school in which pupils explore their identity and are connected to their homeland and their roots. They saw us facing challenges of faith, such as Eliezer's battle with cancer. He weighed less than forty-five kilos (a hundred pounds), but Eliraz bought him a cane and walked to synagogue with him. We educated our children to love this land and our country, our people with all its different kinds of individuals, and our splendid Jewish heritage.

I didn't think I could be an example of love of country to them, because for many years I had felt that I hadn't done enough for my country. What had I done, after all? I didn't dry any swamps or

319

pave any roads. I hadn't even served in the army. I made aliyah to something ready-made, a country already built and developed.

Today I have no such pangs of conscience. I gave, twice. I paid the price of our existence here, I paid my debt to the state. Despite all the sorrow and pain and longing, I know this was the most appropriate death for my sons. If I could wake them up for just a moment and ask, I have no doubt that each of them would say that he was willing to give his life again, so that children in the north and south could sleep safely, play on the playground, and enjoy a peaceful life.

My boys Avichai and Elyasaf serve in combat reserve units, and continue to fight for the land that my grandfather and grandmother dreamed of in the Atlas Mountains, but didn't have the privilege to see. They fight so that we can realize the dreams and aspirations of past generations and the generations to come. Unfortunately, the battle for our existence is still not over.

Ten years after Uriel fell in battle, a strange incident took place. An anonymous visitor approached the gate of Givat Ze'ev, asked the guard if he knew the Peretz family, and said, "Give them this, and say that I can't continue any longer." The guard came to my house with the package. I opened it and found a chain holding Uriel's dog tag, a protective charm he had received from his grandfather, and a bullet. This chain symbolized three generations: grandfather, father, and the son/grandson who continued to fight the battle for survival.

To this day, I have no clue as to the identity of that person who touched my son. But I do know that death has many circles aside from the family, and it affects a wider circle of friends. Sometimes it takes many years before they are able to open their innermost hearts. This messenger may never contact me, perhaps because it's too much for him to bear.

I don't like the question "Will we have to keep on fighting forever?" because in my opinion, it's a question that leads to despair, that weakens. I prefer to keep my eyes on the good and on the light. I prefer to say: we've had the privilege of building a state, we returned to the land of our forefathers, and we're here, Jews over many generations, living and doing everything in order to live. We dream of a life of peace: is there any mother in the world who wants to see her children die? We dream of building families here, of building homes, creating, developing, and living a life of freedom. That's our aspiration, but the reality that is forced on us frustrates its realization.

In this reality, faith is our source of strength. It gives us encouragement and support, although questions of faith arise that we can never answer. Why do good people suffer? Why did I have to bury two sons? Why did my righteous husband die of a broken heart? Why me?

The questions go on and on. But they have no answers. One thing is clear, sharp as a knife: my sons are gone, my husband Eliezer is gone, and I'm here carrying on. Living. That's a fact. Now I face a different question: how do I continue? What sort of substance can I infuse into my life? What meaning do I give it? As I learned from my sons' deaths, a life isn't measured by its length. My loved ones died young, but they instilled rich substance into their lives during the short time allotted to them, and left their mark not only on us, but on many others in this country.

Uriel's death was a private disaster, mine and my family's. When Eliraz fell, the second son in our family, our privacy was taken away. Everyone said, "It's not your son who fell, it's the son of the entire Jewish people." I try to take comfort from that. Maybe his death brought people together, bridged factions and camps, maybe this was the sacrifice that was required? After all, he fell on Passover eve, at the time when our forefathers offered the Passover sacrifice. Maybe this is what had to happen in order to provoke a change in our people. In order to create unity, even for just a few days – unity through the pain of the entire nation, as we experienced.

But it's hard for me to accept. Why did the sacrifice have to be a child, a husband, a father, a young man who still had so many dreams? I don't have the answer.

In *The Lonely Man of Faith*, Rabbi Joseph Dov Halevi Soloveitchik writes a chapter on the meaning of suffering in which he says: "Suffering comes in order to raise the person, to purify and sanctify his soul, to cleanse his thoughts and refine them from superficial excess and rough limitations; to refine his spirit and broaden the horizons of his life." Indeed, out of suffering I have found a new melody.

As part of my efforts to bolster my strength, I looked for verses in the Tanach that would support me and express my pain, one verse for each of the boys I lost. After Uriel fell, it was hard for me to accept the rabbinic saying *"Hashem natan v'Hashem lakach"* (The Lord gave and the Lord has taken away, Job 1:21). I was pleased when our friend, Attorney Avi Bar-Yosef, proposed a verse from Lamentations (2:13): "For your brokenness is vast as the sea; who can heal you?" This verse made me feel that God shared in my pain, which is as vast as the sea that has no boundaries. Sometimes it rises like the sea, yet sometimes it is a source of calm. In this verse, even the all-powerful God, the One Who strikes the blow, says, "Who may heal you?" – as if in the understanding that it's not a wound that can be healed, that there is no remedy for the magnitude of this wound.

After the death of Eliraz, a fighter of the caliber of King David's soldiers, I connected with King David's lament over the loss of his son. At first, when the child falls ill, the king fasts, mourns, and sits on the ground. But after his servants inform him that his son has died, he gets up, gets dressed, eats, and bows down before God. His servants try to understand the meaning of his behavior, and I've adopted his answer for myself: "He said, 'While the child was still alive, I fasted and wept, for I said, "Who can know? Perhaps the Lord will be gracious to me, and the child will live." But now that he is dead, why should I fast? Can I bring him back again? I may go to him, but he will not return to me'" (II Samuel 12:22–23).

I can't bring back Eliraz, Uriel, or Eliezer, but I know for sure that I will go to them. I will go to them as my beloved son Eliraz taught me, holding my head up high, standing straight and proud.

My relationship with the Holy One, blessed be He, is similar to that of a couple dancing a tango or a slow dance – one minute they move close to each other, the next they push apart. In one moment my soul feels powerfully connected and wants to rely on Him, the next He is distant and leaves me on my own.

In difficult times, I turn to Him: "Only You can send me comfort," and He sends it, in His own way. A divine way. Several months after Eliraz was killed, we celebrated Bat-El's engagement party and wedding. From my point of view, it's not a given that every relationship will end up in marriage, and when it did happen in this case, I thanked the Creator for the bounty He sent us, for the blessings and the joy. That's comfort.

It wasn't a test of death that the One on High gave me. Instead, He put me to a much harder test: the test of life through suffering.

CHAPTER 27

A Living Tombstone –
My Mission

The three of them left the world while still young – Uriel at twenty-two, Eliraz at thirty-two, and Eliezer at fifty-six – but in their short lives, they accomplished a great deal.

Uriel managed to do a lot. With all the pain over his dying at a young age, I don't feel that he missed out. In the time allotted him, he did significant things. No moment of his life was spent in vain. He fulfilled his wish of becoming a fighter in the Land of Israel and serving in the elite reconnaissance unit. Even before he began his army service, he was able to fulfill a personal dream that he had held onto since his childhood in Sharm. He flew to Palma de Majorca and dived there at a special scuba diving site. He met many people who carry his memory in their hearts. Did he have time to love? I will never know.

He wrote this message on military notepaper: "When I think about the winter, I think about Orit. Why? Because winter reminds me of loneliness, cold, freezing hands and wet hair, and there's no one to warm me with a smile, a phone call or letter."

I don't know who Orit is. I don't know whether he was writing this while thinking about his winter with Orit, or the winter he passed without her. But the knowledge that he did perhaps have the chance to love gives me a fragment of comfort; yet, it intensifies my sorrow that Uriel never had a chance to build a home and have children. I imagine him with a wife and children. He most probably would have continued on in the army. He wanted to be the first Moroccan chief of staff, so he would have remained in the military. I imagine him after Eliraz's death, hugging me and supporting me. Maybe he would have become a second father to Eliraz's kids. Maybe.

Now, when I hug those four children, my heart breaks. Had Uriel left children, something of him would have remained with us. On the other hand, when I see the tears in the eyes of these fatherless children, I say to myself that perhaps it's better this way. Perhaps God acted kindly with me when he took Uriel at twenty-two, before he could give me grandchildren. I don't know what's better, but I do know for sure that Eliraz's kids will continue his path. Through them, I see both life and death. They give me many moments of joy. Thanks to them, I sing and dance, jump and bounce around like a little girl. But together with this happiness comes deep pain, the pain of missing out. How? How is it that I have the privilege of watching them grow up, of seeing little Gili, who is already able to say the word *Daddy*, while my son never heard her speak?

I have both types: one son who fell without leaving a home or family, and another one who fell and left behind a widow and four orphans.

Missing Uriel is expressed in the simplest ways. He loved cheesecake, so every time someone brings a special cheesecake, I would so much like for him to be able to taste it. When a new highway tunnel was inaugurated in Jerusalem, I thought how happy and proud he would have been to see this. How could it be that he didn't have the opportunity to drive through it? How can it be that he didn't dance at Eliraz's wedding? Recently, when I visited his grave just before the beginning of the school year, I asked Uriel how it was possible that he would not be escorting his nephew, Or-Chadash, to first grade.

I know these thoughts are not logical. Had Eliraz not lost his older brother, he wouldn't have given his oldest son the name Or-Chadash, whose initial first letters combine to form the word *ach*, "brother."

But who's looking for logic? Is there logic in burying two sons? I need Uriel so much right now, after Eliraz has become his neighbor on Mount Herzl. Eliraz continues living through his four children, while I continue Uriel. It's my role, my mission. I think I would have dedicated my life to this even if he had brought children into the world.

This mission – to continue Uriel's path – was born during the shivah. I gave Uriel's soldiers a notebook and asked them to write down thoughts and memories. I didn't open the notebook. People told me, "Why bother opening it? You'll just find simple Golani slang, stuff like 'Brother, I would die for you,' or 'Brother, I'm crazy about you.'" So the notebook sat on a bookshelf in my home like a forgotten knick-knack.

A few months later, on Yom Hazikaron, Eliraz – then in the officers' training course – was stationed at Mount Gilo and asked me to come speak to the soldiers.

"Eliraz," I objected, "I don't know what to talk about."

"Just come, Mom," he asked. "Come and strengthen us."

"What should I talk about?" I asked. On the appointed day, I decided to open the notebook that had been filled by members of the backup team of Golani Brigade's 51st Battalion.

I began to read, and was astonished at what they had written about their commander, Uriel Peretz. His soldiers wrote, "The test of a commander is the test of a human being." Everyone emphasized the fact that Commander Uriel was humane, ethical, sensitive, aware of each soldier's problems – from a toothache to a sick mother, or a brother starting first grade. They wrote that Uriel's door was always open, and that there was no end to the personal interest he demonstrated. He had asked each soldier what he wanted to be, and helped them to advance both emotionally and professionally.

I was very impressed by those "simple" Golani soldiers. They described the long path Uriel had walked, a path that produced good citizens of the State of Israel as well as passionate soldiers, and in that order: first a citizen, and only afterward a soldier. "We weren't afraid to go out into the front line of battle in Lebanon," they wrote, "because we knew who we were walking behind. Uriel gave us what every fighter is looking for, a feeling of security."

I chose quotes from these letters, and started to construct lesson plans for a leadership module that I call "Respectful Leadership." Today I travel all over the country – to IDF bases, youth groups, girls' and boys' religious high schools – speaking and lecturing, with the goal of inspiring leaders who see human beings in front of them.

Because the IDF loves summaries, here is a summary of my lecture on the ten challenges of the commanding officer:

1. Set goals in the spirit of "Know from whence you have come and to where you are going" (Ethics of the Fathers 3:1). Work constantly to achieve them.

2. Be an example in behavior and actions.

3. Be sensitive, attentive, and approachable. Build a supportive atmosphere for the soldiers and take care of their physical and emotional needs.

4. Transmit combat procedures and patterns of behavior that fit the spirit of the IDF. Your job is to build soldiers, layer by layer.

5. Develop the soldiers' battle readiness and aim for constant improvement of their professional level.

6. Create a sense of shared pride by promoting solidarity within the squad, company, and unit, and by weaving an integrated social fabric.

7. Work toward steadily improving performance while learning from and drawing appropriate conclusions about operations.

8. Inspire the soldiers to believe – in themselves, their unit, and their officers – and to be dedicated to their mission, commander, and team.

9. Develop and improve motivation by building trust.

10. Aspire for excellence.

These are the things I learned from Uriel and from other officers I've met. I'm no general – far from it – but I ask commanders to carry out these points with restraint, self-control, moral integrity, and a sense of humanity, while preserving respect for the soldiers and for all human beings.

The person who pushed me to undertake my educational mission in the army was Gabi Ashkenazi, former IDF chief of staff. At the parting ceremony honoring his service, I made the following remarks:

> *Mount Herzl. A state ceremony, placing a flag on the grave of the last soldier buried on this hill – the grave of my son, Eliraz Peretz, deputy commander of the Golani Brigade's 12th Battalion, who fell on the eve of the Passover Seder.*
>
> *Chief of Staff Gabi Ashkenazi strides toward the grave. Beside him are my children, Eliraz's wife Shlomit, and myself. A chilling moment. We walk in silence, without words. You can hear the heartbeats.*
>
> *The chief of staff slows down, his legs heavy, faltering in the march toward my son's grave. He stops, lowers his gaze. A look of pain and sorrow that I'll never forget. In a choked voice, he says, "This is a difficult occasion. I*

can't believe that I'm doing this to you – my last flag on the grave of a soldier, on the grave of your second son."

The pain is sharp. Out of the corner of a damp eye, I see the chief of staff of the Israeli army – this strong, professional man, who has seen battles and lost fighters – standing beside me (a mother, one citizen) in pain and grief. The occasion is not easy for him. "It was on my watch," he says. "It belongs to me." He places the flag and salutes.

Then, like a father who treats his children equally, he remembers. In this plot lies another son, my son, First Lieutenant Uriel Peretz, who fell in Lebanon. Again I hear: "He fell on my watch as major-general of the northern command." He places the flag and salutes.

Remembers, and never forgets!

Honored guests,

I'm sharing this moment with you, a private, painful moment, because on that occasion, it wasn't the chief of staff who stood beside me, the supreme commander. It was Gabi the human being. It was human pity and nobility of spirit that moved him. It was just like me, when I go to the gravesite. It's inconceivable for me to go to just one son. The second one is always waiting for a hug and a visit.

That's what you were like, Mr. Chief of Staff, sir, like a father to my children. It wasn't just the fallen soldier you saw before you, but his entire family. This broad viewpoint enables us to understand the wonderful connection you have woven with the bereaved families.

You have considered them and the fallen soldiers as an inseparable part of building the IDF spirit.

I'm sure that each family has moments from their inter-actions with you that it will preserve forever – moments such as the phone call on holiday eves, when you wish us a happy holiday and a good new year, when you ask and take an interest in all the members of the family; when you asked about my husband Eliezer's heart, which stopped five years ago from his inability to stand the pain of his oldest son's death.

I recall special conversations, such as the one a few min-utes before Hadas's wedding ceremony, when you called to congratulate us and apologized for not being able to attend. In the same breath, you added, "I remem-ber you as a girl, sitting shivah for your brother, quietly shrinking into a corner, a girl whose entire world had collapsed. But now the moment of joy has arrived." "Mom," said Hadas, "how can he remember that from nine years ago?"

Yet you remember! The images of the younger children sitting shivah are engraved in your memory. On our memorial days, you always called to encourage and strengthen us, and at the same time, to tell us about meeting Eliraz during an exercise up north in the bitter cold: "I saw your boy, and he's fine…" There was so much love and joy and encouragement in that sen-tence. You never relax, but continue to ask what you can do to help, to encourage and push us to continue, continue to live a life of action.

From you I drew the strength to continue. You encour-aged me to meet with IDF soldiers and deliver your messages: "Fight for every soldier, not with every soldier," "Only nesharim, eagles, in Gamla – no neshirot, dropouts, in the IDF." I owe my leadership lessons to you, to the path you have carved out.

Like your fighters, I also felt a sense of responsibility toward you. When Eliraz fell and you asked me to continue, I took it as an order. You can't refuse the chief of staff. I was your soldier, too.

Honored guests,

This is a special time, a time to say thank you. Thank you, Mr. Chief of Staff, for the privilege of knowing you, the privilege of having five of my six children serve under your command, for the moments of pleasure you gave us, whether through words of encouragement or through your support.

You have been given an essential characteristic of an ethical, outstanding leader: knowing how to touch hearts. You spoke to us as equals. Even when you occupied the highest position, you were not arrogant. The general's overall view never blurred the personal connection. In every meeting with you, you gave us the feeling that we were the most important people there.

Your behavior with the members of the bereaved families inspired esteem and admiration. You were an example to your commanders and soldiers in your special attitude toward the family of the bereaved, following the maxim "Watch me, and follow my lead" – always sensitive and empathetic, kindhearted and open. This behavior was not exhibited on one lone occasion. This

*was your way of life, a way that strengthened our faith
in the IDF and its commanders.*

*I salute you with honor, as you saluted my sons, and
give you the blessing that I gave them when they went
out to battle: "May the Lord bless you and keep you;
May the Lord make His face shine upon you, and be
gracious to you; May the Lord lift up His countenance
to you, and grant you peace."*

In recognition of my lifework, my project of leadership education, I was awarded the Menachem Begin Prize. These were my
remarks at the awards ceremony:

Honored guests:

*I stand here today – excited, aching, and thankful.
Excited about this august occasion; aching over the
absence of my loved ones, my sons and my husband,
who are not here with me today; and thankful for the
honor of being a partner in a project that strengthens
our national spirit.*

*The award I am receiving today is not mine. It belongs
to my sons Uriel and Eliraz, who fell in the defense of
our homeland, and to Israel's fighters throughout history.
They are the ones who deserve the honor. The award is in
honor of the parents who have buried their children with
their own hands. It belongs to the widows and orphans,
to the brothers and sisters who continue, in the shadow
of loss, to carry on the spirit of the fallen and their heritage, and who act with determination and perseverance
to pass on this heritage to the coming generations.*

*From where did my sons draw their powerful love
for this homeland? From where did they draw their*

strength and bravery when they went out to be first in line to face the enemy? From faith, complete and pure faith in three principles that were their guiding light: the Torah of Israel, the People of Israel, and the Land of Israel. The faith in our right to live a life of freedom in our land.

The fighters of Israel, my sons among them, continue in the path of the Maccabees. They knew then as they know today that we are asked to stand guard to protect our people from the enemies who plot against us. The Greeks, Hezbollah, Hamas, Ahmadinejad, and all those who would do us harm are referred to in the Passover Haggadah: "In each and every generation, they rise up against us to destroy us, but the Holy One, blessed be He, saves us from their hand." As Judah the Maccabee said to his fighters: "For the victory of battle stands not in the multitude of the army; but strength comes from Heaven. They come against us in much pride and iniquity to destroy us, and our wives and children, and to lay waste to us, but we fight for our lives and our Torah. The Lord Himself will overthrow them before us. You, do not be afraid of them" (I Maccabees 3:19–22). Each generation has its enemies, each generation has its heroes, and each generation has its dead.

I didn't have the privilege, as my sons did, of being born here in Israel. But I did have the privilege of watching my sons put on IDF uniforms, stand beside the Western Wall, pray, and sing, "Our feet stood within your gates, O Jerusalem" (Psalms 122:2).

I saw them fighting in Gaza, in Lebanon, in Jenin, everywhere they were required to be, always in front.

They've always led, because that's what has to be, that's what has to be done. Because, as they said, "It's our turn, Mom, and we are the ones who have to carry the torch now." I was filled with pride, and I thank them and all the soldiers of the IDF for the privilege of being a free citizen of my homeland. For the privilege of my sons being able to protect me and my people, to protect the Jerusalem of our forefather Jacob.

I share this feeling of pride, this love for our land and this dedication with the youth and the IDF soldiers. All this I do out of optimism, joy, and hope. This is my sons' philosophy in today's reality, in which everything is framed as a question. Today, people are afraid of positive statements about the Jewish people, the Land of Israel, and the IDF. I tell the youth the simple story of my sons and of all the children of this land, and I demand of each of them to take up the idea: "You are the Maccabee," because we are worthy! Because we have no other land.

Since the death of my son Uriel twelve years ago, I have made it my goal to pass on his torch to our wonderful youth: the flag that enfolds within it values of commitment, giving, responsibility, dedication, and love for others; the aspiration for excellence, love for our land and its landscapes; and mainly, belief in the justness of this path.

Eliraz's death intensified my commitment and belief in the need to teach these values, because his death, twelve years after his brother's, is testimony that the continued struggle for our existence is not over. Over his grave, I asked those present not to construct buildings in his *memory, but to build the spirit. I asked them to take one of his qualities and implement it in their lives. That will be our answer to our enemies.*

Our spirit is strong, and even if I hurt and cry over the deaths of my sons and my husband Eliezer, I am not broken. You can't break a spirit. It grows stronger and takes on new forms of giving and dedication, of connection to this land and our heritage. Out of the darkness that visited our family and many other families in Israel, every day I choose to spread light. Like the Chanukah menorah that we are commanded to place in the window facing outward, toward the public domain, I serve as a kind of lighthouse lighting the way for all passersby and saying to them, "Follow my light."

Each one of us is asked to light his personal light and raise it up high, to join the communal light of our people. Together we can banish the darkness from our lives. We can spread the light through simple, humane acts that are free of self-interest, motivated by faith in the truth of this path, by responsibility, and by love for people and homeland. These are the lights that build a nation.

After Uriel fell, we began to talk about him at the Shabbat table and in everyday conversations, because I felt, as in the verse from Jeremiah (31:20), "For whenever I speak of him, I do remember him still." His name is always on my lips, and now this verse applies to Eliraz as well. I'm a walking tombstone for my two sons, but unlike the tombstone on the grave, I'm not silent, I'm a living, breathing memorial. I'm the tombstone of their lives. My path is to live them, with them.

CHAPTER 28

A New Path –
A Principal No Longer

The secular elementary school in Givat Ze'ev occupied a central place in my life, not just because it's right next to my house. It was my second home and my mission in life. But after Eliraz fell, I felt that I had to leave.

I had begun to consider leaving long before that. Over the prior two years, I had watched the number of students drop as the population grew older. In addition, an influx of religious families came to our settlement, and there was talk about closing my secular school, or unifying it with another school in the area. At that point, I knew I would not be the one to end my life's work. I couldn't close the gates of this school where my sons had grown up, whose development was intertwined with my family's life.

One month before Eliraz was killed, I shared my deliberations with him, and he said, "Mom, move forward. You have a lot to offer." Still, he understood the important place the school occupied in my life and how hard it was for me to consider leaving.

Luckily for me, the merger plan was put off by a year. I told Eliraz, and he said, "You see, Mom? You earned one more year."

Then Eliraz fell, and my situation was very different than it had been when Uriel died. When I buried my first son, I had support – Eliezer, my husband. I had someone with whom to share the pain. When Eliraz fell, however, the full weight of the pain fell on my shoulders, and so returning to school was harder as well.

I did return to school after the shivah, in deep sadness. The period after Passover demands intense work, getting ready for the end of the year and at the same time preparing for the upcoming year. The daily encounter with the students, their eager voices in the corridor led me to feel that these kids deserved a principal who radiated a higher level of enthusiasm and cheerfulness than what I was able to give them at that time.

The strain grew with the death of my beloved secretary, Sima Yom-Tov, who had worked alongside me throughout my career. I felt overly surrounded by death. So I announced that after years of serving as principal, the time had come to leave. I was going on to pursue a new path.

I'm not leaving the educational system, because I can't leave something that's an inherent part of me. No other job has more influence on the formation of the future generation of this country than that of the educator. I started the 2010–2011 school year in a new role in the Ministry of Education: Jerusalem district supervisor of values education in the Department of Society and Youth.

I began my new position with a heavy heart and not a little trepidation. I had asked the school not to organize a farewell party for me. I had had enough of leave-takings, and knew I wouldn't be able to stand any more. On the last day of school, I sent a letter to the parents. I wrote that "there is a time for every purpose under the heavens" (Ecclesiastes 3:1), and that after investing twenty-seven years of my life in TALI Secular School Number One, the time had come for me to end my role as principal, so the school could benefit from leadership with new energy.

I told them that the death of my son Eliraz had added to my pain over the death of my oldest son Uriel, and over the sudden death of my husband, who had also felt that the school was his home. I chose to conclude my letter quoting the words of Rabbi Nechuniya ben Hakanah as recorded in the Mishnah (*Berachot* 4:2). Rabbi Nechuniya prayed each day when he entered the study hall: "When I walk in, I pray that no mishap occur because of me. When I leave, I give thanks for my portion." When I came into the school every day, I prayed to the Creator that no student would come to harm. Now, as I leave, I thank the Holy One for granting me the privilege of educating a generation, and for the opportunity given to me to reach the inner core of my students."

I took up my new post in the Department of Society and Youth when it was headed by Zevik Alon, whom I have known for many years. His daughters attended my school, and he was one of the first parents to connect with the TALI concept, so I felt that I was going to a familiar place. When I started my new position, he presented me with several challenges. I had worked in formal education my entire life, and now I was observing the informal side of the educational system – premilitary training for youth, student councils, and youth groups. This gave me a broader, more general view of education, following the student from elementary school until induction in the military.

As part of my new job, I meet with youth, recount my personal story to them, and talk with them about coping during crises. I talk about spiritual strength, love for the Land of Israel, giving, and other values. I meet wonderful youngsters who connect to the pain, and through it understand the price of our existence in our country. My work in the department also enables me to focus on raising motivation for performing meaningful military service. In addition, I direct a new project at the Ministry of Education, the Social Bagrut Certificate, which aims to develop the students' involvement in social and volunteer programs.

The feedback I receive from schools regarding my meetings with youth encourages me tremendously. I often ask myself, as Eliraz did, why I came into this world. What is my mission? What am I supposed to do? I have no answer. But when a student comes up to me at the end of the meeting and says, "Miriam, you inspired me, you gave me strength and direction," I feel that I gained from this student as much as he gained from me. Each of us in turn both gave and received.

This is why even on the hardest days, before a memorial ceremony or when I wake up and my head is spinning, I don't allow myself to stay in bed. I have never required a minimum number of participants at these meetings. I believe in lighting single candles. When I see a spark ignited in the heart of one person, I'm sure it will spread to others.

I also meet with a wide range of adult groups. I call these encounters "The Song within the Grief," because with these groups, I talk about how one can find the ray of light from within the valley of death, from inside the blackness. I describe how from within the depths, one can see the outstretched hand of God sent to you to pull you out of the pit.

The first day of my new job, in my new office, was not easy. I couldn't believe that September 1 had arrived, and I wasn't standing at the school gate to greet the first-graders. There's a huge difference between the hallways of the Ministry of Education and the revitalizing clamor of kids. I also miss the ringing of the bell, the ceremonies, and the teachers' meetings. I even look back at the bureaucratic details with longing and love, and so I try to go out into the field, visit schools, inhale the smells of the classrooms, and absorb something of the students' vitality and energy.

The encounter with new people and different content – social rather than pedagogical – inspires me, gives me ideas, and sweeps me up into the joy of activity and creativity. Although I'm building my role within the department slowly, at my own pace, I already have a dream, a new project.

At meetings with youth and soldiers, I have found that they don't always identify with the stories of great heroes. It's hard for them to connect to stories of bravery that seem larger than life, and I've found that the simple stories of anonymous soldiers are the ones that inspire them the most.

In this regard, I would like to research the stories of fallen soldiers that we have never heard of or had the opportunity to know. I'd like to collect the key phrases they left behind, about love of our homeland and the justice of our path, quotations that will inspire our soldiers, that we can use to educate the next generation. If implemented, I plan to call this project "Values in their Words."

Uriel wrote, "With all the thorns and barbs that have scratched my body, you could put together a three-foot hedge. But these aren't just ordinary thorns – they're thorns from the Land of Israel, and whoever lives in this country must know how to accept these thorns with love."

Eliraz wrote, "You must give your all. If you love, you must love all the way. If you're a friend, you must be a friend to the end. If you're a combat soldier, then you're there to the end and you give your all, even when it comes at your personal expense or at the expense of your home leave. That's what's called, in lofty words, dedication. It means that you give of your body, your strength, your means, and your heart for people or causes other than yourself. What is extraordinary is when you do this not occasionally, but continuously, day in and day out, moment by moment."

These are examples that I found in the circle close to me, in the drawers of my two sons, but they're just a drop in the bucket. Almost every family opens drawers or computer files and finds jottings, thoughts, even poems. After a soldier is killed, every quotation takes on special, almost prophetic significance. But we have to remember that these sentences, which echo like prayers, were written while the boys were alive and still in uniform. They wrote them while they were dreaming of completing their service as best they could, of being discharged, and then starting a new chapter. In life.

CHAPTER 29

There Is an Eden

There is a Garden of Eden, I think. There is a good place where they have gone, and from which they will perhaps return one day, when the resurrection takes place. But I didn't give my children names that incorporate the name of God so that they could get to Eden so quickly.

When I had trouble during my first birth, Eliezer stood outside the door and prayed for protection from the angels: "Michael on my right, Gabriel on my left, Uriel in front." He vowed that if God would stand before me and I would have a safe delivery, he would call our son Uriel. I was the one who suggested Eliraz's name. I had dreamed that I was told a secret, and because Eliezer had planned to call him Eliyahu, after his kabbalist grandfather, we combined these into Eliraz, which relates to Elijah the Prophet, a man of secrets.

Eliraz was killed on Shabbat Hagadol, the Shabbat before Passover, when we read in the Haftarah portion (Malachi 3:23–24): "Behold, I will send you Elijah the Prophet." The end of the sentence reads, "that he may turn the heart of the fathers back through the sons, and the heart of the sons back through their fathers." That verse is deeply symbolic for me. It doesn't read, "turn the heart of the son," but rather "the heart of the sons," in the plural. Two sons. Both of them are in Eden, together with their father.

Did we make a mistake by giving them names with a holy connotation? Would other names have promised them a different fate?

There is a Garden of Eden on high, while here on earth, there is life. After Eliezer died, I stayed in bed for two months. Every morning, with my last drop of strength, I stood before the mezuzah. Not the one up in my room, but the one on the ground floor, at the entrance to the house, where I could look up at the heavens, where nothing came between me and the Master of the Universe. I shouted to Him: "God, I want to live! Please send me a cure!"

I inherited my survival instincts from my mother. In the *ma'abarah*, the immigrant camp, even while burning with fever from pneumonia, she got up to serve us lunch when we came home from school. While recuperating in the hospital following an operation, she traveled by bus from Be'er Sheva to Kiryat Shemona to pay a shivah call, and returned to the hospital after the visit. That required an enormous amount of strength, and she had it. I never saw my mother lying in bed helpless.

I'm not like her, and my children have seen me confined to my bed because of illness. But even when I'm bedridden, I'm able to rise. Sometimes more quickly, sometimes slowly. Even when I was hospitalized for an extended period of time and the doctors weren't able to come up with a diagnosis, I got out of bed every morning and encouraged myself: "Miriam, I realize you are dizzy, but you will walk to the end of the corridor and back." The next day I walked the corridor twice, and on the third day, I asked my kids to take me out to the yard, to breathe some air. The will to live is that strong in me.

I don't make an effort to be a hero; I just make an effort to live. When I see how much the kids worry and hurt, I say to myself, "Stop it, they've suffered enough," and I force myself to stand up, not out of heroism, but out of a powerful will to live. So it's strange to me that others view me as inspiring.

When I'm asked to come and strengthen others, I feel like asking, "What are you talking about? Touch me, I'm flesh and blood, fragile and broken." When I attempt to avoid their requests, they say, "True, you may not be stronger than anyone else physically, but you are strong spiritually." But even this justification moves me to protest. How can you define a strong spirit? Am I exceptional because I keep on living? We live whether we want to or not. We all get up to a new day. The question is what do we do with that getting up, and with the new day into which we have arisen?

I believe that there is a goal in the fact of our very presence in this world. Every human being was created in order to make the world a bit better than what it is right now. Every person comes into this world with a mission. For example, I believe that a person who says "Good morning" to a stranger in the street has done something good. With that offhand greeting, he has sent a small ray of light that brightens the stranger's world. I believe that if we all look inside ourselves, we will find many rays of light. Our job is not to keep them to ourselves, but rather to discover them and diffuse them. That's how we'll make the world a better place.

The definition of "mission" is beyond me. It embarrasses me. I only know one big mission, and that belonged to Moses, who led the Israelites to the Promised Land. The key word in his mission was *hineni* – "Here I am." I'm here, I'm committing my entire soul without any interest in personal gain, out of deep belief in the task I've been given, out of belief in God and in the mission I am performing.

If every one of us would explore for himself – as my sons Uriel and Eliraz did – basic questions such as who am I, what am I, why am I here, and what is the uniqueness that I bring to the world, action and a sense of mission would emerge from that inner exploration.

My mission was not in the sacrifice of two sons. This is not the way I chose to express my love for homeland and country. This is the way that was forced upon me and upon my nation. As I see it, serving as the principal of a secular school, though coming from a religious home, in a period of deep divisions between secular and religious Israelis, and creating an open dialogue out of love and recognition that we are all children of one people is my small contribution to my small world. Each of us, in our own way, bears individual responsibility for his personal and communal life. This was expressed in what Eliraz told me after Uriel was killed: "Mom, now it's my turn to continue," he said, and I imagined the chain of generations that began with Abraham, Isaac, and Jacob. I understood that he had to fulfill his destiny so that this chain would never come to an end.

Our history is stained with blood. Even in the time of the Maccabees, the best of our sons died, and mothers sat shivah. But when you are able to rise above the personal pain and see the continuity of history, you understand that now it's your sons' turn, your own turn. For this reason, I never explored the question of "why" – not the first time I buried a son, and not the second time either.

To be honest, that's not strictly true. During the first few days, I did ask why. It's impossible not to. After Eliraz fell, I imagined that God's computer was stuck on the Peretz family, maybe something in the system had gone wrong. It wasn't normal for death to strike me yet again. I had already paid the price. I had already given Uriel, and Eliezer had died of a broken heart following his first son, so how could it be?

A few days passed, and I realized that this question wasn't leading me anywhere. With time it took on another tone: what did this suffering intend to tell me, what were these travails meant to teach me? This is the big inquiry of my life. It still hasn't ended. This inner search leads me to new understandings about life. I look at things differently. I've learned to value the small things in life, and every second becomes a precious moment that will never return. I imagine myself drowning in a sea of pain that chokes me and threatens to overcome me, but still fighting to hold my head above the water, still singing my song, Miriam's song.

My boys were killed and this is a sorrow that can never be forgotten. I don't know how long I'll live. I don't know what will happen tomorrow. But today, at this very moment that still lives between my hands, maybe I have the ability to do something good? Maybe I'm sinning to God if I burrow inside my pain instead of using the small moment He has given me in order to help, or at least to try?

This understanding was born inside me after Uriel fell, and it was sharpened when Eliraz fell. Maybe it was hidden inside me always. Others will decide that. But today I try to look for the good in every moment. I find it and value it.

Unfortunately, I was made to stand yet another test at the time of Eliraz's death, which was different from Uriel's because our privacy was shattered. Eliraz became a symbol. We were still deep within our mourning; we didn't read newspapers or follow the media reports. But I was told that a senior reporter had written on his Facebook page that we were a family of jihadists. He wrote that he was tired of hearing the mantra of "the Israeli people – Israel Defense Forces – Israeli children – divine sacrifice." He wrote that Eliraz wasn't killed for his sake.

Following this, reporters and photographers came to visit and asked for my response. "Response to what?" I asked. I had no idea what they were talking about. It all seemed like vanity of vanities. Eliraz was no longer, and something inside me had died.

They told me about the reporter. I couldn't believe what I was hearing. Us? A family of jihadists? We were bloodthirsty? War-mongers? I had educated my children to die? I had encouraged

Eliraz to die like his older brother? But I had taught my kids to live! To live in happiness!

When they asked my son Elyasaf this question, he replied, "Tell that reporter that we'll continue living in Israel. We'll fight for it and defend it so that he can continue expressing his opinion. That's what we learned from Eliraz," he asserted. "Selfless love, love that expects no compensation."

But his response didn't satisfy them, and again they pushed me. "So, Miriam, what do you say?" they pressed.

In one moment I gathered myself together, and I answered: "Look, I grew up in a simple, modest Moroccan home. I was taught that when you like someone, you invite him to eat. So I invite that guy to have a meal with us. That's all."

A few days passed, and after Shabbat was over he called me. He asked for my forgiveness. I said, "There's nothing to forgive." It wasn't me talking, it was Eliraz speaking through my voice. Once he had written an article about anger, and he explained that it was cruel to turn your back on one who asks for forgiveness.

On the other side of the line I didn't hear a voice; rather, I pictured a person's eyes. A person in pain, an individual who loves Israel in his own way. I saw my own brother, a son of my people, who said what he did and then apologized. Eventually he wrote me a moving letter, in which he said, "We won't argue the fact that this is our country." This is our point of connection, the Land of Israel. And we both know that it's our right to live here. To me, there is no connection greater than this.

Some people tried to stir things up, to fan the fire. Unfortunately, this is the culture of dialogue in the State of Israel. When someone expresses a view that isn't accepted by the other, personal barbs fly. This isn't the way of the Peretz family. My attitude is exactly the opposite: disagreement is good. We don't have to agree with each other. It would be disastrous if we all agreed. But when we disagree, we have to show mutual respect. If I was able to respect that journalist, and if despite our disagreement, I was able to find the common ground between us, as members of one people living in this precious land – that's enough for me. Out of this disagreement, I developed a warm connection with the journalist. We still disagree, but we know that neither of us hates the other. On Yom Kippur Eve, I was touched when he called and again asked for my forgiveness. If God forgives, how could I possibly refuse to do so? I am unworthy. I viewed this as a test from God.

If I passed this one small test that God put me to – a test of restraint and love – I owe my thanks to Eliraz. He loved people. He always viewed each person in a positive light, and considered everyone his brother. On Mount Herzl, at his funeral, I asked: "Don't construct buildings in his memory. Take one of his good qualities and try to implement it in your daily life. In this way, you'll build your spirit." In my behavior toward that journalist, I felt I was carrying out what I had asked from others.

In my imagination, I picture my two sons standing beside their father, their grandmothers and grandfathers, and I feel that they are well protected. They are not alone. But the first rain brings endless weeping. Maybe they're cold, maybe they're wet. The hot wind of the *hamsin* also brings tears. Sometimes I think perhaps they're in a better place than I am, because I'm in a place of suffering where my soul is being battered – a place that makes me get up each morning to a new struggle for life – while they are in a place that is only good, I have no doubt of that.

I talk to them and shout at them and invite them to come to me, and they do. I hear Eliraz saying to me, "Mom, keep on going, it's okay." Sometimes he says, "I had to go." I have chills when he says, "I prepared Shlomit. She'll know how to bring up the kids, she'll keep going. I love you all so much, Mom." I see Uriel, with his glasses and white teeth and giant smile, saying to me in his simple language, "What's the big fuss about, Mom? We did what you taught us to do, to be faithful to our path, to march in front. I'm here, Mom, taking care of Eliraz." Eliezer sends me a rescuing angel every time I need help, and I apologize to him: "I'm sorry, Eliezer, that I don't do enough to memorialize you, because I dedicate myself fully to the kids."

I want to invite them to me over and over again, but sometimes I have pangs of conscience. Maybe I'm disturbing their rest? Maybe I'm bothering them? Days pass, and they step back. They move away in body, but not in spirit. With every day that begins and ends, the distance in time grows, but the spiritual distance grows shorter. They are up in heaven – almost half of my family is up there, in God's commando unit – and I'm down here. Stretched between us is a thread of love, of longing, memories, prayer, and everything they left down here inside people's hearts.

Sometimes I look down at the prayer book that is already wet with tears, and I can't understand how it is still in one piece. When I read the verse in the book of Job (5:7), "Sparks fly upward," I think about the members of the Peretz family who flew upward before their time. Sometimes I lift my eyes to the ceiling – the ceiling of the synagogue that Eliezer built that has windows through which I can see the heavens above. I pray that my quiet voice will penetrate the thick cement walls, fly upward, and reach that place.

Because there is an Eden. I know it.

Five Years Later

Four years ago, one year after Eliraz was killed, a delivery man from Yediot Aharonot Publishing arrived at my home, with a box containing the first copies of my book, *Miriam's Song*. I opened the box, took out a copy, and cradled it in my hands. "This is the Peretz family Passover Haggadah," I said.

With this statement, I felt that I had completed the task I had set for myself. Eliraz was killed two days before Seder night. On Passover, the Torah commands fathers *v'higadeta l'vincha*, "tell your children" – to recount the history of our people to their children. But Eliraz was gone – who would tell the story to his four children? Gili was only two months old when her father died. What would she know?

I knew that the children wanted to hear about their father. I saw them listening to me, eyes wide, when I made the seemingly offhanded comment that they were as mischievous as he had been. But every time I opened the photo albums and talked to them about my memories, I felt like I was dying. I said to myself, "Eliraz, you should have been the one sitting here with your children, seeing with your own eyes how they have grown. It should have been you telling them about our family history – that's the father's job, that's what *v'higadeta l'vincha* means."

Every time I saw Eliraz's four children, I felt as if two beings were occupying my body at the same time. On the one hand, I was Miriam the grandmother, who sang, danced, played, and enjoyed spending time with her grandchildren. On the other hand, I was Miriam the mother, who had lost her son Eliraz. These two entities mingled within me, pain and joy surged inside at the same level, without conflict. Sometimes pain overcame joy, at other times joy overpowered pain, coexisting alongside each other in the same person, the same woman.

Later, Rabbi Eli Adler of the Otzem premilitary academy, which Eliraz attended, published a special version of a Passover Haggadah in memory of Eliraz, with his biography and photographs. I felt hardly capable of such a challenge as writing a Haggadah commentary. Even when I held the first copy of *Miriam's Song*, I was certain that it would be a history for our family only, especially for Eliraz's children. I was afraid of forgetting. The years that had passed since the death of Uriel, my oldest son, had proven that pain and sorrow overcome images of the past. So I started working with Smadar Shir while Eliraz's death was still fresh, before the pain became enveloped in silence. Throughout the shared project, even when we touched the most painful issues, I knew I had to do it. I did it for Eliraz's children and for the next generation of the Peretz family, that I wish had remained anonymous.

I never imagined that just days after the book left the presses and was sent to the bookstores, I would become a well-known and talked-about personality, a kind of symbol, a lodestone from which people could draw encouragement and comfort.

Me? All these years I had done nothing but concentrate on my own family. I had been content to stay inside my small shell. I liked being a private person. Who was I to suddenly start receiving a flood of phone calls, letters, emails, and invitations to lecture all over the world?

Yet the flood began immediately. Friends of mine from high school, who hadn't previously made the connection between Miriam Peretz and the Miriam Ohayon who had attended Comprehensive "B" High School in Be'er Sheva with them, contacted me, saying, "We've been looking for you for years." Thanks to the book, we organized an active What'sApp chat group and a reunion. I was very excited to meet my friend Dalia Cohen from elementary and high school days – long ago, when I was a new immigrant, she had given me her hand-me-downs. People my age, over sixty, called to say, "It's so lovely that you took us back in time to stories from our days in the *ma'abara* [immigrant camp]." They said they would give the book to their children so that the next generation would understand what they had gone through in the camps.

Men and women I didn't know told me, "You've brought honor to the Moroccans" – but I was embarrassed. Me? I was born in Morocco, but I hardly symbolize Moroccan culture. I don't symbolize anything. Others told me that they connected to the belief in God that Uriel and Eliraz exemplified so powerfully. They categorized *Miriam's Song* as a book about faith. That embarrassed me, too. I had only meant to describe what I felt. How could I be a symbol of faith? My faith also includes many doubts, highs and lows, uncertainties, and questions for which there are no answers.

Most embarrassing of all were the random people in the supermarket or on the street who asked me to give them my blessing, as if I had some kind of special power. But I did it with love. I've always given my blessing sincerely and from the heart. My children joked, "Mom, they've turned you into Baba Miriam," and I laughed. Who was I to give my blessing? After all, it's mainly in the realm of the kitchen that my hands have proven their efficiency.

Jokes aside, I gave this some serious thought. Who was I to bless strangers? I had taken my own children to the greatest rabbis in the State of Israel to ask for their blessing. I had given them my own mother's blessing each morning and evening, and each time they left the house. But at the moment of truth, what happened to all those blessings? Who received them? Which soldier merited them? I believe that the Holy One, blessed be He, hears the prayers of pain.

On Yom Kippur Eve, Rabbi Benny Lau called me and said, "In another few hours I'll begin the fast, and I'll be reading your book." I was moved to tears. I glanced up to Heaven and asked, "God, how is it that on the holiest day of the year, the rabbi will be holding my book in his hands?" Then I thought, maybe it's all for the best. Maybe this is what will encourage God to take a look down here, to look at all the bereaved mothers like me and do everything in His power so that no mother, in Israel or around the world, will have to bury her son.

Rabbi Lau asked me if I knew how he had received the book. I answered, "No, how should I know that?" Then he began to tell the story, and I remembered.

A few days earlier, on Rosh Hashanah Eve, as I was busy in the kitchen preparing for the holiday, the phone rang. A male voice said, "Hello, Miriam Peretz? This is Avi Wartzman, vice mayor of Be'er Sheva. I want you to be my mother!"

I smiled and said, "Sorry, I already have six kids."

"I know," he replied. "But I'd like to come visit you, and you'll be my mother."

I looked around at the chaotic kitchen. "I'm sorry," I excused myself. "It's almost Rosh Hashanah, and I'm very busy. Can we meet after the holiday?"

But he insisted. "I don't care. I'll come and wait outside until you have time for me."

He came, book in hand, and said, "When I read it, I felt like you were my mother." We sat in the living room and talked for three hours, my cell phone buzzing incessantly in the background. Relatives and friends called to wish me Shanah Tovah, a happy New Year, but I didn't answer. I was completely focused on my conversation with Avi Wartzman. He said, "See? Even now you're behaving just like my mother – you're talking directly to me." After the holiday, he ordered four hundred copies of the book for the Be'er Sheva municipal social workers. He told them, "When you go visit the homes in Shikun Dalet, the hard-knocks neighborhood where Miriam Peretz grew up, remember that behind every door there may be another little girl like her." He was the one who had given a copy of the book to Rabbi Benny Lau. The rabbi said me, "I don't usually read every book that people bring me, but Avi said 'This is a must' – and he was right. I'm beginning Yom Kippur in fear and trembling, with your book."

One day, I received a call from a representative of a public housing company. The moment I heard the name of the company, "Amidar," I was taken aback, and began to murmur apologies. The man asked why I was apologizing. I related: "When I was a child in the immigrant camp, we used to curse your company. We thought of it as the rich owner of all the apartment blocks, exploiter of the poor. I have to admit that when I was a teenager, when we moved into an apartment in north Shikun Dalet, we didn't pay the rent regularly – not because we didn't want to, but simply because we had no money."

He listened, and said that he had been deeply moved when he read the book. He was especially touched by the description of Passover Eve, when I stood in line, coupon in hand, to get a bottle of cooking oil, a package of matzah, and a box of sugar, and I was so grateful to the State of Israel for taking care of my family. He added, "I wish more people would learn to appreciate our country and what it gives, instead of whining and complaining."

A high school student sent me an urgent text message: she was about to take her math matriculation exam, and she was quaking with fear. She wrote that she would enter the exam room reciting the words that Uriel had said on his first day of first grade. He had trouble getting on the bus because he was short and the step was high. But when I tried to help him, he said, "Mom, I can do it!" This student was also saying to herself, "I can do it." I wished her good luck on the test.

Another girl, this one from Sderot, wrote that during Operation Protective Edge she had read my book in between air-raid sirens, running with it into the safe room. The book was what gave her the courage to overcome the fear that whistled over her head. Most readers said that they read the book in one breath, swinging between joy and sorrow, while others revealed that when they reached the parts about Uriel and Eliraz, they couldn't continue and had to take a break.

Very quickly the book began to be distributed as a gift for high school graduates and officers' training courses, and to defense ministry employees. The characters of Uriel and Eliraz became a national legacy. I would meet soldiers, and out of their shirt pockets they would pull little notes with quotes from the book. I would see Uriel's sentence peeking out from behind their insignia: "With all the thorns and barbs that have scratched my body, you could put together a three-foot hedge. But these aren't just ordinary thorns – they're thorns from the Land of Israel...." On Uriel and Eliraz's tombstones, I found notes with quotations from the book. When I went to lecture at an officers' training course, one of the women soldiers asked if she could speak with me in private. We moved off to one side. Carefully, she took out a wrapped object from her purse. Slowly she peeled off the wrapping and said, "This was my boyfriend's wallet. He was killed in Gaza." She carefully opened the wallet and showed me a small piece of paper with Uriel's quote about the thorns of the Land of Israel.

I was deeply moved. I knew that soldiers were carrying Uriel and Eliraz's sentences with them. I knew that they were penetrating many hearts.

How I wish that my two sons were alive, and that no one was citing them.

Many people wrote that actually, the chapters about my husband Eliezer were the ones that moved them, and the more they mentioned him, the more intensely I felt his absence. When Uriel fell in battle, he stood by my side and we coped, the two of us together. When Eliraz fell, I had to handle it alone. I never stop missing Eliezer. I'm sixty-one years old, and I know I'll grow old without him. Now, after the children have all left the nest, this should have been our time together. When I see couples walking down the street, hand in hand, I shout out to God: "Couldn't you have given me that? You had to take that from me, too? You couldn't give me the pleasure of growing old together?"

Every single day, the neighborhood postbox and my email account are filled with letters from readers, who recount how much this book strengthened them and filled them with inspiration and faith. At first I was surprised – why my story? After all, there are people out there with much more powerful stories than mine. Eventually, I realized that every person walks around with his life story percolating in his head. For years on end, he searches for a listening ear that will permit him to open up and share. Unintentionally, I became an address for those who found it difficult to express their feelings. They wrote, "You speak as if from within our own hearts. We are coping with the same anger and pain, and when we see you continuing your life and hear you speaking, it gives us strength. It proves that even out of great tragedy, we can go on. We can even smile."

I didn't choose this reality – it was forced on me. But I admit that there is something to this wide, warm embrace of the public. I don't ask for this embrace, but I let it in, I allow it to come close and penetrate my soul. Usually it doesn't end with just a hug. The person standing before me wants to bend my ear with the story of his life, and when I hear things like "You're an inspiration" or "You're a hero," I pinch myself on the arm. Look at me. Am I really a hero? I'm flesh and blood, just like everyone else.

In my own eyes, I'm no hero at all. But if a hero is someone who chooses life – then yes, I've chosen. If a hero is someone who continues to love the Land of Israel and the Jewish people – then yes, I love them. And if a hero is someone who wants to give and do good, only good – then yes, I'm a hero. This double death has strengthened me. My two graves have taught me to pursue values of giving and lovingkindness, love for the Land of Israel and the Bible; they've made me sensitive to every individual. Sometimes I place my hand on my heart and I wonder how that organ continues to function. Every knock on the door shrunk my heart. Every death notice shattered me to smithereens. But in the five years since Eliraz was killed, my heart has grown larger and wider. I shouldn't have kept on living – from my point of view, it's a miracle I'm still here. It's Divine Providence, it shouldn't be taken for granted. Every day I thank God in Heaven for continuing to believe in me, for continuing to bless me with life.

* * *

During these five years since Eliraz's death, I've been invited on many trips abroad. The first was for a festive fundraising dinner given by the Friends of the Israel Defense Forces (FIDF), held at the famous Waldorf Astoria Hotel in New York City. For the first time in my life, I gave a speech in English, and my knees shook at the magnitude of the occasion.

I began my speech by describing the announcement of Eliraz's death, and I said that the knock on the door didn't stop life – it gave life a different meaning and intensity. When the Hezbollah killed my son Uriel and the Hamas killed my son Eliraz, they harmed only the bodies of my sons, not their spirits, their souls, or their faith. No enemy can break the spirit of the Jewish people, and no bullet can murder faith. Sometimes we take the existence of the State of Israel for granted, as a self-evident fact. But the deaths of my sons, and of thousands of other soldiers, bear witness to the fact that the continuous struggle for our existence has not ended. Our sons are a rare breed – they are the generation of revival that knows the meaning of independence and a state.

This generation has chosen to defend our freedom, and is willing to sacrifice its life on behalf of that value. My family has had the honor of participating in the defense of the State of Israel, and even though grief struck me twice, I never give up, because the spirit – of my sons, of the Jewish people, of faith and hope – lives on, inspiring a new generation. We are the eternal people – and as the saying goes in Hebrew, *Am hanetzach lo pochek mi'derech arukah* – "The eternal people do not fear the long road ahead." On behalf of my sons and all the fallen soldiers, I told the FIDF, *Am yisrael chai v'yihiyeh la'ad!* – "The Jewish people live, and will live forever!"

FIDF dinners were organized to raise funds on behalf of IDF soldiers. They were held around the United States, including New Jersey, San Francisco, San Diego, Los Angeles, Boca Raton, Houston, and Las Vegas. I never dreamed that my passport would collect so many stamps. Although these trips were difficult, both physically and emotionally, I went feeling that I was performing a mission on behalf of the State of Israel. Every time I get on and off a plane, I tell myself, "Miriam, this isn't possible. You're not supposed to be in these places. Uriel should have come here on a trip after the army, and Eliraz should have been here with his wife, Shlomit, for their tenth wedding anniversary or some other happy occasion." I try to see the world through their eyes, and usually I'm able to do so, because miraculously – I have no other explanation – almost everywhere I go, I have greetings from Uriel and Eliraz.

It happened when I was inside the Walmart on 34th Street in New York City, looking for presents for my grandchildren, Eliraz's children. A woman I didn't recognize came up to me and said in English, "I know you from somewhere." I replied that I was from Israel. She switched to Hebrew and after a short conversation, back to English. "Oh, my dear!" she said. "You're Miriam Peretz, Uriel and Eliraz's mother!" After the dinner in Houston, a young man from the Israeli embassy approached me and said, "Nice to meet you. I was one of Uriel's soldiers." In Teaneck, as I left Keter Torah synagogue following Friday night services, a young man said, "You don't know me, but during officers' training course I slept in the bunk above Uriel." I was invited along with Avi Berman, president of OU Israel (the Union of Orthodox Congregations in Israel), to Shabbat lunch in the home of Rabbi Shalom Baum. Among the guests was a young woman who said, "I served in Eliraz's brigade," and proceeded to tell me about him.

Were these miracles? Or living greetings from my sons? It's as if they are beside me, everywhere around the world.

Through the book, students in many schools in Israel and abroad were exposed to the characters of Uriel and Eliraz. They made films, media presentations, and booklets. Yavne School of Sydney, Australia, prepared an exhibit with a special room in memory of each boy. At their Yom Hazikaron ceremony, students and community members walked through the rooms. When I received a printed booklet documenting the exhibit, I acknowledged that it held a grain of consolation. The Talmud says, "The dead are condemned to be forgotten" (*Pesachim* 54b) – but my children are not forgotten. On the contrary – Eliraz's death led to heightened awareness about Uriel. True, I'm the person responsible for this rebirth, but it's important for me to emphasize that the reason people connect to them and to me is not because I'm telling a story of pain and loss. That isn't the main thrust of my narrative. The significant part is the choice of life and hope.

My latest trip was a few months ago, to Panama. I flew there with my sons Avichai and Elyasaf, at the invitation of the Jewish community and sponsored by David Harari, Ikey Badash, Shimon Hafetz, Meir Malka, and Rabbi Yigal Tsaidi, director of Jewish programs at Einstein School in Panama City. Community representative Ezra Cohen was waiting to meet us at the Panama City terminal. He asked, "What can I do for you? A manicure or pedi-cure? Maybe a massage? We just want to spoil you."

I was astonished. For years I'd been running around Israel and the world on a volunteer basis, meeting with a wide variety of communities, but I'd never heard such a welcoming sentence. During our week-long stay in Panama, we had the opportunity to get to know this warm Jewish community. We participated in their happy occasions, attending *brit milah* ceremonies and prayer ser-vices, as well as the Yom Yerushalayim (Jerusalem Day) ceremony at Einstein School. Two lines of children dressed in blue and white waved Israeli flags as they marched into the auditorium. What had we done to deserve this honor? The students sang the words "The mountain air is clear as wine" from "Jerusalem of Gold," and there in Panama, I felt as if I were breathing the air of Jerusalem. Even in Israel, my home, not all schools mark Yom Yerushalayim with such an exciting ceremony. We encountered an audience that identified with our pain and listened in silence to our family story, as well as our analysis of the challenges that Israel faces today. One of the most significant of these is the challenge of unity. How can we unify all the groups in our country – religious and secular, Ashkenazi and Sephardi, Arabs, Christians, and Druze – into one nation, the nation of Israel?

In a fascinating meeting with the vice president of Panama, who also served as minister of foreign affairs, we became virtu-al ambassadors. My sons told her about how they had fought in Gaza during Operation Protective Edge (July–August 2014), and about the IDF's code of battle ethics. She embraced me warmly, and I told her, "You're a woman, and so am I. Who knows better than we what our children mean to us? We aspire to life, not to death and war." I asked her to help us, in her own way, to achieve the peace we so longed for.

In my speech in Panama, I said that when I received the announcement of Uriel's death, the first thought that flew into my head was what would happen if one day someone said the name "Uriel," but no one knew who that was. I was so afraid, and then I adopted the verse, "For whenever I speak of him, I do remember him still" (Jeremiah 31:19), even though speaking of him makes me weep. Speaking in English and in Moroccan, I told the WIZO women the story "Three Gifts" which I used to tell my mother. My English is very basic – in high school I slept through English classes, and now I pay the price. I don't differentiate between past and future tense. But they understood me, and the story touched them deeply. At *seudah shlishit*, the third Shabbat meal, when I was expected to speak on a new topic, I described the immigrant camp and the toolbox of life skills I had inherited from my mother, who grew up in a cemetery in Morocco, where her father worked as the guardian. I ended with the story of the Baba Sali, thanks to whom I didn't abort Uriel. Out of the blue, someone in the audience raised a hand and identified herself as the Baba Sali's great-granddaughter. What a small world. I told her that when Eliraz was little, his eyes were crossed. Her great-grandfather gave my husband drops of holy water to sprinkle on his eyes, and said, "Don't worry, he'll be fine."

My sons are memorialized in Israel as well. In Petach Tikva, a new religious high school was named Amit Eliraz, and I'm in close contact with the students and teachers there. When Eliraz was killed, I asked that the only buildings erected in his name be educational and religious institutions, and this wish is still being honored today. The Ashkenazi community in the Mishab neighborhood of Givat Ze'ev, where I live, felt a connection to his life, and decided to establish Beit Eliraz ("Eliraz House"), a synagogue and religious community center. Construction has been delayed as donations are still needed, but in my mind's eye I can already picture the children who will come to pray at Beit Eliraz, and the soldiers who will use the event hall for meetings and lectures.

* * *

The five years that have passed have brought happy occasions: my daughter Hadas gave birth to two more sweet girls, Eliraz and Ma'ayan. My daughter Bat-El had a daughter, Carmi. We also celebrated two weddings – Elyasaf married Noa, and Avichai married Hani. If I could, I would continue to focus only on my family life, which vacillates between celebrations and memorials. But in March 2013, I found myself face to face with Barak Obama, the president of the United States.

It was Passover Eve. In Moroccan households, you shouldn't get too close to the housewives in the week before Passover – that's the time when the pressure is at its peak. In remembrance of the Children of Israel who were slaves in Egypt, every Moroccan housewife takes on a massive cleaning project. Just try to imagine this scenario: I'm toiling away, organizing cupboards and scrubbing the oven, my clothes stained with bleach. I wash sheets and air out blankets. I make the children brush off their shirt fronts after each meal to make sure no crumbs of *chametz* are carried into the bedrooms. In the middle of the chaos, the phone rings.

"Hello, we're calling from the president's residence."

Without a second thought, I replied, "I'm in the middle of Passover cleaning. Don't try to trick me, I'm in no mood for jokes." With that, I hung up.

Barely two minutes passed, and the phone rang again. "Mrs. Peretz, President Shimon Peres would like to invite you to dine with Barak Obama."

I still couldn't believe my ears. "Okay, okay. Let's talk after the holiday."

The phone rang once again. It was my son Avichai, and he said that Tomer Reichman, who had been Uriel's sergeant, was now working in President Peres' office. "Tomer called me and said that the president wants to invite you to dinner, but you keep hanging up on them."

I explained to Avichai that I had been sure someone was playing a joke on me. I added, "They said on TV that the dinner honoring Obama would take place on Thursday night, which is when we're planning to go to synagogue for the third annual memorial ceremony for Eliraz."

Avichai replied in an assertive tone. "Mom, the brothers and sisters will go to the synagogue. You'll go to the president's residence for the dinner with Obama, and the next day we'll all go to Mt. Herzl together."

How did I deserve the honor of dinner with the president of the United States?

The planners of the Obama visit had decided that on Friday, 11 Nissan, at nine a.m., the American president would lay flowers on the graves of Theodor Herzl and Yitzhak Rabin, and traffic would be blocked off in the entire area. The presidential visit fell on the same day as the annual memorial ceremony for Eliraz. Defense ministry officials called to ask whether I was willing to postpone the memorial ceremony, as the security arrangements required Mt. Herzl to be empty of visitors. I explained that with all due respect to Obama, I could not change the date of the memorial ceremony – it was an issue of halachah. But I was willing to move my ceremony from nine a.m. to eleven a.m., so as not to interfere with the presidential visit. I contacted the memorial department of the Ministry of Defense, and they willingly assisted me. In order to avoid conflicts with the Obama security arrangements, they decided that the participants in Eliraz's memorial ceremony would park in a nearby parking lot, where they would undergo security clearance. Then they would be bussed to Mt. Herzl under police escort.

After I obtained all the necessary permits to hold the ceremony, I thought to myself how symbolic it was that we would be there together. Obama had come to talk about peace – it was fitting that he should be aware that my children, Uriel and Eliraz, had paid the price of peace. Obama should come to Mt. Herzl, I thought, and see that we have other national heroes besides Herzl and Rabin – all those fighters that are buried on that hill. That's the appropriate way to end a visit to Israel.

The media reported the preparations for the presidential visit, expanding on the topic of the dinner, to which a select one hundred guests were invited. Then, in the midst of the tumult of Passover Eve, I received the official invitation to the dinner with Obama. I asked in embarrassment if I should prepare something, or wear something special. The secretary said the dress code required a jacket.

A jacket? Me? I wore a black skirt and an old jacket that Eliezer had bought me ages ago. I phoned Eliezer's friend Asher Kadosh, and when I told him I thought I might die of embarrassment, he reassured me. "My good friend Chaim Cohen, who is a friend of President Peres, is also invited to the dinner," he said. "Don't worry, he's a *dialna* Moroccan – 'one of ours.' He'll help you fit in to the scene."

Tomer Reichman awaited me at the entrance to the president's residence. I put my arm through his, and we felt like a royal couple walking down a red carpet. The only place I had even seen such a sight was on TV, while watching the Oscar ceremony in Hollywood. I walked into the reception room, and saw Knesset members Tzipi Livni, Yair Lapid, and Shelly Yachimovich; Nir Barkat, mayor of Jerusalem; and Israel's chief justice and chief rabbis. What did I know about royal etiquette? I felt out of place. This was the memorial evening for my son Eliraz. What was I doing there, in a jacket and heels?

The guests were invited to adjourn to the dining room, and I continued to wonder how I fit in at this event. I was placed at a round table with State Comptroller Joseph Shapira and representatives of the US delegation. As we made small talk, I darted a sideways glance at the menu that was set on the table. From

364 S Miriam's Song

my point of view, the dinner was timed perfectly. It was a few days before Passover, when we remove every last crumb of food from the house, and I was starving. In my family, the week before Passover is not just a week of spring cleaning. My kids call it the "week of famine." Ever since I had received the invitation, I hadn't wasted a thought on whether I would have a chance to say a personal word to the president of the United States, as I was certain that he would prefer to talk to people who were more important and well-respected than me. Miriam – I said to myself – this is your chance to enjoy a delicious meal. My imagination conjured up the gourmet presidential meal that would satisfy my empty stomach.

The menu was in English, and I couldn't understand all of it, but I did manage to identify the words, "Tower of tomatoes in pesto and olive oil sauce." Tower? I wondered. It sounded wonderfully bounteous. But when they brought me my serving, my face fell. There was no tower to be seen. Instead, on the plate sat a single cherry tomato, sliced into thin strips, and on each strip was a pinch of basil. This was what they served to honored guests? A sampler? In every ordinary Moroccan household, the hostess places twenty different kinds of salads on the table for hors d'oeuvres. Where was the traditional *berbera*, the red beet salad? Where was the famous *matbucha*, the roasted sweet pepper and tomato salad? Where were the spicy carrots? They certainly have something to learn from us Moroccans, I thought. I wondered if President Obama had ever eaten a real Moroccan meal.

From my seat, I sneaked a peek at the head table: Prime Minister Binyamin Netanyahu, beside him President Barak Obama, President Shimon Peres, and Sara Netanyahu, the prime minister's wife. With my very own eyes I watched as Obama mopped up hummus with a tiny pita – he, too, had been served a sample. When he had entered the dining hall, I had noticed that he was very tall. There was something about him that radiated royalty, as if he had stepped out of a legend. But faced with a plate of food, he ate and laughed just like any ordinary guy.

The meal continued, but I was still so famished I could eat a bear. In desperation, I attacked the basket of cookies that was brought to the table. Just as I stuffed a particularly large specimen into my mouth, I noticed President Peres and President Obama walking up to me. I jumped out of my chair. Heaven help me, I thought, does it have to be right at this moment, when my teeth are full of crumbs?! Just when I'm finally enjoying the food?!

President Peres introduced me to Obama – "This is Miriam Peretz." Obama said, "Yes, I heard about you. You're the mother of the boys." We shook hands. I was touched: the president of the United States knew about Uriel and Eliraz? With crumbs in my teeth, in my halting English, I said: "Mr. President, tomorrow is the memorial ceremony for my son Eliraz. When you stand beside the tomb of the great visionary of our state, Theodor Herzl, I will be standing beside the tomb of my son, Eliraz. This is no coincidence. See what a heavy price we pay in order to fulfill the dream."

Obama nodded, and I continued: "Mr. President: Mt. Herzl, the place where my sons are buried, is my home, and theirs. I ask you to do everything in your power so that I can continue living in this land, in security and peace, and so that my grandchildren won't have to pay with their lives."

Perhaps I'm exaggerating, but I thought I noticed Obama's eyes grow moist. In that moment, I said to myself once again: Uriel and Eliraz, you are here. The only reason that I'm here is thanks to you.

Then the president asked graciously, "May I give you a hug?"

"Of course," I replied, and I felt his embrace was heartfelt. Setting aside his political positions and opinions, he was a gentleman – fatherly, sensitive, and attentive. It was a heartwarming moment. Before me stood the most important man in the world – Obama, the human being.

A few months later, when I returned to the US to speak in New York, I stood in the middle of Times Square, watching the waves of humanity, and I asked myself: How many of you red-blooded Americans have had the privilege of shaking the hand of your very own president? Thanks to Uriel and Eliraz, I had enjoyed an even greater honor – a hug from him.

* * *

My frequent trips around the world have led me to encounters with many wonderful families, whom under different circumstances I certainly never would have met. It's how I met the Chipkin family of Johannesburg, and Hagit Hadar of Brooklyn, who hosted us lovingly in her home, as well as at the Magen David School, where she works as a teacher. In peaceful Monsey, I and my daughters Bat-El and Hadas were guests in the home of Fay and Doron Cohen, who give generously to Israel. In Teaneck, I was hosted by Becky and Avi Katz, and every morning I watched as the head of the household sat in front of the beautiful landscape of his yard and studied Talmud. In Los Angeles, I found a second home with Naomi and Daniel Silverman. Every year they make sure to send me a photo of the first flowering of the tree that stands at the entrance to their home. The pink spring flowers fill me with joy.

I've gotten to know the many different types of Jews in the world, their deep love for Israel and their warm hospitality. I visited the home of Esther and Jerry Williams in Lawrence, in the Five Towns area of New York State. I had hoped to rest there, to gather my strength after a long week of giving leadership classes and speeches, and before my return flight to Israel. But as the verse says, "Many are the thoughts in a man's heart, but it is God's plan that will stand" (Proverbs 19:21). After three days in Esther's home, the weather forecasters announced on the news that a powerful storm was about to hit the area – Hurricane Sandy. At three

Friends of the IDF dinner, USA

Keren Hayesod dinner, Sydney, Australia. Left to right:
Fentahun Assefa-Dawit, Greg Masel, Bruce Fink, Dennis Prager,
Johanna Arbib, Miriam Peretz, Gary Perlstein.

Haim Saban and his wife, Friends of the IDF dinner, USA.
(Photo courtesy of Friends of the IDF.)

Israel's 67th Independence Day ceremony at the home of Reuven Rivlin, the President of Israel. On the left, *Prime Minister Benjamin Netanyahu.* On the right, *Minister of Defense Moshe Ya'alon.* (Photo courtesy of Tomer Reichman.)

Israel's 67th Independence Day ceremony at the home of President Reuven Rivlin. Left to right: *Noa Peretz, Nechama Rivlin (wife of the President), Miriam, President Reuven Rivlin, Elyasaf Peretz.* (Photo courtesy of Tomer Reichman.)

Miriam with participants in the torch lighting ceremony on Israel's 66th Independence Day. Front row center: *Knesset Chairman Yuli Edelstein;* to his right, *Limor Livnat,* to his left, *Jerusalem Mayor Nir Barkat.*

Israel's 67th Independence Day ceremony at the home of President Reuven Rivlin. Left to right: *Prime Minister Benjamin Netanyahu, President Reuven Rivlin, Miriam, Minister of Defense Moshe Ya'alon, Former Chief of Staff Gadi Eizenkot.* (Photo courtesy of Tomer Reichman.)

*Knesset Chairman Yuli Edelstein presenting medal to
Miriam at the torch lighting ceremony*

*Israel's 67th Independence Day ceremony at the home of
President Reuven Rivlin.* (Photo courtesy of Tomer Reichman.)

With President Reuven Rivlin and his wife Nechama.
(Photo courtesy of Tomer Reichman.)

Israel's 67th Independence Day ceremony at the home of President Reuven Rivlin. (Photo courtesy of Tomer Reichman.)

Dinner in honor of US President Barack Obama's visit to Israel, at the home of President Reuven Rivlin. Left to right: *President Obama, Shimon Peres, Miriam.* (Photo courtesy of Chaim Cohen.)

Miriam with President Barack Obama at a dinner in honor of the US President's visit to Israel, at the home of President Reuven Rivlin.

(Photo courtesy of Chaim Cohen.)

Avichai and Chani   *Elyasaf and Noa*

Eliraz's children at Avichai's wedding holding their father's photo.

The granddaughters. Gili Bat-Ami, Aluma Eitam, Hallel Miriam holding Maayan Eitam, Shir Zion, Eliraz Eitam (sitting),Carmi Issachar.

The Peretz family at Avichai's wedding

Miriam and the children. Left to right: *Hadas, Avichai, Miriam, Elyasaf, Bat-El.*

Shlomit and Eliraz's children

p.m., Avi Berman arrived and announced that all flights were canceled due to the storm, and that he had found me the final seat on a flight to Geneva. I laughed. I saw a cloudy sky with some light winds, with no signs of a storm, so I couldn't believe that something was about to ruin the calm of my mini-vacation. We drove to the home of Tony Magdar in Long Beach, and looked out over the ocean. It looked perfectly fine to me.

We returned to Lawrence. Our hosts didn't appear too worried, so why should I worry? After dinner, as I was sitting in front of the TV along with Jerry, I noticed water seeping under the door and into the room. I pointed this out to Esther, who rushed to get a towel and slip it into the crack under the door. One towel and a second – but the water kept streaming in. I turned to look out of the big picture window into the yard, where I saw a towering tree sway from side to side. Suddenly it collapsed as if made of straw, and crashed to the ground.

Water began to flow into the room from all directions, and in a matter of seconds the water was up to my knees. Working quickly, I began to pick up the photo albums that were stacked on the bottom shelf of the bookcase and pass them to Esther, who set them on the table. Albums, I thought, contain precious memories – and memories mustn't get wet. The water continued its slow rise, and then the electricity cut off, plunging us into thick darkness. Wet and trembling, I lifted my eyes up to Heaven in prayer: "God, what's going on with you? I left my family and came all the way here just to do some good. I wanted to meet with congregations and give the people hope. Is this how You're paying me back? Do the disasters have to follow me all the way to Lawrence? Weren't the disasters that hit me in Israel enough for You?" In the pitch black, freezing cold, I had a tough conversation with the Creator of the Universe. "What are You thinking by bringing this storm? I bet even You can't see me through all this fog."

Quickly we climbed up to the second story, where the water couldn't reach us. We wrapped ourselves in blankets, and the whole night long, I listened to the whistling of the wind. The sounds of explosions and breakage echoed in my ears incessantly. It felt like disaster.

The next day, the sun shone as if nothing had happened. The sky cleared and the storm passed, but the electricity still wasn't working, and it was bitter cold in the house. We made our way downstairs to assess the damage. Tiny fish swam across the lawn, while children's toys littered the road. The phone lines weren't operating, but when I went out for a walk just to warm up a bit, as I passed the home of the mayor of Lawrence, I noticed I had cell reception. My call went through to Maddy, a family friend who worked as an air hostess for El Al. Whenever I flew, Maddy always made sure to be working on my flight. She's a regular fountain of youth – with her it's laughs and jokes the whole time. I told Maddy that the house where I was staying was flooded and cold, and she proposed that I come to Manhattan, to the hotel where the air hostesses were booked. "I asked for a big room," she said. "You can stay there with me until the flight back to Israel."

I was pleased. My hosts arranged transport, but when I arrived at the hotel, I found Maddy downcast. She related that the hotel was fully booked due to Sandy, and the air hostesses were being transferred to another hotel, where she would be given a small room. "No problem," I told her. "The main thing is for it to have electricity and heat. We'll manage."

We arrived at the other hotel. We were given a tiny room, and we stored the suitcases in the shower, because otherwise there was no room to move. In order to use the bathroom we had to take out the suitcases. I, as usual, was looking on the bright side – I was happy just to have a bed, heat, and a roof over my head. But Maddy felt guilty and tried to make it up to me. The next morning she got up early and rushed out to buy kosher food. When she got back to the room, she announced, "Miriam, I've brought us some good stuff for breakfast. We can't eat in the room because it's so small. Let's go down to the other air hostesses' room. It's more spacious, and they have a coffeemaker."

The air hostesses' room was indeed more comfortable. Maddy set out the food on the table: bagels, Philadelphia cream cheese, sliced pineapple and mango, and cakes. I thanked God for such bounty – out of the bitter cold He had sent me Maddy, and now I was warm and I had a bagel and a cup of coffee. What else could a person want?

Suddenly the door opened, and a young girl came in. I assumed that she was a stewardess. She and Maddy held a conversation, and my gaze latched onto her as if I knew her. I couldn't take my eyes off her, and the questions nagged at me incessantly: Had I taught her in some framework? Had she served in the army with one of my children? Meanwhile, the voice of reason ordered me not to pry.

"I know you," I said. "We've met before, haven't we?"

"No," she replied. "I don't know you."

I asked her name, and she replied, "Muriel." I asked where in Israel she was from. "Ramat Gan," she replied. I really didn't know any Muriel from Ramat Gan. But still, I thought, I do know this girl. I just have to find out how. Muriel was exhausted after a long flight. All she wanted was to drink a quiet cup of coffee, while pushy me wouldn't stop interrogating her. Something inside me pressed me to solve the riddle.

"I really miss being at home on Shabbat," I said. Then I asked Muriel, "What do you do here on Shabbat?"

"Oh, wow," she exhaled. "That's a long story."

"What could be such a long story?" I wondered. "All I asked was what you do here on Shabbat."

"Before, on my Shabbat breaks in New York, I would go out partying. I went to clubs all over the city. Now it's different – I try to be in Israel on Shabbat. Shabbat is precious to me. I enjoy it so much."

I asked her what had changed, but she dodged the question. "Never mind. It's a long story."

I remarked that we seemed to have plenty of time. "Tell me what led you to change your lifestyle," I encouraged her.

"My life changed," Muriel said, and despite her exhaustion, she began to tell her story. "I'm from a nonobservant family. I traveled around in places that had no connection to Judaism. On one trip in South America, I wasn't feeling well, so I had to stay back while my friends went on a trek. Someone brought me a book, and it had a powerful influence on me. Since then I've become more connected to Judaism, and I'm working on becoming more observant."

"What's the name of the book?" I asked, my curiosity rising. "Maybe it'll convince me to become more religious, too."

Muriel shrugged. "I'm sure you haven't heard of it," she quipped. "You shouldn't read it, anyway. It would be hard for you."

"Try me," I insisted, and out of the corner of my eye, I saw that Maddy was burning with curiosity as well.

"It's about a woman who lost two sons," Muriel explained. "But it's not tragic. Just the opposite – it says a lot about inspiration and faith."

At that point in the conversation, I was certain that she was talking about me. Maddy, silent throughout the conversation, was on edge just like me.

"What's this woman's name?" I asked.

"Miriam Peretz."

Still, I didn't reveal my identity. I asked her, "What would you do if you met this Miriam Peretz?"

"I'd give her a big, loving hug," she replied.

I kept my expression blank, and got up to make another cup of coffee. Then I came to stand before her and announced,

"Muriel, I am Miriam Peretz. I'm the mother of those two boys, Uriel and Eliraz."

Muriel was astonished. Maddy was dumbstruck.

I gave Muriel a hug, and when she hugged me, I felt as if we had always known each other. Who would ever have believed that at the height of the hurricane, while everyone around us was fleeing their flooded homes, we would come together as if we were one soul? Together, we returned home – to Israel.

Some people call such things "coincidence," but as the verse asks, "Will two walk together unless they agree?" (Amos 3:3). What were the chances that after Hurricane Sandy, I would arrive at a random hotel in New York, meet an air hostess who had read my book, and discover that thanks to Uriel and Eliraz's story, she had become more religious and begun to keep Shabbat?

My term for such incidents is "the hand of God." I believe that God has opened a window for me to meet new people. At every such "coincidence," I felt inspired, surrounded by God's presence and love. He never left me. Even in the midst of the storm, He was with me, as if to say, "Miriam, I took your most beloved away from you, but I'm the One Who gives you others to love, in My own way."

I would be lying if I said there was no comfort in that. This is the proof that the souls of my children continue to exist through people who never knew them when they were alive. Thanks to the souls of Uriel and Eliraz, their circle of acquaintances has grown – and so has mine. Sandy didn't just arrive for no reason. She had a goal – to enable souls to come together and prove that even out of destruction, we can rebuild.

* * *

In these five years, I have unwillingly become a symbol of spiritual strength. I am overcome with requests for encouragement and support. Sometimes I say to the Holy One, blessed be

He, "As if it weren't enough that You took my children away from me, You gave me a new role. I never prepared or studied for it, but I fulfill it in faith and love." I, who lost life, ask Him to enable me to grasp onto life.

In these five years, I've learned to love people more than I did in the past. I've learned to listen, and I've adopted a positive outlook, choosing to view everything on the bright side. I've learned that there are so many stories that we don't hear. Maybe it's my role to lend a willing ear, and thus to give someone a moment of joy and hope. At such moments, I say to the Creator: "I accept Your judgment, because out of deep darkness, I've developed a great ability to give to others."

Whenever I visit a house of mourning – whether they buried their loved one in a uniform, after illness, or in some other disaster – the first thing they ask me is why. Why my child, why my family. I try to explain that there is no answer to this question, nor will there ever be one, and that I have no explanation for the existence of such suffering. I don't say it's unjustified to ask, "How is it that my most religious, my most successful child was killed?" I try to explain that this is actually a very legitimate question, especially for people who feel that they follow the path of Torah, believe in God, and are dedicated to good deeds and mitzvot. But, I continue, such questions don't permit you to rise up. They push you down. They weaken you and prevent you from growing.

What can encourage you to grow is a different question. "Now, after my child was killed in battle, murdered, or died of disease, or after my husband died before his time – where should I take my life?" In other words: Since we were given life, what should we do with it? Are we going to waste it? I intend to take advantage of every moment to perform meaningful deeds. I believe that every individual can and should discover his strong points, and use them for action. Every person was created with strength and talent. Grief is the moment to grasp these inborn talents and develop them, in order to bring good into the world.

Although I have accumulated so much experience with death, I'm unwilling to become a symbol of grief. I am willing to be a symbol of grasping life, because the disasters that hit my family inspired in me a powerful will to do so, and I feel that God is helping me. In my imagination, I picture God plucking my soul from my body, over and over again, and saying to Himself, "Now that her soul has been uprooted, I'll fill her heart with good things."

Any mother who buries the fruit of her womb would prefer to die. But as it says in Ethics of the Fathers, "You live despite yourself, and you die despite yourself" (4:22). If you are still alive, and if, despite the logic that says that a parent shouldn't bury his child, you wake up in the morning to a new day, there is one central word in your life: choice. The reality that you are alive is a fact, but you are the one who decides whether you stay in bed and cry all day long over the bitterness of your fate, or do something with the life you have. Because God is the One Who offers you to "choose life" (Deuteronomy 30:2).

Every single day, I go through this process of choice. Some days my soul bleeds. I feel like I'm choking, that I don't have the strength to contain the pain. On such days as well, I order myself, sometimes force myself, to hold on to something positive. In every reality, I search for and find that ray of light – because that single, thin ray can only be found by someone in the deepest, darkest abyss.

My advice to bereaved mothers: Always leave the door to life open, even if it's just a tiny crack. Try not to close it off entirely. At first I left a narrow opening, just enough to let in some air. Eventually, when you leave the door to life open to the world, you allow joy and love to come inside – into you.

It's not easy to leave that door open when death is fresh. All you feel like doing is closing yourself up, disappearing. But in my experience, when the door of life is open, when the door of the heart is wide open, rays of light filter through, and they help you grow stronger.

I also say to bereaved families: People who have lost a loved one start life all over again. Like an infant learning how to walk, they must take life step by step, using the toolbox of life skills they have accumulated over a lifetime.

Fortunately or not, my toolbox was full. I had collected these tools ever since I was born, thanks to my mother, the cemetery caretaker who lived alongside the dead. In the immigrant camp I collected more skills for my toolbox in Israel. When people ask me, "Where do you get your strength?" – I look back on my life, and reach the conclusion that everything I experienced before Uriel's death helped me cope with that tragedy. When he died, I acquired the skills to cope with Eliezer's death; and when they informed me about Eliraz, I knew that I was already experienced with death. I thanked God I had the skills that would enable me to begin walking forward – I knew what an army funeral was, and I knew what shivah was with thousands of visitors. I knew who my real friends were, the ones who remained with me after the house emptied out. I knew that I could go on, as I had after Uriel was killed. That advance knowledge kept my fear of the unknown in check.

But when Eliraz fell, despite all the experience I had accumulated with grief, I discovered that I needed new tools in order to cope by myself, without Eliezer. I had to cope with the death of my son, as well as support Shlomit, his widow, and his four children, now fatherless. I knew what it was to be a widow, but I had no idea what it was to become a widow at such a young age, with four little kids still attached to your apron strings. Shlomit's pain stabbed at my flesh even more than my own. I knew some of what she would go through. How I wished I could take that pain away from her and experience it in her place.

Did experience make the pain any easier? There is no simple answer to this question. The pain is pain and the loss is loss, but the coping is different. When I received notice of Eliraz's death, I accused God: "Wasn't it enough that you took Uriel and Eliezer? Are You, the One Who is greater than all others, the all-powerful and awe-inspiring, battling against little me? What is the power dynamic between us? It's not fair!" But in the same moment, in the midst of all that shock and pain, I realized the greatness of the Creator. I understood that I was as inconsequential as an ant walking across the earth; I understood the insignificance of humanity. Eventually, I learned to say to God: "I accept Your judgment. I'm not trying to fight You, or even argue with You. Little me is asking only one thing from You: mercy. Have mercy on me. I beg You, don't touch my children or grandchildren. Let me be their ransom."

In the past few years, I've held a constant dialogue with God. I discover His mercy in every step of my life, in every angle and situation. On Rosh Hashanah eve, I was standing in the kitchen, slicing meat, and I almost cut off my finger. At the last second, the knife fell from my hand, as if an invisible wall had sprung up between it and me. I lifted my eyes from the sink, looked through the window to the skies, and said to God: "Thanks for thinking of me. Thanks for having mercy on me, for permitting me to stand in synagogue this Rosh Hashanah without a bandage on my hand. I could have been seriously hurt, but at the crucial moment, You were here with me. Thanks for Your kindness to me."

There's nothing worse than to lose two sons. Yet I, who experienced the worst that could possibly happen, am busy all day long finding God's kindnesses. One day I decided to do an exercise. I took a piece of paper and drew two columns. At the top of the first, I wrote "List of my complaints to God," and for the second, "List of God's kindnesses." The first list was short: Uriel, Eliezer, and Eliraz were taken from me before their time. The second list was practically endless: my daughter Bat-El got married, little Gili danced and sang at their wedding, Uriel's friend came to visit, my daughter-in-law Shlomit invited me to spend Shabbat at their home, despite a slipped disc in my back I can still go up the stairs and climb up to my children's graves, I can open my eyes, stand on my feet, enjoy the blossoming of the trees, laugh with my rambunctious grandchildren – and the list goes on and on.

My dance with God has become a daily event. I feel a deep connection to Him. I get up from bed after a sleepless night, I see the sun in the window and say, "Thanks for what I have right now." Not for the good that might come tomorrow or the next day, but for now. I say, "Thanks, God, for not forgetting me, for never being too busy for me. You're always available to listen to my pain."

* * *

When we started to work on the English translation of *Miriam's Song*, I was surprised to discover that the story about Eliraz's meatballs wasn't there. I tortured myself – how could I have left that out? That story means so much to me. It was a moment of walking out from the darkness and into the light.

Because I believe in "better late than never," here it is now.

When Eliraz fell in action, we sat shivah for only one and a half days, because it was so close to Passover. After we finished the shivah, shell-shocked and in pain, my daughter-in-law Shlomit asked if I would spend Shabbat at her house in Eli. Before, such invitations used to fill me with great joy. To be a guest in the home of my son and his wife was pure pleasure. It's wonderful for a mother to see that her son has built a family and a home with kids running around inside. This is the goal of our lives – to watch as the next generation continues. But Shlomit's request – "Come visit" – petrified me. How could I go to Eliraz's home when he wasn't there? How could I go into his room and see the bed in which he would never sleep again? How could I stand before Eliraz's shelf full of books and know that he would never again flip through them? How could I stand in their kitchen and know that Eliraz would never again return from a military operation and stand there cooking a meal for his wife and children, the special meal of a father who had just returned from battle? I didn't feel capable of taking that step and entering their home.

While I was stalling and searching for the right answer, I heard my grandson Or-Chadash, who was then six years old, say to his sister Hallel Miriam: "What fun! If Grandma comes, she'll be bringing us meatballs, of course!"

The last words struck me like lightning. Meatballs! My son Eliraz loved my meatballs dearly. When he came back from the fighting in Lebanon, he would go straight into the kitchen, and at the sight of the pot on the gas – meatballs in tomato sauce – he would smile radiantly. He would gobble them straight from the pot, standing up, not bothering to spoon some onto a plate or mix them with rice. "Sit down, take a plate and a fork," I would plead, but he would reply, his mouth full: "It's a shame for them to lose their taste on the way to the plate." Those meatballs were home, they were life.

But now, how could I make meatballs that Eliraz would never eat? How could I continue making the dishes he so loved? Something similar happened when my oldest son fell in action. For years I couldn't bear to taste the cheesecake that Uriel had loved.

Another minute passed, and I gave in. True, Eliraz would no longer eat my meatballs, but his children wanted them. How could I refuse them the enjoyment?

This happened on a Wednesday, and we arranged that on Friday at ten a.m., a taxi would come to take me to their home. On Thursday I asked my neighbor to buy me some ground beef, and when she brought the meat to my home, I instructed her, "Don't show it to me, just put it in the refrigerator please." Before she left I remembered something. "I'd appreciate if you could chop an onion and some parsley, and add the *ras el hanout* spice to the meat – it's in the kitchen drawer." She can do it all, I thought, I can't touch that meat.

On Friday at four a.m., I woke up in panic. I'd forgotten the meatballs! The taxi would be arriving at ten. What should I do?

I went downstairs, opened the front door, and stood outside in the pitch blackness. I looked up at the dark skies and demanded: "Look, You have to help me make those meatballs! Please, just give me the strength to make some meatballs."

I didn't ask for encouragement or for the strength to overcome. All I asked was for my hands to be able to make the meatballs for my grandchildren.

I went into the kitchen, took the package of meat out of the refrigerator, and placed it on the countertop, but I couldn't touch it. I walked around the house, back and forth, from the living room to the kitchen and from the kitchen to the living room. I tried to touch it and pulled back, because inside myself I knew that the moment I made the first meatball, I was accepting His judgment, and accepting the fact that Eliraz would never eat them.

I went back to the kitchen. In the window I saw the first ray of light, and I continued speaking to Him: "Give me the strength to make meatballs for Or-Chadash, for Hallel Miriam, for Shir-Tzion, and for little Gili." As I was praying, I rolled the first meatball, and while I rolled, memories welled up inside. I remembered how Eliraz ate his first meatball, at seven months old. He didn't really eat it, but shredded it into bits, sucking up the tomato sauce – and he was thrilled. Maybe he managed to get a tiny morsel into his mouth. At age one year, he would dismember the meatball and mashed it all over his hair and face. At two years old, he was eating them joyfully, and at thirty-two, in just a few minutes he would devour ten meatballs on a full plate of rice.

I continued rolling meatballs and asking for his forgiveness. "I'm sorry, Eliraz," I murmured, "for making meatballs that you will never eat. I'm sorry, son, that I'm continuing."

The pot filled up with meatballs in tomato sauce, with a few tears mixed in. Before Eliraz fell in battle, I used to make meatballs in ten minutes. But that day, it took me more than an hour. That's how it is when you bury a child. Even the simplest actions, like getting dressed and brushing your teeth, demand superhuman strength, both physical and emotional. Every little activity makes you weep rivers. I made a pot of rice, got into the taxi, and when I reached the settlement of Eli, Or-Chadash ran out joyously to meet me, his sisters trailing behind.

They didn't say, "Grandma, we're so happy you came." They just asked, "Grandma, did you bring us meatballs?"

That's when I knew that Eliraz was right. The meatballs were a symbol of life.

Since then, I make Eliraz's meatballs for his children, for his friends' children, for Uriel's friends and their children. I do it with great pleasure, because I remember that five years ago, I couldn't do it. I make the meatballs that Eliraz won't eat, for the many kids who are called "Eliraz" after him. I know of fifteen already, and sometimes they come visit me. My daughter Hadas also called her daughter Eliraz.

Recently, the doctor who did an ultrasound examination on my daughter Bat-El identified her as my daughter, and he wrote on the photograph: "Dear Grandma Miriam, when can I taste some of your meatballs?"

* * *

After Uriel was killed, I began to volunteer for the IDF, giving classes and lectures on the topic of leadership. I traveled all over the country, from Gladiola Post on Mt. Hermon all the way down to Eilat. I met many soldiers, I was exposed to different units, and

I earned the title "Mother of Golani." After Eliraz was killed, and after the book was published, more and more people were exposed to my story, and the media gave me the title "Mother of the Boys."

Then came May 2014, and I was asked to light a torch on Mt. Herzl at the yearly ceremony on Yom Ha'atzmaut, Israel's sixty-sixth Independence Day.

The request reached me in a strange manner. I gave a talk in Jerusalem to a special forces unit of the marines. One of them asked me a question that challenged me profoundly – was it worth the price? He asked, "Today, in view of the atmosphere prevailing today in this country, don't you think that your sons' death was unnecessary?" We had a deep discussion. I talked about my desire to influence reality, and to see the positive in our country. I finished the talk with a feeling of satisfaction, and then I looked at my phone. Ten text messages flashed on the screen: "This is Yitzchak Zonenstein from the government public relations office. Please get back to me ASAP."

What did he mean, ASAP? Should I call him right away, even though it was eleven p.m.?

I called the number, and a male voice answered. "Hello, Mrs. Peretz. The torch-lighting committee has chosen you to be one of the torch lighters. The topic of this year's ceremony is 'Time for Women,' and all the lighters are women who have done something significant and inspiring."

I laughed. Then I said to Yitzchak, "I think you've made a mistake. I don't know how to light a torch. I only know how to light memorial candles. Maybe you're looking for another Miriam?"

"It's no mistake," he replied. "The committee has chosen you unanimously."

"That can't be," I argued. "I'm Miriam Ohayon from the Hatzerim immigrant camp. I made aliyah from Morocco to a state that was ready and waiting. What have I done to help establish it? I'm not deserving of such an honor."

"The committee has decided that in your own special way, you help give bereaved families the strength to keep on living," he asserted. "You symbolize the power of life in our people."

I hung up the phone, called my kids, and heard shouts of excitement: "Wow, Mom! That's out of this world! What an honor!"

"I don't want this honor," I replied. "I don't deserve it. It must be a dream, it can't be real."

After these conversations, I went down to the living room, to the wall where the photos hang. I stood in front of the photo of Uriel and Eliraz, and said: "My dear sons, I've just had a phone call from the office of public relations, and they informed me that you were chosen to light a torch on Yom Ha'atzma'ut. It's not me, it's you, my dead sons. You will light the torch of life, the torch of hope, faith, and continuity." For an entire hour I stood in front of the photos and cried. The next morning, at six thirty a.m., I went to Har Hamenuchot (Givat Shaul cemetery) and Mt. Herzl to visit the graves of Eliezer and the boys. Weeping intensely, I told them about the phone call. I wanted to hear what they had to say. "I need your advice," I told them. "I need your embrace."

At such an early hour, Mt. Herzl is a silent paradise, with colorful flowers decorating the graves. You can hear the chirping of the birds. I stood there and begged, "Uriel, Eliraz, give me a sign that you can hear me."

Suddenly I heard my phone ringing, piercing the silence. I took it out of my purse and recognized the voice of my grandson Or-Chadash. He had woken up early and missed his grandma. When I heard Or-Chadash shout, "Grandma, how are you?" – that was the sign I had been waiting for. That's the boys' reply, I thought. Dear Mother, we're proud of you. Carry that torch with pride. We'll be there.

That day I began the long process of preparation. I met the other torch lighters. I was thrilled to meet Adina Bar-Shalom, the daughter of Rabbi Ovadia Yosef. "What an honor it is to sit beside you," I said in embarrassment to Geula Cohen, who to me is a symbol of this country. "Miriam," she said, "it's such an honor for *me* to stand beside *you*." I met Maxine Fassberg, general manager of Intel Israel and a vice president of the international Intel Corporation. I had a long talk with Paralympic athlete Pascale Bercovitch. We met with Minister of Culture Limor Livnat. I admit that my heart skipped a beat at the sight of each torch lighter who came along with a husband or partner. More than ever, I missed my Eliezer, who had always been proud of me. I knew that if he had been with me, undoubtedly he would have said, "I'm not surprised at all."

During the preparations, I exuded strength and power, as if I was planning to climb Mt. Everest. But the day before the ceremony, when I arrived at Mt. Herzl for the dress rehearsal, I saw that my hill had completely changed its look. I no longer recognized it; it was no longer the same hill that was my second home. There was a huge difference between my hill of the dead, the hill of longing and pain, and the hill I saw before me – decorated in blue and white flags, bathed in background music, full of joy and celebration.

That's when the floodgates opened for my tears.

The bus arrived at the tent from which we would make our entrance onstage. The other torch lighters all climbed off the bus, cheerful and singing. As for me – my legs failed me. I couldn't get off the bus. I stayed behind, unable to control my weeping. I felt like screaming, "This isn't for me! This hill that's witnessed funerals, the tears of mothers and fathers, the wailing of children on their parents' graves – what does all this celebration have to do with me?"

Somehow I got off the bus and into the tent. I went over to a corner, and everything burst out of me. My painful cries and heavy groans shook the tent. The women came up to comfort and embrace me – but I was not to be calmed.

They called us to go on stage. "Imagine the audience sitting on the grandstand," they said – but I couldn't see any audience. I only saw what was behind the grandstand – the best of the IDF's young soldiers who were buried there. I saw my sons' graves.

I began to read: "I, Miriam, daughter of Ito and Ya'akov Ohayon" – and I lost it. I took a sip of water, and asked if I could try again. "I, Miriam, daughter of Ito." There, I made it through the opening. I continued: "...am honored to light this torch in honor of the fallen, and among them, my two sons" – and again I lost it. How could I continue?

Five attempts. "I can't do it. Try to understand me," I cried. "I give up. Please leave me alone."

The pain at that moment was as intense as when they had died. In my mind's eye, I pictured their caskets being lowered into their graves.

I didn't want to light any torch!

Luckily, at that moment Orna Barbivai came up to me and embraced me. She was the first woman in the IDF to obtain the rank of major general, and was chosen to light the torch in honor of her position as head of the IDF Manpower Directorate. She wasn't wearing a uniform, but it was a military embrace. An embrace that I had learned to recognize. She said, "Miriam, you can do it. You taught us that you can." I asked her to hold my hand so that I would be able to read the sentences on the page – I was shaking that badly.

On my sixth try, I was able to read the entire text. I did it! My shout echoed over the ceremony area: "I did it!"

I didn't know that this entire occasion had been filmed for television. When news announcer Oshrat Kotler saw the images on the screen, she burst out in tears. She stopped the broadcast, and said, "What a brave woman."

Then the moment of truth arrived. The torch-lighting ceremony takes place at the conclusion of that terrible day – Yom

Hazikaron, Israel's Memorial Day for IDF soldiers. How could I switch from memorial to rejoicing in the blink of an eye? At the beginning of the day I stood on Mt. Herzl, at the main ceremony, standing beside the graves. Just like every other year, I'm torn by the question of which son's grave I'll stand beside during the siren. I decided to stand beside Eliraz, and as I stood there, I heard the prime minister speaking, saying that on this hill, that evening, Miriam Peretz would light a torch.

I bent down to Eliraz's grave and asked, "You hear, Eliraz? The prime minister is talking to you – to you and Uriel."

After the memorial ceremony I went home. Hundreds of people came and went, and at four p.m. my daughter Hadas said, "Mom, the taxi will arrive at five. You'd better start getting ready for the torch lighting." I felt confused. Just a minute ago I had been sitting in the yard with friends, talking about Uriel and Eliraz. Now I had to go up to my room, get dressed, and put on makeup. How could I make such a sudden transformation? When I got back to the living room, now dressed in a black suit and heels, I was a different Miriam. Beside the staircase stood the friends who had come for Yom Hazikaron, and they looked like they had come to see a bride going down the stairs toward her *chuppah*. It was a surrealistic, even slightly frightening sight, and I prayed to God with yet another request: "Tonight, among the flags and the lights, among the thousands of people celebrating and rejoicing, let me see Uriel and Eliraz sitting in the audience. You have to help me. Don't let me see the graves."

I was afraid that I would shake or stumble. But the moment I heard the voice of Yehoram Gaon, the master of ceremonies, announcing my name, with the song *Poh b'eretz chemdat avot* ("Here in the beloved land of the forefathers") playing in the background, my feet carried me forward. I walked onto the stage with dance steps as if the weight of years had been lifted, as if the pain and longing had disappeared. With each step, I sang to myself

Hitnaari, me'afar kumi – "Shake yourself free, rise up from the dust" (from *Lecha Dodi*, song of welcoming Shabbat from Friday night services). For just a moment, I was once more Miriam Ohayon the redhead, full of life and happiness. I heard my father's voice whispering in my ear, *Ya binti* – my dear daughter, and I saw my mother, Ito, placing both hands on my head to bless me. The audience filling the ceremony area seemed like one big family, uniting in a loving embrace. When I lit the torch and reached the standard phrase recited by all torch lighters, *l'tiferet Medinat Yisrael* – "For the glory of the State of Israel" – I knew what the price of glory was. I saw Uriel and Eliraz standing before me, and I told them, "You are the glory. Thanks to you and your friends, we have a state, and today we're celebrating its independence."

* * *

The torch-lighting ceremony reinforced my connection with the prime minister. Since I respect him, I've never called him "Bibi." To me, he's Mr. Binyamin Netanyahu.

He was Israel's prime minister when Uriel fell in battle, and he called to comfort and to encourage me. I didn't even attempt to hide my excitement at the sound of his voice and words. Later, I was invited to join Torah classes at the prime minister's residence. He often said that I conveyed a message of love for the Land of Israel, of faith and hope. Four months before the 2015 elections, a few minutes before Shabbat began, he called me and asked me to join the Likud without running in the primaries, in a sure position, and then to run for the Knesset with him. I replied, "Thank you very much for thinking of me, Mr. Prime Minister. I'll think about it."

In my heart I knew my answer would be negative, but I always like to leave the door partially open.

I consulted with two close friends, Asher Kadosh and Ze'ev Hever (Zembish), and the opinions were balanced on either side.

On *motzaei Shabbat*, journalists began to call, asking if it were true that the prime minister had called me, and whether I was really running for the Knesset. I don't lie, so I didn't deny it, but said only, "I also heard such a rumor." Of course, I couldn't make any formal declaration until I had given the prime minister my answer. Still, the Sunday morning newspapers carried the headline, "Miriam Peretz runs for the Knesset."

On Sunday morning I called him and said, "Mr. Prime Minister, I'm very, very thrilled by your request. It's a great honor. But ever since my sons were killed, I've chosen to continue focusing on educational work – in my meetings with IDF soldiers, members of the security forces, youth, bereaved families, and communities in Israel and worldwide. I'm afraid that politics will distract me from the path that I've chosen. I'm not willing to give up even one meeting with IDF soldiers, youth preparing for military service, or bereaved families, in order to attend political meetings and debates."

The prime minister listened, and replied, "I respect that. Continue on your path."

Two months before the elections, I received another phone call from his office. They informed me that the prime minister was planning a visit to the Bnei David premilitary academy in Eli, the settlement where my son Eliraz's family lives. They invited me to join the prime minister in his visit, but I explained that I was very busy with my work. A few days later, they called again and said, "We would like you to know that the prime minister is going to the academy today, and he'll be visiting the room dedicated in Eliraz's name."

I could hardly ignore that. I called Shlomit, my daughter-in-law, and told her that the prime minister was arriving that day. "I'd be very pleased if you would come to the meeting with the kids," I added.

Shlomit and the kids had just moved into a temporary trailer home, because their house was undergoing complete renovation. She told me that while packing and unpacking, she had found a box of Eliraz's letters, in which she had seen a letter addressed to "Bibi."

It was eight a.m., and the visit was planned for eleven a.m. I was hoping that Shlomit would be able to find the letter by then. She did.

Eliraz had written this letter seventeen years previously, in 1996, when he was eighteen years old, a student in the Atzmona premilitary academy in Gush Katif. At the time, the media was busy waging a tar-and-feather campaign against Prime Minister Netanyahu. His whole life, Eliraz had never been one to stand by idly – involvement was his outstanding character trait. He wrote:

> *To our prime minister, Mr. Binyamin Netanyahu,*
>
> *Greetings and happy holiday.*
>
> *RE: Respect for you and for the prime minister in general:*
>
> *My name is Eliraz Peretz. I completed my high school education at Himmelfarb High School, and right now I'm awaiting my draft call-up (impatiently), and study-ing at the Otzem premilitary academy in Gush Katif.*
>
> *One of the first topics we studied in the academy was respect for the prime minister, as part of the principle of respect for every individual as a human being.*
>
> *In the past few weeks, the government's honor and your honor as a human being has been openly vili-fied, mainly in the manner in which you have been addressed. It's particularly painful that ministers and Knesset members, who are supposed to be the elite of*

our nation, have sinned in their slander and weak defamation of your honor.

The consequences of this are damage to our national honor and the undermining of our status as a nation – in front of our people, and mainly, before our enemies and the entire world. Our enemies rejoice and are strengthened by these exact words.

I feel that I am personally harmed when your honor is harmed, both as a human being and as our prime minister. You are the person who symbolizes, implements, and carries our entire people, in all its facets, on his shoulders.

I and my friends in the academy have protected your honor as best we can, to ensure it wouldn't be harmed. At the moment, our power is limited. Still, we want to encourage you, and insist that people should stop damaging the honor of the prime minister of the State of Israel, which unfortunately could lead to assassination.

My comrades, my teachers, and I consider you as the strand that connects the entire Jewish people in all areas.

Push onward with pride! My purpose is to strengthen you! Stick firmly to your goal!

Our eyes are on you. We are prepared at every moment to be called to defend the flag.

Yours with esteem and love for the nation,

Eliraz Peretz

After Eliraz wrote these words, his friends said, "You're making a fool of yourself. Not only is your handwriting illegible, but do you really think that the prime minister will read your letter?" In response to their reactions, he stuffed the letter in a drawer and never sent it.

I arrived at Eli. Shlomit was already there with the four kids. Binyamin Netanyahu hugged each of them, and Shlomit said, "Mr. Prime Minister, I have here a letter that should have reached you seventeen years ago, but was never sent."

The prime minister read the letter, and we saw that he was deeply moved. "Was there any other kid in Israel who was concerned for my honor as a human being?" he said.

Two days later, I was invited to the ceremony honoring outgoing Chief of General Staff Benny Gantz. The prime minister and his wife also attended the ceremony. After it was over, I approached Mrs. Sara Netanyahu, with whom I had often spoken in the past. After Eliraz was killed, she invited me to their home, and before the torch-lighting ceremony she sent a representative to see how I was managing the difficult day of Yom Hazikaron, to check whether I needed support. "You have no idea how moved the prime minister was by Eliraz's letter," she said.

I replied that yes, I had seen the tears shining in his eyes.

At the time, just before the March 2015 elections, Binyamin Netanyahu and the Likud Party that he headed were in a poor position. The media predicted that they would win only twenty mandates. A reporter asked Netanyahu, "If you're elected as prime minister again, whom will you call first?" He replied, "My first phone call will be to Miriam Peretz."

This question was broadcast on the radio and on television. Many people thought it was a pre-election gimmick. "The prime minister won't be calling you," they told me. I smiled to myself. Why should he call me? I was sure that Netanyahu's first phone call would be to Barak Obama.

The elections took place on a Tuesday. I spent the day in a room with no cellphone reception, busy with final preparations for the upcoming wedding of my son Avichai. That night, at two minutes past ten, I left the room for a moment. Immediately, my phone rang. "The prime minister is looking for you urgently," a voice said, and they put him on the line. I heard him say, "Good evening, Miriam. I've called to tell you that the Likud will be forming the next government."

I was astonished. "Mr. Prime Minister," I asked, "to what do I owe the honor of you calling me?"

"I remember Eliraz's letter," he replied. "I remember the words, *'Push onward with pride! Stick firmly to your goal!'* I felt an obligation to fulfill Eliraz's will."

I was moved beyond words. "Mr. Prime Minister," I finally said, "I'm happy for you, and I'm happy for the Jewish people. I trust you. You carry the entire nation on your shoulders – young and old, religious and secular, workers and unemployed, Arabs, Druze, Christians – the entire broad spectrum. I pray that God will grant you the wisdom and understanding to lead and unite this nation in all its diversity. My wish for you tonight is that you'll bring us to times of peace, and that you'll be proud of us, your children."

Binyamin Netanyahu, who lost his brother Yonatan (Yoni) in Operation Entebbe, is a prime minister who knows bereavement. He knows – like myself and my children – what it is to pay the highest possible price for love of the Land of Israel, and why we pray for the day when peace will reign.

* * *

In the summer of 2014, Operation Protective Edge dragged me back in time to Eliraz's death. Again the fighting took place in Gaza, which is where Eliraz was killed. More soldiers died, and the cycle of grief continued. I felt that everything was closing in on me. Once again I experienced sleepless nights full of worry, and I did the best I could – attending funerals of the fallen and visiting bereaved families.

I was called up to battle, in a manner of speaking. In Sderot, I met soldiers from Bahad 1 base who had lost their commander in battle. I met with youth in bomb shelters, and visited bereaved families. Strangers came up to me and said, "We want to contribute somehow. Can we drive you on your visits to the bereaved?" So every day I had a volunteer driver. I joked that I had a daily "hunk on duty" who drove me around the country, often while the sirens were going off. This enabled me to visit ninety percent of the families whose world caved in during Operation Protective Edge. Each time I entered a home, I remembered those knocks on the door of my own house. A knock that changes your life, that slices it in half, into before and after, and in the after, nothing is ever the same.

There are no words that can comfort, certainly not in the days immediately following the death. In that stage, the family still describes the deceased as living, because their consciousness has not yet digested the loss. Each family copes in its own way. There's no comparison between them, and so I tried to speak to each family in its own language.

We made a trip to comfort the parents of Staff Sergeant Shawn Carmeli, in Ra'anana. On the way, we decided to stop in Herzliya, at the home of Staff Sergeant Eitan Barak, the first soldier to lose his life in Operation Protective Edge.

While our car stood at a stoplight, we heard a siren. I jumped out and ran to hide on the side of the road. In the skies above me, I saw the trail of the Iron Dome. Then I noticed an Arab woman taking shelter beside me, along with her two crying children. They looked like two scared chicks. "Don't be afraid," I said. "It will pass." What a crazy reality, I thought. Possibly, members of this very woman's family were fighting in Gaza against our soldiers.

But as long as she's here beside me, we're sisters in distress – we're both just women who want to live, and to protect our children.

What's the difference between us? If the similarities are greater than the differences, why can't we have peaceful relations?

After the siren faded, we visited the home of the Barak family, where Eitan's sister was waiting. Her pain cried out to Heaven. She could not accept the death of her brother, and she asked me how she could go on living from then on. Her parents asked, "Tell us about the horror that awaits us."

I talked to them about the first Shabbat without him. The first time you sit at the table and see the empty chair, you'll understand that this is what death means. When you want to eat something that Eitan loved, it will stick in your throat. In a few weeks, you'll begin preparations for Rosh Hashanah. You'll buy gifts for everyone except Eitan, and you'll realize that he's never coming back. I mentioned other situations that reveal the loss that becomes more tangible from one day to the next. But I still felt that this family wanted to know more about what to expect.

In such moments, when I'm looking for the answer, I turn to God, and I ask Him to put the right words in my mouth. I asked the father a seemingly random question: "What do you do for a living?" He replied that he was an insurance agent. He explained that his clients always tried to get the highest percentage of disability possible, so that they would be awarded the largest possible remuneration.

I told them: "The moment they knock on your door, you become disabled. But unlike in the insurance business, in this case the percentage of disability isn't decided by any committee. You're the one who'll decide that percentage. On some days you'll feel one hundred percent disabled – at the memorial ceremony, on your son's birthday, when you escort your daughter to the wedding canopy, times when his absence particularly stands out. On other days you'll feel only five percent disabled. That's when you feel strong enough to leave the house, go visit friends, or sit in a restaurant – and that's fine. Don't fight the good days, don't be afraid of them. Grief is a permanent disability, and you are the only ones who can decide its degree."

I felt that I was speaking in terms from the father's world, and that he understood me. Later, I met these parents at one of the events organized by Irit Oren-Gonders (Lieutenant Colonel-Reserves), director of the Or Lamishpachot Association ("Light for Families"). They got dressed and left their home, and came to the event. I knew that on that day, perhaps in contrast to many other days, their percentage of disability was low, and I was pleased.

I drove to Ashdod, which was under constant bombing attack, to comfort the parents of Sergeant Ben Vanunu, a Golani fighter who was killed in Sejaya. A young woman opened the door, and when I asked who the mother was, she answered, "That's me."

"You're Sarit Vanunu?" I hugged the bereaved mother. "You look like a little girl."

We sat in the kitchen. Her husband Ilan was at the prayer service. Ben's girlfriend showed me a message he had sent her on her cellphone, with a quotation from Eliraz about giving: "If you're in a combat unit in the army, then you're there all the way. You give it all you've got."

I was thrilled to see that Eliraz's spirit was still alive. When I saw other quotations, I couldn't help but wonder: Did the spirits of Uriel and Eliraz fight in Operation Protective Edge? Of course, I answered my own question.

I traveled to Holon, to the family of Sergeant Benaya Rovel, a combat soldier in Battalion 101 of the parachute brigade. The person who had invited me to the Rovel family was Ma'ayan, who was engaged to Benaya's older brother Yarin. She sent me a text message: "We are planning to get married in a month, but the family is talking about postponing it. Would you be willing to come and give us some encouragement?"

I walked into the home and announced, "Even if you don't invite me, I'm coming to the wedding."

The parents asked how they could rejoice during the year of mourning, but I said, "You'll complete the shivah, you'll start a new life, and at the wedding, we'll all dance and rejoice."

While I was sitting in the mourners' tent, a siren went off, and we all ran into the shelter. Ada, Benaya's mother, grasped my hand and said, "It's not finished. Quite possibly, another one of our soldiers was killed just now."

I kept my promise. Although that same night I flew to the United States on a speaking tour, I managed to attend the wedding with my daughter Bat-El and her husband Matan. We wept at the *chuppah*, especially when the groom broke the glass and sang the song, "If I forget you, O Jerusalem." I recalled my own personal breakage, the destruction of my personal Jerusalem. Then we danced, because it's a mitzvah to rejoice with the bride and groom, and to me, that is the dance of life. Perhaps the bereaved mother went home and wept for her son after the celebration, but to live means to rejoice. There's a time for happiness, and a time for pain. A time to bury a son, and a time to marry off a son.

Aviram Shaul, brother of Staff Sergeant Oron Shaul, who is officially defined by the IDF as a fallen soldier whose place of burial is unknown, asked me to meet with their mother Zehava. I went to visit them during the shivah in the settlement of Poriah Illit in northern Israel. On the way, I wondered what I was about to face. What could I say to parents who had lost their child, but who have no grave to visit?

I said everything I could possibly say, and when I left the home of the Shaul family, I thought, "God, I'm complaining about my bitter fate, but I have a grave – I have two graves, I have a place where I can go to cry." I reproached myself: "Where are your proportions, Miriam? There is grief bigger than yours – the grief of a mother who has no grave to weep over."

During Operation Protective Edge, I also traveled to visit wounded soldiers. I was very touched when I came to the room of Lieutenant Colonel Roi Levy, commander of Golani Brigade Reconnaissance Battalion, who was severely injured in battle. I knew Roi, as he had come to comfort me after Eliraz's death. He had told me about Uriel, who inspired him to persevere during the challenging basic training course for the special forces unit. According to Roi, in difficult moments, he looked at Uriel and thought, "If that little guy can walk around with such a big smile, then so can I."

I told Yehudit, Roi's mother, about this, and added that "Golani is a family."

She hugged me and cried. We both cried when I said, "Be glad that he's only injured. Be glad that he's alive. You have something to hold on to, you have hope."

During Operation Protective Edge, famous singer Ya'akov Shwekey came from the United States to perform in Caesarea in front of the wounded soldiers. Sharon Daniel of Givat Ze'ev, who represents him in Israel, invited me to attend, and for the first time in my life, I visited the giant amphitheater. Shwekey sang, the audience was thrilled, and suddenly he mentioned my name and invited me up on stage.

Me? What was a sixty-one-year-old woman doing, hanging around in the Caesarea amphitheater? I had no business being there.

I walked up the steps to the stage, afraid I would fall off.

I had no idea what to say. I stood there looking out over the audience, which was huge, and suddenly an idea flashed through my head. Throughout Operation Protective Edge, the media was hungry for a victory image. I pointed to the people sitting in front of me, and I said, "You are my victory photo! A nation that is able to sing and be happy even as missiles are whistling over our heads – that's the victory image of the Jewish people throughout history."

I spoke in a mixture of Hebrew and English, and I spoke from the heart. I spoke to thousands in the same way that I speak at home. I don't need the Caesarea amphitheater to say that to me, there's no happier sight than young people who come from all over the world to show their support for us, the Jewish people, in this land. To me, there's no sight more moving that that of wounded soldiers sitting in their wheelchairs, singing joyfully, clapping their hands, and continuing with their lives.

* * *

In the five years that have passed since Eliraz was killed, each week I've met with some one thousand individuals, both soldiers and civilians. Even when I don't feel I have the strength, even when my health is shaky, I travel to the bases and to the brigades, and any place I'm needed. The officers' training courses visit Jerusalem as part of their educational seminar, and on Thursdays I meet them at Binyanei Ha'umah convention center. I see their desire to hear my story – not just about the pain, but about the coping, the choice of life and hope. I hear their need to know and learn about the values that guide my life. They ask me many questions – Why must I continue to live in this blood-soaked land? Why must I serve in the Israel Defense Forces? Why must I endanger my life to defend my homeland? Through the stories of Uriel and Eliraz, they find the answer to their questions. I add: "I've come to speak to you because you play a part in the image of my life, in the image to which I aspire." My goal is to be able to attend the wedding of my grandson Or-Chadash, Eliraz's oldest child.

When Eliraz stood under the wedding canopy with Shlomit, he didn't make the usual vow, "If I forget you, O Jerusalem." Instead, he vowed, "If I forget you, my brother Uriel" – then he lifted up his foot and broke the glass. Shlomit and Eliraz named their oldest son Or-Chadash, after Uriel – both contain the word Or, which means "light." Today Or-Chadash is eleven years old, and he is the splitting image of his father. He still wears the Golani cap, and a Golani flag still hangs in his room.

Last year on the holiday of Sukkot, Or-Chadash sat in our sukkah together with my children Bat-El, Avichai, and Elyasaf. I felt incredibly sad, because the sukkah always reminds me of the last holiday of Sukkot we spent as a whole family, when Eliezer sat at the head of the table with Uriel to his right and Eliraz to his left. Now we sit in the sukkah, and Uriel, Eliezer, and Eliraz are no longer with us – but Or-Chadash is here. The family conversation rolled around to the topic of the army. I asked Or-Chadash if he wanted to serve in Golani, and he replied, "I'm not sure." I was surprised, because I knew how deeply the spirit of Golani runs in his veins. I asked why he wasn't sure, and he answered, "Grandma, I'm my mother's only son. Someone needs to stay with her and my three sisters. I'll serve in the army in a position that's right for me. Maybe by then, there won't be any more wars, and the army won't need soldiers."

A shiver ran through me. In my mind's eye, I saw images from the past – Eliraz hugging his father, and in parallel, I saw Or-Chadash hugging his mother Shlomit. What a heavy responsibility he has, as the only male in the family. I prayed: God, hear the request of this little child in this sukkah where we sit today. May it be a *sukkat shalom*, a sukkah of peace.

This is what I say when people ask me "why." I tell the soldiers that I'm certain that when he stands under his wedding canopy, Or-Chadash will follow in his father's footsteps and vow, "If I forget you, my father Eliraz and my uncle Uriel, and all the fighters of the IDF." When I hear his voice and the shattering of the glass, I'll look with pride to Heaven, and I'll shout silently to the Hezbollah in the north and the Hamas in the south: "You see! My son's spirit lives on. You cannot kill the spirit of Jerusalem – they dreamed of Jerusalem, and they fell for Jerusalem. Tonight Or-Chadash is adding his own stone to the rebuilding of Jerusalem, the city of kindness and friendship, where one day we will live in peace and love."